MODERNISM, LABOUR AND SELFHOOD IN BRITISH LITERATURE AND CULTURE, 1890–1930

Morag Shiach examines the ways in which labour was experienced and represented between 1890 and 1930. There is a strong critical tradition in literary and historical studies that sees the impact of modernity on human labour purely in terms of intensification and alienation. Shiach, however, explores a diverse series of efforts to articulate the relations between labour and selfhood within modernism. She examines the philosophical languages available for thinking about labour in the period. She then gives an account of the significance of two technologies, the typewriter and the washing machine, central to a cultural and political understanding of labour. Through readings of writings by Sylvia Pankhurst and D. H. Lawrence, Shiach shows how labour underpins the political and textual innovations of the period. She concludes with an analysis of the 'general strike' both as myth and historical event. This study will be of interest to literary, cultural and historical scholars alike.

MORAG SHIACH is Professor of Cultural History and Head of the School of English and Drama at Queen Mary, University of London. Her publications include *Discourse on Popular Culture: Class, Gender and History in Cultural Analysis, 1730 to the Present* and *Hélène Cixous: A Politics of Writing* as well as a wide range of articles on cultural history, cultural theory and modernism. She has edited Virginia Woolf's *A Room of One's Own* and *Three Guineas* as well as an anthology *Feminism and Cultural Studies*.

MODERNISM, LABOUR AND SELFHOOD IN BRITISH LITERATURE AND CULTURE, 1890–1930

MORAG SHIACH

CAMBRIDGE UNIVERSITY PRESS

PUBLISHED BY THE PRESS SYNDICATE OF THE UNIVERSITY OF CAMBRIDGE
The Pitt Building, Trumpington Street, Cambridge, United Kingdom

CAMBRIDGE UNIVERSITY PRESS
The Edinburgh Building, Cambridge, CB2 2RU, UK
40 West 20th Street, New York, NY 10011–4211, USA
477 Williamstown Road, Port Melbourne, VIC 3207, Australia
Ruiz de Alarcón 13, 28014 Madrid, Spain
Dock House, The Waterfront, Cape Town 8001, South Africa

http://www.cambridge.org

First published 2004

Printed in the United Kingdom at the University Press, Cambridge

Typeface Adobe Garamond 11/12.5 pt.   *System* LaTeX 2_ε [TB]

A catalogue record for this book is available from the British Library

Library of Congress Cataloguing in Publication data
Shiach, Morag.
Modernism, labour, and selfhood in British literature and culture, 1890–1930 / by Morag Shiach.
p.   cm.
Includes bibliographical references and index.
ISBN 0 521 83459 7
1. English literature – 20th century – History and criticism.   2. Modernism (Literature) –
Great Britain.   3. Lawrence, D. H. (David Herbert), 1885–1930 – Political and social views.
4. Labor movement – Great Britain – History – 20th century.   5. Working class – Great Britain –
History – 20th century.   6. Pankhurst, E. Sylvia (Estelle Sylvia), 1882–1960.   7. Labor movement
in literature.   8. Working class in literature.   9. Self in literature.   I. Title.
PR478.M6S55   2003
820.9′355 – dc21   2003055138

ISBN 0 521 83459 7 hardback

For Michael, James and John

Contents

Illustrations

Acknowledgements

The labour of this book has been part of my life for a number of years. During that time I have been fortunate to benefit from the support of a wide variety of colleagues and friends. I would like to thank my colleagues in the School of English and Drama at Queen Mary, University of London, and particularly those who read, responded to, and advised on parts of this book while it was in preparation: Michèle Barrett, Lisa Jardine, Elizabeth Maslen, Chris Reid and Jacqueline Rose. Viv Gardner and Bill Schwarz offered encouragement at a vital stage, and I am grateful to them both. Many people contributed suggestions of useful and relevant texts, or offered other helpful information, and I would like to thank Howard Finn, David Glover, Joanna Labon, Catherine Maxwell, Michael Minden and Chris Willis. Early versions of the work in this book were presented to a wide variety of audiences, and I thank the people who invited me to present this work to conferences and seminars in Britain and in the United States: Tim Armstrong, Amanda Dackombe, Geoff Gilbert, Tracy Hargreaves, Peter Hulme, Matthew Kibble, Tim Mathews, Rachel Potter, Alan O'Shea, Suzanne Raitt, Miri Rubin, Trudi Tate and Joanne Winning. I am grateful to Anne Fernihough, Caroline Howlett and Hugh Stevens, whose invitations to contribute to books they were editing helped me to focus key parts of this research project. I would like to thank the School of English and Drama at Queen Mary, University of London for support with research expenses associated with the project, and Queen Mary, University of London for granting me the sabbatical leave necessary to undertake the research. The anonymous readers for Cambridge University Press offered extremely helpful advice for which I am very grateful. Michael Moriarty responded to this project as it developed with great insight and great care, and I thank him for his invaluable support.

Parts of chapter 2 were originally published as 'Modernity, Labour and the Typewriter', in Hugh Stevens and Caroline Howlett (eds.), *Modernist Sexualities* (Manchester: Manchester University Press, 2000), pp. 114–29 and I am grateful to Manchester University Press for permission to re-produce these. Parts of chapter 4 were originally published as 'Work and Selfhood in *Lady Chatterley's Lover*', in Anne Fernihough (ed.), *The Cambridge Companion to D. H. Lawrence* (Cambridge: Cambridge University Press, 2001), pp. 87–102 and I am grateful to Cambridge University Press for permission to reproduce these.

I am grateful to Dr Richard Pankhurst for permission to reproduce drawings and unpublished writings by Estelle Sylvia Pankhurst. I am also grateful to the House of Commons, to the National Portrait Gallery, to the Women's Library, to Leicester Museums and to the Bridgeman Art Library for permission to reproduce these drawings. I am grateful to the National Portrait Gallery for permission to quote from material related to portraits by Estelle Sylvia Pankhurst. I am grateful to the Museum of London for permission to quote material in the David Mitchell Suffragette Collection.

Introduction

'There is no point in work unless it absorbs you'

D. H. Lawrence

How and why does human labour matter to modernism? This book is concerned with modern labour, and specifically with the ways in which labour was experienced, imagined and represented in the years between 1890 and 1930. 'Labour' is one way of designating human productive activity. My choice of this term is, of course, a modern one: our capacity to think of human work as an abstraction, as 'labour power' rather than as the activity of a concrete individual, only arises in the context of modern industrial production.[1] The word 'labour' turns our attention to productive activity that is paid and that takes place outside the home, since it seeks to capture human activity within the terms of wages and employment.[2] Talking in terms of 'labour' also carries important value judgements about history and about politics, and thus risks both homogenizing the historical period we are studying, and reproducing its hierarchies and exclusions. This is a particular problem for the analysis of women's work, which assumes so many disparate and unpaid forms that it can be invisible, or at least invisible as 'labour'. The relations between women and 'labour' will thus be a recurrent theme of this book.

When I talk of 'modern labour' I am drawing attention to the specific forms labour assumes within the historical process of modernization. In that sense, modern labour has a long history in Britain, stretching back for two hundred and fifty years. But I am also using the notion of 'modern labour' in a much more historically constricted sense, to refer to labour as it was experienced in the moment that, within literary studies, we know as the moment of 'modernism'. 'Modernism' is a cultural expression of the intense development of key aspects of modernity, to the point where they are reconfigured as an internal critique. Modernist cultural expression vigorously repudiated key aspects of modern life as it was experienced in the early years of the twentieth century, drawing on the creative imagination to generate new understandings of time, of history, and of selfhood. By focussing this study on the years between 1890 and 1930, we will be able to see this cultural contestation of the meanings of labour in particularly vivid form.

As societies and cultures become industrialized, urban, secular and democratic, the experience of work is crucially modified. As we shall see, this produces a wide range of responses, many of which stress the fragmentation and mechanization of labour in the modern period. Modern labour is often experienced, and represented, as oppressive, intense and deadening, and as such we might assume that it would be seen as the negation of the individual. In fact, however, cultural responses to modern labour are often marked by a complex, but persistent, desire to read selfhood in and through the activity of labour. In the many different forms of writing and of visual representation that are explored in this book, we will find an effort to articulate the relations between labour and selfhood, expressed in ideas of fulfilment, absorption, vitality, will, species being and agency.

This book is organized in terms of a number of key questions, and it is the aim of each of the chapters to advance our understanding of these questions, and to suggest at least some answers. The first question is concerned with the languages and images available to people in the modern period for thinking about labour, and specifically with how these developed in the early years of the twentieth century. What were the distinctive ways in which writers and artists sought to capture the activity of labour in the period: how did they set in play existing philosophical, political and cultural traditions and how were these modified? I will also consider how specific technologies reconfigured the understanding of labour and selfhood. If modern labour is mechanized labour, then how do different forms of technology create or inhibit the articulation of selfhood? Thirdly, how do the experience and the significance of labour in the period vary according to gender? Is the connection between labour and liberation understood differently for men and women? And finally, I will ask how an attention to the idea of labour might modify our readings of cultural texts of the period, and particularly of literary texts where this question has been systematically marginalized in recent critical work.

I have suggested that the period from 1890 to 1930 interests me particularly because it is a moment of energetic and polemical critique of key aspects of the modern experience. In this sense, my periodization is driven by a cultural preference for the innovative and iconoclastic. But this period also helps to focus larger historical questions. For example, if modernization is closely bound up with the development of democracy, this is the moment at which the expansion of the franchise makes modernity an achieved fact. Eric Hobsbawm has written powerfully about the period from 1875 to 1914 as the 'Age of Empire' asking us to reflect on the continuing resonance of this period in our contemporary world: 'we . . . are no longer in it, but we do not know how much of it is still in us'.[3] Although I have chosen to start at the slightly later date of 1890, the force of Hobsbawm's question is very real: we do still live to some extent in the shadow of this period, and it is useful to remember that familiarity as much as the more explicit sense of strangeness generated by detailed study of these early days of the twentieth century.

These 'early days of the twentieth century' still contain many of the values and ideas of the 1890s, and writers on the Edwardian period have often begun their analyses with the final years of Victoria's reign, in order to identify some of the key industrial, international and cultural conflicts that characterize this period. Thus, for example, in *The Edwardian Temperament*, Jonathan Rose begins his research with the year 1895, a moment when he can begin to discern the putting in place of the characteristic Edwardian 'turn of mind'.[4] The Edwardians are, indeed, at the heart of this study, and most of the writers I will discuss reached maturity in this crucial first decade. Rose writes, rather caustically, of the extraordinary openness to new ideas and new sensations in this period, suggesting that the Edwardians 'resolved psychic conflicts by believing in everything' (210). I would suggest that this multiplicity was rather more painfully experienced than Rose indicates, but, nonetheless, it is part of the fascination of these early days of the century that so many different modes of understanding the world were seriously and assiduously explored.

In terms of the specific areas with which this book is concerned, ending in 1930 has a clear rationale. By the thirties, D. H. Lawrence was dead, Sylvia Pankhurst had transferred her energies from the labour movement to the international struggle against fascism, the general strike of 1926 had been defeated, and the typewriter had become an everyday technology with a clear role in business and in the arts. Also, in the 1930s, the cultural images and arguments explored in this book were substantially modified. The philosophical, political and cultural eclecticism I explore below gives way to a more structured set of approaches to the study of labour, expressed in more rigidly defined disciplinary spaces. Both politically and culturally, labour assumed a greater prominence in the thirties, and in an increasingly polarized political landscape across Europe, exploration of the complexity of labour gave way to attempts to capture its larger historical symbolism.

The decision to pursue my research into labour and selfhood up to 1930 also reflects my unease with the widespread representation of the Great War as a cultural and social watershed, an event that brought a period to an end. There is a rich and diverse body of historical and cultural criticism on the significance of the Great War for British culture in the rest of the twentieth century, and I do not seek to deny the power or the pertinence of such work.[5] Clearly, the War marked the lives of all who lived in that period, and led to conceptual and political challenges in many areas of British life. It also, of course, had very specific consequences for the organization of labour as the absence of so many young men at the Front led to the recruitment of new workers, many of them women. But in the course of my research for this book, I have been struck not by the sense of rupture generated by the War, but rather by the effort at continuity. Writers carry on arguments about labour and selfhood they had articulated before the War, and with real vigour and commitment. Sylvia Pankhurst and D. H. Lawrence, for example, are emphatically marked by the War, both personally and culturally, but it does not bring to an end the kinds of questions they were seeking to ask about labour and selfhood in the early years of the century. Also, when we find the War explicitly invoked as a key historical event, for example in discussions of the General Strike, this is done in order to create a sense of historical continuity rather than to suggest a traumatic disruption.

In studying labour and selfhood between 1890 and 1930, I am trying to capture distinctive aspects of modern labour over these forty years. Writing at the end of this period, Adriano Tilgher said that the modern era was one in which 'the conception of man as primarily a worker has spread its roots into every field of thought'.[6] The nature and significance of work certainly changed significantly during the long and uneven process of industrialization in Britain, and one expression of these changes was the increasing identification of an individual with the forms of paid labour in which he or she was employed. Krishan Kumar has pointed out that the idea of 'unemployment' as a particular mode of social being 'was first elaborated and analysed in the 1890s', and this new concept provides some indication of new ways of thinking about labour and about selfhood.[7]

The organization of labour underwent significant structural modifications from pre-industrial to modern times. The pre-industrial period was characterized by variety and instability of work. Work was seasonal, and periods of intense work could be followed by periods of slackening, where work was sought in a number of different fields. The whole household was likely to contribute to the sustenance of the family, and much of the work was likely to take place in the home. In the early period of industrialization, paid wages were still likely to be only a part of a household income. Instability was still a common facet of working practices, and even skilled workers had to cope with periods where work was slack, or non-existent. There were also high levels of casual labour in most branches of industry. Again, however, all family members were likely to contribute to the household income, with women and children often earning money through work undertaken in the home.

In the early years of the twentieth century, 'the occupational composition of the working classes changed substantially' with very significant increases in the numbers of men working on the railways and in the mines.[8] Those in work now found themselves less subject to irregular and uncertain patterns of employment: mechanization meant that work had to be undertaken regularly, as the cost of interrupting production could be significant; and widespread unionization was an effective means of protecting employment practices. Paid employment now became a much more significant proportion of family income, and was very likely to be undertaken by men. Women's employment will be discussed further below, but it is worth noting here that while twenty-five per cent of married women were employed in 1851, by 1911 only ten per cent were in employment.[9] The concept of the 'family wage', developed in the middle of the nineteenth century, presented a model of household income in which men earned sufficiently high wages that women were not required to contribute to the household income. Trade unions campaigned, often unsuccessfully, to secure this level of remuneration in the early years of the twentieth century. They also campaigned systematically to eradicate casual and sweated labour, seeing both as a threat to the high wage levels they sought. This frequently amounted to attacking women's right to work in specific industries, as we will see below, but it also meant systematic criticism of significant sections of immigrant workers. David Feldman has discussed the significance of 'sweated labour' in debates leading up to the passing of the Aliens Act, which sought to reduce Jewish immigration to Britain in 1905.[10] We can catch something of the intensity of this debate in Robert Sherard's 1905 study of child labour, *The Child-Slaves of Britain*, where he writes:

What is the cause of this, do you ask? The continuous pumping of alien filth from the kennels and ghettos of Europe, Asia and America into the East End of London through the sewage pipes of the steamship companies. . . . Faces that were not with us at Agincourt peer at you from every doorway.[11]

The language of 'slavery' Sherard employs in his title serves to create a link between the communities from which he withdraws so emphatically and forms of labour that are the antithesis of self-realization, and thus of modernity.

In the same period when work begins to be grasped as the defining aspect of human individuality, however, it is actually declining as a proportion of that individual's daily life. The passing of the Ten Hours Act, regulating working hours in industry, in 1847 was followed by campaigns for a nine-hour day in the 1870s and an eight-hour day in the 1890s. Paul Thompson points to the fact that the average working week was reduced from something over sixty hours in the nineteenth century to fifty-three hours in 1911, while John Burnett indicates that the figure is further reduced to forty-eight hours by 1920.[12] This reduction in working hours was accompanied by the significant growth of a leisure industry. The number of cinemas in Britain increased rapidly in the early years of the cinema, the mass-circulation press more than doubled in size, while new and bigger Music Halls were built across Britain. Broadcasting and motorized transport both opened up new forms of leisure as the century developed. The tension between the persistent attempt to articulate labour as self-realization, and the very real reduction of the time spent on labour by almost all workers, is part of the fascination of this period.

One reason for a reduction in working hours was greater 'efficiency' in many branches of industry. Efficiency was actively sought in many areas of industrial and social endeavour in the period; and this quest reached a particular form of articulation in the movement known as 'Taylorism'. 'Taylorism' was named after Frederick Winslow Taylor, who published his *Principles of Scientific Management* in 1911.[13] As James F. Knapp has argued, Taylorism is:

not a single theory, but rather a number of associated practices, ranging from technical procedures for machining steel, to time and motion studies, to recommendations about pay incentives, to philosophical generalizations about the relevance of scientific 'law' to economic production.[14]

Taylor sought to design structures of management and forms of production that would eliminate 'awkward, inefficient, or ill-directed movements' (*Principles*, 7). His method was to reduce labour to its simplest components, to devise the most efficient method of carrying out each minute part of a task, and to devise pay structures that would reward workers for modifying their habitual work routines in favour of those known to be more efficient. 'Time and motion' studies were the means by which managers could measure each aspect of a production process to arrive at the most efficient method of operating. This process involved fragmentation of the labour process, detailed and constant measurements of workers' actions and productivity, and the redesigning of fundamental aspects of the labour process. Taylor was clear that the successful implementation of scientific forms of management would mean the reshaping of the worker, and the eradication of habitual working methods, but argued that 'our duty, as well as our opportunity, lies in systematically cooperating to train and to make this competent man' (7).

This process of fragmentation and measurement, in which control of the labour process shifts from worker to manager, was readily understood as simply the culmination of that process of the division of labour that began in the eighteenth century, in other words as the epitome of modern labour. This seems to be the view of Harry Braverman, whose *Labor and Monopoly Capitalism* (1974) was such an influential account of the fate of work in the twentieth century.[15] But this fragmentation, and 'degradation' of work is only part of the story of labour in the early years of the century. The search for efficiency certainly commanded widespread cultural and political support,[16] but the implementation of Taylorist principles was always rather uneven. Traditional practices survived in many branches of industry, and the acceptance of new working methods was very closely allied to the actual realization of higher levels of wages. 'Waste' was not removed from either the practice, or the imagination, of labour in these early years of the century.

The period between 1890 and 1930 has often been seen as particularly significant for women, and is frequently represented as the historical moment when women gained access to key aspects of modernity. As Rita Felski has argued 'the emancipation of women is presented as inseparably linked to their movement into the workplace and the public sphere'.[17] Adding access to the vote, of course, adds to the sense of this as a crucial moment in British women's history. In an account of the relations between feminism and early modernism, Ann Ardis once more identifies labour as a key site of women's emancipation in the period, as 'women enter the workplace in significant numbers for the first time'.[18] As we will see, there was indeed an acute sense in this period that labour was a central issue for women in a quite new way. But the participation of women in the labour force did not change as dramatically as these judgements might suggest.

The percentage of women in the workforce changed very little between 1850 and 1930, staying at around thirty per cent for most of the period. It actually dipped a little in the last quarter of the nineteenth century and then climbed back up gradually over the opening decades of the twentieth century.[19] What did change was the participation of married women in the workforce, which declined substantially, and also the fields of work in which women were likely to participate, which expanded significantly.

As we have seen, the participation of married women in paid forms of labour fell in this period. This was partly because of a commitment to raising the earnings of male workers to the point that they could financially support a whole household, a central part of Trade Union policy in the second half of the nineteenth century. This policy developed in the context of a growing sense within working-class communities that for married women to work was a threat to 'decency' and respectability. This sense was reinforced by policies of the state, which assumed a male breadwinner in the way it designed and implemented social policies: for example, National Insurance regulations limited the access of married women to employment benefits.[20] Concern over levels of infant mortality also created very significant pressures on working mothers, expressed by the passing of the Factory and Workshop Act of 1895, which restricted women's early return to work after giving birth. Finally, many trades and professions, including teaching and the civil service, operated a 'marriage bar', which required women to leave their employment at the moment of their marriage.

The female working population in the early years of the twentieth century, then, consisted mostly of young single women. As they had done since the nineteenth century, many of these women worked in domestic service: John Burnett suggests that in 1901, forty per cent of women who worked still worked in domestic service (*Useful Toil*, 140). But new areas of employment did also open up, including, shop work, clerical work, nursing and teaching. Following the passing of the Sex Disqualification Removal Act in 1919, a number of professions and learned societies also became open to women for the first time. In the context of a general expansion of the clerical workforce in this period, it is striking that while only one per cent of clerks were women in 1851, by 1951 sixty per cent of clerical workers were female.[21] During the First World War, women also entered new forms of employment in munitions factories. This move was surrounded by anxiety, on behalf of both employers and Trade Unions, and Veronica Beechey argues that engineers working in the industry before the War:

> eventually reached a series of agreements with the employers and the government that women should only be allowed to enter the industry as unskilled and semi-skilled workers.[22]

If women did succeed in gaining access to training, and consequently to skilled forms of labour, they were required to leave at the end of the War.

Despite these restrictions on work in the munitions factories, however, women still had access to relatively higher rates of pay and shorter working hours, particularly if they had previously been employed in domestic service. One of the women whose autobiographies were collected by John Burnett writes quite explicitly about the benefits of this munitions factory work, asking, 'what would she find in this great new venture? She already had a feeling of a new freedom, and of time to think' and adding that she was 'enjoying a freedom that she had not known for a long time, having been like her sister in domestic service' (*Useful Toil*, 125–27).

This narrative of liberation through labour is far from the universal experience of labour for women in the early years of the twentieth century, however. Deborah Thom has argued that between 1900 and 1920 'visual and verbal representations of the working woman changed' in such a way that women's labour became overwhelmingly associated with the evils of sweated labour.[23] 'Sweated labour' refers to labour involving long hours, very low rates of pay and unsanitary working conditions, and was the site of considerable agitation in the early years of the century. We have seen that sweated labour was associated with immigrant communities, but it was also associated with women, who were held to be driving down wages by agreeing to work in such dreadful conditions. An exhibition of 'the sweating system at work', organized under the auspices of the *Daily News* in 1906, concentrated almost exclusively on women's labour, involving as it did forty-two women and only two men.[24] The National Anti-Sweating League, which was set up after this exhibition, was to campaign vigorously for the establishment of Boards to regulate industries felt to be particularly liable to employ sweating. And Deborah Thom points out the first Trade Boards set up to regulate pay in sweated industries dealt overwhelmingly with areas of employment strongly associated with women ('Free from Chains', 89).

This identification of women with the low pay and poor working conditions associated with sweated labour produced a number of, sometimes opposed, political responses. Sally Alexander has discussed the importance of the economic position of working women for the Fabian Society.[25] The Society formed a women's group in 1908, and much of their campaigning was concerned with women's labour, and particularly with sweated labour.[26] Many women active in the Trade Union movement supported the introduction of a minimum wage to combat sweated labour, and also supported a broader range of 'protective legislation', designed to secure better working conditions for women.

Other parts of the feminist movement in this period, however, saw protective legislation as generally bad for the industrial status of women workers, since it would make it difficult for them ever to earn the same level of wages as men. Denise Riley suggests that the Open Door International for the Economic Emancipation of the Woman Worker, founded in 1926, saw legislation designed to protect the working mother as antagonistic to the interests of working women as a whole.[27] Many of the women who took up this position had come to feminism through the suffrage movement, and were broadly committed to equality of treatment for men and women.

Despite the poor rates of pay for women in the early years of the century, the difficulty of access to training, the insecurity of many jobs, the certainty of having to resign on marriage and the dreadful physical conditions in which many women worked, there is a persistent desire among women in this period to find some form of liberation, or fulfilment, through and in modern labour. Clementina Black wrote in 1915 of 'that wave of desire for a personal working life which forms so marked an element in the general development of modern women'.[28] Three years earlier, Rebecca West wrote more succinctly of 'the women who are alive: the working women'.[29] Both suggest that work is the space in which modern women might re-imagine themselves, and make themselves 'alive'.

There are a number of books that have explored arguments and ideas related to the present study in recent decades. David Meakin's *Man and Work: Literature and Culture in Industrial Society* (1976) is a wide-ranging exploration of the ways in which work has been represented, and experienced, as an integral part of human identity. Meakin argues that 'consciousness is born of that active confrontation with nature', and his book examines the historical emergence of particular narratives and images for understanding the activity of human labour.[30] The burden of Meakin's argument is the degradation of work in the modern period, and he explores traces of alienation and rootlessness across a range of writings. He argues forcefully for the importance of returning to the social and political conditions in which we would be able once more to grasp work as 'the natural centre of a whole and integrated existence' (156). Meakin's polemic is engaged and engaging. It is regrettable that he gives almost no attention to women's labour, however, for as we shall see attention to women's work may offer a rather different sense of what is possible at any given historical moment in terms of imagining labour and selfhood.

Ruth Danon's *Work in the English Novel* (1985) is a study of the ways in which work enters the imaginative landscape of narrative fiction in Britain. She is concerned to explore the 'gospel of work' as represented in eighteenth- and nineteenth-century fictions, examining both its utilitarian and its idealist modes. She begins by discussing the aspiration to integrate life and work in *Robinson Crusoe*, and then explores the fictional realization of this integration through the domestic space in *David Copperfield*. Her study ends with a discussion of the challenges of modern labour, understood in terms of instrumentality and the limits of 'vocation'. Her key text here is *Jude the Obscure* where, she argues, 'physical labor, which provided, in earlier novels, the primary model of integrated work, has become alienated labor'.[31] This narrative of decline, towards instrumentality and alienation, means that this book has little to say about the ways in which such decline was actively challenged in the twentieth century, ending instead with a sense that labour and life cannot be integrated in the modern world.

James F. Knapp's *Literary Modernism and the Transformation of Work* (1988), however, is centrally concerned with representations of labour in the early years of the twentieth century. Knapp describes the aim of his study as bringing into relationship with each other 'the formal experiments of modernist literature, the institutionally sanctioned criticism of that literature, and the transformations in the nature of work which are generally associated with the term "scientific management"'.[32] He provides fascinating and detailed readings of key modernist texts, and develops a cogent overall argument about the impact of Taylorism in those early years of the century. Using Taylorism metonymically, to figure all aspects of labour in the period, however, does reduce the general historical scope of this study, and Knapp is rather forced into the general conclusion that 'while modernist literature spoke loudly against the degradation of all kinds of work, it nevertheless tacitly accepted contemporary assumptions about the instrumentality of reason' (18). Indeed, as the book progresses, it becomes less and less concerned with the details of forms of labour and more concerned with the prevalence of instrumental reason.

Anson Rabinbach's *The Human Motor; Energy, Fatigue and the Origins of Modernity* (1992) has been very influential for this study, although relatively few traces of this work actually remain in my final text. Rabinbach's work explores the idea of the human body as a machine as it develops throughout the nineteenth century. This involves detailed exploration of theories of energy and fatigue, of the scientific measurement of work and of exhaustion, or failures of energy and of labour power. Rabinbach's vigorous engagement with texts in different genres, from scientific treatise to imaginative literature, made me aware of the importance of being open to multiplicity and to the messiness of cultural history. The historical and geographical scope of Rabinbach's study, however, while undoubtedly part of its originality and importance, meant that it was not easy to bring the detail of his argument into my own work. I certainly recommend this text to anyone interested in the broader European context of studies of work in the early years of the twentieth century.

Finally, two further texts, while not drawn on explicitly in this study, have reassured me about the potential and the importance of labour as a topic in cultural history. Richard Godden's *Fictions of Labor: William Faulkner and the South's Long Revolution* (1997) shows the ways in which careful attention to the history of labour relations within a particular culture can illuminate our readings of complex literary texts.[33] And Keith Thomas's *Oxford Book of Work* (1999) constitutes a compelling record of the multiplicity of cultural responses to work, and demonstrates the extraordinary range of texts to which our critical energies could now be turned.[34]

In the first chapter of this book I consider philosophical explorations of modern labour and selfhood, which are of particular relevance for the writings I will explore in the rest of the book. John Locke's discussion of the relations between labour and individual property at the end of the seventeenth century is analysed as a key text for understanding the language of possession in relation to the language of labour. We then turn to Adam Smith's inquiry into the origin of the wealth of nations, an inquiry that placed human labour at the centre of an understanding of value. A reading of aspects of G. W. F. Hegel's philosophy leads to a more general argument about the mutual implications of labour and selfhood in his work as well as in the writings of Arthur Schopenhauer in the early years of the nineteenth century. This is followed by a detailed analysis of the significance of labour in the cultural and political writings of Thomas Carlyle and Karl Marx, and then of John Ruskin and William Morris. The chapter concludes with an analysis of labour and selfhood in the writings of three thinkers writing in the period with which this study is concerned, Friedrich Nietzsche, Olive Schreiner and Sigmund Freud.

The second chapter is concerned with the ways in which our understanding of labour is inflected by technology. Given the concern of this book with 'modern labour', it is important to examine the impact of mechanization, since the fragmentation and alienation caused by machinery are often seen as the defining qualities of work in a modern society. I have chosen two very different technologies, the typewriter and the washing machine, which are nonetheless both part of our sense of what makes a world modern. In my analysis of the typewriter, I consider the reorganization of clerical work in the period, the use of typewriters by creative artists, and the symbolic and narrative role of the typewriter in a range of fictional texts. In examining the washing machine, I discuss the significant technological and social developments in laundry in the period, and then consider the metaphorical associations with washing, and with dirty laundry, in imaginative texts of the period.

The third chapter is concerned with the work of Sylvia Pankhurst in the first twenty-five years of the twentieth century. Pankhurst is probably best known as a suffrage activist, and as part of a family of suffragettes. Her connection to that movement gives me an opportunity to reflect on the ways in which labour entered into the texts and the arguments of one of the most important political movements of the period in Britain. Pankhurst also had a particular interest in working women, and her essays, poems and paintings are the subject of detailed discussion. I consider Pankhurst's essays on working women in relation to journalistic and political traditions for the representation of women's labour, discuss the extent to which she was able to think of her own creative labours as 'work', and finally develop a detailed reading of her paintings and drawings of working women.

The fourth chapter is concerned with the importance of labour for the imaginative writings of D. H. Lawrence. Lawrence is considered as a modernist writer, but one with a particular interest in theories of selfhood and in the social and cultural significance of labour. Lawrence's repudiation of egoism, and his commitment to vitalism, are read in relation to the changing significance of labour within his writings. His vitalism is also connected to aspects of suffrage thinking and activism. The chapter considers the concern with 'neurasthenia' as a failure of will and a disengagement from labour in the early years of the century and connects this to Lawrence's short story, 'England, My England'. It then explores Lawrence's repudiation of a Freudian 'unconscious', and concludes with a consideration of the importance of labour in Lawrence's novel, *Lady Chatterley's Lover*.

In the final chapter, I examine the 'general strike' as an event and as a process with an integral relationship to the imagining of human labour in the early years of the twentieth century. The general strike is a distinctively modern form of political activism, relying on the gathering of large groups of workers into a single workplace, and also relying on modern communications both to initiate and to sustain it. My particular concern is with the forms of temporality implied by the process and the experience of the general strike. I examine the writings of the French political theorist, Georges Sorel on the general strike and consider their relation to the philosophical writings of Henri Bergson whose work was of great significance for many modernist writers. I consider the nature of syndicalism in Britain, and then examine the writings of John Waugh Scott, a philosopher who sought to understand both labour and selfhood in new ways. The chapter concludes with an analysis of the significance of the 1926 General Strike in a range of fictional writings.

I discuss a wide range of writers in this book, and consider a great variety of texts, including philosophical writings, novels, poetry, journalism, political theory and visual arts. I do not claim that these texts exhaust the range of ideas and aspirations associated with labour between 1890 and 1930. I do, however, suggest that the cumulative effect of my readings is to make us aware of both the importance and the complexity of 'labour' in this period, something that has been largely overlooked in recent literary and cultural histories of the period. If these readings also help us to understand more of our own conflicted and yet intense relations to the activity and the significance of human labour, they will have served their purpose.

CHAPTER ONE

Philosophies of labour and selfhood

My discussion of the relations between modernism, labour and selfhood from 1890 to 1930 begins in this chapter with an exploration of philosophical writing from the eighteenth to the twentieth centuries. The theorization of human labour has long been a concern of philosophical writing, and the relations between labour, individuality and political power have particularly fascinated philosophers concerned with the nature and the limits of the modern state. There is something perhaps a little perverse about this initial turn to the philosophical in a study that is largely concerned to develop a cultural history based on the formal and imaginative complexity of cultural representations. In the book as a whole I have sought to avoid giving theoretical or historical priority to any one mode of writing, believing that we may be better able to grasp the passions, the pains, and the fantasies associated with the activity of human labour at any given historical moment if we attend to different forms of cultural activity and different modes of representation. My decision to situate this project initially in relation to traditions of philosophical writing is, in that sense, a methodological compromise. I do not intend to suggest that the texts I discuss below give us an overview of the relations between labour and selfhood from the eighteenth century to the twentieth. At any given moment in that period different imaginings and theorizations of labour were competing, transforming and emerging, in ways that would require much more close-grained readings to uncover. Rather, the texts I have selected for discussion below set in play ideas, aspirations and arguments that will emerge in a variety of forms in the cultural texts that make up the focus of this study. Since my particular focus in this book is the ways in which labour and selfhood could be thought, imagined or experienced together in early twentieth-century Britain, I will concentrate on philosophical texts that clearly had an impact on political and cultural arguments and texts within that national context.

A number of insistent questions and themes emerge from the philosophical texts I have chosen, and these will re-emerge throughout the following chapters. The defining aspects of 'modern labour' are found by many writers to lie in the division of labour: that increasing tendency to break labour down into ever-smaller constituent parts. The rapidity with which this fragmentation took hold of many forms of the labour process, and the interaction of this with increasing mechanization led many writers to anxious speculation about the alienating and destructive tendencies of modern labour. This anxiety about the subjective and social costs of mechanization is, however, met, and to some extent answered, by a vigorous organicism that emerges in so many of the texts I will discuss in this chapter and also throughout the book as a whole. Here labour is understood as the energy of will, as the process of growth and creativity that drives both the individual and the human species. At its most extreme, this tendency develops into a vitalism that sees a life force driving all of nature and of culture, and also sees labour as the space in which this vital energy could receive its fullest expression.

The philosophical explorations of labour I discuss in this chapter are also engaged in a series of explorations of political legitimacy and of political subjectivities. I begin my discussion with John Locke, whose exploration of the capacity of labour to bestow ownership underpins many much later articulations of the relations between labour, property and selfhood. When I turn to Hegel, and to Marx, I am interested more particularly in the ways in which labour enters into arguments about the nature and the meaning of freedom, as both an ethical and a political category. The fact that political structures move definitely towards the representation of 'labour', with the formation of Labour parties and Communist parties throughout Europe between 1890 and 1930, makes the relations between labour and political selfhood of particular interest for this study. The idea of labour as the source of economic value intersects in the period with arguments about labour as the source of ethical value and of political legitimacy, although once again these ideas are crucially inflected by anxieties surrounding the fragmentation and mechanization of modern labour.

The tensions between labour as self-fulfilment and labour as self-sacrifice that emerge in so many of the texts discussed in this chapter will find fuller textual expression in many of the poetic and fictional texts I discuss later in this volume. Modernist texts so often strive to give the fullest possible expression to the destructive tendencies of modernity while simultaneously working to transcend these in the organic or vital energies of aesthetic form. The capacity of labour to embody both the drive towards creation and the certainty of ever-increasing alienation was to fascinate many writers in the early years of the twentieth century, and to energize many aspects of the broad cultural project of modernism. The very particular role of artistic labour within this dynamic was to prove a compelling issue for many writers of the period. D. H. Lawrence and Sylvia Pankhurst reflect on the physical arduousness of artistic labour, but also show an acute sensitivity to the ways in which it is quite unlike other forms of modern labour since it is still only occasionally mechanized, and almost never fragmented. This specific quality of artistic labour was indeed to form a central part of Hannah Arendt's later study of *The Human Condition* (1958), a powerful critique of the tendency of modern philosophers to elevate 'labour' as an ethical and political good and thus to incorporate all aspects of human behaviour under the yoke of necessity:

We have almost succeeded in levelling all human activities to the common de-nominator of securing the necessities of life and providing for their abundance. Whatever we do, we are supposed to do for the sake of 'making a living' . . . The artist is thus the only 'worker' left in a labouring society.[1]

As we shall see in chapter 2, however, the capacity of technology funda-mentally to transform artistic labour was already informing the cultural imagination of modernism profoundly and the special quality of artistic labour was in question throughout the period.

The final recurring philosophical and political question to which this study will return is the proper employment of women between 1890 and 1930. The intensification of many forms of industrial labour led to frequent legislative interventions designed to protect women workers throughout the nineteenth century. Such protection led to women's exclusion from many forms of industrial labour and their secure implanting in lower-paid forms of manual labour. The drive to protection was underpinned by a series of arguments about the relations between labour and the human condition that were, as we shall see, frequently gendered. This apparent incompatibility between women and labour interacts curiously with the historical emergence of women into new forms of labour, such as typing and secretarial work, and also with the slow opening up of the professions to women. Once more, attention to labour allows us to map the historical and cultural tensions that drove the modernist cultural imagination in quite distinct ways.

The sudden, spectacular rise of labor from the lowest, most despised position to the highest rank, as the most esteemed of all human activities, began when Locke discovered that labor is the source of all property.[2]

John Locke's philosophical legacy is now perhaps seen primarily in terms of his epistemological arguments developed in the *Essay Concerning Human Understanding* (1690). These are concerned with perception, innate ideas, the relations between essence and language, and the nature of personal identity. Yet it is his *Two Treatises of Government* (1690) that contain what have been described as 'the most influential statements he ever made' concerning individual property and human labour.[3] Locke's theorization of the development and legitimacy of civil government begins with the assumption that men are both free and equal. This would seem to imply that all men have an equal right to use all the land and resources provided for mankind by God, and yet Locke's overall argument seeks to defend both the legitimacy of private property and its centrality to the development and sustenance of sound civil government. The legitimacy of private property, for Locke, is founded on the activity of human labour.

Locke's point is that natural resources are of no use to mankind until they have been appropriated; food must be ingested if it is to nourish, and this amounts to taking possession to the point of mixing resources and the body indissolubly. This appropriation is generalized in the activity of labour, since this amounts to a mixing of 'the *Labour* of his Body, and the *Work* of his hands [which] we may say, are properly his' with nature, in order to create ownership.[4] Having added his labour to raw materials and resources, the resulting product becomes the possession of the given individual and this is legitimate and according to reason, provided that there is enough and as good left in common for others.

This model also holds good, Locke argues, for the enclosure and possession of land: '[God] gave it to the use of the Industrious and Rational, (and *Labour* was to be *his Title* to it)' ('Second Treatise', 333). Locke argues that mankind has been commanded by God to labour and to create riches from the earth, and thus that 'subduing or cultivating the Earth, and having Dominion we see are joyned together' (334). By creating good out of what would otherwise be barren and neglected, mankind follows divine command and gains individual possession of land. In his 'First Treatise', Locke had already argued that the command to labour was the most fundamental connection between the divine and civil society:

God sets him to work for his living, and seems rather to give him a Spade into his hand, to subdue the Earth, than a Scepter to rule over its Inhabitants. *In the Sweat of thy Face thou shalt eat thy Bread*, says God to him. ('First Treatise', 208)

And this general command to labour also becomes the means by which ownership of property can be legitimated.

Locke is clearly aware that the requirement to leave as much and as good in common may pose problems in the context of late seventeenth-century Europe, but he argues that across the world as a whole, and particularly in America, there is still ample uncultivated land that could be made productive. Such uncultivated land offends against the general requirement to labour and thus to increase value, and Locke suggests that 'the increase of lands and the right imploying of them is the great art of government' ('Second Treatise', 339). Labour and the creation of value are thus fundamental human capacities, but they must always be limited by the recognition that mankind should not consume excessively to the point where goods or artefacts are spoiled and wasted. At first, this would seem to imply a natural limit to both the appropriation of land and the production of goods to what could satisfy the needs of the individual. But Locke notes that the invention of money sets mankind free from this limitation: 'And thus *came in the use of Money*, some lasting thing that Men might keep without spoiling, and that by mutual consent men would take in exchange for the truly useful, but perishable Supports of Life' (343). Thus, private property, enclosure of land and accumulation of wealth in the form of money are all legitimated by the original process of mixing labour with nature to create value. And civil government is then understood as existing primarily to preserve the ownership of property set in place by such appropriative acts of labour.

In Locke's account of the formative role of labour in the establishment of the structures of civil society, there is little attention to the details of the labour process or to the subjective meanings of labour. As Johannes Rohbeck has argued, 'Locke does not describe the labour process in the sense of a developed agrarian or skilled trades production which presupposes specific means of production', but rather he imagines labour as an originary, and largely solitary, act.[5] The social relations of labour receive very little attention. For example the fact that the labour of a servant, and the goods it produces, are the property of that servant's master receives almost no discussion, but is simply assumed as part of the order of things: 'the Grass my Horse has bit; the Turfs my servant has cut; and the Ore I have digged in any place where I have a right to them in common with others, become my *Property*' ('Second Treatise', 330). The horse, the servant and the self are all assumed to confer ownership on the same individual through the solitary act of labour. Within this act, Locke finds the fundamental relation between the divine and the realm of civil government, and he thus produces an account of mankind that puts the necessity of labour at the heart of what it means to be human.

Some eighty years later, when examining the nature and causes of the wealth of nations, the political economist Adam Smith was also to consider the relationship of labour to the fundamentally human. For Smith, the fundamental human capacity lies in the tendency to barter, truck and exchange, but this can only be understood in relation to the role of labour in the production of value and in relation to the historical division of labour.[6] Labour, Smith argues, is 'the real measure of the exchangeable value of all commodities' (*Wealth*, 26) and further anything that is bought with money, or through the bartering of goods, is actually purchased by labour to the extent that labour is the only original source of value:

Labour alone . . . never varying in its own value, is alone the ultimate and real standard by which the value of all commodities can at all times and places be estimated and compared. It is their real price; money is their nominal price only. (29)

But, for historical reasons, the exchangeable value of any commodity is more commonly expressed in money rather than in terms of the quantity of labour embodied in it. These historical reasons are connected to the division of labour, which Smith sees as fundamental to the creation, and the increase, of wealth.

The division of labour is what happens when manufacturing processes are broken down into their constituent parts, each of which is undertaken by a separate operative. Smith's example of this process, famously, is the manufacture of pins, and he details meticulously the various aspects of this manufacture and the formidable increases in productivity that can be achieved when it is broken down into its constituent parts of drawing out wire, straightening it, cutting it, and so on. By dividing the manufacture of pins into eighteen distinct operations, Smith calculated that it was possible for ten people to manufacture 48,000 pins in one day. This increase in productivity is brought about by increasing dexterity in individual operatives who are now able to concentrate all their energies into perfecting a small number of movements, by investment in specialized machinery, and also by the removal of time-consuming transfers from one activity to another by an individual worker. As Smith puts it, workers who are obliged to turn from one type of activity to another gain 'the habit of sauntering and of indolent careless application' (8).

The increasing tendency towards the division of labour in all branches of industry is, Smith argues, the source of increasing productivity and wealth. It is also what creates the need for money as a means to ensure the distribution of goods and services, since almost no individual worker could now hope, through his own labour, to meet all his needs. More worryingly for Smith, such division of labour also produces a potentially damaging set of consequences for the individual worker. Kathryn Sutherland has pointed out the extent to which Smith's text assumes a tight relationship between labour and selfhood, to the extent of assuming that 'we are the jobs we do, that personality is a function of work'.[7] Smith is indeed concerned that the increasing manual dexterity of workers might be accompanied by a significantly reduced capacity for concentrated or critical thought. His remedy is to some extent cultural: education and cultural goods are to offer some sort of compensation for the aspects of the human personality that are negated by modern labour. This creates a potential tension between work and the human that will be more fully explored in later philosophical and political texts, but it also suggests that culture might come to have an increasingly central role in the protection of boundaries of the human.[8]

Smith's other approach to the potentially negative consequences of the division of labour lies in a confident assertion of the possibility of sustained economic growth. Smith suggests that high wages are the necessary result of a successful economy, and argues that technological innovation makes it possible to sustain high levels of profitability in the fact of high wages (*Wealth*, 78). Conversely, he sees starvation or oppressive working conditions as symptoms of economic failure. His vision is of a workforce that is well paid, productive and steady and he does not support undue intensification of labour as it is likely to lead to exhaustion rather than to increasing productivity: 'great labour, either of mind or body, continued for several days together, is naturally followed by a great desire of relaxation' (73).

Like Locke, Smith has constructed an account of modern labour based on innate characteristics of the human personality, and on the centrality of labour to the production of value. Unlike Locke, however, he has foregrounded the importance of the labour process, and of the relations of production to productivity and to wealth at any given moment. Both Locke and Smith have a tendency to naturalize labour and the production of wealth, and also to conflate the human and the masculine. Despite the prominence of women in both domestic and industrial labour in the periods when both are writing, they produce a vision of a very masculine *homo faber*. This rhetorical coupling of men and labour will produce very particular difficulties for women writing later in the nineteenth or early twentieth centuries as they try to imagine the possible relations between women, labour and the essentially human.

The relationship of work to selfhood as well as the individual and social effects of the division of labour were also central to the philosophical writings of G. W. F. Hegel in the early years of the nineteenth century. Hegel studied the writings of Adam Smith, and had a detailed knowledge of British political and economic reform which fed directly into his 1821 study of law, morality and ethical life in relation to the state.[9] He also had a close and critical knowledge of the philosophical tradition of German Idealism which formed the terms and the methods of his exploration of the ways in which subject and object could confront and know each other in the practical and the conceptual world.

Hegel's philosophical explorations of consciousness and self-consciousness, the individual and the state, ethics and politics have been profoundly formative for a wide range of philosophers and social theorists since the early nineteenth century. His interest in freedom has made his work important for a revolutionary tradition broadly concerned with the possibility of liberation, while his historical interrogation of the institutions of the state has made his thinking crucial for organicist philosophers of individual and political continuities. And his dialectical method, which sees in the unfolding of contradiction the energies and the forms of new individual and social identities, has given us the most significant and tenacious theoretical account of historical change of the last two hundred years.

Hegel's explorations of the capacity of human reason to grasp its own unfolding and to perceive its own historical being were profoundly shaped by the philosophical legacy of Immanuel Kant, whose critiques had provided both a method and a rationale for the philosophical interrogation of reason as a grounding of certainty. Hegel's first major philosophical text, *Phenomenology of Spirit* (1807) is a study of the way the mind appears to itself; a study in which the emergence of selfhood has a crucial role. The volume begins with an account of the forms of knowledge available through unmediated sense perception and then develops progressively towards an analysis of self consciousness, where a consciousness strives to construct coherence and system, through the entry of desire where a self encounters the need both for recognition and for differentiation and towards reason and ultimately towards absolute knowing. As Richard J. Norman has argued, 'the theme of work, understood both as theoretical work and as practical work, is central to the *Phenomenology*' since, as we shall see, it is in the activity of labour that Hegel is able to glimpse a crucial mutual implication of reason, selfhood and freedom.[10]

The necessary progression from the consciousness of sense impressions towards some lived version of selfhood carries, for Hegel, certain specific requirements: these include recognition, freedom, work and discipline. For Hegel, indeed 'all modernity consists in coming closer to freedom on the concrete, practical level'.[11] The ways in which these categories are implicated in and through the category of selfhood can be most readily grasped in that section of the *Phenomenology* where Hegel deals with 'the truth of self-certainty' through a reading of what has come to be known as the 'master/slave dialectic'.[12] Hegel begins this part of his discussion by considering the conditions under which self-consciousness can begin to grasp itself as such. At first, he represents this process as the playing out of a logic of desire that seeks constantly to supersede an other as soon as it is recognized as such: 'self-consciousness is thus certain of itself only by superseding this other that presents itself to self-consciousness as an independent life: self-consciousness is Desire' (*Phenomenology*, 109). Hegel goes on to argue that 'a self-consciousness exists *for a self-consciousness*' (110), and that this offers a crucial glimpse of the notion of Spirit which will be the unity of these opposing self-consciousnesses: a possibility that can be grasped only much later in Hegel's systematic argument.

This idea that self-consciousness is a social fact leads Hegel towards the category of 'recognition' as a fundamental aspect of self-knowledge. He has argued that self-consciousness exists only if and when it exists for another, which is to say that it exists only in being acknowledged. This observation is both conflictual and complex. Firstly, in this fact of recognition the self is lost because it becomes an 'other' for the self that perceives it. Secondly, however, in this very process the self is confirmed because it refuses to see the other as essential and sees rather the simple affirmation of itself: 'this ambiguous supersession of its ambiguous otherness is equally an ambiguous return *into itself*' (111). Though self-consciousness had first been experienced through the exclusion of all extraneous objects from the self, this exclusion becomes problematic, and even impossible, when that other object is also a self. The initial confrontation of two selves does not reach its true philosophical meaning immediately, since 'they have not as yet exposed themselves to each other in the form of pure being-for-self' (113). The confrontation of self with self only assumes its true philosophical meaning when these selves have grasped the meaning of freedom in the most extreme sense of refusing their own embodied contingency: 'the individual who has not risked his life may well be recognized as a *person*, but he has not attained to the truth of this recognition as an independent self-consciousness' (114).

The notion that human selfhood is so markedly haunted by conflict and by death has proved to be part of Hegel's enduring legacy, and the ethical and political implications of such a model of subjectivity have been reworked in numerous philosophical traditions. Within the structure of the *Phenomenology*, however, this haunting is immediately answered by Hegel's very different theorization of the mediation of such conflict through the social fact of human labour. Hegel introduces this discussion of labour through the figures of the lord and the bondsman (often translated as the master and the slave), and the possibilities of selfhood that might be presented to them both. The lord and the bondsman are a displacement of the murderous encounter of selfhoods outlined above, in the sense that their inequality is an expression of the fact that one self has submitted to another and accepted a relation of radical inequality.

Initially, Hegel suggests, we might assume that the lord has the more achieved version of selfhood since he can relate himself mediately to the bondsman who exists both as a thing (since he is dependent) and as an independent being (since he is a consciousness). The lord thus achieves his recognition in and through another consciousness, but yet Hegel argues that 'for recognition proper the moment is lacking' (116) since the outcome of this encounter is a recognition that is one-sided and unequal. The very dependence of the bondsman that seemed to make it possible for the lord to achieve pure enjoyment of the thing is in fact his undoing, since 'what now confronts him is not an independent consciousness, but a dependent one' (117).

For the bondsman, on Hegel's model, the possibilities of selfhood are ultimately more promising. Firstly, living in a state of fear or of dread produces the perception of freedom that Hegel had already argued was attached to the sensation of risk, of putting one's life at stake and thus challenging the contingency of the present moment. Hegel suggests that 'through his service he rids himself of his attachment to natural existence in every single detail; and gets rid of it by working on it' (117), and this is achieved not simply through the social fact of dependence but also in and through the experience of labour. Hegel argues that through work 'the bondsman becomes conscious of what he truly is' (118). Work is a temporal and practical process through which the other can be glimpsed and it also creates a product in which the fact of otherness can be captured in a way that confirms the self-consciousness of the worker:

Desire has reserved to itself the pure negating of the object and thereby its un-alloyed feeling of self. But that is the reason why this satisfaction is itself only a fleeting one, for it lacks the side of objectivity and permanence. Work, on the other hand, is desire held in check, fleetingness staved off; in other words work forms and shapes the thing. The negative relation to the object becomes its *form* and something *permanent*, because it is precisely for the worker that the object has independence. . . . it is in this way, therefore, that consciousness, *qua* worker, comes to see in this independent being [of the object] its *own* independence. (118)

In the practical activity of making, of producing a finished object, the worker becomes aware that being-for-self belongs to him, and that he thus exists essentially in his own right.

And so Hegel's conclusion to this section would seem to be that in work, where the bondsman might expect to find alienation and a reflection of his dependence, he in fact 'acquires a mind of his own' (119). But we should treat this conclusion with some caution, since this 'mind of his own' is still some way from the articulation of reason and freedom to which Hegel aspires. Both lord and bondsman are marked negatively by the unequal relation that defines their being, and Hegel insists that for the bondsman ultimately 'having a "mind of one's own" is self-will, a freedom that is still enmeshed in servitude' (119). Self-will as a distorted and negative articulation of the selfhood that might be expressed in and through the experience of labour is a motif that will return repeatedly in the texts and arguments explored in later sections of this book, and will also receive a strikingly different treatment in the discussion of Arthur Schopenhauer below.

Before following through this trajectory of human labour and will, however, I would like to return to the question of the division of labour which structures so many accounts of the specificity of modern labour. As Raymond Plant has argued, Hegel was not indifferent to the social and individual costs of such fragmentation, but sought rather to save 'the inner life of man within the commercial system'.[13] Hegel's model of historical development allows us to glimpse continuities within apparently radical disjunctions, and his account of labour equally sustains a vision of collective relations within and through the fact of fragmentation. In other words, although modern labour produces isolation and fragmentation it is also the space in which a new version of the social becomes imaginable.

Thus, Hegel writes about the division of labour that 'this abstraction of skill and means makes the *dependence* and *reciprocity* of human beings in the satisfaction of their needs complete and entirely necessary' (*Philosophy of Right*, §198). Although the integration inherent in a particular form of the labour process may have broken down, new forms of cooperation develop that will themselves be sustained by new forms of social institution. We become consumers of human effort that is not simply our own but a collective and cooperative effort. Also, Hegel follows Locke in seeing an intimate connection between the fact of human labour and the institution of private property, and thus sees a connection between labour and the structures of the modern state: 'The development of the modern state is therefore shown by Hegel to be a rationally discernible development from human labour' (Plant, *Hegel*, 94).

But this complexly interrelated and reciprocal system of needs mediated by the institutions of the state can still feel like loneliness, and Hegel acknowledges that the modern worker may simply not grasp the network of relationships through which he, and it always does seem to be a 'he', is integrated into society. The modern worker may not feel a sense of belonging, and for Hegel it is part of the function of the state to represent and even to construct this belonging through transparent forms of participation. The integration that is no longer discernible in the everyday experience of labour can then be refigured in and through the institutions of the state.

Arthur Schopenhauer's philosophical contributions to the understanding of labour in the early years of the nineteenth century provide further terms and ideas for the exploration of work in the modern period. The most significant of these terms is 'the will', which Schopenhauer understood as the essence and the substance of all forms of life. Schopenhauer was writing in relation, and in vigorous response to, both Hegel and Kant. He sought to understand the formative role of human subjectivity in the construction of certain forms of knowledge, but also aimed to connect this incipient idealism to an understanding of human existence and human knowledge as fundamentally embodied. His major text, *The World as Will and Representation*, which was first published in 1819 and then continually revised until just before his death in 1860, sought to establish the conditions of possibility for perception of the world as 'representation' or appearances, but also of the world as thing-in-itself, through the activity of the will. *The World as Will and Representation* was first translated into English between 1883 and 1886, and Schopenhauer's images and ideas informed significant aspects of philosophical and cultural debate in Britain in the late-nineteenth and early twentieth centuries.[14]

For Schopenhauer, 'the will' does not refer to consciousness or to the intellect, but refers rather to the energies and process associated with the continuation and the development of life in all its forms. We know the will through our experience of action, movement, and growth, and such knowledge is 'immediate' in the sense that it is not a matter of intellect, reflection or reason: 'we know what we will because our action itself expresses our will'.[15] The will is not a mental act, but rather an energy that drives all life forms: 'The animal feels and perceives; man, in addition *thinks* and *knows*; both *will*.'[16] Schopenhauer argues that the body is the condition of knowledge of the will, and that the 'knowing subject is individual precisely by reason of this special relation to the one body' (*World*, 1, 103). This does not mean that will is in any sense a distinctively human property. Will is expressed as much in gravity, in crystal formation and in plant growth as in any human action, and is a blind and irresistible urge or drive. It is not subject to the processes of birth and death, since individuals are the temporal realization of that which knows no time.[17] Both generation and death are to be understood as part of life, and thus as expressions of will, and Schopenhauer argues that 'only in degree does constant excretion differ from death' (*Philosophical Writings*, 131).

Schopenhauer's philosophical categories stress the epistemological significance of embodiment, while connecting the individual body to large and impersonal forces and energies: 'knowledge, which is the conditional supporter of the whole world as representation, is nevertheless given entirely through the medium of a body, and the affections of this body, are, as we have shown, the starting point for the understanding in its perception of this world' (*World*, 1, 99). The stress on embodiment and on the energies that drive forward species and structures, suggest interesting connections between Schopenhauer's philosophical categories and the activity of human labour. Human work might perhaps be understood as one expression of this blind and unconscious striving that creates and re-creates the living world, a striving that also finds expression in the sexual impulse and act. In labour, the will finds expression, and by embodying the energy and direction of this will in its growth and activities, the human species is particularly well realized through the activity of labour. Schopenhauer certainly suggests such a connection when he writes that, 'not merely man's actions, but even his body, are to be regarded as the phenomenon, the objectification, of his *will*, and as its work' (*Philosophical Writings*, 15). This coupling of will and work will re-emerge in numerous texts of the early twentieth century, which will draw on the vitalism of Schopenhauer's representation of human energies, but graft on to it a sense of will more connected to ideas of agency and purpose.[18]

Interestingly, however, Schopenhauer's analysis of work as an expression of will refers overwhelmingly to the animal, rather than the human, worlds. Thus, for example, he discusses birds building nests and spiders spinning webs as examples where will is at work, producing activity that sustains life without any rational knowledge of the future to guide such activity. He discusses the minute divisions of labour within the beehive or the anthill, once more stressing that while such activity draws on particular local forms of knowledge it takes place without any sense of an end beyond the end of sustaining life: 'all parts work merely for the continued existence of the whole, which alone is the unconditional aim or end' (*World*, II, 345).

There seem to be two distinct, but nonetheless related, reasons for Schopenhauer's reticence before the activity of human labour. The first expresses something about the specificity of modern labour, particularly as it depends on mechanization and on the division of labour. In the early pages of *The World as Will and Representation*, Schopenhauer sets out some distinctions between knowledge, understanding and abstract reason, and the examples he chooses to illustrate these distinctions are suggestive of his wider judgements about modern labour:

An experienced billiard player can have a perfect knowledge of the laws of impact of elastic bodies on one another, merely in the understanding, merely for immediate perception, and with this he manages perfectly. Only the man who is versed in the science of mechanics, on the other hand, has a real rational knowledge of those laws, that is to say, a knowledge of them in the abstract. Even for the construction of machines such a merely intuitive knowledge of the understanding is sufficient, when the inventor of the machine executes the work, as is often seen in the case of talented workmen without any scientific knowledge. On the other hand, as soon as several men and their coordinated activity occurring at different times are necessary for carrying out a mechanical operation, for completing a machine or a building, then the man controlling it must have drafted the plan in the abstract, and such a cooperative activity is possible only through the assistance of the faculty of reason. (*World*, 1, 56)

One must not be misled here by the contrast between the 'mere' under-standing and real rational knowledge. Schopenhauer's clear preference is in fact for non-reflective forms of knowledge, since 'virtue and holiness result not from reflection, but from the inner depth of the will, and from its relation to knowledge' (58). Indeed he goes even further, in describing reason as 'feminine, receptive, retentive, and not self-creative' (86), all terms that seem to designate the antithesis, and even the death, of will. Modern labour has, then, become inappropriately reliant on reason, on abstraction and on forms of knowledge that are removed from the intuitive physical knowledges of the skilled workman: Schopenhauer compares the 'reflecting European' adversely to the natural man in this respect (56). Labour that is inherently dependent on reason, abstraction and fragmentation, cannot, for Schopenhauer, comfortably express the movement and the logic of the will: thus his preference for spiders, ants, and bees.

But Schopenhauer's engagement with the activity of human labour also follows another path, connected to his understanding of the 'will-to-live'. The will-to-live is not simply an impulse to self-preservation, which would only be the affirmation of the individual, but rather the processes through which 'the will wills life absolutely and for all time' (*Philosophical Writings*, 13). The will-to-live is expressed through the numerous activities and labours undertaken to preserve and to reproduce life within the organic and the inorganic worlds. Again Schopenhauer illustrates this force first in the lives of insects and animals, conceding that when we turn to the human race 'the matter indeed becomes more complicated and assumes a certain seriousness of aspect' (*World*, II, 357). Given the relentless drive of this will-to-live, the individual is spurred on to meaningless but ceaseless exertion: 'every living thing works with the utmost exertion of its strength for something that has no value' (357). Life presents itself as a drudgery to be worked through, as a ceaseless tumult of activity where the sheer power of the will-to-live overwhelms the desires or aims of any individual. Having begun by drawing on the creative and embodied energies of the will to suggest an intense relationship, even to the point of identification, between the human and all other forms of life, Schopenhauer here seems to arrive at the melancholy effects of such an urgent and impersonal will. As his argument continues, Schopenhauer in fact finds some respite from the imperiousness of the will both in aesthetic experience and in mysticism. But it is clear that such respite can never be found in the activity of human labour, which is either the expression of a feminine and non-creative abstract reason, or is the painful and enforced living through of a remorseless will to life: 'whereas everyone would really like to rest, want and boredom are the whips that keep the top spinning. Therefore the whole and each individual bear the stamp of a forced condition' (359).

Thomas Carlyle, who was also writing in the first half of the nineteenth century, shared Schopenhauer's commitment to non-mechanistic theories of human history and behaviour. Carlyle's extensive writings on contemporary history, his literary translations and commentaries, and his polemical and challenging philosophical speculations, were to have a profound impact on the ways in which nineteenth-century Britain could perceive or imagine itself. Carlyle was strongly influenced by German literary romanticism and philosophical idealism, and constantly sought to capture the forces and energies within the social and the human that could not be captured by mechanical or materialist models of society or the individual. He believed in the presence of an animating spirituality that was the expression of God's will, a belief he connected to a supernatural moment of revelation he experienced in the early 1820s. His work sought to do justice to this recognition of divine will, to insist on a notion of justice that could not be reduced to a matter of calculation, and also to see in the human condition something more profound than the pursuit of happiness.

One of the most fascinating and unsettling expressions of Carlyle's philosophical, political and ethical thinking can be found in his text of 1833–34, *Sartor Resartus*, which despite its conceptual and formal complexity, was to become one of the best-selling books of the Victorian Age.[19] This text concerns itself, at one level, with the philosophy of clothes; but clothing quickly comes to be understood as a metaphor for all types of disguise and of studied self-presentation so that the volume in the end is able to explore all the major institutions and forms of belief in early nineteenth-century Britain. It begins by introducing the character of Professor Teufelsdröckh and his history of clothing, proceeds to create a biography of the Professor apparently derived from a series of autobiographical fragments, and then ends by considering the philosophical and social implications of this history of clothes. *Sartor Resartus* is a profoundly intertextual piece of writing, and echoes of other writings, as well as numerous citations, can be found throughout. It also teases the reader with the layers of subjectivity that mediate different aspects of the text, so that it is often hard to attribute aspects of the text to any recognizable or coherent subjectivity. Nonetheless, *Sartor Resartus* does construct an amalgam of the speculative, the bizarre and the dogmatic that is characteristically the voice of Carlyle himself, and if we examine the moments where the text turns particularly towards the question of human labour we can find a coherent and forceful argument about the centrality of labour and of practical activity for mankind's realization of himself.

In the first book of *Sartor Resartus*, the Professor introduces the idea that mankind is essentially a practical species whose practicality is expressed in his use of tools:

'But, on the whole', continues our eloquent Professor, 'Man is a Tool-using Animal (*Handthierendes Thier*). Weak in himself, and of small stature, he stands on a basis, at most for the flattest-soled, of some half-square foot, insecurely enough; he has to straddle out his legs, lest the very wind supplant him. Feeblest of bipeds! Three quintals are a crushing load for him; the steer of the meadow tosses him aloft, like a waste rag. Nonetheless he can use Tools, can devise Tools: with these the granite mountain melts into light dust before him; he kneads glowing iron as if it were soft paste; seas are his smooth highway, winds and fire his unwearying steeds. Nowhere do you find him without Tools: without Tools he is nothing, with Tools he is all.' (Book 1, chapter 5)

In transforming and subduing nature through the use of tools, then, mankind finds both definition and affirmation of himself. This idea is strongly developed in Carlyle's characterization of the creative and self-constituting affirmation he names 'the everlasting yea'. Such affirmation can never simply be rhetorical or solipsistic. Carlyle insists that conviction is worthless unless it is expressed in deliberate and practical action. Doubt can never be dispelled except through action, and only in dedicating himself forcefully to the practical action that lies to hand can mankind hope to access the spiritual realm. The ideal, Carlyle argues through the Professor's voice, is either within the here and now or it is nowhere. Thus he insists that committed and arduous work is the most reliable route to spiritual certainty: 'Up, up! whatsoever thy hand findeth to do, do it with all thy might. Work while it is called today; for the Night cometh, wherein no man can work' (Book 2, chapter 9).

This position is further explored in the fourth chapter of the third book, where Carlyle writes in praise of the toiler, honouring his labour and regretting only his ignorance. At this stage of his argument, Carlyle admits of a distinction between the man whose toil is primarily practical, and he whose work involves the search for spiritual illumination or the Bread of Life. The manual labourer is given a heroic disposition and a socially necessary role: 'Venerable to me is the hard Hand; crooked, coarse; wherein notwithstanding lies a cunning virtue, indefeasibly royal, as of the Sceptre of this Planet. Venerable too is the rugged face, all weather-tanned, besoiled, with its rude intelligence; for it is the face of a Man living manlike'; but Carlyle admits to honouring the man who toils for spiritual insight yet more highly. His aim in constructing this opposition, however, is to overcome it through the imagined sublimity of the man who will toil equally on both fronts: 'unspeakably touching is it, however, when I find both dignities united'.

Carlyle's commitment to labour takes a rather less benevolent turn in his 1839 study of Chartism. In this text he sets out to examine the social and industrial conditions that may have led to the anger and radicalism expressed in the Chartist struggle for the franchise in the 1830s. His aim is to understand whether the conditions of labouring people represent a pathology of the social, or whether the discontent expressed by these labouring people is itself a pathological response to a rational social situation. Typically, Carlyle's answers to these questions are complex, mobile and undermined by an irony that haunts the text. He has little time for the orthodoxy of Poor Law Reform and its self-presentation as disinterested justice. Nonetheless, he is prepared to contemplate its necessity while acknowledging the harshness of removing outdoor relief and driving the poor into Workhouses. His argument is that though the present arrangements may be harsh, they do at least bring an end to an earlier phase of relief for the poor which had served simply to reward the unthrifty and the idle.

Carlyle is insistent about the social and the ethical requirement for labour. Unlike his argument in *Sartor Resartus*, he is here explicitly examining the duties of the labouring poor, and his rhetoric is consequently harsher and more strident. His identification of the duty of mankind is inflected in this text by his attention to the many social institutions which will step in, and punish the individual who does not internalize Carlyle's version of his basic duty. He writes, for example that 'for the idle man there is no place in this England of ours';[20] that 'he that will not work according to his faculty, let him perish according to his necessity'; and that 'work is the mission of man in this Earth'.[21] Once more, the act of labour is associated with the fulfilment of a human identity that is specifically masculine. In struggling for a decent wage and submitting to the proper authority of a political or social superior, the workingman is working towards a 'manlike place and relation' (*Chartism*, 22). In working, man makes himself ruler of at least part of the world of nature, and gains a kind of mastery, and Carlyle insists that man must 'honour his craftsmanship, his *can-do*' (22).

But honouring, as Carlyle is aware, is not enough. After a fervent denunciation of the fecklessness of the Irish and a celebration of the Saxon virtues of diligence, Carlyle is left with the realization that there is no effective social institution for the rewarding of hard work. This is partly the result of the dissolution of the social to the point where cash payment is 'the sole nexus between man and man' (57). The tendency of capitalist social relationships to erode the fabric of justice and to threaten the viability of human virtue which Carlyle discerns here is reminiscent of Adam Smith's recognition of the socially pernicious consequences of the economically beneficial process of the division of labour. And Carlyle's proposed solutions also have something of a flavour of Smith: the social unrest expressed in Chartism is to be alleviated by widespread emigration and by the development of universal elementary education. Once more culture is to assuage the erosion of the human that economic relations have so remorselessly begun.

In his 1843 comparative study of medieval and contemporary societies and their institutions, 'Past and Present', Carlyle is once more exercised by the individual and social significance of labour. This text is another sort of response to the dilemma outlined above concerning the ethical and social damage produced by the dominance of the cash nexus. The comparison between medieval and nineteenth-century institutions, cultural forms, and collective practices is all to the benefit of the earlier period. This is no complacent celebration of human or technological progress, but a serious and thoughtful reflection on what may have been lost in that 'progress' that will find echoes in the work of Ruskin or Morris later in the century. Yet Carlyle's position is far from accepting, and he seeks to imagine how the social and the ethical might be maintained as significant and weighty presences in the contemporary structure of the everyday. One important site for this imagining is in the field of human labour, and Carlyle returns to the activity of human labour insistently throughout the second half of his study. Thus, for example, he writes that 'idleness alone is without hope: work honestly at anything . . . There is endless hope in work.'[22] Work is represented as far more significant than the achievement of happiness, and as more essential than the most elevated cultural expression, 'The spoken Word, the written Poem, is said to be the epitome of the man; how much more the done Work' ('Past and Present', 192). Work contains nobleness, and even, Carlyle suggests, sacredness. A man perfects himself through the act of labour, he argues, and 'the whole soul of man is composed into a kind of real harmony the instant he sets himself to work' (223). But the price of this harmony is abstraction. Attentiveness to the concrete social and economic relations of Britain in his study of Chartism had led Carlyle to a practical and theoretical paralysis in the face of willed idleness and un-productive labour. Only by withdrawing from the conditions under which modern labour was being performed could Carlyle retrieve the imaginative possibility of labour as a sacred and secure form of self-realization.

The complex relations between labour as a creative and self-creating process and labour as a forced or alienated condition, also structure Karl Marx's extensive writings on labour from the 1840s to the 1870s. The centrality of 'labour' as an economic, cultural and historical category, and its importance for the development of Marx's thought, have been the objects of significant critical and theoretical attention. C. J. Arthur, for example, sees 'labour' as the connecting thread between the three traditions of thought that are fundamental to Marx's writings: German philosophy (particularly Hegel and Hegelianism), political economy, and French socialism.[23] We have already noted the significance of human labour for aspects of Hegel's thought, but as we shall see, Marx's arguments draw on the general structure of Hegel's philosophical method to suggest the role of self-estrangement in the development of human productive activity and thus of human history. Marx also draws on the work of Adam Smith, as an example of a tradition that illuminates the centrality of human labour to the economic process without understanding its historical nature, and in particular without understanding the historical nature of capitalist labour relations. Finally, Marx draws from French socialism a rhetoric for the condemnation of the inhuman and destructive effects of the division of labour; a rhetoric that is powerfully expressed, for example in the writings of Charles Fourier: 'nine-tenths of civilized men are worried about the present day because they are obliged to devote themselves to loathsome work that is forced upon them'.[24]

In order to grasp these different traditions as they operate within Marx's writings, and also as they inform later works broadly in the Marxist tradition, I will examine Marx's discussion of labour primarily with reference to two texts: the *Economic and Philosophic Manuscripts of 1844* and the first volume of *Capital*. The manuscripts were unpublished in Marx's own lifetime, and did not appear in print until the 1930s, so one obviously cannot claim any direct influence of these texts on philosophical or imaginative literature of the early decades of the twentieth century. Nonetheless, these manuscripts do give us some access to the ways in which the Hegelian arguments explored above actually entered philosophical and political writings later in the nineteenth century. Also, the residues of Hegelianism in later texts by Marx here find a more distinct and more developed articulation, which allows us to see more precisely the ways in which Marx's economic and philosophical categories draw on particular assumptions about the human species, nature and labour.

The burden of Marx's argument in the *Economic and Philosophic Manuscripts* is the nature of estranged labour, and the process through which both the activity of labour and the products of labour come to seem alien to the worker. In developing this argument, however, he also brings into focus important assumptions about the nature of labour and its relation to human 'species being'. Marx borrows this notion of species being from Feuerbach, and in particular from *The Essence of Christianity* (1841) where Feuerbach had argued that religious feeling is more properly understood as the externalization of aspects of man's properties as species being.[25] The de-mystification implicit in Feuerbach's movement from the divine to the human appeals to Marx, and he draws on the notion of species being to ground his arguments about the ethical and historical relations between social structures and the practices of labour.

In the *Economic and Philosophic Manuscripts*, Marx discusses labour as a mediating activity between man and nature: 'Man *lives* on nature . . . nature is his body with which he must remain in continuous interchange if he is not to die'.[26] The capacity to make of nature part of his own body is the basis for both universality and freedom, and constitutes the specificity of man's species being. Labour is not, on this account, simply undertaken to fulfil a particular or immediate need. Indeed, Marx, like Schopenhauer, sees this as a crucial point of distinction between the animal and the human, arguing that only human life activity can be understood in relation to consciousness and will, and thus to freedom (113). Human productive labour is not simply an activity aimed to satisfy a particular need, but rather, 'the whole character of a species – its species character – is contained in the character of its life activity; and free, conscious activity is man's species character (113). Human productive activity 'is the life of the species. It is life-engendering life' (113).

Marx repeats the point in a number of subtly different formulations, each stressing the relations between consciousness, freedom and human labour, arguing, for example that 'in creating a *world of objects* by his practical activity, in *his work upon* inorganic nature, man proves himself a conscious species being', and further that 'man produces even when he is free from physical need and only truly produces in freedom therefrom' (113). Human labour is the place in which man's relation to nature is acted out, and the terms of this relationship are governed by consciousness, universality and freedom as the central elements of human species being:

It is just in his work upon the objective world, therefore, that man first really proves himself to be a *species being*. This production is his active species life. Through and because of this production, nature appears as *his* work and his reality. Man duplicates himself and contemplates himself in a world he has created. (114)

This vision of human labour as creative, and as a central and stable point of connection between the human and the natural worlds, does of course have its charms. For Marx, it is very much the ghost that haunts the bulk of his writings about labour, since these writings deal overwhelmingly with the estranged condition of human labour in industrial capitalism. Before examining Marx's account of the ways in which this powerful connection between labour, man and species being is undone, however, it may be worth thinking about some of the limitations, or problems, internal to the vision itself. Firstly, the transformation of nature into the inorganic body of man and the argument that through labour nature becomes part of mankind have little to say about the possibly conflictual nature of this relation. Marx is quite clear that the relationship between man and nature is reciprocal, in the sense that man relies on the materials nature provides and is thus obliged to tend and to husband these. But there is no ethical dimension to this relationship on Marx's account, and nature becomes the site of the externalization of man's species being, wherein man 'duplicates himself'. The only limit to this process of ownership, transformation and projection is pragmatic. There are clear traces here of Marx's indebtedness to Hegel's philosophical method, since Hegel sees the process by which man separates himself from nature, and thus nature becomes an entity 'for' man, as an integral part of a progressive narrative of self-realization. But the very abstraction of Hegel's history of spirit in the *Phenomenology*, may in fact save him from the pressing political and ethical questions that arise when Marx puts practical activity, rather than Hegel's consciousness or spirit, at the centre of this process of historical unfolding.

Secondly, Marx's representation of productive activity is strongly gendered, and his articulation of the relations between consciousness, freedom and labour risks erasing women from the vision of species being. Whereas Schopenhauer's will could be realized in sexual activity and in reproduction, Marx's account of labour stresses manual labour and the production of objects. As we shall see, this emphasis develops into quite particular concerns with the employment of women and children in industry and with the economic consequences of 'unproductive labour'[27] when Marx turns to the examination of nineteenth-century capitalism. But it is worth noting that the problem of women's labour exists in the very founding argument about species being and freedom, which can never really be understood as addressing anything other than manual labour and the production of artefacts. Despite the fact that women have been centrally involved in the mediation of nature through labour and in the production of a wide range of domestic and agricultural artefacts, the language and the images in Marx's text struggle to encompass that activity of women's labour, particularly as it would be imagined in the mid-nineteenth century. It is not that Marx excludes women's labour from his argument about species being, freedom and universality, but rather that he doesn't pay it any attention. The dilemma this creates for subsequent activists and theorists is substantial. This dilemma is to some extent precisely historical: at the very moment Marx is theorizing the disjunction between labour and freedom some women are experiencing their connection in particularly vivid ways, suggesting that one story of what happens to labour in industrial countries from the mid-nineteenth century simply cannot be told.[28] But it is also a dilemma about the limits of the imagination and how it informs our sense of freedom or even of any kind of alternative practice. If we do not see women when we try to imagine species being, we have given ourselves a very significant problem of the imagination. If we do not articulate this absence we compound the problem by naturalizing it. This is the dilemma that we will see Sylvia Pankhurst addressing later in this book.

The correlation between labour, consciousness and freedom that Marx sees as expressive of species being is not, however, what he finds in nineteenth-century industrial society. On the contrary, Marx argues that 'in his work . . . [the worker] does not affirm himself but denies himself' and 'the worker only feels himself outside his work, and in his work feels outside himself . . . When he is working he is not at home' (110). Nineteenth-century labour is experienced as a negation of the self, as a curtailment of the relationship between man and nature and as a negation of freedom: 'In tearing away from man the object of his production, therefore, estranged labor tears from him his *species life*' (114). And this fundamental transformation of the nature and the significance of human labour is, for Marx, the result of the transformation of the worker into a wage labourer.

As a wage labourer, a worker does not own the products of his labour, and thus 'to an increasing extent his own labor confronts him as another man's property' (67). Further, this labour then appears to him as something outside himself, '*something alien*, as a power independent of the producer' (108). It is not simply that the labour no longer belongs to him because it is embodied in an object that belongs to someone else, but that it is now foreign to him, and even opposed to him as an independent power. In this estrangement of the object form the worker, there is a loss of selfhood: 'labor in which man alienates himself is a labor of self-sacrifice' (111). This, for Marx, amounts to forced labour.

Such self-sacrifice creates a further level of estrangement where 'one man is estranged from the other' (114). The worker has become machine-like, and his life activity, which should be the grounding of his species being, has become a mere means to his existence. Thus, as the act of production is turned against the worker, so too is the worker alienated from his own species, mankind. As the worker sinks to the level of a commodity, whose labour can be bought and sold, the objects produced by his labour appear as alien, and even as oppositional to him.[29] He produces beautiful things, but his own life is one of privation and the very act of production becomes an experience of active alienation. Thus the worker feels himself only in the most basic animal activities of eating, drinking and procreating, while his own creative energies are turned against him in the process of labour.

Marx develops some of the implications of estranged labour further in *The German Ideology*, which was co-written with Engels between 1845 and 1846. Once more the argument begins with the assertion that mankind is distinguished from animal life through the capacity for purposeful labour, particularly labour that controls and transforms nature. Marx and Engels then quickly turn their attention to the oppressive conditions under which work is performed, and the destructive effects of this for individual workers. Thus they state that for nineteenth-century wage earners 'labour has lost all semblance of self-activity and only sustains their life by stunting it'.[30] But here the negation of the self-affirming properties of labour is not read simply as a loss, but rather as a radicalizing moment in a revolutionary narrative: 'only the proletarians of the present day, who are completely shut off from all self-activity, are in a position to achieve a complete and no longer restricted self-activity' (pp. 92–93). This inaugurates Marx's dialectical analysis of the social and political significance of the estrangement of labour under capitalism that will shape his writings over the following decades. The dialectical structure of his argument allows for negation as a creative process, where estrangement is followed by new forms of consciousness and new modes of social relationship. Labour is described as a condition forced upon the proletarian worker, who 'is sacrificed from his youth upwards' (85) and who is stunted rather than sustained by his productive labour. But this very diminishing creates the possibility of new forms of social relationship, and the loss of particular historical forms of consciousness or selfhood can also be the condition for the creation of new and progressive forms. Thus, for example, abstract labour, wherein the particular activities undertaken matter less than the economic relations that subtend them, can for the first time be lived as an historical experience: labour has ceased to be tied to a particular individual at a particular moment, and this abstraction 'appears to be actually true in this abstract form only as a character of the most modern society' (144). This new relationship to labour creates the need for revolutionary intervention, since 'the proletarians, if they are to assert themselves as individuals, will have to abolish the very conditions of their existence hitherto . . . namely, labour' (85). As G. A. Cohen argues, for Marx 'the wage-worker's indifference manifests his alienation. But it also betokens a birth of freedom.'[31]

This allows for a rather different approach to the relations between labour and freedom in Marx's later work, which nonetheless shows the traces of his early concern with labour, universality and species being. Much of *Capital* is taken up with an intellectually and rhetorically powerful critique of the forms of degradation typical of modern labour, including intensification, mechanization and extension of the working day. Yet Marx also sees in these very processes the possibility of liberation, and he does so in a double sense: seeing in the very estrangement of man the 'freedom of detachment'[32] while also arguing for the necessity of developing productive capacities to the point where it becomes possible to imagine the end of labour determined by necessity.

Capital: Volume One was published in 1867, and was first translated into English in 1887. Its arguments and its vibrant images were thus available to political activists, philosophers and creative writers in the early years of the twentieth century. In this text, Marx once more begins his consideration of the labour process with a discussion of the particularity of human labour. He argues that 'primarily, labour is a process going on between man and nature'[33] and then suggests that the main difference between human and animal labour lies in the capacity of the human worker to create an object that exists previously only in his own imagination. So purposive will and the physical transformation of nature are the defining aspects of human labour. So too, Marx argues, is the making of tools, which allows for the development of increasingly complex labour processes and Marx borrows from historians of ancient civilizations the notion that the development of the instruments of labour can be read as an indication of the state of development of any particular civilization.

When he comes to describe the relation between man and nature, however, Marx's language in *Capital* is significantly more robust than in the earlier manuscripts. As he describes the process by which labour transforms nature he writes:

Living labour must seize on these things, must rouse them from their death-like sleep, must change them from potential use-values into real and kinetic use-values. Bathed in the fire of labour, appropriated as embodied labour, and, as it were, animated for their functions in the labour process. (176)

The exchange between nature and man has here become a matter of violent injection of energy and direction into an otherwise passive and 'death-like' nature. Nature is brought to life by the contact with the transformative capacities of human labour.

The production of use-values is, however, only part of Marx's concern, since his aim is to understand the production not simply of objects but of commodities, that is to say of objects that are produced and exchanged within particular social and economic relations characteristic of capitalism. The form of the commodity depends on its relation both to use-value and to exchange-value, the latter being an expression of the labour embodied in it. But, as Marx argues, the complexity of the relation between these two aspects of value within the commodity form is extremely hard to grasp, and there is always a tendency to naturalize the commodity rather than to understand it as the expression of a social relationship:

the mystery of the commodity form is simply this, that it mirrors for men the social character of their own labour, mirrors it as an objective character attaching to the labour products themselves, mirrors it as a social natural property of these things. Consequently the social relation of the producers to the sum total of their own labour presents itself to them as a social relation, not between themselves, but between the products of their labour. (45)

Having addressed this mysterious form of the commodity in early sections of *Capital*, Marx is in a position to develop an argument about the relations between labour as the production of use-value and labour as the production of exchange-value, and specifically to arrive at his theory of the production of surplus value. The exchange-value of any commodity is determined by the amount of labour time socially necessary for its production, and within capitalist social relations labour habitually produces a value greater than its own, that is to say it produces not just sufficient wealth to ensure the subsistence of the worker and his family but also 'surplus value' which is the property of the owner of the means of production. The object of the owner is to extract the maximum possible surplus value from any particular worker, or from the labour process more generally. Thus, Marx argues, 'the inherent tendency of capitalist production is towards the appropriation of labour for the whole twenty-four hours of the day' (259) and much of the burden of his critique is aimed at finding the most effective ways in which to overcome this tendency. He discusses in rich historical detail campaigns and legislation aimed at reducing the working day, and also notes their only partial success. His particular concern is with the tendency to bring young children and women into industrial forms of labour, requiring them to work long hours in conditions that are injurious to their health. Mechanization greatly exacerbates this tendency, while also reducing the worker to 'nothing more than the extant material conditions of production' (408). Marx is clear that mechanization is not driven by any desire to lighten the load of the industrial workforce, but rather 'machinery is to cheapen commodities, and to diminish the part of the working day in which the worker works for himself while increasing the part of the working day which he gives to the capitalist for nothing. Machinery is a means for the production of surplus value' (391).

The tendency of Marx's argument in *Capital* is towards the reduction of human labour, at least of human labour as organized under capitalism. He sees the reduction of working hours, and the removal of specific categories of workers from industrial production as the legitimate aim of political struggle. Labour as an activity emerges in this account as burdensome, forced and destructive of the social and moral lives of the workers. He writes, for example, with real distaste about the ways in which young girls 'become rough, foul-mouthed boys before nature has taught them that they are women' (500).

Yet such fragmented and burdensome labour also carries the potential for overcoming the conditions that produce it. Although Marx is critical of the efficacy and the scope of Factory Acts designed to reduce the working hours of women and children, he nonetheless observes that such legislation did in fact result in significant technical innovations in specific industries. And technical innovations themselves required the development of a more skilled work-force and the provision of technical schools which brought ed-ucation and training to a significant percentage of (male) workers. Similarly, although the increasing regulation of the working day comes into conflict with traditional modes of organizing time it does also help to overcome the worst excesses of seasonal or casual employment. The fact that such developments carry both increased exploitation and potential liberation within them is an illustration of Marx's argument that, 'the evolution of the contradictions within a historical form of production is the only historical way in which these contradictions can be resolved and a new form come into being' (527). Indeed, Marx suggests that there is more at stake here than the historical development of any particular form of production. He had already suggested in the *Economic and Philosophic Manuscripts* that emancipation of workers contained within it real and general human emancipation, and in *Capital* he sees the playing out of contradictions within industrial forms of labour as carrying within it larger forces of human liberation:

By ripening the material conditions of production and the social combinations of the productive process, it ripens the contradictions and antagonisms of the capitalist form of production, thus simultaneously ripening the factors that tend to revolutionize the old society and the factors that tend to build a new one. (544)

At the heart of such ripening towards revolutionary change is the industrial worker, whose labour produces the surplus value that is the dynamic energy of capitalism.

Such disruptive dynamism is some way from the social and economic preferences of John Ruskin, who wrote extensively about labour and selfhood from the 1850s to the 1880s. Ruskin, a close friend of Carlyle's from the early 1850s, was born in 1819 of Scottish parents. His early intellectual training at Oxford led him to an enduring interest in architecture and in the visual arts. His voluminous and polemical writings represent a sustained attempt to think through the social and economic conditions that can allow for the creation of significant and vital cultural artefacts. His interest in modern painters, particularly Turner, made him acutely aware of the contestation and the formal challenges of cultural expression in the modern world. Equally, his architectural writings, particularly inspired by the architectural history of Venice, explored the ways in which materials and craftsmanship could be mutually enabling given the right sort of communal and familial relationships within any particular society or at any given moment. Throughout his writings there is a fascinating and often productive tension between an almost visceral sensitivity to new social and cultural movements and forces and a determined clinging to institutions, relationships and concepts that seem to enable the perception of order, continuity and community. Much of this productive tension is played out in and through his analysis of the relations between labour and selfhood.

Ruskin's writings on labour have often been read through the notion of 'the gospel of work', that nineteenth-century valorization of work as inherently good and as spiritually uplifting that has framed many cultural histories of representations of labour in the period.[34] Certainly, one of Ruskin's early expositors, writing in the 1880s, begins by drawing attention to Ruskin's conviction that 'life without industry is guilt' and connecting this to the much broader sense of work as a spiritual value.[35] Ruskin certainly writes in ways that would support such an overall judgement. For example in a lecture to the Working Men's Institute at Camberwell, delivered in 1865, Ruskin argues forcefully that work is its own reward: 'the best grace before meat [is] the consciousness that we have justly earned our dinner',[36] and he develops this argument towards the conclusion that the Lord of work is God, while the deity who presides over wages is the Devil ('Work', 37).

Yet such value in work can only emerge in the context of a rightly ordered society. Ruskin believed that labour would always be hierarchically arranged, with different classes undertaking different sorts of work and with the division between mental and manual labour absolute:

Here we have at last an inevitable distinction. There *must* be work done by the arms, or none of us could live. There *must* be work done by the brains, or the life we get would not be worth having. And the same man cannot do both. ('Work', 42)

He was certainly concerned that all forms and levels of labour should be worthwhile and should be justly rewarded, but Ruskin did not challenge either the division of labour or the vertical divisions of his society. Ruskin argued that labour should be both enabled and directed by a benevolent aristocracy, who could ensure social stability and the proper division of labour.[37] Skilled labour should be organized through Guilds, who would ensure effective training and just reward. Manual labour should be honest, useful and cheerful and should also be fairly rewarded. Ruskin opposed both the intensification of labour and the proliferation of useless goods driven by an irresponsible mercantile capitalism.[38] Instead of competitive individualism, which Ruskin saw as both destructive and divisive, he advocated a truly political economy, which would arrange relations and activities within the state in the interests of a complex community, and in support of enabling and sustaining familial bonds. Despite his own complex and driven relation to the family, Ruskin saw it as the founding institution of economy, of labour and of selfhood: a conviction that left him silent on the sexual division of labour.

Ruskin wanted to see a world in which labour was regular, sustainable and fairly rewarded, but he could not sustain any argument about how this might be achieved, other than through a generalized and universal repudiation of the contemporary. His discussion of the 'laws of justice respecting payment of labour' proceeds carefully and methodically, until he contemplates the tendency of money to sever the bonds between use-value and exchange-value.[39] His vision of stability, hierarchy and justice is hard to sustain in the context of economic relations that produce flux, instability and forms of exploitation of which Ruskin is all too aware. Ruskin sought for ways in which to overcome the division between work and life, so that work could become a stable and fulfilling site of self-expression, since 'no man can retain either health of mind or body without it' (*Unto this Last*, 101). By the 1870s he embarked on a series of projects aimed at healing the breach between work and life. He himself worked both as a street sweeper and as a road mender.[40] He also helped to found the Society of St George, which was formed to arrange for the purchase of land upon which willing men and their families could be set to work: an initiative that would flourish again within the context of Distributism in the 1920s.[41] Ruskin believed that useful work was essential to mental and physical health, but also that work must always be carried out in the interest of the larger social body of which the individual was only a minute expression. Order, hierarchy and stability were the conditions of useful labour, and the individual worker must always in some sense defer to the fulfilment of such conditions:

[Ruskin] neither sees the feasibility nor admits the desirability of abolishing from work those qualities of self-sacrifice which imply the subordination of the present interests of a narrow self to the longer interests of the larger social self.[42]

William Morris, artist, designer and social and cultural theorist, also put the condition of modern labour at the heart of his cultural and political project. As we will see, many of his anxieties as well as many of his stylistic preferences show traces of Ruskin's writings. Yet his work was also profoundly shaped by Marx's critique of modern labour, and in particular by Marx's analysis of alienation as the inherent social and psychological condition of such labour. He drew importantly on Marx's sense that labour and liberation must be connected in any political project. Rather than sustaining Marx's dialectic, however, which saw the negation of the self-affirming properties of labour as also a radicalizing moment in a revolutionary narrative, and the playing out of contradictions within industrial forms of labour as carrying larger forces of human liberation, Morris could see liberation only in the renunciation of the material conditions and the social relations that sustained modern labour. In his distinction between 'useful work' and 'useless toil', Morris developed an account of the social and subjective centrality of labour at the same time as he constituted an historical critique of labour as it could be performed in late nineteenth-century Britain.[43]

Morris certainly believed that mankind was meant to labour. He argued that our livelihood will never be simply given to us by nature, but rather 'we must win it by toil of some sort or degree' ('Useful Work', 117). On the other hand, he was also convinced that the tendency to see in all forms of labour an ethical or social good was a serious error which could lead to the valorizations of exploitation as well as of repetitive and deadening forms of labour. There are, Morris argues, two types of labour, one of which offers both pleasure and fulfilment, while the other offers only exhaustion. It is, he argues, 'manly to do the one kind of work, and manly also to refuse to do the other' (118). The gendering of this relation to work is a topic to which I will return below, but right now I simply want to stress that Morris is clear that the relations between labour and selfhood can only be grasped in the context of a careful consideration of the forms and contexts of labour.

The barriers to useful and pleasurable work can be found, according to Morris, in social inequality and in the productivist logic of commercial capitalism. The existence of a rich and leisured class leads to a number of distortions: their appetite for consumption leads to the creation of useless goods and to wastefulness, while their refusal to work leads to an intensification of labour for others. But Morris does not believe that greater social equality and a more even distribution of labour will in themselves reduce the burden of useless toil, at least not while we remain caught in a 'merciless logic of expansion' (125). This logic is driven, he argues, by manufacturers whose primary aim is not the production of goods but rather the production of profit. The result is work that is both joyless and enervating:

Our present joyless labour, and our lives scared and anxious as the life of a hunted beast, are forced upon us by the present system of producing for the profit of the privileged classes. (126)

Such frantic and futile labour is the target of Morris's critiques, and against this joyless condition he writes of the conditions that might restore what he sees as the natural pleasures of work.

Morris does concede that the physical and mental effort of work always carries within it an element of pain: 'there is certainly some pain in all work, the beast-like pain of stirring our slumbering energies to action' (118), but he nonetheless argues that work, when properly arranged, is both fulfilling and pleasurable. To be useful, Morris argues, labour must be directed towards some useful end: the product of this labour must have inherent use-value. It is also important that any given worker should undertake a variety of activities throughout the working day. Morris insisted that 'to compel a man to do day after day the same task, without any hope of escape or change, means nothing short of turning his life into a prison torment' (129). The division of labour, on this analysis, loses any place in a narrative of progress, and Morris sought both in his writing and in his own cultural practice to challenge specialization and fragmentation of the labour process. He believed each worker should do both mental and manual labour, and that each individual should acquire the range of practical and intellectual skills necessary to sustain themselves in comfort. Finally, work should be undertaken in the most pleasant environment possible so that the health of any worker is not undermined. These conditions, having a useful end to the labour, variety of employment and pleasant surroundings, need, finally, to be supplemented by sufficient rest, by which Morris means not simply rest sufficient to recuperate but leisure sufficient to the further development of the individual personality. The achievement of this sustainable relation to labour will, Morris argues, require sacrifice: something will have to be renounced. As so often in theorizations of the relations between labour and selfhood, fulfilment through labour can only be bought at the cost of giving up aspects of the self and its pleasures. Here, what Morris would have us give up is ready access to cheap and varied commodities, a sacrifice he argues we should assent to for the general good: 'we should be contented to make the sacrifices necessary for raising our condition' (133).

Morris's argument in 'Useful Work and Useless Toil' received a fuller imaginative treatment some five years later in his utopian fiction *News from Nowhere*.[44] This text imagines a future where key economic institutions and social practices of the nineteenth century have been fundamentally transformed. The narrator of this fiction is introduced to the nature and significance of these changes by a series of different characters. The first character the narrator encounters in this new world is a waterman who offers to take him across the Thames. The narrator offers to pay him, and the waterman's response to this financial incentive to labour introduces the first recognition of the profound disjunction between their two worlds that the narrator is to discern: 'he laughed loud and merrily, as if the idea of being paid for his work was a very funny joke' (190). This willing and friendly worker acts as a guide to the manners and mores of his time, introducing his guest to a world of collaborative labour and easy-going collectivism.

The guest is particularly perplexed by the seemingly universal enthusiasm he finds for hard work: work is seen in this future world as a desirable and scarce good rather than as a source of suffering. In this text, we are invited to imagine a moment when labour has lost all association with pain, as even the more arduous and repetitive aspects of labour can be experienced as 'pleasurable *habit*' (262). The reward of labour, the narrator is told, 'is *life*. Is that not enough?' (262). The rhetorical effort Morris has to make to expel any association between labour and suffering is considerable, sufficient indeed to introduce an uneasiness into the relaxed consensual imagining of this utopian fiction. As one character insists that 'happiness without daily work is impossible' the narrator reflects that 'I thought the old boy was preaching a little' (263). The need to insist undermines the sense of obviousness the fiction elsewhere tries to achieve. As the old man goes on to develop a detailed denunciation of the productivist logic of nineteenth-century industry, the tendency towards intensification of labour and the distortions brought about by global capitalism, he becomes increasingly 'peevish' and crusty (266). The negative energies associated with nineteenth-century industry seep into this utopian world, leaving an unsatisfied anger.

Indeed, as *New from Nowhere* unfolds its version of community, family and labour, it becomes increasingly marked by this coercive rhetorical style, at once compelling and, to use Morris's own term, joyless. Part of this joylessness, at least for many twenty-first-century readers, is connected to Morris's radically limited capacity to re-think the relations between gender and labour. Women are explicitly confined to the realms of domestic and agricultural labour. Whilst men multi-task, women are fulfilled by the local and the familial. It can of course be argued that Morris deserves credit for at least seeing that domestic labour could be both challenging and fulfilling[45] but it is nonetheless true that his valuation of manly labour leaves little space for women to challenge the divisions and fragmentations of their relations to work in the period. Morris's imagining of the pleasures of labour assumes the gendered division of labour as much as it relies on the renunciation of the dubious joys of cheap and plentiful commodities.

To move now from a consideration of Morris to an examination of the philosophical legacy of Friedrich Nietzsche may seem perverse, since Nietzsche displayed a real antipathy to the claims of socialism to offer any kind of model of human liberation, and never, it would seem, actually read any works by Marx, to whom Morris was substantially indebted.[46] Nonetheless, Nietzsche does provide a crucial bridge between the philosophical categories and concerns of Hegel and Schopenhauer and the cultural milieu of early twentieth-century Britain: a bridge that both assumes and negates much of the philosophical legacy of Morris or of Marx. The strident and insistent egoism of Nietzsche's philosophical project, with its repudiation of existing moral norms and cultural forms, as well as the stylistic innovations of his philosophical prose, were certainly to prove a source of cultural and philosophical inspiration for a striking range of writers in the early years of the century, including George Bernard Shaw, T. E. Hulme, D. H. Lawrence and Jack Lindsay.[47]

Nietzsche's philosophical writings examine the history of morality, of religion and of philosophical beliefs, with the aim of mapping moments of energy, innovation and vitality. Nietzsche's model of history is explicitly antithetical to the Hegelian model of an unfolding system of historical stages. Indeed, in *Twilight of the Idols*, Nietzsche writes 'I mistrust all systematists and avoid them. The will to system is a lack of integrity' (1, 26). Instead, Nietzsche's understanding of history stresses the moment, the explosive energies of a particular individual or event against the backdrop of repetition and conformity. The rhythm of this expression of vitality has little in common with the temporality of labour, with its structured repetitions.

Nietzsche writes with anger and with profound scepticism about the elevation of work to an ethical good. In *Twilight of the Idols* he explicitly associates such elevation of work with a period of cultural and spiritual weakness:

Periods should be measured by their *positive energies* – in which case that Renaissance period, so extravagant and fateful, emerges as the last *great* period, and we, we moderns with our anxious self-welfare and brotherly love, with our virtues of work, unpretentiousness, abiding by the law, scientificity – accumulative, economical, machine-like – emerge as a *weak* period. (IX, 37)

It is interesting to see Nietzsche articulate his perception of the mutual implication of selfhood and work, even if it is in terms he is determined to repudiate. An anxious concern with the self, mechanical labour and the gospel of work are seen by Nietzsche as part of the same negative philosophical paradigm and the same period of cultural weakness. In an earlier text, *Daybreak* (1881), Nietzsche's sense of the hopeless spiritual and ethical lot of the industrial worker was even more forcefully expressed. Nietzsche addresses the 'factory slaves' with the ironical observation that there may be no contradiction between fulfilment, freedom and their dependent condition, 'provided, that is, they do not feel it to be in general a *disgrace* to be thus used, and *used up*, as a part of a machine'.[48] There is a clear sense here that Nietzsche sees the conditions of factory labour as destructive of the self, and as using up the vital energies of the human. He writes of mechanical labour and the pursuit of wealth through intensified production and asks 'how great a sum of *inner* value is thrown away in pursuit of this external goal!' (*Daybreak*, 206). Nietzsche advises factory workers to resist the 'flutings of the Socialist pied-pipers' (206) who offer nothing but hope, and argues instead that industrial workers need to recover their sense of significance and control by leaving their jobs in Europe and going abroad, 'better to go abroad, to seek to become *master* in new and savage regions of the world, and above all master over myself' (206).

Despite the polemical energies of Nietzsche's writing, his solution here is far from revolutionary. Emigration as a solution to 'the labour question' was, after all, the staple of nineteenth-century fiction as much as of social policy. Faced with the phenomenon of modern labour, Nietzsche's response is one of withdrawal. There is no way of connecting industrial labour to achieved selfhood, so the industrial labourer must become the colonial pioneer, and travel the globe in search of self-mastery. Nietzsche does at times seem to be aware of the sterility of this conception of modern labour, and denounces it implicitly in *Twilight of the Idols*: 'The stupidity, the fundamental instinctual degeneration which is the cause of *all* stupidities nowadays, lies in the fact that there is a labour question' (IX, 40). But this insight gives way in turn to a denunciation of the process of democratization that leaves the question of labour as a human activity precisely unexamined.

Industrial labour leaves Nietzsche with very little new to say, but the rhythms of labour do also lead him to a rather different series of assessments of the connections between work and the human body, articulated in relation to the twin poles of idleness and boredom. Practical activity is of substantial philosophical importance for Nietzsche, largely because it is the only place in which individuality can be articulated. Nietzsche writes, particularly in his earlier texts, under the influence of Schopenhauer's imagining of a continuum between human and non-human forms of organic life. Schopenhauer understands the individual not as an autonomous and rational selfhood, but rather as a particular historical articulation of a vital force. Nietzsche is thus particularly resistant to the idea that human identity can be grasped in relation to consciousness, seeing consciousness rather as the last development of the organic, and thus the most incomplete part of it.[49] He is profoundly interested by materialist accounts of human development, and looks to physiology to provide the language of pathology and symptom through which he will conduct his cultural critique. The relations between practical activity and the possibilities of innovative thought are of vital philosophical importance to Nietzsche, and it is thus all the more striking that the forms this practical activity might take remain a little abstract. The labour process, in particular, is a form of practical activity that haunts Nietzsche's texts in the form of negation, as idleness or boredom, rather than providing the focus for a substantial philosophical inquiry.

It is well known that Nietzsche found the rhythms and energies of walking particularly compatible with the activity of philosophical inquiry: moving at a steady pace providing both perspective and space for reflection, as well as ensuring a bodily consciousness in the process of thought. Duncan Large points out that the early working title for *Twilight of the Idols* was in fact 'Müsiggang eines Psychologen' ('Idleness of a Psychologist') and the etymology of the word 'Müsiggang' lies in the concept of a leisurely stroll (*Twilight*, xix–xx). This might seem likely to lead Nietzsche to a general endorsement of the pursuit of leisure over the discipline of work, but in fact in his writings of the 1870s he had responded with real hostility to the cultural and individual costs of idleness. In *Untimely Meditations*, in an essay dealing specifically with the work of Schopenhauer, Nietzsche asks:

What is it that constrains the individual to fear his neighbour, to think and act like a member of the herd . . .? With the great majority it is indolence, inertia, in short that tendency to laziness . . . men are even lazier than they are timid.[50]

The same point is made also in *Twilight of the Idols*, where Nietzsche insists that above all, the individual must never 'let himself go'. He argues that there must be constant struggle with mediocrity and conformity, and identifies laziness explicitly with the deadening effect of the habitual (IX, 47).

So Nietzsche's philosophy is vigorous and strenuous, even if it cannot always be understood in relation to a finished product. It is the overcoming of the habitual and the subduing of impulses of decay that Nietzsche celebrates here, rather than the active creation of any new philosophical or cultural object. It is then perhaps an attempt to think the activity of labour outside an economy of production, far less an economy of exchange. And part of the very complex logic of this attempt to think work within a very different economy lies in the ways that Nietzsche mobilizes the concept, and the affect, of boredom. In *Twilight of the Idols*, boredom is figured as the psychic expression of mechanical conformity: '"What is the task of any high-school education system?" – To turn man into a machine. – "By what means?" – He must learn to be bored' (IX, 29). But in the earlier *Human, All too Human*, Nietzsche had mapped a much more profound series of connections between boredom, human need and productive labour:

Boredom and play. Need forces us to do the work whose product will quiet the need; we are habituated to work by the ever-new awakening of needs. But in these intervals when our needs are quieted and seem to sleep, boredom overtakes us. What is that? It is the habit of working as such, which now asserts itself as a new, additional need; the need becomes the greater, the greater our habit of working, perhaps even the greater our suffering from our needs. To escape boredom, man works either beyond what his usual needs require, or else he invents play, that is, work that is designed to quiet no need other than that for working in general.[51]

Work has here become largely divorced from the satisfaction of a material need, and has become rather an unexamined habitual response to the experience of boredom. Boredom is the symptom of a transition from work as the expression of human need to work as a habitual search for consolation. But there is no consolation in this knot of work, boredom and play (itself just another form of work). Instead, the recognition of the impossibility of satisfying, or even expressing, the self through or at work, can only lead to a state of longing: longing for 'a blissful, peaceful state of motion; it is the artist's and philosopher's vision of happiness' (*Human*, 254).

Nietzsche's repudiation of idleness, if not his scepticism about the relations between work and selfhood, certainly find an echo in the writings of women actively addressing feminism or the 'woman question' in this period. Idleness seemed to many of these women not a philosophical or political choice, but an enforced state that left women with no socially useful role. The most developed and forceful articulation of the anxieties surrounding women's enforced idleness can be found in the writings of the South African novelist and essayist Olive Schreiner, and particularly in her 1911 publication, *Woman and Labour*. This text was profoundly influential for a wide range of feminist thinkers in the early years of the twentieth century. Vera Brittain described it as the 'Bible of the Woman's Movement';[52] while Barbara Hutchins, in her 1916 exploration of *Conflicting Ideals of Woman's Work*, referred to it as the 'most brilliant and inspired expression' of the view that women have an absolute right both to work and to equal pay.[53] The powerful symbolic significance of Schreiner's text can also be seen in D. H. Lawrence's novel of 1915, *The Rainbow*, where Ursula's involvement in the suffrage movement and her aspirations towards personal freedom are invoked in the context of excited reading of 'some work about "Woman and Labour"'.[54]

Woman and Labour was the result of thirty years of thinking and writing by Schreiner about gender and modernity. Schreiner first came to prominence in Britain in the 1880s through her novel, *The Story of an African Farm*. This novel explores the material and the psychological costs of isolation as well as the ambiguous but compelling visions of freedom that are associated with mobility and with change. The characters and situations in the novel are clearly located in the specific geographical and social context of late nineteenth-century South Africa, but the novel's articulation of frustrated ambitions and incompletely realized life projects resonated powerfully with readerships in Europe and the United States. Schreiner's fictional explorations of women and the specific dilemmas modernity presented to them frequently focussed on labour as a mode of self-expression as well as a means towards financial autonomy. Thus, for example, in the short story 'The policy in Favour of Protection —', Schreiner presents an erotic triangle, in which two women are both in love with the same man.[55] At the beginning of the story the older woman is occupied writing an article and is interrupted by the younger woman who asks for her help. The older woman agrees to help, by severing her connection with the man they both love, and concludes this emotionally fraught encounter with the words: 'Now you must go; I have my work to finish' (*Dream Life*, 78). The rhetorical insistence of her ownership of work is important at this moment of erotic renunciation. The gesture is repeated again at the end of the story, which has seen both women frustrated in their aspirations towards marriage, and the older woman forces herself back to work, to finish an article on free trade and protectionist principles. The broader implications of this concluding image of freedom and protection are considerable. The explicit reference is economic, but the question of protection has hung over the relations between the two women as well as the relation of marriage, and the possibilities of freedom to love and to live fully are explored at a number of levels in the story. Work here appears as a stable point, as an occupation on which other identities can be founded, but also as a form of sublimation of sexual and maternal passions.

Schreiner's importance as a theorist of work and selfhood was acknowledged well before the publication of *Woman and Labour*. She published a two-part article on 'The Woman Question' in the New York *Cosmopolitan* in 1899 which anticipated many of the arguments made in *Woman and Labour*[56] and her 'thoughts about women' were issued as a pamphlet by the Women's Enfranchisement League of Cape Town in 1909.[57] Schreiner's arguments about modernity, progress, gender and labour receive their fullest articulation, however, in *Woman and Labour* where she is able to situate her arguments about work in the context of a developed historical argument about cultures and their histories.

Schreiner's argument about woman and labour begins with an extensive discussion of parasitism: that state of useless dependency that is the characteristic of particular social groups and particular stages of cultural development. In our primitive state, she argues, man and woman are both fully and usefully occupied: 'side by side, the savage man and the savage woman, we wandered free together and laboured free together. And we were contented.'[58] This observation hovers between cultural history and comparative anthropology, as Schreiner's observations on savage culture are often informed by her observations of native African cultures. Schreiner sees the development of civilization as necessarily connected to the division of labour, which she sees largely as a natural expression of different human capacities. Thus although the end of nomadic existence leads to more arduous forms of labour for women, 'we endured our toil, as man bore his wounds, silently; and we were content' (*Woman*, 35).

Schreiner's assumption is that women at this stage move naturally and happily towards forms of labour that are associated with domesticity and maternity, feeling powerfully their social usefulness. Naturalizing the sexual division of labour in this way, Schreiner is drawing partly on the philosophical and scientific writings of Herbert Spencer. Spencer had written about the tendency of women to undertake menial and laborious tasks, while men confined themselves to warfare and to hunting, in his two-volume study of *The Principles of Ethics*, insisting that this division of labour was 'fully approved of by the women themselves'.[59] Spencer's overall philosophical project led him to naturalize such social trends through the evolutionary model of adaptation between an organism and its environment. The attraction of Spencer's theorization of social change as a process of evolution and adaptation, for Schreiner as well as for other writers concerned with the 'woman question', has been widely acknowledged.[60] Spencer's work offered a model of social change which acknowledged the impact of biology as well as of culture on any given social structure. It thus allowed women writers to begin their account of culture with a sense of the human as an embodied existence rather than as an abstract category, and it is this dimension on which Schreiner draws as she talks about women's socially useful role in primitive societies. Spencer's work did also, however, tend not simply to naturalize but to ossify such sexual division of labour, as, for Spencer, even arbitrary divisions can be reinforced by convention to the point of becoming natural laws.

So although Schreiner is indebted to Spencer's cultural history, and powerfully influenced by his sense that the individual organism will tend to defer to larger social needs, much of *Woman and Labour* is in fact an argument against the sexual division of labour as it is manifested in early twentieth-century industrialized societies. Schreiner's critique of the division of labour in the modern world is explicitly connected to an argument about the impact of mechanization. Mechanization had displaced many individuals from the sphere of productive labour, and had thus created the phenomenon of unemployment for substantial categories of male workers:

There has arisen, all the world over, a large body of males who find that their ancient fields of labour have slipped or are slipping from them, and who discover that the modern world has no place or need for them. (43)

This is, however, met by the opening up of new forms of labour drawing more explicitly on intellectual rather than on physical strengths. Schreiner thus argues that although some men are driven to mental and physical collapse by intensification, particularly of mental labour, men are overall able to find new and demanding forms of labour even in the modern world of mechanization. Mechanization has also, however, removed many categories of labour from within the home, leaving women with fewer forms of socially useful labour: 'there is a silently working but determined tendency for the sphere of woman's domestic labours to contradict itself' (52). Women's role as child bearer is much less socially necessary as infant mortality declines, and machine production has transformed many areas of domestic labour including food production, laundry and cleaning. For women, then, Schreiner sees a real threat of 'inactivity and degeneration' (123).

Parasitism is Schreiner's term for this state of inactivity, and she sees it as unhealthy both for the individual and for the culture as a whole. Female parasitism had always been connected with broader social oppression; slavery or other extreme forms of social inequality having been necessary before aristocratic women could achieve exemption from labour. But Schreiner suggests that the phenomenon is both more widespread and more destructive in its modern manifestation, where women are 'sinking slowly into a condition of more or less complete and passive sex-parasitism' (77), which leaves them entirely dependent on their sex functions, decorative and decadent. This is the anxiety that had fuelled discussions about marriage in texts such as *The Story of an African Farm*, where the relations between marriage and prostitution are painfully explored.

The reduction of most women to a state of passive dependency is seen by Schreiner to amount to a 'clogging' of individuality that will lead to more general forms of social degeneracy. Schreiner insists that 'only an able and labouring womanhood can permanently produce an able and labouring manhood' (107), and thus argues that it is vital for the interests of men and of women that women find a socially useful role within industrialized societies. Women's work will preserve modern societies from decadence and enervation, provided that that labour is 'active, virile and laborious' (106). The movement towards the 'family wage' in particular branches of industry, where employed males are to be paid a wage sufficient to provide for the whole family is, Schreiner argues, no sort of solution to this dilemma, but rather risks exacerbating it. Economic and social relations must ensure not simply material subsistence but also psychological fulfilment.

Thus, Schreiner argues that 'the female labour movement of our day is, in its ultimate essence, an endeavour on the part of a section of the race to save itself from inactivity and degeneration' (123). It is also an attempt to save the culture more generally from degeneracy by ensuring that activity and purposeful employment are available to all. This may involve individual acts of sacrifice, where women give up the chance of marriage or childbirth for themselves, sustained by 'this abiding consciousness of an end to be attained, reaching beyond her social life and individual interests' (128). Spencer's vision of the organism's drive to adapt to the unfolding interests of the species here returns with vigour, infusing Schreiner's coupling of labour and selfhood with an undercurrent of sacrifice and loss. Schreiner's final invocation, 'today we are found everywhere raising our strange new cry – "Labour and the training that fits us for labour"' (283), however rousing, cannot dispel this sense of suffering and sacrifice as the lot of the women who might make this aspiration a social reality. Certainly, the texts about women's labour which we will explore in the following chapters never lose this sense of self-negation and sacrifice even as they articulate their compelling visions of individual freedom. The choice between parasitism and masochism never comes out as a very comfortable one.

The energy that drives such oscillations between work as self-fulfilment and work as self-sacrifice is also a fundamental part of Freud's thinking in the late 1920s, particularly as it relates to the history and the limitations of 'civilization'. In 'The Future of an Illusion' (1927) and 'Civilization and its Discontents' (1929–30), Freud develops an argument about the psychic and social costs of the sublimations and repressions necessary to the establishment and the maintenance of civilizations.[61] These essays are fundamentally concerned to understand the emergence and development of human civilizations, as well as their role in supporting the general human search for happiness, which is understood both as the pursuit of pleasure and the absence of suffering. Freud believes that the increasing control of nature is central to any narrative of civilization's development since such control holds out the hope that many sources of human suffering, such as disease, starvation and premature death can be overcome. Nature frequently opposes man, thwarting his ambitions and undermining his plans, and Freud sees the practical and technological benefits of cooperative labour as fundamental to the human desire to form kinship groups, and later complexly structured societies.

Freud argues that 'the communal life of human beings had . . . a two-fold foundation: the compulsion to work, which was created by external necessity, and the power of love ('Civilization', 290), and he thus puts practical labour at the heart of the ethical, social and psychological dramas of living as a social being. The image of 'compulsion' is central to this drama as Freud stages it across the two essays. Work is part of a story of increasing control of nature, material improvement and progress, but it also drives the development of social structures that can lead only to frustration, disappointment and guilt. Such emotions are part of the disintegrative tendency Freud sees in his contemporary society, but they are also the expression of compromises, adjustments and sublimations that are the very foundations of that society. This knot cannot readily be unpicked, and Freud returns to it at a number of moments across the two essays.

In 'The Future of an Illusion' Freud sees a stark and destructive opposition between the needs of civilization and of the individual. He argues that civilization has 'to protect everything that contributes to the conquest of nature and the production of wealth against men's hostile impulses' (184). These impulses are particularly powerful in the mass of working people who are spontaneously idle:

It is only through the influence of individuals who can set an example and whom masses recognize as their leaders that they can be induced to perform the work and undergo the renunciations on which the existence of civilization depends. (186)

The point is put rather more gently in 'Civilization and its Discontents', where Freud simply notes that 'as a path to happiness, work is not highly praised by men . . . The great majority of people only work under the stress of necessity, and this natural human aversion to work raises most difficult social problems' (268). The gendered nature of this claim appears to escape Freud, but he does return later in the essay to the question of the conflictual relations between the working individual and the workings of civilization in a way that is illuminating. He argues that women are forced into a position of hostility towards civilization, as a perhaps ironic consequence of the fact that they 'laid the foundations of civilization by the claims of their love' (293). In the sexual division of labour, women assume the interests of the family and of sexual life, while 'the work of civilization has become increasingly the business of men' (293). Although Freud does not challenge such a tendency, he does show the disintegrative and aggressive responses it is likely to unleash, including that fact that men 'to a great extent [withdraw] from women and sexual life' (293).

Labour is, then, part of Freud's story of civilization as a frustration of individual impulses and as a source of compulsion. But Freud has a powerful sense that this is not all that can be said. Civilization does also at least hold out the promise of some kind of precarious balance between instincts and social needs; a balance in which labour would have a central role. Freud first approaches this idea through the very particular category of artistic labour. He has already conceded in 'The Future of an Illusion' that art is inaccessible to most members of his own society, 'who are engaged in exhausting work and have not enjoyed any personal education' (193), but he is interested in this creative labour as a possibly viable form of fending off suffering by displacement of libidinal energies:

The task here is that of shifting the instinctual aims in such a way that they cannot come up against frustration from the external world. In this, sublimation of the instincts lends its assistance. One gains the most if one can sufficiently heighten the yield of pleasure from the sources of psychical and intellectual work. When that is so, fate can do little against one. A satisfaction of this kind, such as an artist's joy in creating . . . or a scientist's in solving problems or discovering truths, has a special quality. (267)

The scientist and the artist can apparently find satisfaction in work precisely in so far as it is freely chosen, does not involve conflictual relations with the external world, and leads to a product that can be experienced as an expression of themselves: in other words in so far as it is quite unlike most forms of modern labour. But Freud does, finally, hold out a hope for labour as part of individuality rather than its negation in a rather tantalizingly under-developed footnote. I will conclude this chapter with Freud's observations on the rewards of labour, developed by him with an explicit nod towards Voltaire's recommendation at the end of *Candide* that we might all be well advised to concentrate on cultivating our own gardens:

The ordinary professional work that is open to everyone can play the part assigned to it by Voltaire's wise advice. It is not possible, within the limits of a short survey, to discuss adequately the significance of work for the economics of the libido. No other technique for the conduct of life attaches the individual so firmly to reality as laying the emphasis on work; for his work at least gives him a secure place in a portion of reality, in the human community. (268)

It is the nature, and the limits, of that 'secure place' that the remainder of this book will attempt to explore.

CHAPTER TWO

Technologies of labour: washing and typing

Our experience of, and our understanding of, labour is crucially inflected by technology. Although we have come to understand 'technology' as a term referring to objects, the machinery and tools associated with a particular field of human endeavour, it is useful to think of it here in an older and rather broader sense as referring also to techniques and habits of labour and the knowledges that inform these, as well as the artefacts that develop or inhibit such techniques. 'Technology' is then what enables us to understand particular forms of human activity as 'labour' as well as what allows us to grasp the historical unfolding of labour practices.

In this chapter I will be concerned with technological innovations in two rather disparate fields of labour: the reproduction of texts and the washing of clothes. Both fields are significant for our understanding of the historical movements of modernity. Historical developments in the forms and methods of textual reproduction have been understood by many critics and historians as an important dimension of the structures of communication, political organization and aesthetic representation that make the 'modern' world seem distinctive and even to some extent coherent.[1] For a cultural critic such as Friedrich Kittler, indeed, technologies of textual reproduction can provide a figure for the basic epistemological and affective shape of any given cultural moment.[2] Similarly, cleanliness and hygiene have frequently been understood as key cultural markers of a 'modern' society, both in the sense that a modern society may offer the techniques and resources to achieve higher standards of cleanliness, and in the sense that self-understanding as 'modern' may involve a repudiation of the 'primitive' quality of dirt.

In the historical moment that this book addresses, significant technological innovations in the reproduction of texts cluster round the development of the typewriter. This technological innovation significantly pre-dates the modernist cultural moment. Nonetheless, it is in the late nineteenth century that the typewriter comes to have a significant material presence in offices and in homes, and it is thus to the moment of modernism that we might expect it to make a distinctive contribution. In this chapter, I will consider the ways in which the typewriter is connected to movements in working populations and practices, as well as the extent to which it enabled new forms of labour. I will also examine the ways in which imaginative texts of the late nineteenth and early twentieth century found forms and narratives to represent the new kinds of working the typewriter might be understood as embodying. As we shall see, typing as a form of labour becomes increasingly visible in the early years of the twentieth century. Whether it embodies a form of liberation and mobility, or simply assures a more mechanical and repetitive experience of work for its operators is a vexed question for many writers in the period. It is a complexly contested technology at the levels of social-scientific research, of the economic relations of publishing and commerce, and of the organization of the workplace throughout the early years of the twentieth century.

My second area of research, however, is characterized by its rather fleeting and embarrassed presence in the cultural texts of the early twentieth century. Although cleanliness and hygiene were important aspects of the scientific and industrial unfolding of modernity, housework might be better understood as modernity's uncomfortable remainder. The very category of 'housework' is of course a result of the process of modernization, and specifically of industrialization, that removes significant categories of labour for the first time from the home.[3] As the production of food, clothing, tools, lighting and heating move increasingly outside the household, a specific range of tasks associated with the sustenance of the family home come to be grouped together as housework. The washing of clothes is part of this residue, if a contested part. Who was to do this labour, and how and where it was to be done was far from clear in the early twentieth century. The number and the size of commercial laundries increased significantly during the late nineteenth century, suggesting that laundry might follow bakery, butchery and agriculture in leaving the home for larger more industrialized locations. But the development of the domestic washing machine led in rather a different direction, towards this labour becoming increasingly associated with the individual housewife and the home. Mapping innovations in techniques of washing, in materials used for laundry and in the social relations between the labour of washing and the individual home onto the fleeting and often uncomfortable presence of dirty washing in the literary texts of modernism will lead to a deeper sense of the possible relations between labour and selfhood in the period: the more invisible forms of labour turning out to be among the emotionally as well as the economically more significant.

The typewriter and the washing machine both reconfigured the spaces and the temporalities of labour in the period. One was rapidly used as a figure for key subjective and economic dislocations and transformations of the early twentieth century, while the other entered the cultural imagination more hesitantly, trailing behind it associations of moral and social dirt. Both raise particular issues for an understanding of the historical meanings of women's labour, bound up as both come to be with that troubling concept: a labour of love.

THE TYPEWRITER: WORKING, WRITING AND WOMEN'S LABOUR

Thinking about the relations between technology, cultural practice and the body has generated interesting critical insights in recent years, particularly in relation to the modernist period. Mark Seltzer's *Bodies and Machines* and Tim Armstrong's *Modernism, Technology and the Body* have drawn attention to the ways in which technologies both produce and express cultural anxieties and fantasies associated with corporeality, desire and death.[4] Anson Rabinbach's *The Human Motor* has compellingly unpicked the ways in which the body is read and organized as a machine, and the consequent deployment of ideas of 'energy' and 'fatigue' to explicate the dilemmas of modern labour. Interestingly, given the overall argument of this chapter, he also argues that the shift from a moralizing to a scientific relation to the working body foregrounded the idea of hygiene: 'fatigue and energy emerged as a modern conceptual framework for expressing the relations between work and the body . . . By the 1860s and 1870s a new literature stressing the hygienic aspects of work began to appear.'[5] In terms of the typewriter as a specific technology, however, the most influential recent critical voice has undoubtedly been that of Friedrich Kittler. Kittler produced two studies in the 1980s, which were translated into English some years later, which gave the typewriter a privileged place within a complex and layered narrative of cultural modernity.[6] The richness and originality of his historical and critical readings have generated a significant level of interest in the materiality of writing as part of a historiographical engagement with the cultural moment of modernism.

Kittler's own theoretical position is shaped by his disavowal of a philosophical and critical tradition of hermeneutical interpretation. Much of the rhetorical and critical edge of *Discourse Networks*, indeed, can be located in

Kittler's attempt to show that notions of interiority, expressiveness and creativity associated with the moment of romanticism are precisely historical, and are radically challenged by the technological and cultural innovations of '1900'. Kittler picks one central cultural figure to embody each of his cultural moments: Goethe for 1800 and Nietzsche for 1900, and round their writings he weaves a series of readings of texts and practices that may seem both marginal and fleeting, but which he offers as exemplary. It is part of the logic of thinking in terms of 'discourse networks' that centre and margin are disturbed, since the aim is to understand the connections between technology, communication and the body both at the level of the everyday and at the level of the culturally innovative. Networks connect the most trivial and the most actively shaped forms of cultural expression in a paradigm that can be captured by the attentive and alert cultural historian.

The discourse network of 1800 is read by Kittler as a project of training individuals to read texts as coherent, expressive and affective. He stresses the significance of pedagogy, and in particular the process of giving sounds to letters so that language can be 'sounded out' to the eager child. The mother has a central role in this production of expressive readers, she is the grounding of this oral and affective bond that ensures a child's entry into the discourse network: 'the origin of language, once a creation ex nihilo, becomes maternal gestation' (*Discourse Networks*, 25); 'primary orality, the Mother, the self-presence of the origin'.[7] Kittler indeed concludes that 'as Nature *and* Ideal, the mother oriented the entire writing system of 1800'(53).

When he turns to '1900' in the second half of his study, Kittler is particularly interested in the technological and cultural innovations that might be read as disrupting the bonds between language, individuality and coherence he has identified in his analysis of '1800'. He thus stresses the increasing interest in failures or pathologies of communication: moments where language seems to break down or to proliferate excessively. He writes about the science of 'psychophysics' as a new mode of understanding the connections between selfhood and the body and stresses its interest in the materiality of language. Psychophysicists, for example, studied the process of memory by asking individuals to memorize long strings of 'meaningless' combinations of letters. The self, language and meaning have here become disconnected in ways that allow Kittler to argue for a much more general uncoupling of writing and subjectivity in the period. In 1900, Kittler argues, we can find a very broad interest in language as material. Far from any notion of writing as the expressive flow of a particular individuality, Kittler finds in a number of scientific disciplines and philosophical texts a fascination with language as process, as differential system, and as fragile fragment. This discourse network is concerned not with writing but with inscription, and not with interiority but with materiality: in both these facets the typewriter is to play a central role. Kittler argues that instead of a play between man and the writing surface 'there is the play between type and its Other, completely removed from subjects. Its name is inscription' (195).

In Kittler's theorization of modernism, then, the typewriter plays a key role. It is a form of writing that severs the link between the eye, the hand and the text. Early typewriters actually made it impossible to see what was being written at the moment of inscription; 'none of the models prior to Underwood's great innovation of 1897 allowed immediate visual control over the output' (*Gramophone, Film, Typewriter*, 203). The typewriter organizes writing into spatially designated and discrete signs, produced at some distance from the writing hand. It mechanizes the act of writing and destroys the illusion of an immediate link between language and the self: 'the typewriter thus unlinks hand, eye, paper, and mind; unlinks writing, hand, and spirit'.[8] The typewriter here becomes the archetypal modernist technology, staging language as process, as structure, and as in a distant and contested relation to the self.

In seeing the typewriter as metaphorically encapsulating the experience of the modern, Kittler is not alone. Mark Seltzer similarly privileges the typewriter as a technology expressive of the modern:

The typewriter, like the telegraph, replaces, or pressures, that fantasy of continuous transition with recalcitrantly visible systems of difference: with the standardized spacing of keys and letters; with the dislocation of where the hands work, where the letters strike and appear, where the eyes look, if they look at all.[9]

Jennifer Wicke also offers a reading of the typewriter as figure of modernity in the context of a fascinating critical analysis of Bram Stoker's *Dracula*. Wicke foregrounds the significance of a range of new communications technologies in this novel, arguing that they are intrinsic to its disturbances and its fascinations:

As radically different as the sexy act of vamping and such prosaic typewriting appear, there are underlying ties between them . . . [My] argument will turn attention to the technologies that underpin vampirism, making for the dizzy contradictions of this book, and permitting it to be read as the first great *modern* novel in British literature.[10]

Wicke draws attention here to the ways in which *Dracula* signals, almost excessively, the tension between the primitiveness of vampire mythology and the fevered excitements surrounding new technology, and in this very oscillation she locates the novel's claim to be the 'first great modern novel'.

As will be discussed later in this chapter, the status of the typist, Mina, in *Dracula* articulates the gendered nature of knowledge and power in the period. Mina is at the centre of the texts and the documents that constitute the novel, with access to knowledges that are both sexual and dangerous. At the same time, however, she is carefully positioned as economically and socially dependent; the willing wife whose knowledges will always be constrained by the fact of her family position. Friedrich Kittler also draws attention throughout his texts to the reconfiguration of gender relations around the typewriter, and also to the recalcitrance of gender hierarchies and the notion of 'sacrifice'.[11] He argues that 'the end of all women's laments is based on the historical fact that script, instead of continuing to be translation from a Mother's mouth, has become an irreducible medium among media, has become the typewriter', suggesting that this severing of the link between language and the maternal offers women a space within the discourse network that is neither the space of the mother nor the space of desire (*Discourse Networks*, 198). As we shall see, however, both maternity and desire haunt fictional explorations of the meaning of the typewriter, to an extent that now seems almost pathological. Kittler sees the typewriter as disrupting the epistemological and affective link between writing and the mother's voice, and he also sees the erosion of the authority of the author as opening up a space for women's writings. Finally, he connects the typewriter historically to new educational opportunities and new patterns of labour for women: 'Apart from Freud, it was Remington who "granted the female sex access to the office"' (352).

Kittler is not alone in seeing the typewriter as having a special significance for women. Christopher Sholes, who designed the first commercially produced typewriter in 1867, said that 'it is obviously a blessing to mankind, and especially to womankind'.[12] Later historians of the typewriter have endorsed this judgement. For example, Frank J. Romano claims that 'typewriting was the opportunity that opened the door for the emancipation of women', suggesting that the employment opportunities it offered contributed to a personal freedom for women as individuals and as a group.[13] There is, of course, an important shift between these two versions: from the typewriter as technology to a consideration of the act of typewriting, of labour. I will discuss the problematic nature of this shift further below, but at the moment it seems important simply to note that discussions of the typewriter as technology quickly map on to more general arguments about the historically changing role of women in the public sphere, and specifically to the idea of 'opening the door for the emancipation of women'.

The typewriter thus plays a significant role in two rather distinct versions of the modern. Firstly, in Kittler's argument the typewriter signals radical shifts in the relation between subjectivity and writing and embodies the gap between the discourse networks of Romanticism and modernism. Secondly, for a number of historians the typewriter becomes a figure of women's labour and their increased participation in the public sphere and as such is read as a tool of social emancipation.

The connection of the typewriter to women's labour is not as natural, however, as some historians would have us assume. In a detailed study of office workers between 1870 and 1930, Margery Davies seeks to challenge the idea that the typewriter was inevitably a woman's technology.[14] She points to a range of factors that led to the expansion of office work, and the increased participation of women in this work, in the early twentieth century. The rapid increase in the size of major companies, the development of national and international markets, the growth of marketing and of 'scientific management' all produced greater volumes of clerical work. More employees were required, and this requirement was partly met by women, who were, anyway, cheaper labour. Those very factors which precipitated the expansion of clerical work also served to make the typewriter a commercially viable technology for the first time. Many writing machines were invented before Sholes's, but his was developed at a time when the expansion of office work meant that investment in this new technology could be secured, and the likely sales could justify the very significant investment. The entry of women to the office and the development of the typewriter were indeed related, but the entry of women into the office was by no means an inevitable result of the invention of the technology of the writing machine.

The association of women with typewriting was in fact initially contested. A report in the *Scientific American* of 1913 set out to measure the aptitude of men and women for the physical and mental labour of typewriting and concluded that:

In general, men surpass women in rapidity of auditory action and, consequently, in speed of work, but are inferior to women, perhaps, in power of sustained attention.[15]

Women's entry into the office, and their increasing role as typists was seen as neither natural nor inevitable.

Despite this initial hesitancy, the percentage of women among clerical workers did increase dramatically in the first half of the twentieth century: from 13.4% in 1901 to 59.6% in 1951.[16] Women's entry into the office coincided with a broad reorganization of clerical work and the production of a much more rigid office hierarchy. The distinction between the secretary and typist was crucial in the early years of the century: the 'secretary' was still more likely to be a man until at least the 1920s and there was little mobility between the two grades. The question of whether this increased entry into the public sphere of the office represented, or was experienced as, emancipation is significantly more complex. The economic, political and individual significance of the entry of women into new forms of waged labour in the twentieth century has been understood in a number of different ways. One version of the position of women within modernity sees wage labour, with increasing literacy and access to the vote, as part of the progressive emancipation of women. This story needs to be treated with some care, however, as there is a tendency to overlook factors which continued to produce relative poverty and professional frustration for women workers. For example, there was clear sexual segregation in clerical employment in the early twentieth century: male and female clerks entered by different doors, worked in different rooms, and were paid different rates. In a study of women working in the offices of the Prudential insurance company in the 1870s, Ellen Jordan stresses that segregation was the norm: women and men were forbidden from mixing at work and women had to be supervised by other women.[17] Women were rarely acknowledged as 'skilled labourers', and were thus paid significantly less than men. The marriage bar, which forced women to resign on marriage, operated until the 1940s, and the number of married women in work actually fell considerably from the late nineteenth century.[18]

Margery Davies, in her study of office workers between 1870 and 1930, acknowledges the relation between employment and feelings of autonomy, but also stresses the material circumstances that drove most women into paid labour:

> For some women, participation in the labor force afforded psychological benefits such as increased independence and self-reliance. This however, should not distract attention from the central fact of working-class life: most women worked because they had to.[19]

Sharon Hartman Strom, in an analysis of office work in the United States, suggests that 'office jobs were the best jobs available to most women between 1900 and 1930', in that they provided reasonable remuneration and comfortable working conditions.[20] Research by both Teresa Davy and Kay Sanderson into the experience of female typists and civil-service clerks, however, suggests that these working conditions did not necessarily lead to any sense of fulfilment. Both report that the women they interviewed saw their jobs as tedious and restricting, and saw marriage, in contrast, as offering 'freedom'.[21]

(TYPE)WRITING MODERNISM

In order to explore further the complexity of these relations between the typewriter, modernity, labour, selfhood and ideas of emancipation, I will analyse a number of fictional texts which include the typewriter and the typist as part of their setting and their metaphorical landscape. Before considering these cultural representations of the act of typewriting, however, I will explore the extent to which modernist writers were actually involved day-to-day with the typewriter as a technology of writing. If the typewriter refigures the relation between subjectivity and writing, does it do so only metaphorically and imaginatively, or does it actually modify the experience of creative writing?[22]

Few studies of modernism have paid significant attention to the material experience of writing, and there is relatively little work on the relation of modernist writers to the typewriter. Kittler, as we might imagine, is an exception to this general rule. He identifies Nietzsche as a central figure in the development of the discourse network of 1900 largely because of his demonstrable historical connection with the typewriter. Nietzsche bought a very early version of the typewriter in 1882 and Kittler says, 'Nietzsche as typist – the experiment lasted for a couple of weeks and was broken off, yet it was a turning point in the organization of discourse' (*Discourse Networks*, 193). Kittler develops this argument further in *Gramophone, Film, Typewriter*, where he writes:

Writing in Nietzsche is no longer a natural extension of humans who bring forth their own voice, soul, individuality through their handwriting . . . A type of writing that blindly dismembers body parts and perforates human skin stems from typewriters built before 1897, when Underwood finally introduced visibility. (210)

As a piece of historical criticism, the claim seems exorbitant. Nietzsche's deteriorating vision did certainly lead him to explore this new technology, but there is scant evidence in his writing that this in itself refigured his relation to language. One or two passing comments are the sum total of evidence Kittler can find for this transformative moment. In a letter to Peter Gast of 14 August 1881, Nietzsche writes: 'I have had to delete the reading of scores and piano playing from my activities once and for all. I am thinking of acquiring a typewriter, and am in touch with its inventor, a Dane from Copenhagen.'[23] Then, in a typed letter of 1882, Nietzsche reflects on the relations between writing materials and thinking.[24] There is, however, no evidence that Nietzsche used the typewriter for more than two weeks. He wrote about the experience only in passing, and developed no explicit account of its significance. We do however have evidence from his childhood of his very strong involvement in the process of writing by hand: 'What he enjoyed most of all was writing. His handwriting was extremely neat, and his poems, his lists, and the memos he wrote for himself all show that he took pleasure in forming letters and laying lines of handwriting out attractively on the page'.[25] We also know that the quality of his handwriting, under pressure from his deteriorating eyesight, was of concern to him late in his life.[26] Nietzsche was producing his work at a period when new mechanical relations to the process of writing became not only imaginable, but realizable. The uncovering of this material about Nietzsche's relation to the process of writing is refreshing and certainly raises new sorts of questions about his work. Yet Kittler's claim that for Nietzsche to develop his ideas about subjectivity, memory and inscription 'it was first necessary to write with and about typewriters' remains finally speculative.[27]

Henry James was also driven to working with the typewriter because of physical disability, in his case writer's cramp.[28] James never in fact used the typewriter himself, but employed a series of secretaries to whom he dictated his work directly on to the typewriter. The best known of these, Theodora Bosanquet, began working with James in 1907. After James's death, Bosanquet published a detailed and reflective account of his working methods. She writes interestingly about James's method of creative composition, suggesting that the act of dictation made his language both freer and more involved. James does not seem to have been alienated by the mediation of this technology, indeed Bosanquet claims that 'the click of a Remington machine acted as a positive spur' to his creativity, though she also notes that any other make of typewriter caused him great difficulty.[29]

Consideration of James's use of the typewriter has not, however, focussed on his relation to the material act of transcription, but has looked rather at the ways in which his method of creation transformed the relations between writing and speech. Sharon Cameron sees James's dictation as crucial to his reworking of ideas of selfhood and consciousness, because of the intersubjective relations it necessitated. Dictation, Cameron argues, 'in effect exteriorises thought and moves it between persons'.[30] On this account, the typewriter's significance is relatively small, compared to the centrality of speech for the development of James's style.

Both Nietzsche and Henry James had strong motivations to explore methods other than handwriting for the composition of literary texts. There is little evidence, however, that this was a widespread concern among literary modernists. Even among poets who were most concerned to explore the affective and semantic significances of typography, the 'visual poets' of the early twentieth century, there was a clear attachment to handwriting as the medium of composition. Although the invention of the typewriter would also seem to have been a necessary prelude to visual poetry, in fact it had little or no impact on the movement. Almost without exception the early poems were drafted as handwritten manuscripts.[31]

A clearer pattern of the developing relation between writers and the typewriter emerges in the pages of *The Author*, the journal of the Society of Authors. We first find discussion of the typewriter in 1893 in a letter bemoaning the difficulty of finding a reliable typist in Paris. The letter ends by suggesting that young women might consider typing as a reasonable career: 'I would not undertake to advise any girl to come abroad on the chance of making a living by type-writing. But I believe that there *is* a good opening for some earnest worker.'[32] In the same year, however, an article in the journal about handwriting reveals that authors were not expected at this point to submit typewritten manuscripts.[33] Between 1899 and 1905 there is a long debate in the journal about the appropriate rates of pay for typists. It is clear from the terms of the discussion that authors feel uneasy both with the financial burden of having to have their work typed and with their new role of employer. During this period, however, publishers had begun to expect work to be submitted in typewritten form.[34] The difficulty of typing, its physical effects, and its monetary worth are discussed in detail throughout this period, and there is little suggestion that creative writers themselves were typing their own work. The situation is changing rapidly, however, and a letter of 1906 claims that 'there must be many members of the society who, like myself, are in the habit of typing their own work'.[35] The numbers typing their own work were likely to have been very small, but over the next ten years regular adverts for portable typewriters begin to appear in the journal, though they are still outnumbered by typists advertising their services to authors.

The transition towards typewriting for creative writers was both slow and uneven. Poets were less likely to use typewriters than fiction writers, though Kittler discusses the fact that T. S. Eliot, who would write *The Waste Land* on a typewriter in the early twenties, was already talking about the capacity of the typewriter to concentrate and pare down his poetic style in 1916.[36] Fiction writers who depended on a regular income from literary journals and popular fiction, who were more immediately dependent on developments in the literary marketplace, were most likely to begin typing their own work. The experiment was undertaken with some caution however: it is nearly ten years after publishing her first novel, *Pointed Roofs* (1915), that Dorothy Richardson makes her 'first attempt' at typewriting:

Dear Bryer
    Hats off. This is my first attempt
Iam drunk but not with Fine. Though an enor
mous one stands in sealed magnificence on
    the table
        I shaal never use a pen again
it is so exciting tomake mistakes in sp
elling and in spacing. My literary style
    will change completely.[37]

We know that D. H. Lawrence was already using a typewriter in 1916 while working on the text that would become *Women in Love*. His biographer, Mark Kinkead-Weekes writes that this 'was to become "one of the labours of Hercules" that went on for month after month . . . by mid-October the revision of the novel was still only two-thirds done. At that stage he decided that enough was enough the typing was bad for his nerves and was making him ill; so he persuaded Pinker to have it completed in his office instead.'[38]

Many writers, however, remained unmarked by the experience of typewriting until well into the twentieth century. Thus A. E. Housman could write to his publisher in 1922: 'If, as I gather from what you say, printers no longer print from MS, then I should be obliged if you did the type-writing, though it will not be more legible than the hand I write literature in.'[39] He would also remark, later that year: 'perhaps type-writing had better be used, but I do not like it, as it makes things look repulsive.'[40]

For modernist writers, then, the typewriter often seemed to be a strange and even unwelcome technology. For Richardson, certainly, it offered the exhilaration of a new relation to space and structure in language, while for Eliot it may have facilitated a certain concentration of language, but for many professional writers it represented an expense and an unwelcome mediation in the creative process.

Despite this rather hesitant professional relationship to the typewriter as a technology of writing, many writers drew in important ways on the historical and metaphorical resonances of typewriting and the typewriter from the 1890s onwards.[41] The typewriter provided a figure for the exploration of new forms of labour and their relation to the possibility of autonomy both for individuals and for women as a social group. The typewriter could also be used either metaphorically or descriptively to explore changing relations to writing, both as a literary form and as a technology.

The earliest appearance of the typewriter in a work of fiction is in Conan Doyle's story 'A Case of Identity' (1891). This story involves a young woman, Mary Sutherland, who is courted by a man called Hosmer Angel, who, having persuaded her to marry him, then mysteriously disappears on the morning of the wedding. It transpires that 'Hosmer Angel' is in fact Mary Sutherland's stepfather in disguise. The stepfather's aim is to leave Mary so distressed that she will not consider marrying anyone else and thus to keep control of her modest inherited wealth. When Mary Sutherland comes to see Sherlock Holmes, he quickly identifies her as a typist by the marks on the sleeves of her dress. She describes her financial circumstances in detail and explains that typewriting gives her a small but reasonable income: 'I find that I can do pretty well with what I earn at typewriting.'[42] The young typist is represented as basically pitiable, she is large, she 'looms', she has a broad face, she is vulgar. Holmes does manage to unravel the mystery surrounding her failed romance, but decides that it would be unwise to tell Mary Sutherland all the facts of the case, and so leaves her in confusion and unhappiness. He solves the mystery by identification of the source of the typewritten letters which had been sent to Mary, remarking that '[i]t is a curious thing . . . that a typewriter has really quite as much individuality as a man's handwriting', and more individuality it would seem than the women to whom the typewriting is sent.[43] This move to create individuality in the face of the anonymity and impersonality of mass-produced cultural forms is familiar enough in the history of detective fiction, with its interest in deciphering and individualizing the apparently random experience of the modern and the urban, but it is nonetheless striking to see this desire develop in relation to the typewriter at such an early stage in the technology's history. The association of typewriting with the vulgar and the pitiable found in 'A Case of Identity' is reinforced in a later Sherlock Holmes story, 'The Adventure of the Solitary Cyclist', where Holmes says to a prospective client:

I nearly fell into the error of supposing that you were typewriting. Of course, it is obvious that it is music. You observe the spatulate finger-end, Watson, which is common to both professions? There is a spirituality about the face, however.[44]

Such spirituality was apparently impossible to reconcile with the habitus of the working woman typist.

In George Gissing's naturalist novel of 1893, *The Odd Women*, the type-writer plays a major role. This novel examines the emotional, familial and economic ties that shape the lives of working women at the end of the nineteenth century. Much of the action of the novel takes place around an establishment known as 'Miss Barfoot's' which exists to provide training for the daughters of educated men. Having taken some secretarial courses, a young women called Rhoda Nunn teaches typing there, and also works in a number of other ways to better the economic and social position of women. Rhoda Nunn encourages Monica, a young shop-worker, to train as a typist as a means towards a greater degree of personal autonomy and of financial security. Typing is represented as both financially and morally better than other forms of labour available to single women, such as teaching or shop work. Indeed, having left teaching to learn secretarial work, Rhoda Nunn declares, 'I was vastly improved in health, and felt myself worth something in the world.'[45] Typewriting produces physical robustness as well as a more secure sense of selfhood.

'Miss Barfoot's' becomes a centre for agitation about the condition of women; a place where there is 'a bookcase full of works on the Woman Question and allied topics' (60). Monica is initially uncomfortable at entering a space so clearly concerned to articulate an oppositional mode of femininity, a mode the novel itself designates 'odd'. She expresses her unease in terms that suggest some recognition of the power relations that both constrain and enable any new form of social identity, worrying that 'to put herself in Miss Nunn's hands might possibly result in a worse form of bondage than she suffered at the shop' (40). The emphasis on 'hands' is striking here, since it follows closely on an exchange where Rhoda has stressed the training of hands necessary for typing, asking whether Monica has ever learned the piano, as a way of gauging how disciplined her hands might already be. Having embarked on instruction in typing, however, things initially seem to go well: 'seemingly contented, Monica worked at the typewriting machine . . . she experienced a growth of self respect' (79).

This narrative of self-realization seems reasonably coherent: work and technology leading to a form of personal liberation. But the novel does not leave this space of activism and autonomy intact. Monica leaves the school, marries disastrously and dies. Rhoda falls in love, but rejects her lover's offer of marriage because it would interfere with her ability to work, and then ends the novel staring disconsolately at Monica's baby. Surrogate motherhood seems to be imaginable in relation to labour in a way that sexual desire cannot. Having begun with typewriting as a form of economic and social liberation, the novel ends with typewriting as a deadening negation of the sexual. Rhoda's debate with her lover, Everard, about the meaning of work articulates the problem for and in the novel:

'What *is* your work? Copying with a type machine, and teaching others to do the
same – isn't that it?'

'The work by which I earn money, yes. But if it were no more than that –'. (208)

The final dash carries much of the ideological and emotional significance
of this exchange. It designates a failure of language to capture the 'more'
to which Rhoda aspires through labour. The element beyond 'the work by
which I earn my money', the element that Rhoda experiences as integral
to her self, cannot be articulated.

Uncertainty about the typewriter as a technology of emancipation is
similarly expressed in *The Type-Writer Girl* by Olive Pratt Rayner (Grant
Allen).[46] The protagonist of this novel, Juliet Appleton is a graduate of
Girton College, Cambridge, who moves to London in search of a job. She
is trained as a typist and sees typewriting as a means to financial autonomy.
Having arrived in London, where she enjoys the energy and the diversity of
urban spaces, she enters an office looking for a job. The male clerks appraise
this woman who has responded to the advertisement for a 'Shorthand and
Type-writer (female)' (21). She is hired and reflects with some relief that,
'[i]n the struggle of life I had obtained a footing' (28). Her experience of
work as a typist is, however, alienating: 'so I continued to click, click, click,
like a machine that I was . . . On the fourth day, however, the rebel in my
blood awoke' (34). Juliet walks out on her job and goes to join an anarchist
commune. The pleasures of the manual labour this involves quickly fade,
however, and Juliet is subjected to sexual harassment, so she leaves the
commune after one week, declaring 'I must go back to London, and be
once more a type-writer' (82).

On her return to London, Juliet approaches a publisher looking for
work as a typist, but he is initially reluctant to employ her since he does not
approve of employing middle-class women who see work merely as a form
of amusement. Juliet angrily rejects this representation and insists that paid
work, and specifically typewriting is essential to her self realization:

'I should hate teaching!' I cried vehemently. 'I prefer freedom. I am prepared for
the drudgery of earning my livelihood in a house of business. But I must realise
my self.' (125)

Freedom, drudgery and selfhood are here woven together in a way that
leaves little room to ponder their incompatibilities. Yet in this novel, once
again, sexuality is to threaten any secure sense of self realized through work.
Juliet dines with her employer, and they begin to fall in love: 'for a week
I was a woman, not merely a type-writer' (179), Juliet says, articulating
a previously silenced tension between her identity as sexual woman and

as working woman. Juliet's employer turns out to be the fiancé of one of her old friends, and Juliet eventually rejects his offer of marriage in a self-denying gesture of sacrifice which seems certain to bring general misery. Having renounced this sexual relationship, Juliet ends where she began, as a typist: 'I am still a type-writer girl – at another office' (98). The energy, potential and excitement of such an identity at the beginning of the novel are, however, now largely clouded by ideas of sacrifice, of repetition and of mechanical labour.

The importance of the typewriter in Bram Stoker's *Dracula* has already been suggested above. In this novel we first encounter Mina in the act of practising her typewriting so that she can assist her future husband. Mina will in fact type up all the diverse and increasingly troubling documents produced during the hunt for Dracula. She sets off for Transylvania declaring herself 'so grateful to the man who invented the "Traveller's typewriter"'.[47] Jennifer Wicke has developed a very persuasive reading of these representations of the typewriter in *Dracula* in relation to the prominence of a range of communications technologies, including the phonograph, shorthand, telegrams and the press within the novel as a whole.[48] The typewriter can certainly be read fruitfully in relation to this broader concern with the cultural technologies of modernity, but what I wish to explore here is rather the way the typewriter in *Dracula* relates to ideas of work, of autonomy and of the sexual.

There is, in fact, very little work in *Dracula*. Even the professionals, the doctors and lawyers, have remarkable freedom and leisure. Dr Seward's declaration that 'I must only wait on hopeless and work. Work! Work!' (96) expresses his mood of helplessness and frustration rather than describing any strong or sustained commitment to labour. Autonomy is equally elusive in the text: Mina's typewriting does not offer financial autonomy, since no-one ever pays her for doing it, but instead reinforces her sexual dependence. Yet despite this economic dependence, Mina does apparently experience typewriting as offering some sort of reassurance, or confirmation of her self: 'I should have felt quite astray doing the work if I had to write with a pen' (450). Mina has to transcribe the intimate writings and recordings produced by other characters in the novel, gaining knowledges that hover on the edge of vampirism. Her work of typing is constantly in danger of slipping into an invisible and sexualized form of labour, and Dr Seward notes in his diary: 'After lunch Harker and his wife went back to their own room, and as I passed a while ago I heard the click of the typewriter. They are hard at it' (289). This almost farcical turn of phrase captures something of the slippages between innocent and sexual forms of knowledge within a novel where all knowledge finally risks being read as indecent.

Ménie Muriel Dowie's *Love and his Mask* (1901) is a much less familiar cultural document of the period. Dowie was a travel writer and 'new woman' novelist, whose fiction sought to map the emotional as well as the intellectual double-binds that stood in the way of any radical re-imagining of the social and familial identities of women in the period. *Love and his Mask* opens with its heroine, Leslie Rose, struggling with a typewriter:

> The working of the typewriter is at any time exasperating. To type something that you feel strongly is an agony, no less. That warring of sentiment with the mechanical acuteness necessary to get the capitals and the stops and the inverted commas in the right place – it is terrible.[49]

Leslie Rose is a young widowed woman, from a wealthy and relatively progressive family, who regularly include theosophists and vegetarians among their lunch guests. She is somewhat educated, possessing like her sisters a 'vast if superficial knowledge' (14), but she does not do any paid work. At the beginning of the novel she is absorbed in writing a letter to a Major-General Riddington, who is fighting in the Boer War and whom she has never met. Her project is to develop with him a new form of intimacy, built on the premise that he will never know the identity of his correspondent. Riddington receives her letters, and then returns from the War injured, and keen to discover the identity of his correspondent. They meet, and much of the novel consists of tense and ambiguous dialogue as the secret is never quite revealed between them.

Leslie is represented as misguided, even as dangerous in the pain she can cause. Her preference for impersonality, which is presented largely as an incapacity to deal with the complexities of personality and relationship, is crucially expressed in her preference for typewriting: 'typing is more impersonal' (77). Leslie's sense of self is constructed through the reading of letters and other texts. She apparently falls in love with Riddington by staring at the letters of his name:

> There it stood. Clear, even, prettily spaced – *his* name, *his* address. The great successful soldier, the modern Rustum; the man with the genius of Attila, of Hannibal . . . *His* name; his beautiful name . . . the man she had never met. (3–4)

Some time after his return from the War, Riddington proposes to Leslie, still unaware that she was the author of the letters he received while abroad. She refuses him, but then nearly changes her mind when she is moved by re-reading his letter of proposal. Later, Riddington sends Leslie the letters he received from his 'unknown correspondent' while abroad and she re-reads them as well:

Warm flushes crossed her cheeks when she turned them over – those typewritten letters – reading here and there a passage. When she came to that in which she had described the love of a woman for her soldier-husband, she read slowly and steadily. It seemed that here was a wisdom, if it *was* wisdom, which she had possessed and lost. She could write of the love of that bride for her departing husband and she could look into her heart and see herself insecure in her refusal of Riddington, for whom she had none of these feelings. It was a shock. (264)

These typewritten letters construct a version of Leslie's selfhood which is both compelling and unrecognizable for her. She had chosen the typewriter for its impersonality, its disconnection from her sense of self: we find her at one point pausing to 'contemplate the finger-tips that had controlled the typewriter' (201) as if they had not even been subject to her conscious control. Towards the end of the novel, however, she actually becomes enmeshed in the personality that has been constructed through these typewritten texts, and the distancing impersonality of the typewriter emerges as just an ironic interruption in the playing out of a quite personal fantasy of desire.

The novel raises interesting questions about the relation between language and selfhood, and the impact on these of typewriting. It sets out to stage a relation of intimacy based on impersonality, which at first seems to offer Leslie the fulfilment that is otherwise unavailable to her in the social milieu in which she moves. Quickly, however, this experiment turns into something destructive and Leslie is described as possessing 'all the blighting inability to give way to feeling that curses high-souled women' (296). Far from representing any real autonomy, the typewriter here embodies the falsities and blindnesses of the modern, and particularly of the modern woman. The novel ends with Leslie (having realized that she is really in love with Toby, a long-term admirer) determining that she should attach less importance to words, which can only be 'about things', and more importance to 'things themselves'. Her typewriting adventure appears to be at an end.

The dangers of modern femininity are also associated with typewriting in a rather later essay by D. H. Lawrence, 'Cocksure Women and Hensure Men', published in 1929. Lawrence's essay is an attack on what he perceives as the dominant mode of modern femininity. He argues that femininity has two basic aspects, the demure and the dauntless, but it quickly becomes clear that he sees the demure as the more natural form. This form of femininity, which he characterizes as 'hensure', involves unconscious and bodily forms of understanding: it is passive, but embodies a sort of strength. His anxiety concerns what he sees as distorted 'cocksure' forms of femininity, which are false, dangerous, and fraudulent:

And when it has collapsed, and she looks at the eggs she has laid, votes, or miles of typewriting, years of business efficiency – suddenly, because she is a hen and not a cock, all she has done will turn into pure nothingness to her. Suddenly it all falls out of relation to her basic henny self, and she realizes she has lost her own life.[50]

Voting, typing and working are here used to stand for the inauthenticity within modern versions of femininity, an inauthenticity that Lawrence sees quite explicitly as a loss of self. The typist as figure of alienated modern femininity has a more specific class location in T. S. Eliot's *The Waste Land* (1922), but the connections between typing, 'pure nothingness' and modern femininity are equally strong. Eliot's typist lives alone, in a chaotic and cramped bedsit. Her breakfast dishes and her washing litter her room, and she eats tinned food.[51] She is unmoved by her sexual encounter with a young clerk, staged in the poem, and indeed she 'makes a welcome of indifference'.[52] Her movements are automatic, her personality void, and as she reaches for the gramophone she expresses the falsity and alienation of mass culture and of modern woman.

Ivy Low's novel *The Questing Beast* (1914) is also concerned with the relations between women and the typewriter, but disavows such seductive metaphorical ascriptions in favour of a more complex mapping of the relations between gender and labour in the period. The heroine of Low's novel, Rachel Cohen, is a clerk who wants to be a writer. She has spent two years working in an office, but has not yet managed to reconcile herself to the labour it involves: 'She felt weak and spiritless. "This is my youth," she kept telling herself. "The best years of my life are being spent in exhaustion and drudgery."'[53] The novel opens with Rachel travelling to work, late and anxious, rushing towards the women clerks' entrance to an insurance office. She angrily expresses her resentment of the physical demands and the lack of creativity associated with typing: 'the effort of typewriting grew more burdensome every day' (142). Rachel fears the impact of the typewriter on the creative process of writing, seeing it as tending towards the formulaic and the clichéd. Creative writing, in this novel, is the antithesis of the typewriter, and the only possible space for the realization of the self. On returning from her burdensome and alienating work, Rachel arrives home to 'write herself out' (33), a process that does not involve the mediation of a typewriter. Rachel eventually leaves her work at the office after publishing her first novel. The gesture might be read as the triumph of self-expression over the deadly repetitions of typewriting, though the fact that Rachel is also pregnant, unmarried and facing a precarious financial future tends to temper such triumphalism with the chill winds of poverty and social vulnerability.

Ellen Melville, the heroine of Rebecca West's *The Judge* (1922), is also oppressed by the boredom of her life as a typist. She sees herself as belittled and constricted by her identity as typist: 'I'll never be anything but the wee typist that I am.'[54] She attempts at first to construct an emotionally fulfilling relationship to her work, 'just as men do':

Her quivering lip said gallantly to the banged door: 'Well, there is my wurrk. I will forget my petty pairsonal trouble in my wurrk, just as men do!' And she typed away, squeezing out such drops of pride as can be found in that mechanical exercise. (136)

The repetitive and subservient nature of her work makes this impossible, however, and Ellen eventually finds such intensity in a passionate but fraught relationship with a lover, Richard Yaverland. West's novel moves away at this point from the modern office to a remote and rural space in which the psychological dramas of Richard Yaverland's family are played out. The relationship ends after Richard's mother's suicide and his arrest for the murder of his brother. Ellen is left alone and isolated, focussing on the possibility of pregnancy: 'She sat and looked at the island, and wondered whether it was a son or a daughter that waited for her there' (430).

This move from the social relations of the woman typist as participant in the workforce to the isolation and intensity of a pregnancy echoes the ending of both *The Odd Women* and *The Questing Beast*. In all three novels, the possibility of having a child emerges at the end of the novel, and constitutes its final image. This may be an attempt to naturalize the copying and reproduction associated with the typewriter, or to answer the mechanical repetitions of typing with a radically distinct temporality of biological repetition. It may also reflect an imaginative working through of the tension Mark Seltzer describes between natural and technological modes of reproduction: 'shifts in the traffic between the natural and the technological make for the vicissitudes of agency, and of individual and collective and national identity'.[55] In narrative terms, however, it works consistently to take women out of the public sphere. The issues of work and autonomy which were so central to the opening pages of *The Judge* are pushed aside in this ending, which has taken Ellen to a space outside the city and into the time of dream, or perhaps nightmare.

The novel does also suggest, however, that Ellen's desire to find a version of her self in or through the work of typing was always already compromised. This much is suggested by her employer's appraising and troubled stare:

It was true that she was an excellent shorthand-typist, but she vexed the decent grey by her vividness. The sight of her through an open door, sitting at her typewriter in her blue linen overall, dispersed one's thoughts; it was as if a wireless found its waves jammed by another instrument. (18)

As a typist, the woman worker becomes available, visible and sexualized. Sharon Hartman Strom suggests that this form of sexual objectification is inherent in the condition of the typist, referring to 'the permeable boundaries between the sexual objectification that women clerks resented (or desired) and the mundane (or important) work they performed every day'.[56] A particularly sensationalist exploration of such permeable boundaries can be found in Tom Gallon's *The Girl Behind the Keys* (1903). This novel opens with its heroine alone and poor in London. She secures work as a typist, and celebrates her good fortune in finding a well-paid and secure position. Her employer insists on the need for complete confidentiality in all her clerical work, and she is quick to stress that she now sees herself as a cipher, acting mechanically and uncritically in her employer's interests: 'you seem to forget that a typist in my position has to become a mere machine; her fingers are the only things that really matter about her'.[57] But she quickly finds herself at the centre of a criminal gang, who are using her as a front for their kidnapping plot. She finds herself typing at gunpoint as her employer tries to bluff the police into believing in his innocence. This woman typist is vulnerable and open to exploitation. She escapes from the adventure, but vows never to work as a typist again. She ends the novel married to the very man whose proposal she had turned down at the beginning of the novel.

Finally, in James Joyce's *Ulysses* (1922), a novel of many permeable boundaries, we also find the typist employed as a figure for anxieties and desires associated with the modern woman. Leopold Bloom, after his masturbatory pursuit of the young Gerty Macdowell muses on the nature of women: 'Those girls, those girls, those lovely seaside girls . . . Longing to get the fright of their lives . . . Sharp as needles they are'.[58] And his eye strays to a typist: 'Typist going up Roger Greene's stairs two at a time to show her understandings' (369). This association between the 'lovely seaside girls' and the typist might seem accidental were it not for the fact that we had already encountered the sexually charged Miss Dunne ('Wandering Rocks') who surreptitiously reads *The Woman in White*, or stares at glamorous pin-ups in between bouts of typing. And indeed we can also find the sexuality of the typist explored in the character of Martha, with whom Bloom corresponds under the pseudonym 'Henry Flower'. Like Leslie Rose in *Love and His Mask*, Martha prefers to type her erotic epistles. Bloom muses on Martha, on her writing, on her work, and on her femininity:

Such a bad headache. Has her roses probably. Or sitting all day typing. Eyefocus bad for stomach nerves. What perfume does your wife use? Now how could you make out a thing like that?
    To keep it up.[59]

Menstruation, the haunting smell of perfumes, marriage and infidelity, impotence and frigidity are all circulating round the central image of the woman who sits typing all day. Her femininity is represented through the activity of labour, but this activity struggles against the powerful longings and the visceral sentiments projected on her by the voracious fantasy life of Leopold Bloom.

WASHING CLOTHES: HYGIENE, DIRT AND THE WASHING MACHINE

If the repetitive and mechanical labour of typing might seem like rather unpromising material for sexual fantasy, sexual associations with the act of washing clothes have a long cultural history. The washerwoman's place within the home, with access to its most intimate forms of dirt, makes her a figure tainted by a moral and social lack of cleanliness. The literary resources of this figure were richly explored by Emile Zola in his 1877 novel, *L'Assommoir*, which produces a compelling narrative of social and individual corruption through the figure of a laundress, Gervaise Macquart.[60] This novel's demarcation of social and geographical otherness is persistently haunted by images of dirt, by noxious odours and by laundry. Gervaise's skill as a laundress is both a marker of her considerable virtues as an honest and diligent worker, but also the key to her ultimate degeneration: she is overcome by the moral and sexual pollution of the laundry, as well as by its heat, steam and noxious chemicals. Zola's interest in the laundress's work is meticulous, and he details the techniques, the machinery, and the economics of washing clothes, as well as drawing richly on their metaphorical weight as figures of disease and degeneration. The problem with laundry, in Zola's novel, lies in its association with the urban and the industrial. Gervaise's early memories of laundry as an outdoor, manual cooperative form of labour are associated with health and vigour. Disease comes with mechanization and urbanization: the dirt and dampness of laundry finding no escape. The 'problem' is not simply labour, but specifically modern forms of labour.

Laundry techniques had changed relatively little from the early modern period until the mid-nineteenth century. Washing clothes then was physically arduous, and very time consuming. In rural communities, washing was done whenever possible in the open air, using river or sea water where these were conveniently available. J. M. Synge, indeed, found women on the Aran Islands in the 1880s still washing their clothes by battering them on the rocks, though he noted this was injurious to health:

I often come on a girl with her petticoats tucked up around her, standing in a pool left by the tide and washing her flannels among the sea-anemones and crabs. Their red bodices and white tapering legs make them as beautiful as tropical sea birds, as they stand in a frame of seaweeds against the brink of the Atlantic . . . This habit of using sea water for washing causes a good deal of rheumatism on the island, for the salt lies in the clothes and keeps them continually moist.[61]

Laundry occupied two or even three days in the week, with at least one day spent washing, while drying, ironing and mangling occupied the remainder of the time. Washing clothes involved plentiful supplies of water, tools for beating or scraping, a utensil for boiling clothes, and some form of cleaning solution, such as lye, soda, 'blue', or soap (though this was taxed in Britain until 1853). Laundry represented not just a significant investment of time, but also of money. In the mid-nineteenth century, a working family would be likely to spend half what they spent on rent on the costs of laundry, while for a middle-class family this proportion was closer to one third.[62] This would include the cost of heating water and of laundry products, and also the cost of either hiring a washerwoman or sending clothes out to be washed.

In the nineteenth century, most families sent out at least a part of their washing, though equally almost all households did some of their washing at home. Home economics books were keen to recommend home laundry, particularly the home laundering of 'linen' including underwear and other personal garments, as commercial laundries were accused of losing and damaging clothes. The laundress was an economically marginal figure in the nineteenth century,[63] and whether she worked in her own home or travelled to other people's houses her work was fluctuating, seasonal, arduous and poorly paid. The development of commercial laundries mechanized the process of washing clothes to some extent, using steam power to agitate and rotate the clothes and thus to facilitate washing, and thus also brought the laundress into the structures of industrial employment. Many early versions of the washing machine were designed specifically for this sort of large-scale cleaning process. Alongside the growth of the commercial laundry, however, there were also considerable changes in the infrastructure of the domestic environment in both middle-class and working-class homes.

The domestic washing machine requires hot and cold running water, and for many models also electricity. The introduction of these services was a gradual process, beginning in the early nineteenth century and not finally being achieved until after the Second World War. Early models of the washing machine, which were hand-cranked, are already being rec-ommended in home economics books of the 1880s and '90s, and were reasonably common in both British and American households by 1900.[64] The electrically powered washing machine, however, was a more gradual entrant into the home. Small-scale electrical motors suitable for home use were not developed until the first decade of the twentieth century, and the technology was initially expensive. Because the US had begun the process of standardizing the electrical supply earlier than European countries, the combination of hot and cold running water and electricity were signifi-cantly more common there in the early years of the twentieth century. The availability of consumer credit also made the financing of such a major purchase a possibility for a wider range of American families. Thus thirty-five per cent of American homes had electricity by the 1920s and by 1941 over half of American residences had a powered washing machine, while for affluent families, the washing machine had entered eighty per cent of homes by 1926.[65] In Britain, on the other hand, only twenty-nine per cent of families owned a washing machine by 1958, while in Germany and France the widespread use of the domestic washing machine was certainly a post Second World War phenomenon.[66]

Acquiring a washing machine was understood to some extent as a 'catch-ing up' with American standards of cleanliness and hygiene. Claire Duchen and Kristin Ross have both written interestingly about the complex inter-section of emotional, medical and political rhetorics surrounding the ideas of hygiene and cleanliness in Europe in the 1950s.[67] Washing, and the home, became associated with the negation of a range of threats, including war, racial difference and social dislocation, and advertisements for soap and cleaning products in the fifties draw on the rich semantic field of 'purity' in their appeal to the housewife.

This appeal to the housewife is in itself expressive of an important his-torical change. It was only after World War One that advertisements for relatively expensive cleaning and household products took to addressing the individual housewife as the potential user rather than her servants. In the early years of the twentieth century, advertisers had invited potential consumers to 'make their servants happier' or to 'ensure they keep their servants', but this appeal did not result in significant sales. The decline in the number of domestic servants, a process that happened unevenly but decisively between 1880 and 1940, on the other hand, was ultimately to lead to a significant rise in the number of machines introduced into the middle-class home and to a consequent decline in the commercial fortunes of the industrial laundry. This privatization of laundry continued inexorably throughout the twentieth century, so that by the end of the century commercial laundry was associated only with the extremes of wealth or of poverty.

The washing machine was a technology that carried associations of modernity, cleanliness, order and autonomy. In the Chicago World Exposition held in 1893, model kitchens included both a washing machine and an ironing machine and the visual effect was one of order and progress.[68] Its integration into the home, particularly in Europe, was a gradual process, dependent on the water supply, advanced plumbing and access to electricity, as well as on the affordability of the technology. The washing machine did not significantly reduce labour time in the early part of the century, though it did reduce its arduousness. Indeed, many women who might have sent a certain amount of their washing out of the house, or employed servants to do it, now had to take charge of the labour themselves, and in the context of the modern home, they worked alone and in a private space. They were also interpellated by the technicians and analysts of 'efficiency' and by a series of initiatives that aimed to adapt the principles of 'Taylorism' to the home. The everyday labour of the household was subjected to a detailed scrutiny, not simply in terms of the quality of its results (wholesome food, clean clothes), but in terms of the efficiency of its operation. Fatigue was to be overcome by a careful choice of technologies and an appropriate and balanced investment of energy by the housewife.[69]

When washing with a machine, women did not have to come into contact so intimately with dirt, but could do so in a mediated and mechanized fashion, and to some extent that broke down the associations between laundry and moral or sexual corruption that had so powerfully informed a text such as Zola's *L'Assommoir*. Laundry has now lost its associations with corruption and decadence and its subtle charge of eroticism, and is a form of labour that is both boring and invisible beyond very particular sites of marketing and domestic science. In the early years of the twentieth century, however, when the mechanized, mediated and impersonal washing of clothes was only beginning to be part of people's experience, laundry was a troubling activity. New categories of women found themselves in contact with the intimate mechanics of washing clothes: the marginal economies of new categories of white-collar women workers meant that laundry costs could not always be met, while lodging and boarding houses often provided erratic and unsatisfactory laundry services. Respectability and cleanliness were powerfully implicated in ways that made the economic and moral position of new white-collar workers precarious.

In literary and poetic texts of the early decades of the twentieth century the washing of clothes provides a figure for the examination of social fantasies, anxieties and fears associated with class and gender mobilities. As we have seen, the techniques and technologies of laundry changed considerably from the mid-nineteenth to the mid-twentieth century, and the invention and the social dissemination of such technologies took place within a rhetoric of 'labour saving' and progress. Washing was to become impersonal, mechanical and, above all, clean. The other side of this progressivist journey towards the technological erasure of dirt, however, was that the washing of clothes became part of the everyday experience of the middle-class woman in quite new ways. From a form of labour that was energetically displaced onto servants or casual labourers, washing becomes part of the everyday labour of the middle-class housewife, and of the more or less economically marginal professional woman. Texts of the early years of the twentieth century show a deep interest in the psychic and social consequences of coming into contact with human dirt.

Perhaps unsurprisingly, the text of Virginia Woolf's in which labour, washing, and hygiene figure most centrally is one in which, as John Mepham puts it: 'against the grain, non-being is given its due'.[70] *The Years* was written in 1937, and thus as a text may appear to fall outside the historical scope of this study. Yet its narrative concern with the years between 1880 and the 1930s actually provides rich material for my analysis of labour and selfhood in this period. *The Years* gives a form to the experience of constriction and enclosure that is the Victorian residue of the modern moment, and also charts the psychological contours of the more characteristically modern experience of social and familial dislocation. Withdrawal and distaste are its characteristic affective states. The novel opens in the 'uncertain spring' of 1880, when Colonel Abel Pargiter leaves his club to visit his mistress.[71] Walking towards her house he is morose and rigid with unease: 'He did not like this bit of the business at all . . . He did not wish to be seen sitting on that doorstep' (*Years*, 6). His psychological unease finds expression in repeated images of dirt, of odour and of washing: 'There was always a smell in the house; there were always dirty clothes hanging on a line in the back garden . . . it was sordid; it was mean; it was furtive' (6–7). Whilst it is certainly true that the polluted air of London rendered outdoor drying of clothes problematic, the attribution of dirt to the drying laundry seems excessive, suggesting the moral pollution of the space rather than the actual state of the laundry. The Colonel nonetheless enters the house. His mistress Mira's sensuality is immediately rendered as she loosens her long coil of hair, letting it fall loose over her shoulders. They kiss, and he begins fumbling 'lower down', when there is a creaking on the stairs. Mira goes out and returns to look anxiously for some money.

> 'How much?' said the Colonel.
> It came to one pound – no, it came to one pound eight and sixpence, she said, muttering something about the washing. The Colonel slipped two sovereigns out of his little gold case and gave them to her. She took them and there was more whispering on the landing.
> 'Washing . . .?' thought the Colonel, looking round the room. It was a dingy little hole; but being so much older than she was it did not do to ask questions about the washing. (8–9)

'The washing' here stands for Mira's economic dependence but also for the sordid and furtive nature of sexual desire that haunts the Pargiters' Victorian home. Dirt and laundry are indeed the first thing Colonel Pargiter encounters on his return to this family home. His first words to his young daughter Rose are 'grubby little ruffian' (12) and Rose places her hand guiltily over the stain on her pinafore. The phrase and the gesture are repeated shortly afterwards as he leaves the room, and the Colonel's distaste and Rose's guilt will be revisited many times. The social and moral stigma of dirt had indeed already been signalled by Rose's sister Milly, 'imitating the manner of a grown-up': 'I think Nurse might have put you on a clean pinafore . . . "It hadn't come back from the wash," said Rose' (10). As with Mira's troubled conversation with the washerwoman who was returning her clothes, this disorder of the laundry seems to figure some much more significant disruption of domestic order.

At this stage in the novel, Mrs Pargiter is lying upstairs, and is seriously ill. Her daughter Delia goes to sit with her, noticing that her face is 'pouched and heavy' (21), and both her skin and her hair are stained, but Delia nonetheless concludes that she looks as if she might go on for ever. Delia is coldly angry with her mother's tenacious hold on this non-life, and the repressions and resentment this anger generates are expressed through images of order, cleanliness and brittle surface. Turning from the stained and heavy presence of her mother's body, Delia finds the bright and brittle visual plane of the mirror, with its dazzling red light, reflecting the evening sky and the brightly illuminated silver and glass bottles all laid out in impeccable order; 'at this hour of the evening the sickroom had an unreal cleanliness, quiet and order' (21). In this uncomfortable oscillation between the stained and the pristine, Delia slips into a fantasy where she stands on a public platform, next to Charles Stewart Parnell, addressing an enthusiastic audience on Irish politics. Here the colour white dominates: a white flower; Delia dressed in white; Parnell very pale. When Mrs Pargiter awakens in a state of confusion she is also to confront the psychological impact of white cloth:

> But her mother was staring at the dressing-table. Some gleam from the lamp outside made the white cloth look extremely white.
>
> 'Another clean table-cloth!' Mrs Pargiter murmured peevishly. 'The expense, Delia, the expense – that's what worries me –'
>
> 'That's all right, mama,' said Delia dully. Her eyes were fixed upon her grandfather's portrait; why, she wondered, had the artist put a dab of white chalk on the tip of his nose?
>
> 'Aunt Eugénie brought you some flowers,' she said.
>
> For some reason, Mrs Pargiter seemed pleased. Her eyes rested contemplatively on the clean table-cloth that had suggested the washing bill a moment before. (23)

The psychological and the economic anxieties circulating round the colour white seem to find their focus in that dab of white chalk on the grandfather's nose. He looms over the domestic scene where mother and daughter swap the small-change of domestic life and worry over the washing bill. The cleanliness and whiteness of this household are dearly bought, but are also symptomatic of a phantasmatic fixity in an imaginary that is always a matter of reflections, surfaces and fearful repudiation of dirt.

The washing of clothes also frames the next episode in the novel, in which Rose is confronted in the street by a man masturbating. Rose manages to escape from the care of her Nurse, who is deep in conversation with 'Mrs C., who came every week with the washing' (25). The Nurse's distracted attention gives Rose the opportunity to leave her house. She walks along the street towards a shop where she will buy a greatly desired 'box of ducks', but in her mind she is a brave soldier riding through enemy lines to deliver a message. Rose's fantasy of heroism is cut short by her encounter with the man who on first meeting 'put out his arms as if to stop her. He almost caught her' (27) and then on their second meeting 'sucked his lips in and out. He made a mewing noise. But he did not stretch his hands out at her; they were unbuttoning his clothes' (28). Traumatized, Rose rushes home, to find everyone unaware of her absence. In the flux of more or less coherent conversation in the drawing room, Rose's sister Eleanor thinks about her day's work among the poor:

Old Mrs Levy, sitting propped up in bed with her white hair in a thick flop like a wig and her face cracked like an old glazed pot.

'Them that's been good to me, them I remember . . . them that's ridden in their coaches when I was a poor widder woman scrubbing and mangling –' Here she stretched out her arm, which was wrung and white like the root of a tree. (29)

The interconnection of these images is striking. The arms that are stretched out towards Rose and towards Eleanor are each in their own way threatening, opening out into the spaces of sexuality and of poverty, while seeming to surround and capture both sisters. Yet they are also gestures of supplication, as if some respite could be found, or some escape might be possible. The drama of this section of the novel is generated primarily by the abrupt dismantling of Rose's fantasy of heroism, mobility and masculinity in her encounter with the sexually predatory man. But I would suggest that this drama is importantly complicated by the labouring women who frame it. 'Mrs C.' is a regular visitor to the Pargiter's house, and her work is meant to keep the Pargiter house free from stains. Old Mrs Levy is one of the sights that 'kept repeating themselves' (29) in Eleanor's mind, a figure who haunts Eleanor with her memories and her judgements. These washingwomen enter the landscape of the Pargiter home only marginally, but they carry with them very significant social and economic meanings associated with stains, dirt and shame.

As the action of *The Years* unfolds towards the 1930s, the Pargiter women become associated more directly with the physical activity of washing. Those of the Pargiter family who live and work independently come close to the odours and the physical realities that had so repulsed the Colonel in 1880. In 1910, when Sara describes a suffrage meeting to her cousin, Maggie, she talks of it happening 'In a room . . . A pale greenish light. A woman hanging clothes on a line in the back garden; and someone went by rattling a stick on the railings' (179), and Maggie picks up and transforms the image, 'sticks rattling on the railings; clothes hanging out to dry, and someone coming in with beetles' wings in her hair' (179). The woman and her laundry are central to these images of the space of suffragism. And these images lead Sara to a fearful meditation on her own body and her own mode of living; '"In time to come," she said, looking at her sister, "people looking into this room . . . will hold their fingers to their noses" – she held her fingers to her nose – "and say 'Pah! They stink!'"' (180). The sticks rattling and the laundry hanging out to dry carry with them a sense of ugliness and squalor that Sara turns aggressively against herself.

Eleanor, on the other hand, having travelled abroad after her father's death, returns to England to be struck by air that smells of soap, and 'How thoroughly people wash themselves in England' (185). Going to visit her brother's house, she finds warmth, sweet smells, friendly domesticity, 'the drawing-room piano . . . strewn with white baby-linen' (187), and Eleanor goes upstairs to wash herself 'methodically but carefully, since they were short of water' (188). But the confident placidity of this domesticity is quickly undermined by Eleanor's fearful insight that such cleanliness may in fact betoken a form of sterility: 'An old maid who washes and watches birds, she said to herself as she looked in the glass' (193). Cleanliness becomes sterility as Eleanor interrogates her own reflection.

As the years pass, such oscillation between fearful fantasy and pragmatic domestic anxiety becomes more pronounced for many of the characters. The novel explores new forms of subjectivity, based on fragment and on memory rather than on the coherent and continuous ego, and opens up complex and ephemeral relations to temporality, but it also charts the minutiæ of domestic life as they develop across the 'years' it so carefully charts. By 1917, Maggie is married and a mother, living a bohemian life: '"We dine in the basement," she continued, turning to Eleanor, "because we've no servants." . . . "And we are extremely dirty," said Renny' (269). Maggie and Renny are visited by Sara whose arrival has been delayed by an unexpected visit from Eleanor's nephew, North. North is about to leave for the front; the potential heroism of his arrival in full uniform being undercut by the fact that when Sara hears him ring the bell she declares 'That's the wash' (271).

As we move towards the novel's end, there is an explicit engagement with technologies of cleanliness and dirt in the modern home. In this final section, the novel's more abstract themes reach a level of urgency in their questioning of the violence of the ego, of the possibility of achieved form or pattern within a life, or of the viability of western civilizations. Eleanor, who is so often found washing, despite her fears of having failed to make or to understand a life reaches the end of the novel able to discern happiness in living relationships. Her niece, Peggy, has a much more troubled sense of the precariousness of human relations. As a doctor, Peggy has achieved the role of the financially viable professional woman that had eluded earlier generations, but she is haunted by the echoes within contemporary London of other worlds quite distinct from and indifferent to her own: 'people toiling, grinding, in the heart of darkness' (368). She foresees tyranny, torture and the fall of civilization, and can confront this vision only by repression and inarticulacy. Against this apocalyptic vision we hear 'Scraps reached her from above. ". . . flats in Highgate have bathrooms," they were saying' (369). The recurring vision of disaster is punctuated by the state of contemporary plumbing. Indeed, throughout the 'present day' section of the novel, images of dirt, stains and smudges jostle with facts about shower baths, electric lights, sanitary towels and running water; the everyday technological conditions of modernist hygiene. Looking at Woolf's *Diary* in the period when she was working on the novel in its earlier incarnation as *The Pargiters*, we find the same sort of oscillation between the aesthetic moment and the temporality of the everyday. She struggles to write, suffering from blinding headaches. Her working day is punctuated by increasingly acrimonious rows with her long-time cook, Nelly Boxall: 'I cannot describe how the Nelly situation weighs upon my spirits . . . I had I think rather a brilliant flash this morning how to compact the rather fluid Eleanor. I shall have a shot anyhow. But Nelly spoils all.'[72] Woolf's work of writing is interrupted by the activity of the electricians who are installing a new 'bath water engine' in February 1934, an improvement presumably to the WC and bathroom Woolf had been so pleased to install in 1926.[73] By 18 February, 'the new electric boiler [is] in and boiling our bath water this morning' (*Diary*, IV, 202), but Woolf is still oppressed by the sense of the sordid as a fundamental aspect of her life, noting a few weeks later, 'a black day, pouring rain, dirt everywhere' (204).

Woolf was acutely aware of the economic, political and ideological significance of domestic technologies. In 1931, she was invited by Margaret Llewelyn Davies to write an 'Introductory Letter' to a volume of memoirs written by members of the Women's Cooperative Guild. Much of Woolf's letter is concerned with her own memories of attending the annual conference of the Guild in 1913, dwelling on the complex interplay of sympathy and boredom, and identification and withdrawal, the event produced in her. In this letter, Woolf dwells at some length on the arduous nature of domestic labour in working-class homes, imagining sympathetically that a working woman might be thinking 'Why in the Lord's name have I not hot water and electric light laid on when middle-class women . . .'[74] But Woolf's attempt to imagine herself in the persona of a working woman is abruptly truncated as she comes to realize the bodily significance of domestic labour, and specifically of washing clothes, 'But after all the imagination is largely the child of the flesh. One could not be Mrs. Giles of Durham because one's body had never stood at the wash-tub; one's hands had never wrung and scrubbed' ('Letter', xxiii).

In the 'present day' section of *The Years*, the affective and symbolic significance of hygiene, work and washing are compellingly, if troublingly, articulated in the sustained description of Sara's Jewish neighbour taking his bath. Sara is living in a lodging house in a street which her cousin's son, North, describes as 'dirty', 'sordid' and 'low-down' (294–95). After a very unsatisfactory dinner, North and Sara are disturbed by the sounds of her neighbour in the bath. North is appalled by the information that Sara will have to use the same bath, '[t]he thought of a line of grease from a strange man's body on the bath next door disgusted him' (322). Sara echoes his disgust, moving towards an Eliotic invocation of the degradation and the corruption of the modern city, '"Polluted city, unbelieving city, city of dead fish and worn-out frying pans – thinking of a river's bank when the tide's out", she explained' (323). The fact of 'a Jew in my bath', with all the associations that brings for Sara of racial difference, and of contamination, drives her out of her domestic space and into the public world, looking for work. North listens to her increasingly excited rendition of her disgust, her fear, her sense of helplessness, and 'the actual words floated together and formed a sentence in his mind – meant that she was poor; that she must earn her living' (325). The need to work and the risk of contamination have been imaginatively yoked together, so that work is the possibility of escape from the sordid experience of poverty but it is also the expression of a completely inescapable contact with humanity and with dirt.

The disgust and the fearfulness associated with dirt and with washing have been sustained throughout *The Years*, despite the technological in-novations that seem to keep them at bay. Whereas in the 1880s washing entered the middle-class home in designated spaces, such as the nursery or the kitchen, by the 1930s all members of the middle-class household could be touched by the technologies of hygiene and the labour of washing. The final section of *The Years* returns again and again to the electricity, the run-ning water and the hot water that were to make each individual home and each individual body the space of hygiene and of order. But it also returns over and again to the fear, the disgust and the sense of compulsion such a privatized battle against dirt might entail.

Fear and disgust are also prevalent in the physical and emotional land-scape of Eliot's *The Waste Land* (1922), as Sara's invocation of the 'polluted city' suggested. The detritus of modern living litters Eliot's landscape, and physical and moral degeneration are the thematic and the narrative poles of his poetic imagination in the poem. Slime, dirt, litter, decay and damp-ness are the markers of spiritual and cultural failure, against which 'The Fire Sermon' tries to imagine purification through fire. Renewal cannot come from water in this section of the poem: since the river is polluted and dirty, it sweats oil and tar. There are indeed two key moments in this section of the poem where characters fail in what might be read as an attempt at purification through water. Firstly, Mrs Porter tries to wash her feet. Mrs Porter enters the poem in lines 197–98, where she is the amorous object of Sweeney's desires: 'the sound of horns and motors, which shall bring/Sweeney to Mrs Porter in the spring'. This image has cut across the echoes of Shakespeare and Marvell in the preceding lines and introduces the discordant and hurried exchanges of the modern world with their urgent but unsatisfactory encounters. Mrs Porter is then glimpsed in the moonlight with her daughter, 'they wash their feet in soda water'. The significance of this is semantically unclear, playing on the tension between soda water as a drink whose contact with feet seems inappropriate to the point of being disgusting, and the washing soda that might cleanse but also destroy living flesh. The image suggests both excess and distress, as if some crucial category mistake is dominating the lives of Mrs Porter and her daughter. The poem moves through fragmented images of loss, violence and sexual corruption in the 'unreal city' that is both metaphorically and metonymically an image of Eliot's contemporary world, and then unfolds the more connected narrative of a sexual encounter between a typist and a clerk as viewed by the mythical figure of Tiresias. The significance of Eliot's choice of a typist for this figure of modern, disconnected and rootless femininity has been discussed above, but it is worth also noting the importance for this scene of 'Her drying combinations'. The young woman comes home to a cramped and sordid room, she eats out of tins, she piles her underwear on to her divan, and she washes her underwear by hand and hangs it 'perilously' out of the window. This washing is expressive of her immodesty, of her sordid life and of the erosion of 'decency' so important to the overall drama of the episode.

Laundry is intimately connected to perceptions of decency in a number of short stories by Katherine Mansfield, which detail the complex interactions of precarious subjectivities and the rituals of everyday life in the early years of the twentieth century. In 'Pictures', we meet Miss Ada Moss, a woman with 'a College eddication' who is now an out-of-work singer living in a room in Bloomsbury.[75] At the beginning of the story it is clear that she is hungry and depressed, waking up to fantasies of decent and substantial food. Her landlady enters her room to collect overdue rent, but Ada Moss tries to put her off with a suggestion that new work is about to come her way. The landlady is unwilling to believe in Ada Moss's coming good fortune, however, because she has become aware of the extent of her fall from the norms and rituals of decency, '[if] she's washing her own wovens and drying them on the towel rail it's easy to see where the finger's pointing' (120). This degeneration is explicitly contrasted with the physical and moral superiority of another working woman in the story, a typist. She is 'beautiful', and appears at the top of a staircase looking down on the aspiring and desperate women below her, mocking them for their belief that they might be able to earn some money that day' (126). Miss Ada Moss fails, as she must, to get any theatrical employment, and ends the story going home with a 'stout gentleman' whose only obvious virtue is his access to money. In 'The Doll's House', which appeared in Mansfield's 1923 collection, *The Dove's Nest and other Stories*, washing is once more drawn on as a figure for social and moral degradation. The story concerns the Burnell family who had also appeared in 'Prelude' and 'At the Bay'. In this family, Mansfield finds the narrative and symbolic resources to explore the disjunctions between inner life and the rituals that sustain more public forms of identity. She uses this family over the different stories to observe the clotted and oppressive nature of the social hierarchies that both constrain and enable individual development. Paralysis, hypersensitivity, self-delusion and occasional moments of warmth give these stories their compelling yet uncanny energy. In 'The Doll's House', the Burnell children have acquired a new doll's house that becomes an object of fascination and envy for other children at their school. The irony of this intense emotional identification with the home as a symbol of security and desirable possession is considerable. One by one, the other children from the school are invited to view the beautiful artefact, all except for two sisters who are deemed to be beyond the pale:

They were the daughters of a spry, hard-working little washerwoman, who went from house to house by the day. This was awful enough. But where was Mr Kelvey? Nobody knew for certain. But everybody said he was in prison. So they were the daughters of a washerwoman and a gaolbird. Very nice company for other people's children! (386)

Kezia, the more troubled but also the more imaginative daughter, defies the prohibition on these girls and invites them to see the precious toy, but this gesture is swiftly and cruelly punished by her aunt Beryl. Beryl's unfulfilled and frightened relation to sexuality is explicitly invoked to explain the ferocity of her repudiation of the little Kelvey girls; once again laundry, degradation and sexuality are uncomfortably knitted together.

In 'The Man without a Temperament', which like 'Pictures' first appeared in *Bliss and other Stories* (1920), Mansfield describes an evening in the life of an English couple, the Salesbys, who have been driven abroad by the wife's ill health. Her emotional and physical delicacy dominate the story. We gradually become aware of the way this couple is perceived by other guests at the hotel, particularly the husband who is mocked, humoured and quietly criticized for his withdrawn, stiff and impatient manner. The story moves between a precarious and empty present and a vital and vivid past that enters the husband's consciousness fleetingly but painfully. He has forced himself to live uncomplainingly within the routines of this frighteningly constrained life, but the effort of repression is vividly expressed in his continual twisting of his signet ring, an ultimately futile chafing against constraint. The main activity of the couple's day is a brief walk, taken at first together, and then by the husband alone. As they walk together, they come upon three girls, who are bathing in tubs of water. They have removed their drawers, and are tramping up and down in the tubs, as if engaged in the vigorous labour of laundry. As the couple approach, the girls flee in consternation, their terror explained only by their shouts of 'The Englishman! The Englishman' (135). The wife is genuinely perplexed about the reason for their flight, wondering whether the fear could have any sort of sexual meaning. We never fully understand either why they were tramping up and down in the tubs or why they fled in such alarm, but the incident is a crucial moment in the story. At this moment the wife decides she can walk no further and encourages her husband to continue alone. The severity of her illness and the futility of his obsessive routines of normality are both powerfully present in this encounter with the children in the tub.

The Englishman's then solitary walk produces responses of spite and derision in those who observe him. The narrative voice concentrates on the immediate sensations and sights that confront him, giving the reader access to his distress and anger only through the powerful interruption of past memories. He has given up his life in England, 'hang it all, old man, what's to prevent you going with her? It isn't as though you've got a regular job like us wage earners' (142), and now is enclosed in the claustrophobic spaces of the hotel and its surrounding streets. The warmth and the dryness that are so important to his wife's health produce thick, stifling dust. He passes the finest villas in the town, and moves towards the poorer parts of the town where the streets are narrower and the air is foul:

At a fountain ahead of him two old hags were beating linen. As he passed them they squatted back on their haunches, stared, and then their 'A-hak-kak-kak!' with the slap, slap, of the stone on the linen sounded after him. (137)

The women are reduced to an animal condition by his reflections, incorporated into the narrative voice through words such as 'hag' and 'squatted' and the guttural sounds associated with the laundry. He finds these women's labour discordant, intrusive, associated with the perceptions of decay and disease that haunt both his walk and the narrative of the story as a whole. Climbing away from these women, he looks down into a valley and sees men cutting grapes: 'He watched a man standing in the greenish shade, raising up, holding a black cluster in one hand, taking the knife from his belt, cutting, laying the bunch in a flat boat-shaped basket' (p. 138). Mr Salesby does not withdraw from this labour, but rather lingers in its rhythms, leaning against a wall and lighting his pipe. In the man's labour he finds a kind of solace, and a possibility of identification, while in the work of the women laundresses, he had found only ugliness, decay and a recession towards the animal. Perhaps Mr Salesby's lack of useful labour and his constricted and constrained life had already led him towards too uncomfortable an identification with the position of the feminine, which is painfully embodied by the washing women. Against this identification, Mr Salesby achieves a moment of calm through the labour of the farmer who collects his grapes and through the reassuring rituals of the smoking of his pipe. Both the manual washing of clothes and viticulture represent pre-modern forms of labour, which mark the remoteness and the temporal paralysis of the story's geographical space, but their psychological and their social meanings are emphatically gendered, and Mr Salesby can only linger over the grapes while he strides purposefully away from the laundry.

Despite the insistent and self-conscious modernity of Mansfield's narrative world, in the matter of laundry she is resolutely pre-modern. The working woman who has to wash her own linen in her lodging house is the only trace of the modern domestication, proliferation and technologization of washing to be found in Mansfield's stories. Otherwise earlier social relations and older techniques seem to structure the memories and desires of her characters. Thus, in 'Je Ne Parle Pas Français' the narrator, Raoul Duquette, recalls his early erotic experience with an African laundress. Raoul is one of Mansfield's more complexly layered characters. He is a writer, and as narrator reflects constantly on the narrative style of the text in which he appears. He is obsessive, solipsistic, fascinated by the liminalities of gender, driven by passions that are fleeting, narcissistic and yet mapped onto fantasies of friendship and love. His memory of the African laundress is introduced as his only significant childhood memory; the one that will both reveal something fundamental about the formation of his character and give us some insight into his 'literary point of view' (66):

When I was about ten our laundress was an African woman, very big, very dark, with a check handkerchief over her frizzy hair . . .

One day when I was standing at the door, watching her go, she turned round and beckoned to me, nodding and smiling in a strange, secret way. I never thought of not following. She took me into a little outhouse at the end of the passage, caught me up in her arms and began kissing me. Ah, those kisses! Especially those kisses inside my ears that nearly deafened me . . .

As this performance was repeated once a week it is no wonder that I remember it so vividly. Besides, from that very first afternoon, my childhood was, to put it prettily, 'kissed away'. I became very languid, very caressing, and greedy beyond measure. And so quickened, so sharpened, I seemed to understand everybody and be able to do what I liked with everybody. (66)

Raoul's intellectual curiosity, his fantasies of omnipotence, and his neuras-thenic languor are all attributed to these childhood sexual encounters. That this illicit and dangerous sexual scene should feature a laundress is surely no longer a surprise, given what we have seen in Woolf's and Eliot's writing. The added charge of racial otherness in these remembered scenes may also call up the crucial role of 'the Jew in the bath' in the last section of *The Years*, and make us aware of the extent to which imaginative representations of washing calls up other fears associated with hygiene and purity. Racial boundaries, gender boundaries, and boundaries between public and private are all anxiously at stake in these moments of modernist hygiene.

Hygiene, as well as racial and gender boundaries, are central to the drama of James Joyce's *Ulysses*. Leopold Bloom has been understood as one of the most 'modern' of the novel's protagonists, given his involvement in adver-tising and the communications industry, his inventive sexual imagination, his democratic aspirations and his complex relation to tradition and fam-ily articulated through representations of his Jewishness. His fascinations with bodily fluids and human smells are viscerally rendered throughout the novel, as are his rituals and habits of purification. He carries a bar of soap throughout the novel, producing it in the 'Ithaca' section, 'to wash his soiled hands with a partially consumed tablet of Barrington's lemonflavoured soap, to which paper still adhered (bought thirteen hours previously and still un-paid for)'.[76] This ablution follows a sustained discourse on the economics and the technologies of the Dublin water supply as well as a list of the sym-bolic and material properties of water that Bloom admires: 'its properties for cleansing, quenching thirst and fire, nourishing vegetation: its infalli-bility as paradigm and paragon' (592). Bloom offers Stephen Dedalus, the artist-figure in the novel, the opportunity to wash himself, since both have arrived at Bloom's house after a long day and night of wandering through the sometimes sordid and seedy spaces of early twentieth-century Dublin. Dedalus declines, citing a fear of water that is connected more broadly to a fear of fluidity in all substances, and particularly in thought and language. This paradigmatic contrast between Bloom the lover of water and Stephen the aesthete of the hard and the concrete is explicitly developed into a contrast between hygiene and genius:

> What impeded Bloom from giving Stephen counsels of hygiene and prophylactic to which should be added suggestions concerning a preliminary wetting of the head and contraction of the muscles with rapid splashing of the face and neck and thoracic and epigastric region in case of sea or river bathing, the parts of the human anatomy most sensitive to cold being the nape, stomach, and thenar or sole of the foot?
> The incompatibility of aquacity with the erratic originality of genius. (593)

Bloom's obsessions with hygiene are then to be understood as the antithesis of genius.[77] His appetite for odours and his fascination with the techniques and technologies of cleanliness are part of the rituals that bind him to the temporalities of the everyday, that stand between him and epiphany.

We first encounter Bloom in the 'Calypso' section of the novel, with the famously nauseating 'Mr Leopold Bloom ate with relish the inner organs of beasts and fowls . . . Most of all he liked grilled mutton kidneys which gave to his palate a fine tang of faintly scented urine' (57). Bloom's pleasure in inner organs soon leads him to the antithesis of such oozing, represented by a working woman whose hands show the traces of washing soda she has used on her laundry:

a kidney oozed bloodguts on the willowpatterned dish: the last. He stood by the nextdoor girl at the counter. Would she buy it too, calling the items from a slip in her hand. Chapped: washing soda. And a pound and a half of Denny's sausages. His eyes rested on her vigorous hips . . . Strong pair of arms. Whacking a carpet on the clothesline. She does whack it, by George. The way her crooked skirt swings at each whack. (61)

The sensual pleasures of the kidneys, and the spectacle of a woman labouring find some kind of erotic centre in those chapped hands with their traces of washing soda.

Stephen Dedalus's sisters carry no such erotic charge in their labour of laundry, but figure rather the poverty that is a constant challenge and reproach to Stephen's self-fashioning as artist. They are not focussed through desiring eyes or through the energizing lens of fantasy, but are simply presented as a moment of drama within the multiplicity of dramas that is a day in Dublin in 1904:

Maggy at the range rammed down a greyish mass beneath bubbling suds twice with the potstick and wiped her brow . . .

Katey went to the range and peered with squinting eyes.

– What's in the pot? she asked.

– Shirts, Maggy said.

Boody cried angrily:

– Crikey, is there nothing for us to eat? (225)

The scene is both comical and grotesque. The squalor and discomfort of their lives leaving only a space for the dark humour that would confound laundry and sustenance.

When laundry re-emerges in relation to Bloom, however, it is once more with a strongly marked eroticism. In the dizzying acting out of identities and histories in 'Circe' Bloom makes an appearance as a 'charming soubrette with dauby cheeks' (491). Wearing female clothing has been held out as punishment, and Bloom is keen to disavow any guilty associations with his transvestism: 'I tried her things on only once, a small prank, in Holles street. When we were hardup I washed them to save the laundry bill. My own shirts I turned. It was the purest thrift' (490–91). The mutual implication of the sexual, the economic and the hygienic in this passage is striking: 'hardup' suggesting both erection and pecuniary deficiencies, the purity of thrift raising both hygienic and moral questions.

Once again, in this text published in 1922, we do not find the technologies of laundry that were becoming so visible and so prevalent, at least in well-off homes. Of course, the action of the novel takes place in 1904 when the labour of washing was still more generally manual. But Joyce seems to want to stress the physicality of such labour, finding in it a rich field of associated symbolisms. Nonetheless, when we are finally made aware of Leopold Bloom's 'ultimate ambition' in 'Ithaca' it is articulated specifically in relation to contemporary domestic space and its technologies. Bloom aspires 'to purchase by private treaty in fee simple a thatched bungalow-shaped 2 storey dwellinghouse of southerly aspect' (633). He repudiates the pleasures of inherited wealth and country grandeur in favour of privatized middle-class domesticity. He fantasizes about the decor, location and arrangement of such a house, but dwells particularly on its modern conveniences: 'bathroom, hot and cold supply, reclining and shower: water closet on mezzanine . . . servant's apartments with separate sanitary and hygienic necessaries for cook, general and betweenmaid . . . pantry, buttery, larder, refrigerator . . . carbon monoxide gas supply throughout' (633–34). The following pages document in overwhelming detail the material costs of such a fantasy, and their impossibility for Bloom, but the narrative of this episode ends by asserting the psychological necessity of such unrealizable fantasy:

It was one of his axioms that similar mediations or the automatic relation to himself of a narrative concerning himself or tranquil recollection of the past when practised habitually before retiring for the night alleviated fatigue and produced as a result sound repose and renovated vitality. (641)

So the psychological health of this protagonist of modernity is intimately connected to fantasies of domestic cleanliness. Bloom's fascination with odours, fluids and oozing matter comes up against his desire for order, impersonality and modern hygiene. The soda-chapped hands of the servant, displaying raw flesh while embodying the rituals of cleanliness, provide one image in which this tension can be played out. That the sight of this working woman creates in Bloom the desire to pursue her suggests the anxiety and powerlessness Bloom feels when confronted by the impossibility of resolving this oscillation between desire as abject and desire as pure. Dedalus may withdraw from the fray in the name of artistic genius, but Bloom is left endlessly repeating the unrealizable fantasy of domestic order, so as to ensure his own 'vitality'.

Vitality is also centrally at stake in Dorothy Richardson's *Pilgrimage*. This series of thirteen novels was published largely between 1915 and 1938, with the final novel appearing in 1967. The novels move unsettlingly between philosophical abstraction and scrupulously documentary naturalism in their formal experimentation with the narration of an individual life. Miriam Henderson's developing selfhood from the 1890s to the early decades of the twentieth century is the subject and the object of these texts. Miriam's sense of self is always precarious, constantly in flux, and articulated very precisely in relation to the technologies of modern labour. Both washing and typing appear at various points in *Pilgrimage*, and are mapped explicitly onto questions of freedom, autonomy and the possibilities of sustaining a narrative of selfhood.

The early novels in the series reveal Miriam's sensitivity to the relations between cleanliness and decency. In 'Pointed Roofs' (1915), Miriam is teaching in a school in Germany when she finds herself subjected to the ordeal of compulsory and collective hair washing. She is physically repulsed by the process: 'For a moment she thought that the nausea which had seized her as she surrendered would, the next instant make flight imperative . . . Tears came to her eyes as she gave beneath the onslaught of two hugely enveloping, vigorously drubbing hands'.[78] The process gradually becomes more soothing through its rhythms and repetitions, and Miriam emerges to say 'Thank you'. Nonetheless, the text records her traumatic self consciousness when faced with the obtrusive fact of wet hair and the necessity of presenting herself in public. The oppressive nature of the way in which these young girls' bodies are subjected to routines of cleanliness and order is returned to at various points, and what this routine would ward off is finally articulated by the school's Head towards the end of this first novel: "'It shall cease – these talks – this vile talk of men. Do you understand? It shall cease. I – will – not – have – it. . . . The school shall be clean . . . from pupil to pupil . . . from room to room. . . . Every day . . . every hour. . . . Shameless!" she screamed' (1, 179). The regime of bodily and personal cleanliness operated by the school is meant to produce a very particular version of feminine passivity, which will serve as a barrier to the articulation of sexual feelings.

As Miriam returns to England, she becomes more conscious of the relations between economy, technology and cleanliness, noting that her sister has gone to work in a house where there is a laundry maid, and musing at length on the toilet arrangements in her lodgings. In 'The Tunnel' (1919), the relations between financial security and personal autonomy haunt Miriam's self-representation, emerging for example in an account of the labour of keeping her clothes clean enough for work. Miriam has been taking her first lessons in riding a bicycle,[79] and this leads to a revelation from her friends that they have been riding on their bicycles round Russell Square in their knickers. They return home, furious that such lack of constraint is not part of their everyday experience, but the discussion continues:

'Yes; and it is not only that; think of never having to brush your skirt.'
'I know. It would be bliss.'
'I spend half of my life brushing my skirt. If I miss a day I notice it – if I miss two days, the office notices it. If I miss three days the public notices it.'
'La vie est dure; pour les femmes.'[80] (148–49)

So not only is the skirt impractical, and physically constraining, it also leads to incessant physical labour of laundering and brushing, so that the women can be inconspicuous and also employable. The ways in which professional work constrains women to particular domestic routines is scrupulously documented across the novels. Miriam notes, for example, in 'The Tunnel' how costly and unfortunate it is that she has never been taught to cook, since she is forced to eat in restaurants, a practice she can barely afford. This generation of women who have been brought up to modest gentility but educated to modest professional autonomy bear the brunt of the transition towards the servantless home. They have not been trained to carry out the basic routines of domestic labour, but are forced to live with only very impractical kinds of domestic support from more or less energetic landladies. Miriam and her friends declare that this constitutes a major impediment to 'living their lives':

> 'And what is our life worth, without late hours? The evening is the only life we have.'
> 'Exactly. And they are the same really. They do their work to be free of it and live.'
> 'Precisely; but they are waited on. They have their houses and baths and servants and meals and comforts. We get up in cold rooms untended and tired. *They* ought to be the first at the office and wait upon us.' (2, 162)

Work and freedom are here in a complex dialectic. Work enables freedom, but also negates it. The women feel that they are excluded from any position in that drama that would recognize their own selves. They become the servant in the office to men who are used to the comforts of servants at home, and the extra labour they have to perform in their homes remains utterly invisible. Miriam confronts this complex invisibility in a section of 'Interim' (1919), where she is caught in painful self-consciousness, unsure whether to acknowledge the presence of an old acquaintance who is now working as a domestic servant, her eye turns to a magazine story. She is at first forceful in her rejections of its representation:

> She guessed the story from the illustrations and dropped into the text half-way through the narrative. No woman who did typewriting from morning till night and lived in a poor lodging could look like that . . . perhaps some did . . . perhaps that was how clerks *ought* to look. (2, 309)

But the final hesitancy is also revealing. What are the possibilities for freedom for the typist in poor lodgings, and could she ever look 'like that'? Miriam's certainties and her tentativeness continue throughout the novel series, as she experiments with different ways of imagining and living herself. The space of the urban and the experience of labour are mutually implicated in ways that set the limits of her pilgrimage. Travelling through the city on a bus in 'Deadlock' (1921), Miriam is aware of a liberation of personalities from their social and gendered habits. She returns to her lodging as to a retreat, a space in which she has the right to be alone and to preserve her visions untouched. Keeping herself apart in her imagination from the challenging sexual and intellectual exchanges with Michael Shatov which will in fact follow this moment, Miriam thinks longingly of the evening ahead and the self-confirming solace it will allow: 'She would have an evening's washing and ironing' (3, 115).

Pilgrimage provides us with very clear evidence of the ways in which the everyday technologies of washing and typing structured modes of subjectivity in the period. These technologies are consistently experienced in the text in relation to labour, to the desire for autonomy and to the overwhelming sensation of social and sexual frustration. Each of these technologies, as we have seen, had the capacity to reconfigure both patterns and places of labour, to re-draw the boundaries between the public and the private, between work and home, and between repetition and creativity. Washing and typing seem constantly to be invoked in the many narratives of self-formation explored in this chapter. Yet they are also, and insistently, hidden, as if they held a charge of desire and of shame. It is, indeed striking, that Miriam's search for the self-confirming solace of washing is imagined in the solitary and private space of her own room where she would seek refuge from the troubling energies of sexual passion.

In the following chapter we will examine this self-confirming solace of labour in the rather different contexts of political activism and industrial manual labour. Sylvia Pankhurst is best known for her activism in the early years of the twentieth century within the suffrage movement, a context in which both labour and selfhood have particular resonances that will be examined below. But she was also active within the broader labour movement, which led her to encounter rather different questions about the relations between labour and political agency. And she was also a painter, an essayist and a poet, and in each of these imaginative forms she had quite distinctive encounters with labour, and specifically with labouring women. The complexity and fascinations of Pankhurst's voluminous cultural productions, and the ways in which they might illuminate the relations between labour, selfhood and the struggle for forms of political representation in the early twentieth century, will be fully explored in the following chapter.

CHAPTER THREE

Sylvia Pankhurst: labour and representation

Sylvia Pankhurst's political and artistic activities in the early years of the twentieth century have produced a varied and challenging archive of texts and images. Her political journalism, her polemical writings, her sketches and drawings and her poetry constitute a sustained attempt to think through possible relations between the activity of labour and different modes of political representation and of political activism.

Pankhurst's work within the women's suffrage movement involved the exploration of possible relations between labour, liberation and women's political representation: an exploration in which questions of identification, of collectivism and of sacrifice were to be central. The possibilities, and the consequences, of identification with working women was an area of recurrent interest to Pankhurst as it was to the suffrage movement as a whole. The fears, projections and fantasies associated with working women have already emerged in the discussion of washerwomen and of typists in the previous chapter, but in this chapter we will focus more specifically on the ways in which political organizations articulated their strategies of identification with working women. This argument will be further developed in chapter 5 when I examine the theorization and the practice of syndicalism in the early twentieth century. Collectivism and sacrifice, as we shall see, are mutually implicated in the texts of the suffrage movement, and both terms are closely identified with positions taken in relation to the activity and the significance of labour.

The suffrage movement is a key part of the political and cultural history of the early years of the century, and its activists, writers and political theorists drew substantially on the philosophical traditions with which this study began to articulate their ideas and their aspirations for political representation, historical agency and economic independence.[1] Pankhurst's subsequent work within the labour movement in the 1920s led her to a more direct engagement with the legacies of Marxism and its articulation of the relations between labour, history and identity, in which collectivism was to emerge once more as both the goal and the recalcitrant moment within her political and her cultural work. Across all these forms of activism, Pankhurst was also involved in the production of a series of literary and artistic texts, including portraits, poems, essays, memoirs and campaigning journalism; texts which allow us to capture something of the imaginative energies bound up in her encounter with the history and the experience of labour.

Estelle Sylvia Pankhurst was born in Manchester in 1882. Her parents were both active in socialist politics, joining the Independent Labour Party on its formation in 1893, and were broadly active within a cultural politics that took as its exemplary figures William Morris, Edward Bellamy, Robert Blatchford and Walter Crane. Sylvia was thus brought up in a family that believed in artistic vocation and social purpose. She also read Charles Dickens, Walter Scott and George Eliot at a formative age: these texts not only sharpened her sense of the writer's role as a social campaigner, but also, she asserts, 'bred in me a great pity for poverty'.[2] Her father died when Sylvia was sixteen, leaving the family in financially precarious circumstances. In 1900, Sylvia went to Manchester School of Art on a scholarship. She then gained a further scholarship to finance study and travel in Europe, and then finally secured a place at the Royal College of Art, in London, in 1904.

The political activism of the Pankhurst family took a decisive turn when her mother, Emmeline, and her sister, Christabel, joined with other women from the Independent Labour Party in Manchester to form the Women's Social and Political Union in 1903 to campaign for women's suffrage. The WSPU was initially affiliated to the Independent Labour Party, a Party to which Sylvia was committed both through her own political convictions and through her friendship, and some would then argue her affair, with James Keir Hardie.[3] After moving to London in 1904, Sylvia set up a branch of the WSPU with three fellow activists: her aunt, Mary Clarke, her landlady, Mrs Roe, and the mill worker, Annie Kenney. In 1905, the WSPU began their campaign of militant activism that was to escalate dramatically over the following decade, particularly after activists began to realize that the election of a Liberal government in 1906 was not in itself going to ensure women's enfranchisement.

By 1906, the WSPU had severed its links with the ILP, believing that the struggle for suffrage must not be subsumed within a broader labour movement struggle where it was unlikely to achieve the necessary prominence. Sylvia was not in sympathy with this move, and the following years were to see her painfully caught between the increasingly autocratic and charismatic leadership of the WSPU, represented by her mother and her sister, and her own commitments to working closely with women in the labour movement as part of a struggle for social liberation and greater equality. The WSPU had many splits and factions over the following years, and Sylvia was often torn by her residual loyalties to her family and her increasing connections to the labour movement. Sylvia remained within the WSPU until 1914, however, and endured numerous episodes of imprisonment and of force-feeding over these years.

In 1912, Sylvia Pankhurst moved to the East End of London, where she helped to set up the East London Federation of the Suffragettes. This organization involved many working-class women, who campaigned for equal pay for women, for the abolition of sweated labour and, after 1914, against the war. The WSPU expelled this Federation in 1914. Sylvia Pankhurst moved into a premises in Old Ford Road, in Bow, East London where she helped to organize a child-care centre, a cut-price restaurant and a toy factory which would provide decent employment for local women. In 1916, the Federation changed its name to the Workers' Suffrage Federation, and its paper, owned and edited by Sylvia Pankhurst, changed its name from the *Women's Dreadnought* to the *Workers' Dreadnought* in 1917. In 1918, the Workers' Suffrage Federation changed its name once more, to the Workers' Socialist Federation, making even more explicit the political distance Sylvia had travelled since 1904. The pro-war stance of most WSPU members had horrified Sylvia in 1914, and her work in the East End then made her increasingly antipathetic to parliamentary struggle as a way of achieving significant social change.

In 1919, the Workers' Socialist Federation affiliated to the newly formed Third Communist International, and was thus part of the process of formation of the British Communist Party in 1920. Sylvia herself was arrested under the Defence of the Realm Act in 1920 on charges of sedition on the basis that material published in the *Workers' Dreadnought* amounted to encouraging mutiny within the armed forces. She was subsequently sentenced to months of hard labour in prison. Her role in the Communist Party was short lived: she was expelled in 1921 because she would not accept the validity of parliamentary activity as part of communist politics, a position Lenin famously dismissed as 'infantile leftism'.[4] It is perhaps ironic that such a prominent suffrage activist should come to be identified with complete antipathy towards parliamentary struggle, but Pankhurst was to sustain her scepticism towards political parties and representative democracy from this time on.

In the 1920s, Sylvia continued to be active in local political campaigns and in political journalism. The *Workers' Dreadnought* published articles on international affairs, on domestic political struggles, on educational reform and on women's health, but it also published fiction and poetry, including Pankhurst's own. This interest in the interrelations between political identities and imaginative representations found fuller expression in the short-lived journal, *Germinal*, which she founded with Silvio Corio in 1923. This illustrated journal published fiction by Gorky, drama by Ernst Toller, poetry by Alexander Blok, by Anna Akhmatova and by Pankhurst, as well as an essay and a story by 'Richard Marsden' (in reality, Sylvia Pankhurst). The journal had substantial cultural ambitions:

The Germinal Circle is intended to assist in the artistic expression of current thought, in order to bring art into contact with daily life and to use it as a means of expressing modern ideas and aspirations.[5]

These aims were further glossed by Pankhurst in the second issue, to stress that bringing art into contact with daily life could only be understood in relation to some form of identification with 'the people': 'I sing of the peoples. I sing of the peoples united; I sing the peoples creative; the peoples alert without master; of themselves they are master.' But in fact, Pankhurst was finding it difficult to maintain a space and a practice in which such identifications could be developed or sustained. She began a sexual relationship with Silvio Corio in 1925, and they lived together in Essex where she ran a Tea Room. Though they were unmarried, Pankhurst had a son by him at the age of forty-five, a matter of some small national scandal: the *News of the World* ran a story about Pankhurst's 'love child', in which she vigorously defended the choices she had made.[6]

From the thirties, Pankhurst's energies were largely devoted to anti-fascism, and in particular the campaign against fascist occupation of Ethiopia. Indeed her personal and her political energies were bound up with the politics of Ethiopia from 1935 until her death in 1960. She founded a weekly newspaper in 1936, the *New Times and Ethiopia News*, which Mary Davis says had 'an extensive circulation throughout West Africa and the West Indies where it was widely quoted in the emerging African nationalist press'.[7] Pankhurst knew many of the leading Pan-Africanist intellectuals and politicians in London in this period. She continued to campaign for Ethiopian independence until its successful achievement in 1954: 'Sylvia wrote that she regarded the campaign to achieve Ethiopian independence as her greatest achievement' (Davis, *Sylvia Pankhurst*, 116). She moved permanently to Ethiopia in 1956, and finally died there in 1960 at the age of seventy-eight.

Sylvia Pankhurst's life, then, was centrally concerned with women's labour, with political activism, with artistic creation and with the possibilities of social liberation. All of these concerns will be examined in this chapter, which begins with a discussion of Pankhurst's early writings about working women. These writings are considered in the light of the suffrage movement's anxiety about social 'parasitism', and its considerable investments in the figure of the working woman. We will then consider the extent to which Pankhurst was able to think of her own artistic and intellectual labours as 'work', and what sort of problems this threw up for her. Finally, we will examine Pankhurst's visual representations of working women, examining both the aesthetic and the political choices involved in the production of such representative images.

WORK, PARASITISM AND SUFFRAGE

In the summer of 1907, Sylvia Pankhurst was 'seized with the idea of going among women workers to paint them at their toil and write articles about their conditions'.[8] Pankhurst had recently completed several years of study at art school, and had been trying to earn her living as a journalist and as an artist. She had also been heavily involved in the day-to day campaigning activities of the Women's Social and Political Union. Pankhurst's journey in search of working women had political, personal and professional resonances whose complexity this chapter will try to disentangle.

Pankhurst spent months travelling to different parts of Britain to meet, interview and study working women. This desire to encounter and to document working women can be understood in relation to the political ideas and forms of organization she encountered within the suffrage movement. The iconography and political strategy of the suffrage movement drew very significantly on the figure of the 'working woman'. Marches and processions organized both by the WSPU and the National Union of Women's Suffrage Societies employed visual representations, including posters, banners and costumes of the range of trades and professions in which women participated. In the precarious struggle to find public modes of representing women which neither sexualized them nor rendered them threatening freaks, the costume of trade or profession seemed to offer an impersonal yet socially meaningful mode of being. Different trades and professions were represented in these processions, with the aim of suggesting women's importance to the economic, material and moral life of the nation. There is undoubtedly an element of masquerade, or forced identification, in some of the ways in which the suffrage movement drew on the figure of the 'working woman': for example Annie Kenney appeared dressed in clogs and shawl long after she had ceased to earn her living in the mills. Yet there is no doubt that women's role as productive, waged labourers constituted a key element in their claim to political representation, not least because it protected them from the damaging and disabling charge of 'parasitism'.

As we have seen 'parasitism' was a central term in Olive Schreiner's *Woman and Labour* (1911). Although this text was not actually published at the point that Pankhurst began her tour, Schreiner had published a two-part article on 'The Woman Question' in the New York *Cosmopolitan* in 1899 which anticipated many of the arguments made in *Woman and Labour*[9] and her arguments and ideas were circulating widely in suffrage publications in the period. Schreiner argued that the fate of women within modernity might be a form of sexual parasitism, where women became economically and socially dependent on the labour of men. This parasitism would lead to a 'clogging of the individuality', a process that would make both self-realization and achieved political identity impossible.[10]

This anxiety about parasitism, and its 'clogging' of individual selfhood, can be found in numerous suffrage texts. Constance Lytton's *Prisons and Prisoners*, a narrative of Lytton's involvement in militant suffragism, was published in 1914. It begins with the rousing invocation: 'Lay hold of your inward self and keep tight hold.'[11] This sense of inner purpose is markedly absent, however, in Lytton's account of her pre-suffrage life of unfocussed and often fruitless struggle to construct a productive and public role for her self. Before her involvement in the suffrage movement, Lytton describes herself in terms that suggest the negativity and decadence of parasitism:

Without doubt I myself was one of that numerous gang of upper class leisured spinsters, unemployed, unpropertied, unendowed, uneducated, without equipment or training for public service, economically dependent entirely upon others. (39)

This is a strikingly negative self-representation: she is part of 'a gang', rather than being an individual; she lacks education, a husband, or property; and crucially she is also 'unemployed'. Since Lytton has described her life as busy with a wide range of activities, she clearly means this to refer to the fact that she is not engaged in any form of paid labour. As part of her conversion to the identity of a militant suffragette, Lytton went through a process of impersonation which she writes about in the text. In order to provoke the excesses of forced feeding she knows are inflicted on prisoners of a lower social class, Lytton adopts the identity of Jane Warton, a working woman of 'unprepossessing appearance' (239). This impersonation may also be motivated by Lytton's sense that the legitimacy of the claim for suffrage is easier to represent through the figure of the working woman:

> it is easy to see that if women are to appeal effectively to a modern parliament for the rights of liberty and representation which so long have been recognised among men, it must be through the working woman, the bread-winning woman. (41)

The sufferings Lytton endures in this role, and their disastrous effects on her long-term health, act to confirm in her a version of her own agency and identity. Having feared the taint of parasitism, Lytton finally constructs a triumphant version of herself that is the negation of all the negatives which characterized her original state, and she achieves this through the mediation of the figure of the working woman.

Elizabeth Robins's novel *The Convert* (1907) also articulates anxieties about female parasitism, in particular the ways such parasitism might block the collective forms of subjectivity imagined within the suffrage movement.[12] Robins's emphasis is importantly different from Lytton's, stressing less a conversion into triumphant selfhood than a conversion away from individual selfhood and towards collective identities. The tension between these two representations of the process of political consciousness is indeed fundamental, not only to suffragism but more broadly to the political and cultural moment of 'early modernism'. Nietzsche's impact on philosophical and imaginative representations of individuality is profound, as will be seen in our discussions of Pankhurst and later of D. H. Lawrence. Bruce Clarke has written a fascinating study of the ways in which such Nietzschean drives towards the authentic and effective articulation of the self interacted with the energies and structures of suffrage activism in his study of Dora Marsden, suffrage activist and egoist.[13] Similarly, Suzanne Raitt has offered a very compelling account of the tensions expressed in May Sinclair's work between evolutionary, impersonal models of change and theories of discipline, sublimation and self-control.[14] The suffrage movement was peculiarly conscious that women had historically found it difficult to achieve a strong sense of either collective or individual identities, and thus the pragmatic political question of how the claims of these different versions of selfhood could be adjudicated was particularly fraught. The idea of 'sacrifice' emerges repeatedly in this context, with its sense of ethical purpose, but also with its sense of loss. The conscious decision to defer individual gratification or expression in the interests of a collective need or identity might be imagined as something very different from the loss or negation of self that results from marginalization, but the evidence from the suffrage literature suggests that it is not, or at least not clearly. Holding on to an 'inward self' while engaging that self in a collective struggle can be experienced either as a harnessing of will to a larger evolutionary process or as painful tension between self-achievement and revolutionary struggle.

Robins's heroine, Vida Levering, is first encountered in the nursery of her sister's house, enjoying a fulfilling and affirmative moment of domesticity: 'so much what the man thinks "feminine", that even the wariest man is reassured' (*Convert*, 12). When Vida leaves the nursery and descends to dinner, however, she finds only the emptiness of social dependency and meaningless chatter : '"All the women", she said, "are trying with might and main to amuse the man, and all the men are more or less permitting the women to succeed"' (28). Vida hears the suffrage movement generally condemned by both men and women, particularly for the ways in which it might offer a public role to women of lower social classes: '"Conceive the sublime impertinence," said Lady John, "of an ignorant little factory girl presuming to stand up in public and interrupt a speech by a minister of the Crown"' (67). Despite such general condemnation of the movement and its activists, Vida and her sister decide to go to a suffrage meeting to 'see for themselves'. At the meeting they experience a powerful, and transgressive, sense of belonging to a crowd which is made up of women and men from different classes: 'Isn't it queer that you and I have lived all this time in the world and have never yet been in a mixed crowd before in all our lives? – never *as part of it*' (91). The boundaries of self and the boundaries of class are both put in question by the experience.

Vida then meets a suffrage activist, and questions her closely about the mechanism by which she managed to align herself with the collective move-ment of suffragism: 'One of the things I wanted to know, if you don't mind – how you came to be identified with the movement' (184). In reply, the woman condemns the weakness and parasitism of upper-class women and their lack of 'sex pride', and contrasts this sharply with the experiences and attitudes of 'those other women, her fellow workers' (191) who, through their labour and through their political activism, are forced to experience themselves as a sex. As part of her conversion to suffrage activism Vida dresses as a poor woman and goes among the destitute:

You'll never know how many things are hidden from a woman in good clothes. The bold free look of a man at a woman he believes to be destitute – you must *feel* that look on you before you can understand – a good half of history. (263)

But this 'impersonation' of a socially and economically vulnerable woman turns out to be not entirely fantastic. Vida has, in fact, already experi-enced sexual vulnerability and economic precariousness. In her youth she was forced to leave her parental home following a scandal, and without training or appropriate education she struggles to earn her living: 'Some girls think it hardship to have to earn their living. The horror is not to be allowed to' (265). Vida's identity has moved throughout the novel from domesticity, to parasitism and then to the vulnerable position of the single working woman. We learn that she had been seduced by an apparently reliable friend. As the novel moves towards its conclusion, the ramifications of this seduction resonate with images of productive labour to construct and simultaneously to negate versions of selfhood. Vida attends a suffrage meeting where a working woman speaks of social distress, of the moral role of women in 'national housekeeping' and of the pernicious inequities produced by unequal pay. Vida identifies with the collective struggle of working women so powerfully that she is able to convert her friend Jean. But Jean is now the fiancée of Vida's seducer and her involvement in the intense identification produced by her conversion convinces her that she must renounce her fiancé and require him to marry Vida.

At this point, it seems as if the outcome of both their conversions to activism is to be painful self-sacrifice and a crippling submission to ideas of duty and respectability. But Vida finally rejects Jean's sacrifice, preferring her own unhappiness and self-negation, expressed in a moment of identification with the sufferings of working women: 'I think of the nail and chain makers of Cradley Heath, the sweated girls of the slums . . . of the army of ill-used women, whose very existence I mustn't mention' (339). The chain makers of Cradley Heath become the objects of an identification that negates the power of the domestic and the sexual, but at the moment of its articulation, this fantasy simultaneously leans towards the sexual vulnerability of those 'unmentionable' women, who are so badly 'ill-used'.

WRITING ABOUT WORKING WOMEN

The project of documenting the lives and experiences of working women that 'seized' Sylvia Pankhurst was thus overdetermined: it resonated with a series of attempts within the suffrage movement to theorize or to fictionalize the process of political identification and agency through representations of the 'working woman'. Pankhurst's writings were at one stage intended as a book 'dealing with the work of women in a large number of trades', though in fact only a fraction of the work was ever published.[15] The research for the book was undertaken in 1907, but the brief extracts which did appear in *Votes for Women* were published some time after, the latest in 1911. The copiousness of Pankhurst's research material, and her inability to finish the book, suggest both the importance and the difficulty of her encounter with working women. The particular trades Pankhurst chose for study were not arbitrary, but expressed her interests as a socialist and as a suffragette. In her extensive research on women and labour, Pankhurst concentrated on fields of work where both women and men were employed, so that she could examine the rationale and impact of differential pay. She also selected jobs which were perceived as physically demanding, and trades which had been condemned as 'unwomanly', so that she could re-insert women workers within the increasingly gendered space of 'productive labour'. A crucial example of such a trade, as Robins's novel might already suggest, was found in the chain makers of Cradley Heath. This industrial town in the Black Country, and these workers, had been part of the iconography and the corpus of social investigation since the mid-nineteenth century, and the appearance of chain makers at a Suffrage Procession was met with great enthusiasm: 'Block three contained the industrial women: chain makers and pit-brow women (who were roundly cheered)'.[16] Cradley Heath was strongly associated with low pay, arduous labour and industrial squalor. As Lisa Tickner argues:

Chainmaking and pit-brow work, more than any other kinds of female labour, were subject to repeated attempts at regulation during the nineteenth and early twentieth centuries. Both were arduous and unrewarding, but both seem to have been thrown into prominence because they were seen as degrading and 'unwomanly'. (*Spectacle*, 309)

Thus, when the social investigator, Robert Sherard, set out to document the sufferings of the 'White Slaves of England' in 1896, the workers, and particularly the women workers, of Cradley Heath were given a prominent place.[17] Sherard begins his account with a commentary on the physically repulsive nature of the town:

It is frankly an industrial town, a town of the Black Country, where, in smoke and soot and mud, men and women earn their bread with the abundant sweat not of their brows alone; a terribly ugly and depressing town. (408)

Sherard draws on the words of women chain makers to describe the poverty and hardship which their trade involves, stressing the difficulty women have in feeding their families on the wages they earn, despite working long hours in a difficult and dangerous trade. He describes the work processes involved and explains the economic relations of the town, including the excessive charges levied on individual workers for the provision of fuel, and the role of contractors or 'foggers' in impoverishing workers. In charging individual workers over fifty per cent of the value of their produce for her services, one particular 'fogger' is denounced by Sherard as employing sweated labour: 'one of a numerous class of human leeches fast to a gangrened sore' (414). In Sherard's writing there is an intensity of indignation and condemnation, expressed through the overall polemic of his critique of 'white slavery'. Yet the women workers are only fleetingly included in Sherard's expansive sympathies: it is inappropriateness rather than injustice that characterizes the women of Cradley Heath for him. Sherard declares his 'manhood . . . ashamed' (411) by the sight of women swinging heavy hammers and he cites with approval the judgement of the Secretary of the Chainmakers' Union that the work involved is 'not women's work at all'. Sherard objects to women's work in chain making on moral, aesthetic and ideological grounds. His evoking of the 'wizened infants hanging to their mother's breasts' (411) or crawling in the dirt among a hail of sparks as their mothers' hammer iron rings, is intended to shock and to embody the unnatural quality of the women's work: these women are toiling at the wrong sort of hearth. The pitiful sight of a sweet little lass 'such as Sir John Millais would have liked to paint' (413) powering bellows for 3d a day captures the distortions and exploitations which preoccupy Sherard in Cradley Heath. The massive, powerful hammer which batters the chain into shape is:

an implement used by slaves most degraded, by starved mothers fighting in sweat and anguish and rags, for the sop of the weazened bairns, who in the shower of fiery sparks grovel in the mire of these shameful workshops. (411)

The burden of Sherard's analysis is the inappropriateness of women's heavy manual labour, and his account forms part of a series of reports and campaigns which sought to limit the extent and arduousness of women's labour. Indeed, as Lisa Tickner has argued: 'The cases of the pit-brow women and Cradley Heath women . . . had come to symbolise the interference of men and the State in the control of women's labour' (*Spectacle*, 296).

When Sylvia Pankhurst wrote about the women of Cradley Heath, or indeed the pit-brow lasses, she did so in the context of her opposition to the series of legislative interventions in women's labour which had diminished the capacity of these women to earn a decent wage, or even to secure employment: legislative action which she represented as particularly intrusive since it had been enacted without any parliamentary representation of women and their interests.[18] Like Sherard, Pankhurst begins her narrative by recording the squalor and ugliness of Cradley Heath: 'the air smells and tastes of soot, and from the low hills on every side rises the smoke of mill chimneys'.[19] Yet from a perception of 'faint gleams of sunshine', Pankhurst moves on to the more pleasing sight of a woman 'in a neat dark dress and hat and white apron' (1): this precise recording of dress will characterize all of Pankhurst's meeting with working women, and will be discussed more fully in the context of her paintings of these women below. Pankhurst walks through the town: attracted by the sound of 'women's voices singing', she looks inside one of the 'shops' in which groups of women work manufacturing chains. She describes the women's labour in some detail, and manuscript amendments to the typescript suggest an effort at precision. She employs technical terms to designate material, tools and techniques of the trade, and stresses the skill, as well as the physical demands, of the work. She talks to the women workers, who report that they find the work broadly satisfying, if demanding, but also say that they can barely survive on the wages paid. They earn significantly less than their male colleagues, largely because they are restricted to producing the cheaper sorts of chain, and Pankhurst meticulously details their earnings and expenses. Like Sherard, Pankhurst observes the presence of children in the shops while the women are at work:

Next door a tired looking woman was making heavy chain. A thin dirty little baby about 18 months old was pulling at her skirts and crying with a dull monotonous wail. A neighbour came in and lifted it on to the hearth. The child stopped crying and stretching out its arms, went to its mother and touched her face. Without a word she put it down on the ground and went on with her work. It clung to her legs, crying again, and she went on working, turning her head to smile at it now and then. (6)

But the pathos and the objectification in this narrative suggest a much more troubled reaction to the relations between the domestic and industrial labour than we found in Sherard's writing. Pankhurst argues that 'the question of the mothers of young children working in the chain shop is both difficult and painful' (18) and indeed she avoids any attempt at answering this question beyond saying it is a matter that can only be settled by the women themselves. The difficulty of the question leads her to consider why these young mothers choose to work in the chain shops, given the meagre earnings they are able to derive after long hours of labour. She concludes that the reasons for working exceed purely rational economic calculation: 'their work in the chain shop gives them a feeling of independence, of having earned something with their own hands, something that no one can dispute their right to' (18). This feeling of independence is reinforced by a sense of pride in technical skills: 'many of the women speak of the technicalities of the work with interest and are proud of their skill in it' (17).

The account Pankhurst gives of the women of Cradley Heath stresses the skill and the physical demands of their chosen trade, but also insists that this work represents some sort of choice, however partial, by the women involved. In spite of low wages and poor working conditions, Pankhurst reports that most women say they enjoy the work. They certainly prefer it to the apparently more respectable and 'appropriate' work of domestic service:

Many women told me that they had wished to put their daughters to something else, but that they had refused to learn any other trade. Many of the girls have tried domestic service in Birmingham and other towns, but have returned to the Black Country to make chain. (17)

The ways in which Sherard connected the smoke and soot and mud of Cradley Heath metonymically to the morals of its women workers are explicitly rejected by Pankhurst. She stresses the gulf between the squalor of their surroundings and the physical vigour and well-being of the majority of the women. Despite a 'ragged dirty white cotton dress' Pankhurst notes that one woman is a 'lithe and active creature' and she notes more generally that 'plenty of fresh air is admitted through the unglazed windows and generally open doors' (17) so that the workers are usually strong and healthy.

Pankhurst does not find 'slaves' but underpaid and sometimes exhausted women who have chosen this form of employment. Yet she struggles with the unambiguously industrial and grimy conditions of these women's work, and is continually drawn to images of light and of nature. The sound of women singing resonates in the text, which ends with a transformative fantasy of pleasurable and happy labour:

I thought of those who live and work in Tibbett's Garden and Anvil Yard and many another dark and dismal spot. I wished that we could bring them forth and spread them over some fresh, green countryside. I thought of them in bright, clean, well built chain shops, well paid and working happily. I seemed to hear the sound of their laughter joined with the tapping of their hammers, I saw their bare arms firm and rounded, the sunshine on their hair, the firelight on their faces, and all the time I heard them singing. (21–22)

If this is the utopian imagination which sustains political activism it certainly risks the transformation of working women into aestheticized icons of liberation; at some cost both to their individuality and to their modernity.

A fraught relation to modernity is not, of course, unique to Sylvia Pankhurst as a socialist thinker. Pankhurst describes her own cultural heritage, growing up in a family with strong links to both the socialist and the suffrage movement, in terms which highlight the importance of pre-modern social forms for the cultural imagination of socialism. Pankhurst cites Robert Blatchford and William Morris as thinkers whose utopian imagination and critique of the distortions and exploitations of industrialism informed her early sense of herself as a socialist. We also learn that Pankhurst's first attempt at gaining paid employment as an artist was a proposed project of illustration for Richard Jefferies's *The Open Air*.[20] Being read Dickens at an early age 'bred in me a great pity for poverty, and a longing, profound and constant, for a Golden Age when plenty and joy should be the gift of all'.[21] As she examined the working conditions of women in the early twentieth century, Pankhurst found herself torn between the need to re-figure these women as conscious agents in their own lives and the power of a political and literary tradition which risked universalizing perceptions of the working woman as unnatural and as a symptom of the distortions of industrialization.

The emphasis of Pankhurst's argument across her various writings, however, is on the ways in which injustices in the industrial world expressed and reinforced broader political injustices, and particularly the injustice of women's exclusion from the franchise. In examining the lives and work of 'pit-brow lassies', Pankhurst was once more intervening in an area which had attracted substantial amounts of social comment and legislative intervention. The presence of women in coal mines had disturbed and fascinated commentators since the mid-nineteenth century, and also increasingly exercised the Trades Unions who believed that women had a tendency to depress overall wage levels within a particular industry. Although the practice of women working underground had ended by the time Pankhurst went to Wigan, many were still employed above ground shifting and sorting coal. Griselda Pollock has examined the peculiar fascinations of these pit-brow women for nineteenth-century commentators, and in particular for the barrister and man of letters, Arthur Munby, whose substantial archive of images and descriptions of working women dwelt overwhelmingly on the pit-brow women.[22] Munby was neither a politician nor a social campaigner, but rather an amateur enthusiast of working women: he secretly married a woman servant, and their relationship involved elaborate forms of role play based on the *frissons* of racial and class differences. Munby's explicit absorption in images and descriptions of pit-brow women, Pollock suggests, offers us some insight into the complexity of the social and gendered meanings of these working women in the period. These women seem to compel Munby because of their relation to dirt and to grime and also because of their physical strength. His collection includes drawings where the enormity of the women's features and of their muscularity is stressed, but also studio-produced photographs of 'Pitbrow Worker in Sunday Clothes'.[23] The proximity of pit-brow women to men while at work, their physicality and their filth all threatened boundaries of gendered identity. In addition, their costume was singular: they wore protective sackcloth aprons over leggings or trousers. This transgressive mode of dress excited so much adverse comment that coal owners actually arranged for studio portraits to be taken and distributed of pit-brow women in their Sunday Best. As we have seen, however, the presence of these images in Munby's collection alongside many images of the women in their working clothes might suggest that this strategy acted to intensify rather than to negate the aura of transgression and sexualization that surrounded these women as workers.

Given the prominence accorded to the unusual dress of pit-brow women, and in particular to their wearing of trousers, it is unsurprising that when Pankhurst, 'in view of the present attempt to prohibit the employment of women upon the brow of the coal mine'[24] set about describing their work she began with a description of their dress. Pankhurst's article on pit-brow women exists in two forms: an unpublished typescript in the *Sylvia Pankhurst Papers* and a version which appeared in the WSPU journal, *Votes for Women* in 1911. The typescript begins with a pit-brow woman at home, rising and dressing to go to work:

She is dressed in a light blue cotton skirt, called a coat, turned up in front and hanging in a bunch of folds behind, a darker blue cotton bodice and a little grey woollen shawl, with coarse black knitted stockings and clogs upon her feet, and on her head the blue 'bonnet'.[25]

The description scrupulously avoids the eroticization that seemed to inhere in so many accounts of pit-brow women. The version which appeared in *Votes for Women* stresses more forcefully the practical considerations which have lead to the pit-brow women's peculiar style of dress:

In the old days they always wore over their stout corduroy knickerbockers, not the ordinary skirt, but something called a 'coat'. The coat, usually made of blue print, is in reality a kind of apron, the fact that it is open at the back being disguised by wide looping folds. Its advantage over an ordinary short skirt is that should it catch in any of the machinery it would be easy to unbutton it and allow it to slip off . . . Now that the machinery is more adequately fenced the skirts are coming back. (37)

Having placed the pit-brow women in the context of home life and re-figured them in terms of rational dress, Pankhurst goes on to describe their work in detail. Both men and women, she points out, are involved in work above ground at the pit: as the tubs of coal are received from below, pushed along tracks, and dragged by cable up a slope to an open shed where they are sorted:

[o]n either side of the belts rows of women stand picking out pieces of stone, wood, and other waste stuff from amongst the coal as it slowly moves past. Sometimes they pick out the waste pieces with their fingers, sometimes they catch at them with an iron hook or rake, and sometimes with a hammer they strike off those which may be adhering to the coal itself. (38)

Again, Pankhurst notes and admires these women's physicality and health: they are 'lithe and strong', 'cheerful and bonny', and one woman has a 'cheery face . . . as bronzed and weather-beaten as any sailor's and her eyes are as blue as the summer sea or her own blue bonnet' (3). They are specifically contrasted, in the typescript, with the anaemic match girls and sewing machinists of the East End of London whose emaciated bodies are symptomatic of a broader social degeneracy and of the destructive consequences of sweated labour.[26] Pankhurst insists that the working conditions of pit-brow women are relatively healthy and that their work, though arduous, is decent. She offers testimony from the women which again suggests choices about employment have been considered and made. One coal sorter says that working at the pit 'brought me out so' (39), by which she means that it made her feel and look better and stronger. The choice of imagery is striking as it expresses that important sense of self-realization that is such a central element of suffrage rhetoric. We learn that this woman's previous employment had been in domestic service, where, we assume, labour and selfhood had been in a significantly less fertile relationship. Pankhurst concedes that 'the work is not what many of us would choose, and the wages are lower than they should be' (39) but also insists that it is healthier and better than many forms of employment open to women. She is clear that even arduous and underpaid work is better than no work: 'One must remember, too, that there is no hardship so great, and no temptation so strong, as that of being without work and without means' (39). This reference to 'temptation', of course, raises the spectre of prostitution, which always haunts discussions of women's economic precariousness.

Pankhurst sees attempts to prohibit women from the pit brow as a negation of their selfhood:

the chief reason for objecting to the attempt to prohibit the employment of women upon the pit brow is that the women themselves, who are fully developed adult human beings, wish to continue their work, and resent this officious and interested tampering with their liberty. (40)

Such 'interested tampering' cannot claim legitimacy because it takes place in a parliamentary context where women are not represented. Pankhurst writes on behalf of these women, re-presenting their labour as healthy and vigorous and re-figuring their bodies not as interestingly fetishized but as banal. Strikingly, however, the articulation of this physical labour as a form of liberation does not remain secure within Pankhurst's own writing. Looking back in 1938 on her visit to Wigan, Pankhurst offers yet another version of these women's labour: its arduousness and physicality proof, not of vigour and strength, but rather of backwardness. The improved working conditions Pankhurst sought in 1911 no longer seem sufficient to negate the brutality of such labour, 'which invention must reduce, and, if possible eliminate, for the liberation of human souls'.[27]

Pankhurst also struggles to articulate a relationship between labour and liberation as she describes work in ceramics factories in the Potteries and in the boot factories of Leicester. What she discovers in both these industries is monotonous and dangerous work done for very low wages. Her report on the Potteries is the most detailed and extensive study of working women Pankhurst produced. She describes the work involved, for men and for women, in meticulous detail:

She takes up a knife in her right hand and applies it to the revolving plate's edge. In doing this she so manipulates the knife that in an instant or two the straight cut edge of the plate becomes perfectly smooth and round. Then, first on one side and then upon the other, she thoroughly polishes the plate with sandpaper, steadying the rotating plate with the right hand and pressing the sandpaper to its surface with the left.[28]

Pankhurst also investigates housing, rates of pay and industrial diseases and accidents. The use of lead in glazes produced severe levels of poisoning, and Pankhurst details the pernicious effects of this poisoning on pregnant women and on their children. Dust is another serious health risk for workers in the Potteries: although Factory Acts had required the installation of 'exhaust fans' to diminish the risks involved in some aspects of the manufacture of pottery, Pankhurst still finds: 'Powdered flint was lying all over the bench and the ring makers, who worked in the same room, were sprinkling handfuls of it from a great bin' (57). She describes encountering a young woman who is near death from consumption:

This woman was extraordinarily emaciated and her arms . . . showed pitiably thin. Her skin was the colour of old parchment, her eyes were prominent, and discoloured, and her dry brittle looking hair hung limply about her face. (57)

These women do not have the vigour, the strength and the shining hair found both in Cradley Heath and at the pit brow, but are rather damaged and prematurely aged by their labour. Pankhurst represents them as passive in their subjection to low pay and dangerous conditions: 'if an opportunity to better her condition should arise, she would take it, but until then she would go on doing the work that came to her' (40). Pankhurst talks to a skilled male worker about his labour in the factory and this man says he would much prefer more challenging and varied work. He suggests that either work in the 'free open-air' (39) or in London would provide more interest and variety, as indeed would being 'an artist and a painter like you' (39). I will return to this question of what sort of 'work' it is to be a painter or an artist below, but it is worth unpacking more fully this man's analysis of the relation between different forms of labour and 'freedom', and how Pankhurst responds to it. Pankhurst is reluctant to accept the man's version of the limitations of his work. She suggests to him that his work produces objects of beauty; that the Potteries offer 'interest and scope' (39) for anyone in search of work; and even that the district has significant beauty for those who can perceive it. However, '[h]e looked listlessly out of the window at the big bottle-shaped ovens and the neighbouring workshops and away beyond them at the stretches of waste ground' and he shook his head in disagreement. Pankhurst does not give up, insisting that the man's skill must give him some sense of satisfaction, but again he says he is dissatisfied and bored by the repetitive and monotonous quality of his work. His reaction leads Pankhurst to ponder on the individual and social meanings of work. She describes as a 'natural human longing' (39) the desire to confront variety and creativity in work, echoing many of the writings on the division of labour discussed in chapter 1. Pankhurst argues forcefully that basic human needs can be expressed and realized in the challenges of creative labour:

How precious is that perpetual desire after the unattainable and that insatiable longing to go one step farther, to do something yet greater still! Is it not this essentially human quality that has led humanity as far on the road to progress and development as it has gone and to which we must look to lead us as far as we ever shall go. (40)

But this idea of self-expression through labour is swiftly undercut by Pankhurst's realization that the women she is observing have no access even to the possibility of such insatiable longing: 'she whose trade is un-skilled, badly paid, and all monotony, nothing to train or strive for, noth-ing but tread, tread' (40). When Pankhurst considers the women workers she can only find a sense of duty and a determination to put up with things:

She spoke of her work as monotonous and uninteresting but as something that had been undertaken as a duty and must be carried through. She was full of common sense and there was not the least trace of whining or repining in her nature. (40)

We have moved some way here from the 'essentially human quality that has led humanity as far on the road to progress and development as it has gone'.

Pankhurst dramatizes in her analysis of these factory workers the tension between collectivity and individuality which is so central not just to her writing but to her political experiences within the suffrage movement. The woman who controls her desires and achieves an absence of whining may be read in relation to the necessary sacrifice which constructs the collective identity of political activism: an association pursued by Suzanne Raitt in her discussion of the complex meanings of 'sublimation' in the period.[29] Pankhurst celebrates the sense of losing the self in a moment of collective identification: 'We were buoyed by delightful triumph in this success, and belief of an early victory for the cause. Self was forgotten; personality seemed minute, the movement so big, so splendid.'[30] But this self-negation does carry risks of eradication, of removal from the 'essentially human' and from the movement of history. Pankhurst is eloquent on the importance of the individual will for the construction, or the realization, of historical agency: 'We are the evolutionary forces, we with our small wills together striving.'[31] The individual will is, however, at best fragile for these women workers in the Potteries with their emaciated and damaged bodies and their overwhelming passivity. Even in death these women are worth little: the Home Office fixed the minimum amount to be paid to a woman's dependants in the event of her death at one third below that paid to a man's. The 'chivalrous care for the interests of women which is supposed to make up to them for their lack of political power' ('The Potteries', 93) has failed, and being represented by no-one, these women workers risk failing even to represent themselves. Sublimation, passivity, and historical agency are mutually, and troublingly, implicated in this part of Pankhurst's analysis of working women.

The women who work in the boot factories of Leicester also seem to face negation. They work in an atmosphere 'intensely bewildering and trying to the nerves'[32] and their work is repetitive and routine. Pankhurst has little sympathy with complaints of male workers in these factories that they are being displaced by women who command lower levels of pay. This is certainly true, but has been exacerbated by past failures of the men to support women's struggles for better pay and conditions, she argues. This culpability is undermined, however, by Pankhurst's narrative of gradual economic decline and diminution of conditions of work within the industry as a whole. She details the life of one woman worker who had managed to acquire the skill of a 'fitter' and had worked independently in a cooperative group. Returning to Leicester on her marriage, she can barely earn enough to supplement the family wage:

the change from the old conditions to the new was fast setting in. The free merry life of the workshop with its singing and laughter had almost disappeared for much of the work was beginning to be done in the large factories where the silent system had been introduced and where the wages were steadily growing less. (27)

Pankhurst here presents these women workers as caught within larger social forces which make independence and financial security increasingly hard to realize. Confronted with their labour and with the stifling and congested atmosphere of the factory, Pankhurst tells us 'involuntarily the thought rises – "how in such a place as this and doing this monotonous work one would pine for the sight of green fields"' (6).

NATURAL LABOUR

When she writes about agricultural workers, Pankhurst employs images of health, strength and organicism extensively. Her account begins with her wandering down a country lane in Northumberland on a still and misty morning, when the grass is heavy with dew and 'you may hear the sound of soft, almost whispering voices, and now and then, perhaps, a gentle laugh'.[33] Laughter and gentle speech already suggest that this version of labour will be seen as less alienated than the submission of factory workers to the 'silent system' in Leicester. As we have seen, for Pankhurst, song and laughter are powerful expression of labour that is fulfilling. The women work collectively and cooperatively. They wear 'old-world peasant costume', including large black straw hats and pink cotton handkerchiefs. Pankhurst returns more than once to the gentleness of these women's voices, comparing them to 'the birds and the little mice that live among the corn' (776/3). Again, she observes the details of these women's labour with care, and captures both the process and the vocabulary of harvest. She stresses the involvement of the whole community in this labour, its natural rhythms, and the sociability of the working conditions. The women are healthy and vigorous, 'sturdy country people' (22) and the work is relatively varied.

Pankhurst does raise the issues of unequal pay in both versions of the article, but this economic inequality scarcely disturbs the harmony of her picture. Given her powerful investment in the healthiness and sociability of agricultural labour, it is a particularly cruel irony that she was to lose her own brother to disease brought on by overwork in agriculture in 1910.

Pankhurst also stresses the harmonious and communal working relations of women involved in the fishing trade, who seem to embody for her not just health and vigour but the very fabric of pre-industrial society:

Full of high spirits, strong, shapely and wellknit, they seem to bring to us a breath of the far off and the unknown and to belong to a life and time infinitely simpler and more primitive than our own.[34]

Again, we are given a detailed description of the women's dress, black oil skin skirts, big waterproof boots, and brightly coloured shawls and bodices, and their work is described with precision:

Each gutter catches up a herring in her left hand, and, holding it with its back touching her palm, sticks her knife into the fish just where the backbone meets the head, and then, with one quick twisting movement, cuts out the stomach and intestines and throws them from her into a small tin basin. (3)

Yet the core of this article is not the work done, but the beauty and the vigour of the workers. When we first encounter them on their way to work at six o'clock in the morning, they are laughing and singing. Pankhurst describes them as happy, as beautiful, as healthy, active and strong (3). Again, the colours of light and sunshine are powerfully evoked: their flesh has been:

turned by the sun to a wonderful ruddy golden hue. There are young women whose hair shines copper and golden in the sunlight to rival that of any famous Old Venetian lady and there are flaxen haired women, daughters of the Vikings, whose features are pure and nobly chiselled and whose deep eyes remind us of the sea. (6)

Pankhurst dwells very little on the details of pay or on any inequalities within the fishing industry, indeed she suggests that these women are paid better than women in the large majority of trades because of the strength of their characters. In a move that undercuts the correlation between industrial power and political representation, Pankhurst offers the vigour and happiness of these women as the force that allows them to achieve relative economic security. Of course, one could read this story the other way round and suggest that relative economic security is conducive to health and contentment, but the thrust of Pankhurst's writing is very much in the other direction. Their labour is arduous and carried out in extreme weather conditions, with any postponement of labour being for the protection of the flesh of the fish rather than the flesh of the women. But Pankhurst naturalizes these long working hours and poor working conditions as a necessary grounding for the heroism of the fisher lassies: in addition to being cheerful and 'ready with a joke or a song', these women 'make no complaint' (12). Theirs is a model of useful and natural labour, where no gap has been opened up between the interests of the self and the interests of the collectivity: unalienated labour comes with a 'constant round of song and laughter' (3).

Yet, despite Pankhurst's fascination with these narratives and images of fulfilled and harmonious labour, her writing does also articulate their fragility. For example, she raises the question of why so many agricultural labourers want to leave the countryside. Within the terms of Pankhurst's article on agricultural labour, indeed, this issue is almost incomprehensible. She talks about the role of changes in farming practices in reducing the need for agricultural labour, but admits that a significant part of the motivation for leaving 'lies with the workers themselves' (19). They go to towns looking for higher wages and because they find village life dull; they are also driven away by the poor standard of housing in the countryside, a reason 'which naturally appeals with special force to the women' (19).

Pankhurst experiences these willed choices by agricultural workers as at best false consciousness and at worst social catastrophe. There is an elegiac note as Pankhurst lists the things which workers will lose when they leave the countryside: 'the sight of the growing corn, the sun rising up over the hills in the early morning, and at midday falling in bright patches between the leaf shadows, ripening the apples' (22). Since Pankhurst describes herself as weeping 'when we returned from rural holidays at sight of the grey streets, with beggars and piteous ragged children'[35] the preference for urban and industrial forms of labour mystifies her completely. Throughout her writing on working women she searches for ways in which forms of modern industrial labour might capture key aspects of rural labour: its sociability, its vigour, its exposure to the open air. Even where the mode of labour seems most resistant to such analysis, Pankhurst will seek to read the actual or the allegorical force of nature within women's labour, as can be seen in her poem, 'The Workgirl' which was published in 1923:

> Soft is thy throat, and covered with the down,
> Fragrant and sweet, that favours budding youth;
> Scornful thy lips unkissed, and shallow yet
> Remaineth thy full eye, by love untouched.

With childishness thy mind is still enwrapt,
Though as a woman's heavy is thy toil;
Not in fair gardens art thou playing free,
Taking thy joyous flight from flower to flower.

Soiled is thy raiment and thy shoes are old,
And in the jolting 'bus beside thee lies
A burden grievous for thy puny strength.

Yet can I see thee with a deeper eye,
Moving thy rosy limbs in artless joy
Swaying thy radiant drapings girt with flowers.[36]

This poem draws interestingly on the sonnet form: its fourteen lines of iambic pentameters staging an argument about the meanings of women's labour. It begins by enumerating the beauties of a woman's throat, and lips, and eyes in ways which echo the eroticized dissection of the body in classical sonnet forms while simultaneously insisting on the 'untouched' nature of this body. The second quatrain stresses the woman's childishness, which lends greater emphasis to the complaint about her lack of liberty: 'Not in fair gardens art thou playing free', and makes her identity as 'workgirl' seem more unnatural. The details of her work are not represented, but rather they are abstracted into 'heavy toil' and 'grievous burden'. The concluding sestet is divided into two stanzas of three lines each, with the crucial 'turn' in the argument coming between these two stanzas. The bedraggled girl with soiled clothes and old shoes is re-figured through the operation of 'a deeper eye' and emerges as rosy, radiant and strewn with flowers.

This figure of a draped woman decorated with flowers echoes important elements of suffrage iconography, and might remind us in particular of some of Pankhurst's own work for the WSPU. Pankhurst designed and organized the execution of a series of murals to decorate the Prince's Skating Rink, Knightsbridge, which was the venue for a WSPU exhibition from 13–26 May 1909. The style of these murals is decorative and allegorical and Lisa Tickner's description of this work as 'dilute Pre-Raphaelite allegory, derived from Walter Crane'[37] expresses the unease that many recent writers have felt when examining Pankhurst's allegorical figures of femininity. The murals were conceived in relation to a text from the Psalms: 'They that sow in tears, shall reap in joy. He that goeth forth and weepeth, bearing precious seed, shall doubtless come again with rejoicing, bringing his sheaves with him.' The sentiment is not inappropriate to a political movement engaged in a long-term campaign which has involved significant degrees of individual suffering including periods of imprisonment, since it aligns the suffrage struggle with biblical conceptions of righteousness and of justice. It also connects to Pankhurst's ideas and fantasies about the moral and social meanings of agricultural labour. The design was executed in the colours of the WSPU, purple, white and green, and thus incorporated representations of ivy and vine leaves, ripe purple grapes, and 'orchid-winged butterflies'.[38] The iconography also included features such as a pelican feeding its young from its breast, which suggested the sacrificial and Christ-like qualities of the suffrage movement, and a dove with an olive branch, another biblical image calculated to express final victory for righteousness after a long period of suffering. One panel of the mural represents a woman sowing grain while another depicts the harvest: here the central female figure is flanked by angels as she stands among a rich array of flowers and leaves. The woman harvester is dressed in the same fashion as the angels: in a loose tunic, with her feet bare and her head uncovered. This figure of 'harvest' functions as the condensation of a number of political and religious narratives within Pankhurst's mural. She expresses sacrifice, suffering, righteous struggle, the victorious conquering of adversity, the triumph of beneficent forces of nature and, in her up-turned head and allegorical centrality and completeness, she also offers an image of personal elevation and individual integrity. The tension between the tears and sacrifice which the mural so powerfully evokes and this elevated figuration of triumph once more stages the difficult relations between selfhood, sacrifice and collectivity which were discussed above, and in a manner that is particularly troubling if the mural's central narrative of an underlying force of justice which is bound to triumph and to find appropriate social expression is questioned.

The darker side of Pankhurst's figuration of harvest as a reaping of the rewards of righteousness can also be found within her own writings. If the harvesting of corn invites images of moral and social good, the harvesting of potatoes is read in terms of social degeneration. Pankhurst's essay on 'The Potato Pickers' was one of the three essays of which a version was published in *Votes for Women*, so she clearly perceived her analysis as having some impact as a piece of persuasive writing in the suffrage cause.[39] The published version is framed by two extracts from the work of Richard Jefferies: in the first Jefferies invites us to look not at 'ourselves' but towards the future and an ideal life; while in the second he talks of his sadness in perceiving repetitive and burdensome labour. We are thus invited to see the potato pickers as symptomatic, both of alienated labour and of the necessity of working to create a better society, rather than to encounter them as individuals with views about the meanings of their own labour. As an urban underclass of casual labourers temporarily working in the countryside, they excite none of the sympathetic identification that is so marked in other aspects of Pankhurst's writings about working women.

Both versions of Pankhurst's essay on the potato pickers begin with a clear, bright autumnal morning: in the published version the lark is singing and the ploughman is whistling; while in the typescript version the lark is nowhere to be heard but the ploughman is still whistling. The horseman drives his well-groomed horses on to pull the plough that will dig up the furrows and uncover the potatoes. His work is repetitive: 'he goes up the fifth potato row, down the third, up the sixth, down the ninth, up the seventh, down the tenth' (26), but within this repetition is the creative calculation about the space needed to turn his horses which makes this work fulfilling, as his whistle surely tells us. The potato pickers follow in the wake of the plough: their 'stooping and bending, bending and stooping' expressing no element of creativity or control (27/34). Pankhurst watches this wearying work for several hours, without apparently seeing anything of the women apart from their general demeanour. As they stop for lunch 'I saw them clearly for the first time' (34). What Pankhurst sees appals her:

They were poor, miserable creatures, clad in vile, nameless rags, sometimes pinned, sometimes tied round them with other rags or bits of string. There were old, old women, with their skin all gnarled and wrinkled, and their purple lips all cracked. There were young women with dull white sullen faces, many with scars or black bruises round the eyes, and swollen, shapeless lips. Their hair was all matted and neglected, and every woman's eyes were fiery red. (34–35)

The rags, in fact, are not entirely 'nameless', since in the typescript Pankhurst had taken some trouble to detail the substance and style of the women's dress: she describes the costume of a number of women, detailing the colour and the fabric in petticoats, skirts, bodices and scarves (28). But these 'poor, degraded creatures' (35) produce an instinct of withdrawal in Pankhurst, who almost buries these women and their work under the weight of images of degeneracy and disease. Wrinkled and gnarled skin contrasts with the ruddy and glowing skin of other rural labourers, while cracked and shapeless lips suggest not only domestic violence but also a more fundamental disorder of character and moral being. Gill Davies has suggested the importance of the mouth as a figure of social and sexual degeneracy in investigative and journalistic writing of the late nineteenth century: 'one recurring symptom of . . . anxiety is a preoccupation with the mouth, both as a focus for appetite and locus of speech'.[40] Pankhurst's potato pickers do not only have purple and shapeless lips, they also have 'loud harsh voices' and 'awful laughter', and even their singing is 'hideous noise' (35). Every mode of expression

which has charmed Pankhurst in other encounters with working women
here repels her. The intensity of her revulsion is so marked that it may need
to be read not simply in terms of a tradition of representation of the labouring poor, but also in terms of a more personal concern with the hideous
female body. In the same issue of the journal, *Germinal,* in which Pankhurst
published 'The Workgirl' she also published a poem called 'The Medusa
of the Dance'. The two poems appear adjacent to each other on the page,
with 'Medusa' on the left-hand side of the page and 'The Workgirl' on the
right, and since both have the same fourteen line form, they could be read
as a sort of distorted mirroring of each other. Medusa has 'thirsty, vampire
lips, vermilion-hued', she has chalk-pink patches which gleam like 'some
leprous evil', or like mildew on a fallen plum. The relentless accumulation
of images of sexual danger, of disease and of a predatory masquerade of
femininity becomes even more explicit as Medusa is described as 'fleshly'
and 'lecherous'. Medusa, her eyes glistening with hate, captures a man in
the dance, and he faints beneath her. So far, so hideous, but once again
there is something of a 'turn' in the last three lines:

> Only thy presence knowing, only fear;
> Drunk with the poison of thy serpent glance,
> His will is thine, Medusa of the dance.

There is just a hint of triumphalism in that surrendering of the will.
Pankhurst has taken us through images of sexual excess and evil to a moment where power has shifted through fear, so that 'his will is thine'. This
fantasy of power triumphant interacts troublingly with the measured and
decorous 'radiant drapings girt with flowers' of 'The Workgirl' as they sit
together on the page.

After reflecting at some length on their hideousness, Pankhurst leaves
the potato pickers to return to their slum dwellings in Berwick-on-Tweed.
But she does not escape from these women and what they represent to her
so easily: 'as I came upon the open road again they overtook me and drove
away past me shouting and singing as though to make the sweet countryside
hideous with the noise' (35). In the typescript version, Pankhurst articulates
the challenge of dealing with women who do not 'belong to the respectable
and self-respecting poor' but are rather part of an amorphous and self-
negating 'army of wrecks and waifs': 'Herein', she says, 'lies one of those
problems that await the free women of tomorrow' (35). Only free women,
she suggests might be able to address the problem of working women who
are not 'self-respecting' but who allow themselves to slip into the mire of
degeneracy. The version of the article published in *Votes for Women* has an

even more striking rhetorical sleight of hand to rid itself of these bruised and sickly potato pickers. After asking whether women could possibly let so many things go wrong in the world if they had the vote themselves, Pankhurst adjusts her focus radically. As she climbs to the top of a steep hill she sees a little house which:

looked warm and cosy as one came in out of the darkness, but the woman who sat knitting there by the fire was sad, because the children she had loved and worked for had gone out into the world, and left her. (36)

This isolated cottage in a rural setting, with a lonely, respectable mother whose work of raising a family is now completed provides Pankhurst with the imagery she needs to end on a triumphant note of assertion of a collective identity through work. The 'great Women's Movement', she tells us, can provide work 'out in the world' for 'her [and] all other women' (36): unless, presumably, they are part of that hideous and degenerate throng of potato pickers.

A PORTRAIT OF THE ARTIST AS A LABOURING WOMAN

Having examined Pankhurst's writings on working women, the rest of this chapter will be concerned with her paintings and drawings. A consideration of Pankhurst's own identity as 'working woman' will be followed by a discussion of the artistic traditions available to her in constructing a visual language of women's labour and the chapter will then conclude with an analysis of the paintings and drawings Pankhurst actually produced as a result of her 1907 tour.

Pankhurst first trained as an artist at Manchester Municipal School of Art where she gained a travelling scholarship which enabled her to study in Venice. She then came top in a national competition for scholarships to the Royal Academy Schools in South Kensington, and spent two further years studying there. It was clearly important to Pankhurst that her art be understood as a form of labour: of her time at art school in Manchester following the death of her father she wrote, 'In spite of our grief and my nervous depression, when absorbed in the work I knew the greatest happiness'.[41] The practice and study of art is here represented as work of sufficient individual significance to counteract both grief over her father's death and her own organic distress which included neuralgia and a number of other chronic complaints. Pankhurst also sees her work as a socially meaningful practice. She had been told by her father: 'If you do not work for others you will not have been worth the upbringing' and she seems to approve and internalize such compulsion to altruism in her approach to her work.[42] Pankhurst articulates her desire for creative independence, but she connects this independence resolutely to a collective struggle for freedom: 'the dream of being an artist in the cause of progress still held me'.[43] Her dream is of a form of self-fulfilment which will also be a kind of political activism, and she believes it might be possible to find this in a career as an artist.

Such an aspiration was by no means straightforward for a woman in the early years of the twentieth century. Paula Gillett and Jan Marsh have both described the substantial barriers to women assuming the identity of 'artist' in the late nineteenth century.[44] Women had problems receiving training in fine art: for example they were not admitted to the Royal Academy Schools at all until 1860. Even when allowed to compete for places at the more prestigious art schools, women students did not have access to the life class, which was seen as an integral part of artistic training for men. They were also excluded from many of the networks of influence, exhibition and reviewing which provided the crucial institutional and ideological support of the art market. For a variety of technical, economic and ideological reasons, women were unlikely to work in oils, but were much more likely to work in the media of water-colour or chalk. Water-colour was seen as a medium of particular importance for an understanding of the history of English painting, but nonetheless it was also seen as an inferior medium, less elevated than painting in oils.[45] Even when women were allowed access to art schools, they were broadly seen as suitable for art training rather than art education, since it was assumed that their future work would be in decorative and illustrative fields rather than in fine art.

In choosing to work in water-colour, and in aspiring to work in public forms of decorative art, Pankhurst was thus following a path which was taken by many of her contemporary women artists. The decorative arts did have a particular significance within a tradition of socialist thought and practice which she greatly admired. Pankhurst's parents, and later her mother, ran a shop selling art objects for the home. They were closely involved with the work of William Morris, who was a frequent visitor to the Pankhurst home. Sylvia Pankhurst cites Morris and Walter Crane as the chief artistic influences on her in her childhood, and since she mentions no other artistic tradition as formative in later years, we have to assume that their work continued to shape what she saw as the possibilities of her work as an artist. Crane had taught at the Manchester Municipal School of Art, and in a book based on a series of his lectures at the School, Crane argued for the importance of decorative art, and specifically of the mural:

'The most important branch of decorative art may be said to be mural decoration, allied as it is with the most fundamental constructive art of all – architecture.'[46] He went on to point out that Italy was the only place to go to see this form of decorative art in its glory and variety. Pankhurst followed his advice when she travelled to Venice in 1902, specifically to study mosaics and frescoes. When she returned she undertook a major project of decoration for a hall which had been dedicated to the memory of her father. She also undertook similar work for the suffrage movement, as has been discussed above.

Certainly in the early years of the century, Pankhurst saw herself primarily as an artist, but her decision to work in water-colour and in decorative forms of art meshed so comfortably with what was expected of women artists at that time that the significance of her art as creative work was and is overlooked. Despite eloquent testimony to the importance of her art by a colleague and friend, 'Sylvia Pankhurst was a great artist. Her work had real greatness, perhaps to compare to Augustus John, only stronger',[47] Pankhurst's artistic career has received little sustained attention. She was herself aware of her marginal status as artist, as can be seen in her correspondence with the National Portrait Gallery over her gift of two portraits of Keir Hardie. Keir Hardie had been her friend, and some would argue her lover, for nearly ten years after she moved to London as an art student, and Pankhurst had undertaken two studies of him in this time, one a water-colour sketch and the other a more complete portrait in chalks (fig. 1). Pankhurst writes to the Director of the National Portrait Gallery that the drawing in chalks is incomplete, really a study for a painting that was never done, and that she offers it only because of the importance of its subject. She claims no merit of her own in the gallery's decision to accept the gift of the portraits, 'I should feel highly honoured that you had accepted my old drawing, only that I recognize the acceptance was not for any merit save its subject', whose place in history she says is important.[48] Pankhurst's own importance as a political figure, far less as an artist, is not mentioned in the correspondence. In an earlier letter to the Director, however, Pankhurst had been rather less willing to disavow the significance of her role as artist. She comments on a request by the suppliers of artists' materials, Winsor and Newton, to use a copy of the chalk drawing for their campaign based on the theme of 'distinguished amateurs'. Pankhurst clearly objects to this description: 'The designation hardly applies to one who abandoned her profession in the hope of becoming more useful and the idea does not appeal to me much.'[49]

Figure 1 'Portrait of James Keir Hardie' by Estelle Sylvia Pankhurst

In the context of the art world's suspicion of 'women amateurs' this unease is hardly surprising. Paula Gillett would certainly suggest that it is the woman amateur who rendered women's acceptance by the art world so difficult in the late nineteenth century, referring to 'the large numbers of female dilettantes whose presence continually frustrated the efforts of those who aspired to professional standards' (*Worlds of Art*, 172). Gillett may be accepting rather uncritically the absolute distinction between these dilettantes and the pursuit of serious art, but she does allow us to grasp something of what was at stake for a trained artist in the designation 'amateur'.

In the context of the suffrage movement, Pankhurst's profession as an artist was publicly acknowledged. When *Votes for Women* provided biographical notes for all forty speakers at a rally in Hyde Park they wrote of Sylvia Pankhurst as follows:

The second daughter of Mrs Pankhurst is an artist . . . Her special line is decorative work, and the beautiful symbolical cartoons at the Prince's Skating Rink Exhibition of the WSPU in 1909 were her work.[50]

Yet one cannot help but notice that her role as the daughter of Emmeline Pankhurst precedes her role as artist. The relation between these two identities was in some turmoil in 1907, at the period when Pankhurst was pursuing her studies of working women. In *The Suffragette Movement*, Sylvia says that her profession as artist offered her the possibility of independence, by which she must have meant more than economic security (215). Since moving to London as an art student in 1904, however, Sylvia had been embroiled in a political movement which was becoming increasingly identified with the personalities of her mother and her sister. Her studies were frequently interrupted by the demands of political activism, particularly after her mother moved to London. Even her journey round Britain was interspersed with frequent demands to help at by-elections or meetings. At this period too, there was a major split in the WSPU following the decision to abolish the constitution of the Union and place effective power in the hands of a very small group, with Emmeline Pankhurst clearly in overall control. Emmeline and Christabel Pankhurst also severed their links with the Independent Labour Party in 1907, though the ILP remained an important part of Sylvia's sense of herself as a political activist. Sylvia must have wondered about her 'independence' as she travelled around painting working women: to what extent did her work give her the means to sustain her own political and familial identities? She certainly reflected on the extent to which this work offered her scope for creativity and innovation as she detailed conversations with women workers in a shoe factory in Leicester:

As the women working there rose from their monotonous task, repeating year in year out the same operation, perhaps machining toe-caps – always toe-caps, they would crowd round my easel full of interest. I was astonished by their oft-repeated comment: 'I should never have the patience to do it!'[51]

Pankhurst is clearly struck that her own labours should seem so painstaking and arduous to women whose work struck her as 'monotonous'.

For Pankhurst, the work of painting and drawing was both creative act and painstaking repetition. It was an activity undertaken in the service of a movement, but also a means to independence: it was both a setting aside and a setting free of 'self'. Some of this complexity can be read in surviving portraits by Pankhurst, and particularly in her two 'self-portraits'. There are two surviving self-portraits of Pankhurst, one in the Museum of London and one in the National Portrait Gallery (see fig. 2). They are similar in style and it is probable that both were done around 1906. Both are unfinished, with detailed drawing of the head and only sketchy outlines of the body. They show a woman with upturned face and an expression somewhere between exaltation and bewilderment. They are done in chalk and charcoal, with a predominance of orange, which links skin tone, hair colour and clothing in a sort of glow. The woman is dressed in prison uniform of brown shapeless serge, though in one of the portraits her cap resembles that of a farm labourer rather than a prisoner.[52] Pankhurst herself describes these images as self-portraits, though they do not closely resemble photographic images of her from the time. On one she has inscribed 'self portrait' and signed it; on the other, rather more elaborately, she has written, 'E. Sylvia Pankhurst. An Impression of Holloway Gaol' and then signed it as well. This doubling of the name, with the intrusion of the 'Impression of Holloway Gaol' leaves us unclear about the subject of the painting. Is she really painting herself, or her prison experience, or Holloway Prison?

Her son's comments on the paintings produce further uncertainty, as he writes of the painting in the National Portrait Gallery: 'It is not really a self-portrait but a drawing of a suffragette by my mother, and I believe she used herself as a model.'[53] The self of these portraits is remarkably elusive: is it the self of the artist, or of the suffrage movement, and why this doubling of portraits neither of which is finished? The further 'interference' caused by the resemblance between one of the paintings and a portrait of a farm girl suggests that Pankhurst's identifications are very fluid at the time when she is painting these portraits, which is also the time she conceived her project of painting women at their toil.

Figure 2 'Self Portrait' by Estelle Sylvia Pankhurst

PAINTING WORKING WOMEN

In order to understand the aesthetic choices Pankhurst made in her paintings of working women, I will now explore the different artistic traditions of
representation which were available to her and on which she drew. Sketches
produced in Pankhurst's youth in the 1890s suggest the early contours of her

visual imagination. For example, she created a series of sketches illustrating famous nursery rhymes. The rhyme 'Bye Baby Bunting' is accompanied by an image of a poor woman, decently dressed and with a clean apron.[54] The woman sits in a simple wooden chair on a bare floor and is lit by light from the fire. The domestic interior in this image is reminiscent of a tradition of genre painting which will be explored below, but it also echoes the moral and pedagogical values of illustrated books for children as they developed in the second half of the nineteenth century. Pankhurst's early notebooks also contain images of knights (of interestingly ambiguous gender), of avenging fairies, of ornate flowers and animals, and of a number of religious subjects, all of which speak to the power of the medievalist revival, associated among others with William Morris, for Pankhurst's imagination. She also produced a number of sketches of young women, dancing and posing, as well as sketches of farm workers gathering hay. Didacticism, charm and fantasy interact in these images to provide a series of concerns and styles distinctive to Pankhurst, but also readable in relation to the cultural context of the 1890s.

It has proved very difficult, however, to find a theoretical or critical language for talking about Pankhurst's paintings of working women, done around a decade later, in 1907. Barbara Winslow's recent study of Pankhurst dismisses her paintings as too derivative, and as insufficiently avant-garde:

Pankhurst's work is traditional; it did not challenge existing portrayals of women – or of men for that matter. In terms of subject matter and use of colour, she was either not aware of or chose to ignore the more avant-garde artists of the nineteenth and early twentieth centuries.[55]

Jackie Duckworth agrees that Pankhurst's style cannot be seen as avant-garde, but suggests nonetheless that her paintings of working women represent some sort of innovation: 'it can be argued that her series on working women was an original concept, that of documentary painting'.[56] Lisa Tickner also suggests that Pankhurst may have been ahead of her time, when she characterizes the paintings as embodying an 'embryonic socialist realism'.[57]

This very concept of 'realism', however, seems to create an impasse for critics of her paintings, who insist repeatedly on the honesty and sympathy expressed in her images, and consequently minimize any sense of the aesthetic choices made in shaping them. Richard Pankhurst talks of his mother as a 'draughtsman in the service of great movements'[58] and goes on to say that her paintings showed sympathy without rhetoric and 'without any attempt to produce works of beauty' (75). Jackie Duckworth argues similarly that:

She recorded these women's lives as a valuable documentation for the future in a style of painting without too much sentimentality or emotion. She painted what she saw, without attempting to beautify or romanticise the subjects for public consumption. ('Pankhurst as an Artist', 44)

This antithesis between a documentary impulse and the distortions of romanticism, has made it difficult to capture the particularities of Pankhurst's work as a creative artist. Yet, it is clear from the range of work that Pankhurst produced that she was making choices about media and styles appropriate to different sorts of work.

Her propaganda work for the suffrage movement tended towards allegorical forms, often with biblical resonances. In addition to her work for the Prince's Skating Rink, Pankhurst also devised the figure of the trumpeting angel that was used on a series of WSPU publications. She also designed the WSPU membership card which depicted a group of working women marching together, with the woman at the front holding aloft a banner demanding votes. The women wear clogs and shawls, one carries a bucket while another carries a baby. They look towards us, though their faces are rather abstractly drawn. Their clothes are recognizably those of working-class women, but they are drawn as blocks of colour rather than as detailed garments. The stripes of one woman's dress and the white aprons worn by the women in front create a lightness of colour tone which contrasts sharply with the dark shawls and clogs. It is a confident style of drawing that draws on familiar icons of female working-class identity to construct its image of women demanding the vote. This decorative style embodying familiar icons of class identity is also found in Pankhurst's work for a proposed campaign by Keir Hardie in support of an unemployment bill. Her poster again shows figures striding towards us, this time both men and women holding a banner which reads 'workless and hungry: vote for the bill'.[59] Both her allegorical and decorative work for the suffrage movement and her propaganda work more generally utilize distinctive styles, which are different from the ways in which she paints and draws the working women she encounters during her research trip. This, at least, suggests that Pankhurst was able to draw on different traditions of representation and to consider questions of specifically aesthetic significance. To suspend such questions in the name of 'realism' is to fail to engage with important aspects of her work.

These aspects include consideration of the different sorts of choices Pankhurst makes in her writings and in her paintings, and the extent to which forms of identification, of objectification and of symbolism vary between these two media. Barbara Green has produced a persuasive argument about the forms of identification staged within the suffrage movement, and how these relate to practices of visual representation and to different forms of looking.[60] Green argues that the characteristically modern '*flâneurs*' gaze, with its combination of roving attention, and disinterested examination, is a particular problem for suffrage activists since it is always resistant to achieved collective identities. Equally, the form of public looking expressed in the gaze of the social investigator, creates a problematic distance between the looker and the subject of examination. The gaze of the *flâneur* and the gaze of the social reformer, which are powerfully historically shaped ways of looking, both construct a complex interaction between the drives towards collectivity and the assertion of individual will and separateness that Green sees as problematic in the context of the suffrage movement. The act of looking, and the practice of embodying that look in an aesthetic object, raise questions of individual and collective identity for both the subject and the object of paintings.

Understanding of the modes of representation available to Pankhurst requires some reflection on the peculiarities of English artistic modernism. Charles Harrison, in *English Art and Modernism 1900–1939* offers a detailed reading of the aesthetic and institutional contexts of art in the early years of the century. He begins with the conflicts at the end of the previous century between artists such as Ford Madox Ford, Hubert von Herkomer and William Morris, who were all broadly committed to the social function of art, and an artist such as Whistler with his commitment to an art based on 'harmony' and 'arrangement', and to a broader aestheticism. Harrison suggests that this conflict was played out over the next twenty years in ways that drew on, and drew in, the broader context of European artistic modernism, but nonetheless remained, to some extent, distinct: 'There was a spectre at the feast of early-twentieth-century English art, an untied loose end of that tradition of care for the representativeness of art's concerns.'[61] This concern with 'representativeness' is at the heart of Sylvia Pankhurst's visual style, and generates quite precise difficulties of style and of framing in her paintings.

Narratives of artistic modernism, like those of literary modernism, have tended to iron out the complexity of competing styles at any given historical moment in favour of a map which identifies particular forms of artistic experimentation as more truly expressive of their moment. Thus we read early twentieth century art in terms of the historical development of Impressionism and the subsequent innovations and challenges of Post-Impressionism: both movements with a powerful hold on our sense of what it is to be modern. As an art student in London in the early years of the century, Pankhurst is certainly likely to have been aware of the work exhibited at the Impressionist Exhibition held in London in 1905. It is true that as a student at the Royal Academy School of Art she may not have been as involved in the analysis and response to such work as would have been common for students at the Slade, which was, as Charles Harrison argues, 'the most important College of Art in London at the turn of the century'.[62] But the activities of groups such as the New English Art Club, and the development of a series of artistic and cultural movements, meant that the London art world, and its art market, were necessarily alert to possibilities of artistic experimentation, and also meant that Pankhurst would have encountered many of these debates and ideas in her years at art school.

The question of how an artist could appropriately represent manual labour was one of broad cultural and political interest at the time. For example, in 1905, we find a man called Lucking Tavener delivering three substantial lectures on artistic traditions for representing human labour to the members of the Walthamstow Brotherhood Church. Tavener begins by asserting that art must serve a moral end. He praises Jean-François Millet for his capacity to elevate agricultural labour 'to a noble dignity which is not usually considered an attribute of that work'.[63] Millet's style is described as simple but dignified, and Tavener approves his representation of types rather than of individuals. Similarly, La Thangue's images of rural labour are mentioned with approval, and Tavener particularly mentions the spiritual elevation his figures can express. The influence of Ruskin on Tavener's preferences and his analyses is clear and explicitly acknowledged: Tavener begins by citing some remarks by Ruskin on the technique and social meanings of Dutch genre art before turning to the more recent French artists for his models.

Such elevated figuration of agricultural labour contrasts sharply with the visual styles employed in a magazine such as *The Graphic*, which concentrated on the distress and sufferings of urban populations. *The Graphic* was founded in 1869, and its visual imagery was shaped both by writings, for example by Dickens or Mayhew, which detailed the ugliness and the horror of the city, but also by the impulse to social investigation expressed in the work of a writer like Charles Booth. Hubert von Herkomer gives expression to both the documentary and the melodramatic aspects of this mode of imagining the working poor in his painting *On Strike* of 1891. This painting depicts a working family standing in a doorway. The man looks sternly into the distance while his wife leans on his shoulder and holds a small baby in her arms. The painting carefully renders the detail of industrial poverty, and simultaneously constructs this poverty as an icon of righteous suffering. The helplessness of the infant, the dependency of the wife and the isolation of the man all interact to create a heightened emotional response. This melodramatic charge which inhabits so many representations of industrial squalor, with its *frisson* of heightened emotion precipitating an anxious withdrawal, was also part of the legacy Pankhurst had to negotiate in her own work.

The aesthetic and the political questions set in play by the representation of working women has been the subject of a recent fascinating study by the art historian T. J. Clark. In *Farewell to an Idea: Episodes from a History of Modernism*, Clark devotes a chapter to the analysis of Camille Pissarro's 1891 painting, 'Two Young Peasant Women'.[64] Much of Clark's interest in this analysis lies in connecting Pissarro's stylistic and technical choices to the quite particular context of French political life in the 1890s, and specifically to Pissarro's twin commitments to modernism and to anarchism. Through this account, Clark also weaves the drama of Camille Pissarro's correspondence with his son Lucien, who was living in England and coming under what his father considered to be the pernicious influence of symbolism and of Walter Crane. We have already seen that Crane, who taught at the Manchester School of Art, was of great importance for Pankhurst in her development of a decorative style. There is thus an interesting sense in which Clark's very precisely located reading of one painting opens out towards a much more general and more explicitly theoretical set of concerns with the aesthetic and the political choices embodied in any particular visual representation, in a way that can help us to read some of the formal aspects of Sylvia Pankhurst's work in the early twentieth century.

It is not possible here to recapitulate what is a deeply layered and complexly structured argument about Pissarro and his place within modernism, but I would like to draw attention to a number of issues Clark raises in his analysis which have a clear relevance to the questions we have been exploring in this chapter. Clark reads Pissarro's work through a series of oppositions: between imaginative sympathy and 'technique'; between monumental figure painting and scenes from everyday life; between surface and the depth that is also history; and between the singular and the uniform, all of which will inform my reading of Pankhurst's images. He also suggests a further fundamental opposition in Pissarro's approach to his painting between a documentary and a decorative impulse: 'the tug-of-war between necessary intensification and easy romanticizing, or between ornament and photography' (61). To restore this sense of conflict to Pankhurst's images, which have been so quickly read as simply 'photographic', would be a substantial critical advance.

Clark connects Pissarro's work to what he sees as a turning point in French political culture, a moment when socialism turns definitively against anarchism, saying:

> There are moments in history when the very nature of class power, and the forms taken by its manufacture of the future, make questions of ethics and rhetoric – questions of representation – primary, or at least unavoidable. (103)

Pankhurst was also producing her work at such a highly charged moment in history, when both class and gender power were the site of significant contestation, in which she was, of course, centrally involved. For her, too, I would argue, questions of representation were primary. Reading Pankhurst's visual style is one way of understanding how she responded to the challenges of such ethical and rhetorical questions. We will find evidence of imaginative sympathy, but also of foregrounded painterly technique; we will find traces of both the monumental and the everyday in her figures of working women; and we will also see Pankhurst trying to find visual strategies to move towards the temporality of history. Her style is decorative, ornamental and sometimes romanticizing, but as Clark remarks:

> The key terms here – 'decoration', 'ornament', 'synthesis', even 'style' – shift wildly in meaning from text to text all through the fin de siècle. And that is because they are called on to do the (magic) work, which modernism still believed possible, of soldering together the aesthetic and the social. (130)

The conviction that labour could be read, above all, as a purposeful human activity, drew Pankhurst also towards the concerns of seventeenth-century Dutch genre painters. The work of Nicolaes Maes in the mid-seventeenth century provides a useful example of such genre painting, which chose for its subject humble forms of labour, often carried out in a domestic setting. Maes's painting 'The Spinner' shows an old woman alone working at her spinning wheel. The interior is sufficiently specified to tell us her economic standing is low, but nothing suggests hunger or suffering. The woman is decently dressed, she looks down at her work in concentration and the whole image is lit by sunlight from a window which is not itself visible in the painting. The careful arrangement of the body in a socially marked space, 'focussed in strong light and fading gradually into shadowed background'[65] and the concentrated absorption in labour are also found in Maes's 'A Woman Scraping Parsnips Watched by a Child'. Here, both mother and child focus on the work being done, but the way that both are captured in the same ray of light allows the painting to suggest intimacy and social cohesion within the very abstraction of labour. Pankhurst frequently paints her working women near a window, absorbed in their work, and with sunlight creating a very clear sense of depth in their interior space. The elevation of the everyday implicit in this style informs her painting of women workers while also creating that important sense of intimacy.

Visual representation of labour may aim to construct sympathy, to provide an allegory of social relationships, to construct a critique of industrialization, or to elevate the labourer as social type. It may also, of course, aim to inform or teach its viewer about the techniques and materials of a particular trade. William Sewell has explored changing representations of 'the mechanical arts', particularly in France, and finds significant historical variation in the arrangement and significance of such pictures. Sewell identifies a tendency in seventeenth-century illustrations towards spiritual elevation of the labouring process, but also finds an explicitly didactic preoccupation with tools and techniques. In the eighteenth century, and specifically in the *Encyclopédie*, human figures become small and inconsequential, dwarfed by images of the tools and equipment with which they worked, and isolated from their fellow workers: 'the odd isolation of workers in the *Encyclopédie* plates signified an opposition to the very notion of a trade community'.[66] By the mid-nineteenth century, Sewell finds the confidence in an ordered and scientific world of work markedly diminished in illustrations that stress the cluttered and chaotic nature of human interaction and of the labouring process in large factories. Sewell ends his analysis in the nineteenth century since 'engravings and lithography were almost totally replaced by photography at the end of the nineteenth century' (286). Pankhurst, however, is clearly an exception to this more general decline, since the documentary impulse in her painting remains strong. She is careful to include relevant tools of the trade she is representing, to show machinery with accuracy, and to suggest the precise organization of a factory space.

PANKHURST PAINTING WORKING WOMEN

In painting working women, then, Pankhurst was responding to a number of traditions of visual representations from high art and from popular journalism. She did not actually produce paintings of all the trades she wrote about: her paintings and drawings deal with agricultural labourers, fisher lassies, women in potteries, in shoe factories and in the cotton mills of Glasgow. The pit-brow women and the potato pickers are striking absences, though those absences may have rather different meanings. Pit-brow women had been so extensively represented throughout the nineteenth century that Pankhurst may have felt reluctant to add to the circulation of these images of muscular and trouser-wearing women. The potato pickers posed a more intense problem for Pankhurst, as she could see them only in terms of degeneration: there seemed to be no possibility of abstracting from their damaged bodies the meaning of 'labour'.

Had Pankhurst's impulse in painting working women been simply documentary, presumably, as Sewell's argument suggests, photography would have been her favoured medium. Instead she followed the more burdensome and time-consuming route of producing a series of paintings in water-colour and gouache and a series of drawings in charcoal and chalk. I will conclude this chapter by examining some of the images she produced, and considering them in relation to the traditions of visual representation outlined above, as well as the broader issues of labour, selfhood and representation which have emerged throughout this chapter and will emerge throughout this book.

In her paintings and drawings of women involved in the pottery trade, Pankhurst presents their working environment with great precision and detail. 'In a Pot Bank: Scouring and Stamping the Maker's Name on the Biscuit China' (fig. 3), depicts a line of working women at a bench. They are bent over their work, absorbed by the precision of their labour. Tools and techniques of labour are rendered in details, while the angle and intensity of illumination stresses the form of the finished cups and jugs laid upon the bench, rather than the faces of the working women. 'In a Pot Bank: Finishing off the Edges of the Unbaked Pots on a Whirler', shows a woman working alone, head bent in concentration, as she puts the finishing touches to a pot. Around her, on a bench, are numerous tools of the trade. She is simply but respectably dressed with a large clean apron. We have already seen in Pankhurst's prose writings on women and labour the importance to her of women's dress. Pankhurst's concern to represent these working women's costume accurately may partly be generated by the very acute sense within the suffrage movement of the importance of dress as part of the way in which women are judged in public spaces.[67] It could, however, also be connected to Pankhurst's youthful representations of domestic and social respectability, signified, as we saw above in the discussion of her illustrations for nursery rhymes, by a clean white apron. Dress does not serve to individuate in Pankhurst's paintings: it does not figure the desire or aspirations of individual women but rather places them within specific class and gendered spaces of decency. Pankhurst's pottery worker looks away from us and is represented as unaware of the look of any spectator:

Figure 3 'In a Pot Bank: Scouring and Stamping the Maker's Name on the Biscuit China'
by Estelle Sylvia Pankhurst

she is concentrated, alone and intact in her labour. There is a monumental quality to this figure, expressed in her framing and in the position of her body, which is simultaneously undercut by her modest stature as she leans over her work. Her apron is illuminated by a shaft of sunlight from the row of windows which runs along the top of the work bench. These windows are clearly necessary to an industrial process that requires precise and careful work, but in the painting they serve to remind us of domestic interiors, and of the ways in which the glow of light can carry associations of elevation or spirituality.

The same lighting effect can be found in 'An Old-fashioned Pottery, Turning Jasper Ware' where the skilled male worker stands a little in front of the woman who is treading the machine that turns the pottery. The arrangement of figures could at first suggest a domestic coupling, but both characters are absorbed in their labour and appear quite separate. Their relations call to mind Pankhurst's reflections on the skilled pottery worker who is nonetheless unfulfilled, and his unskilled female assistant who cannot even rise to the point of aspiring to self-realization through labour. Near the male worker are a series of tools, and an open book with a ruler balanced on top: he appears to be making plans or calculations. The young woman looks into the middle distance while she carries on with her repetitive labour. Yet aspects of the image also undermine any sense of the woman as marginalized, which appeared so clearly in the narrative account. Pankhurst has rendered the space beyond the woman in some detail, and our eye is drawn to the door beyond her. This creates a tension in the painting between the clearly iconographic, and brightly illuminated, foreground and the more obscure further reaches of the factory. But as we struggle to read the significance of this, we cannot help but pause to consider, and to register the significance of, the woman worker.

'Old-fashioned Pottery: Transferring the Pattern onto the Biscuit' (fig. 4) shows two women working at a bench, with their heads bent down in concentration. They are watched by a man who stands in half-shadow. They are both lit up by sunlight, which also catches the glaze of their newly decorated pottery. The grain of the wood on the bench and the door is indicated with care, as are the details of brick and woodwork on the walls, in ways that suggest the human scale of craft labour rather than the impersonal production of a factory. It is indeed striking that two of these finished paintings focus on work in an 'old-fashioned' pottery, where skilled labour is still foregrounded. As we will see below, the images of work in newer factories are much less detailed, showing the work processes and the finished products, but leaving the women themselves obscure.

Figure 4 'Old Fashioned Pottery: Transferring the Pattern onto the Biscuit' by Estelle
Sylvia Pankhurst

Figure 5 'In a Leicester Boot Factory' by Estelle Sylvia Pankhurst

Pankhurst's charcoal and pastel drawing of a woman trimming leather in a shoe factory, 'In a Leicester Boot Factory' (fig. 5) also obscures the woman's face. She is seated at a bench, in front of a window with the sunlight illuminating her head and arm. The details of the work are hidden by her body, though we can see pieces of leather and the outline of a machine. The image is one of absorption and concentration. This woman is clearly in an industrial environment, but is working alone. This isolation can be read as increasing the sense of control in this woman's labour since there is no evidence of supervision or of a broader industrial context within which her work may be shaped. In her neat dress, her concentration and her isolation this woman might be read as a figure of skilled labour and even of social autonomy. But the absence of any facial expression rather undercuts such a reading since there is an uncomfortable sense of something missing in this painting: our visual field is dominated by sunlight and by the spatial contours of the painting rather than by the woman who is at its centre. The sympathetic identification this painting seeks to secure in its use of light and its choice of object is suspended, as if we were waiting for the woman to turn round.

The painting of a group of women working in this same factory is unusual in Pankhurst's work because it represents labour as social: although the women are not interacting in any way, but they are seated close together at their benches, facing each other. Representations of working women in suffrage publications nearly always feature individual women, who are presented as typical of their labour, so this effort at figuring collectivity is striking. Here perhaps the challenges of constructing a collectivity that is more than imaginary are entering Pankhurst's visual imagination. Once more, however, we are not allowed to read emotion or mood in the faces of the women, and their bodies, arranged formally in an industrialized space, do not express any individuality. Neither collective nor individual identities are particularly vigorously realized in this painting which seems to be more interested in the geometry of its spaces than in the particularity of its labouring bodies.

In examining the images of fisher lassies at work, we might expect to find something of the vigour, energy and robust sociability that Pankhurst associated with this form of labour in her writing. Surprisingly, however, these women also seem absorbed and isolated. One woman who is cutting herrings is wrapped in layers of clothing, and her face is turned away. She is surrounded by barrels of fish and a huge crate of herrings awaits processing. In another painting, two women who work together packing fish are also rather obscured by their clothing, and one has her back turned to us. Their posture is upright and static and they seem fixed by the beam of light which illuminates their heads and their arms.

The women agricultural workers painted by Pankhurst are figured in a rather different style, though they too seem caught and fixed by the framing of the painting. Pankhurst uses blocks of colour and employs a looser painting technique to suggest the natural landscape in which they labour. The farm machinery we see is big and heavy, and the women are dwarfed by it: an effect particularly marked in the painting where a woman is standing below ground level while feeding a threshing machine. Pankhurst's chalk drawing of a young woman farm labourer shows us the woman's face and torso, though the rest of the body disappears in vague outline. Her arms are raised, but her hands are completely missing. Perhaps Pankhurst's particular difficulty with completing portraits is emerging here, but it may also be that the attempt to represent both facial expression and active labour is what defeats her. Despite Pankhurst's aspiration in her writing to find in women's work a kind of agency, where work brings an awareness of selfhood, she cannot seem to figure this visually. The women slip towards abstractions of labour, and painterly precision is reserved for the tools and the locations of their labour.

Finally, there is one other group of workers to whom Pankhurst turned her artistic attention: women working in a cotton mill in Glasgow. Pankhurst produced no sustained descriptive writing about these women, though it is clear from remarks throughout her published work that she found the cotton mills alien environments and the women unhealthy and exhausted. Her painting of a young woman, 'In a Glasgow Cotton Mill: Minding a Pair of Fine Frames', unusually depicts a figure looking directly towards us. The woman's face is represented in considerable detail, and her expression is one of sorrow. She sits on a basket, apparently posed for the painting with her hands neatly folded on her lap. Her age is very hard to determine, since her small stature might suggest youth, but her lined face suggests maturity. It is an image of striking passivity: the woman's body is dominated by the massive looms and she seems fixed both by the space in which she is working and by the arrangement of the painting. Her dress is once more represented with care: a striped long skirt, a clean blouse and a long dark apron. This neat and orderly dress suggests some sort of control and 'respectability' even within this alien industrial environment. Despite the look towards us, however, it is an uncomfortable sort of interpellation by passivity that this painting stages: it invites the gaze of the social reformer with its dialectic of sympathy and withdrawal rather than any form of identification. We are drawn by the pity of it but repelled by its immobility and by the dehumanization expressed in the woman's proximity to a massive machine whose rhythms constitute the meaning of her labour. Pankhurst's second painting of the cotton mill, 'Changing a Yarn Package', is again rather a dark imagining of labour. The windows that can be seen in the painting are far away at the end of an enormous frame and their light does not really enter the painting. A bare-footed women is turned half towards us while she changes yarn on the frame, but once again her expression is sorrowful and blank. Her raised arms do not suggest vigour but rather exhaustion since they are bent awkwardly with just sufficient elevation to reach the machine. This woman is alone and there is no sign of any other human presence in the cotton mill. The look invited by this painting, and staged within it, is a rather blank abstraction, an intellectualized response to the fact of alienated labour.

For Pankhurst there did not seem, finally, to be any tenable way of looking, and indeed she stopped painting not many years after this tour of Britain in search of working women at their toil. Pankhurst talks about this ending of her career as a painter in ways that suggest the decision was not a very explicit one: 'I was working on what was to prove, though I did not realize it, a last, unfinished effort of a big picture.'[68] This last 'unfinished effort' took place in 1911, not even half-way through Pankhurst's life. The suffrage movement and the socialist movement absorbed all of Pankhurst's energies and time for the following decades, and her abandoning of her work as a painter may be read as simply an unfortunate result of the urgency of political activism. Yet that 'unfinished effort' does also suggest a problem internal to her work as a painter: something that could not be represented, or at least could not be completed. Charles Harrison draws attention to the increased emphasis on self-expression among artists which followed the Post-Impressionist Exhibition of 1910–11, quoting Desmond MacCarthy's introduction to the catalogue of the Exhibition:

In no school . . . does individual temperament count for more . . . its methods enable the individuality of the artist to find completer self-expression in his work than is possible to those who have committed themselves to representing objects more literally.[69]

The self-expression of individuality was increasingly disavowed by Pankhurst, however, in her commitment to a collectivist political theory and practice. Her work with the East London Federation of the Suffragettes involved the establishment of collective forms of living and working, including cheap workers' canteens, a day nursery and a collective toy factory. Her imagination turned away from the vigour and freedom of labour for the individual and towards the freedom represented by a historical progress beyond the existing divisions of labour. Thus, for example, in 'Co-operative Housekeeping' a fictional text of 1920, Pankhurst writes of the fulfilment of accepting collective social provision of domestic labour and of child-care, a position she could not have endorsed a decade earlier.[70] Her political activism, in both the suffrage and the socialist movements led her to an increasing suspicion of self-expression: individual will was represented as a kind of egoism and Pankhurst increasingly stressed the need for sacrifice in order to construct the conditions of collectivity. Her painting was just one of many necessary sacrifices: 'as an artist the world has no real use for you; in that capacity you must fight a purely egotistical struggle'.[71]

Pankhurst's revulsion from this 'purely egotistical struggle' will find an echo in the writings of D. H. Lawrence, which will be discussed in the next chapter. We will see how Lawrence's commitments to vital and embodied forms of selfhood are conceived through a series of arguments about the nature and the significance of modern labour, and also about the perniciousness of egotistical forms of will. In the concluding chapter we will see crucial aspects of Pankhurst's thinking about the labour movement, collectivism and political change reconfigured within the particular contexts of syndicalism and the practice and theory of the general strike. Identification with labour, and the capacity to represent the energies and aspirations of the labour movement, are a central and continuing part of modernism's negotiations with labour and with selfhood.

CHAPTER FOUR

D. H. Lawrence: labour, organicism and the individual

We have now seen how Sylvia Pankhurst's political thinking and her activism, as well as her imaginative and creative life, were formed through particular engagements with the category of 'labour'. Work was, for Pankhurst, the source of ideas about the possibility of collective identities and also about the sustainability of a notion of agency, understood as the capacity to work consciously and productively to remake aspects of her contemporary world. In this chapter, I will once more explore the significance of labour for the thought and the imaginative writings of a central cultural figure of the period. In turning to the work of D. H. Lawrence, I will be examining someone who is part of the broad canon of formally innovative modernist writers, but also someone who is importantly connected to some of the key philosophical traditions for the analysis of labour and selfhood with which this study began. D. H. Lawrence's writing engages with modernity, selfhood and the activity of human labour in distinctive and complex ways. His search for models of human subjectivity based on the particular properties and patterns of the human organism intersects with convictions about historical change and social structure to generate original and often disturbing models of the meanings and the nature of human labour. The aim of this chapter is to discern the movement of Lawrence's thought and writing in order to understand the role that labour plays in his models of history and of selfhood. The challenge is to connect this quite particular trajectory to other cultural and philosophical texts of the period in ways that allow us to understand more about the social and discursive categories of the last century. My assumption is not that Lawrence's texts are exemplary, far less typical, but rather that in his writing one can discern the traces of other cultural engagements with selfhood, history and labour and that through them we may come to understand important aspects of the cultural history of the early decades of the twentieth century. In reading Lawrence's texts my desire above all is to maintain their strangeness, and not to plead their case. My hope is that this distanced relationship to his writing will allow me better to understand it as a historical text.

The importance of labour for Lawrence forms part of James Knapp's argument about the relations between modern labour and literary modernism in *Literary Modernism and the Transformation of Work*.[1] Knapp's important study maps, in particular, the ways in which modernist literary texts responded to the rationalization and fragmentation of work under the influence of Scientific Management. For Knapp, Taylorism constitutes the primary rhetorical and ideological framework for the experience of labour in the early twentieth century, with its rigid demarcations between physical and mental labour and its reduction of much work to 'mindless mechanical function' (7). This transformation of work is related by Knapp to a transformation of subjectivity, as he examines the institutional, the educational and the political structures put in place to produce the modern worker. Knapp's central argument about literary modernism, and about Lawrence, is that they failed to find an oppositional mode in which to critique the pervasive fragmentation and functionalism of Taylorist versions of labour:

While modernist literature spoke loudly against the degradation of all kinds of work, it nevertheless tacitly accepted contemporary assumptions about the instrumentality of reason, and so reproduced within itself a social discourse which would deny to art any authority to address social and economic issues. (18)

Knapp suggests that Lawrence's antipathy to mechanization and his commitment to the idea of the organism actually leave him unable to grasp the conditions of modern labour other than through an instinct of withdrawal. Knapp argues that Lawrence creates characters who can never do more than act out the pathologies of their own historical moment, who can never imagine or sustain any radical critique: 'his characters often speak about their true, deep selves, and yet that talk mostly functions as resistance to the social codes which are in fact shaping their words, their actions, even their feelings' (89).

While much of Knapp's reading of Lawrence is both historically and critically acute, his observation that Lawrence's resistance to the new order of work 'assumed a form which has made him a curiously problematic figure' (75) leaves a significant space for the further exploration of both this curiosity and this problematic. Lawrence's views on work changed in fundamental ways over the course of his writing career. His commitment to organism takes a number of different forms, and these have diverse and complex implications for the ways in which he is able to imagine the experience of human labour. His very explicit engagement with Nietzschean ideas of individuality place him in a philosophical trajectory which includes his exploration of pre-Socratic Greek philosophies, while his interest in comparative anthropology and religion offer a number of images and narratives that cannot simply be seen as the waste products of Taylorism. To see all of Lawrence's heterogeneous attempts to articulate a poetics of the organism as simply a reproduction of the Taylorist division between manual and mental labour is to risk conceding hegemonic coherence to a Taylorism that was always in itself both partial and riven.

These 'heterogeneous attempts', which I will explore below, have been interestingly connected to the philosophical and political concerns of the suffrage movement by Bruce Clarke in his study of *Dora Marsden and Early Modernism: Gender, Individualism, Science*, a connection that is particularly pertinent in the context of my discussion of the suffrage movement in the previous chapter.[2] Marsden is a fascinating figure, whose career weaves together the political context of the suffrage movement and the literary experimentations of modernism in quite distinct ways. After a period of militant suffrage activism within the WSPU between 1909 and 1911, Marsden then moved on to a career writing for and editing a series of influential and innovative magazines, including *The New Freewoman* and *The Egoist*. Although both the suffrage movement and egoism were to be sources of consistent anxiety for Lawrence, Bruce Clarke makes a very convincing case for the idea that Lawrence and Marsden shared important philosophical reference points in their individual projects of constructing new forms of modern culture; reference points that Clarke connects through the category of 'evolutionary vitalism' (121). Reading Lawrence through Marsden, Clarke develops an account of Lawrence's investments in matter, energy and life and in particular of Lawrence's non-egoistic theorizations of individuality. In a broad-ranging and very persuasive reading of Lawrence's 'Study of Thomas Hardy', Clarke explores the interaction of images and arguments derived from evolutionary biology and from thermodynamics and considers their mobilization by Lawrence in support of a project of creative wastefulness. Perhaps unsurprisingly, given the overall emphasis of Clarke's study, he also points out the central role of the suffrage movement within Lawrence's argument as he connects Lawrence's concerns in this essay to the broader philosophical and political commitments of early modernism: 'Lawrence joined a major sector of early modernist culture in advancing an evolutionary vitalism as a plausible response to the threat of entropy' (163).

One major omission in Clarke's reading of Lawrence, however, is any sustained attention to the category of 'labour' which, as I will argue below is central both to the argument of 'Study of Thomas Hardy' and to Lawrence's creative output as a whole. Clarke refers us to Knapp's study, and endorses its critique of Lawrence's instrumentalism, but he does not develop his insights into the complexity and variety of vitalist thought within Lawrence's work in ways that help us to understand Lawrence's persistent and productive engagement with modern labour. Clarke helps us to move philosophically and imaginatively from suffragism to Lawrence, seeing important continuities within their apparently diverse cultural and political commitments, but further work is needed to understand how the category of 'labour' might inflect or infect this continuity. The aim of this chapter is to constitute just such a philosophical and critical map of Lawrence's engagement with vitalism, organicism and modern labour.

'SO SHALL MAN FOR EVER COME AND GO, GO TO HIS WORK'[3]

Lawrence's 'Foreword' to his novel *Sons and Lovers* (1913) contains a forceful expression of his philosophical and ethical non-conformity. Beginning with John's Gospel and the foundational metaphor of the Word made Flesh, Lawrence develops in this essay a counter-Gospel in which the Flesh stands for all that is originary, unknowable and unutterable while the Word designates all forms of conscious human knowledge which are seen as derivative and contingent. Lawrence argues that there is a necessary hierarchy of Flesh and the Word, and that human cognition can only securely address the Word: 'When we say "I", we mean "The Word I am," this Flesh I am is beyond me' (467). We often, Lawrence suggests, misrecognize this hierarchy and attribute agency to ourselves as rational individuals when we are simply playing out the logic of our species being.

The ramifications of this ethical and philosophical position are worked out in Lawrence's metaphors. Thus, for example, Lawrence compares conscious and cerebral forms of being to the fruit of an apple tree, which is a creative and productive expression of the fruit tree, but is also transient and prone to rotting. The apple blossom in its fragility and beauty then designates the miracle of creativity. The seed, however, encompasses all the qualities of fruit and blossom since it carries them all within its self. The relation between microcosm and macrocosm is such that each replicates the other, so that the seed contains and produces an apple tree as an apple tree contains and produces a seed. The seed is thus the closest to the Flesh, for Lawrence, because its boundaries are beyond the imagination and it partakes of the temporal space of the infinite.

The logic of this image brings Lawrence to a consideration of the relations between woman and Flesh, both being expressed through the ontological peculiarity of the seed:

So we take the seed as the starting point in this cycle. The woman is the Flesh. She produces all the rest of the flesh, including the intermediary pieces called man – and these curious pieces called man are like stamens that can turn into exquisite coloured petals. That is, they can beat out the stuff of their life thin, thin, thin, till it is a pink or purple petal, or a thought, or a Word. (470)

The Word is thus an expression of the Flesh, but it has become thin and immaterial to the point of being insubstantial; a vision that might also be an illusion. Woman, in this model, mediates the Flesh, and stands in for the eternal in relation to both the father and the son. The mother, in so far as she is Flesh and seed is the Father, is also the mediator of the Father and the point of access to the eternal: 'In her we go back to the Father: but like the witnesses of the Transfiguration, blind and unconscious' (471).

This complex and refracted relation to the mother as symbol, as archetype and as flesh has particular resonances in relation to the narrative of *Sons and Lovers* which I will not discuss further here, but it also connects to one of Lawrence's many attempts to think through, or to represent imaginatively, the activity of human labour. From his imaginings of flowers, petals and blossom on the tree, Lawrence moves next to a scene of bees in the hive. The hive is here the family home, though whether considered from the point of view of the son or the father is at first unclear. The woman is the queen bee, who is the source of energy, of transformation and of creative production. The worker bee is a son who homes home to the queen bee as the foundation and origin of his being. But the worker bee must continually leave the hive; he must 'for ever come and go, go to his work'.

The model here is both dynamic and organicist. There is a force that compels the bee towards perpetual activity, towards leaving and re-entering the hive and renewing both the hive and the flowers through his labours.[4] Lawrence expresses the playing out of this compulsion thus, 'so God expels him forth to waste himself in utterance, in work, which is only God the Father realizing himself in a moment of forgetfulness. Thus the eternal working' (472). Here work, word and selfhood interact in a continually mobile process of exchange between father and son. The son wastes himself in work, though whether this is the creative waste of which Lawrence will write in his 'Study of Thomas Hardy' or waste in the sense of failed creativity is not clear. The Word is the work of the son, which is a sort of waste of his self, but it is also the self-realization of the father who achieves this only in a moment of forgetfulness. But what is being forgotten here: the self, the son or the work? Lawrence continues to develop the image, describing the moment when the son engages in work, which is language, as a moment of delight and joy: 'as if the Father took delight in seeing himself for a moment unworking, for a moment wasting himself that he might know himself' (472). The son's work, then wastes both his own self and the self of the father, but only the father comes to knowledge, admittedly through the mediation of forgetfulness, through this process and he does it by the activity of 'unworking'.

There is a conscious pushing towards paradox in this writing, which insists on polarities and hierarchies while simultaneously undoing them through the fluidity and resonances of its imagery. This becomes even clearer as Lawrence describes the individual flower, in so far as it is an expression of species being, as a 'waste of productiveness' which is also a 'moment of joy', of saying 'I am I'. This assertion of the brute fact of particularity and being is immediately undercut, however, by labour and by language. The flower that is a Flower is the 'selfsame waste' as that of the labour embodied in 'every table or chair a man makes', and this activity of manual labour is also a 'fixing into stiffness and deadness of a moment of himself' (472). The 'I am I' that follows this twist of Lawrence's 'I' looks very much like a misrecognition, a comforting illusion rather than the secure conviction of particularity and individuality.

So the waste expressed by the flower in its moment of blooming, which is also an expression of its connection to the infinite, is the 'selfsame' waste as the deadened and inert embodiment of human labour in the table or chair. Perhaps, but it cannot be identical since only in the case of the flower is this waste connected to perception of the infinite. The waste that is a property of work is a deadening and fixing process in which the recognition of the self has become illusory. Thus, when Lawrence writes 'Now every woman, according to her kind, demands that a man shall come home to her with joy and weariness of the work he has done during the day' (472), woman has become part of that deadening and alienating process at least as much as she is part of the dynamism and creativity of the hive.

If the dynamic exchange of energies through continual work and continual return to the hive is not sustained both the man and the woman will be destroyed. Indeed if the mother is not renewed by such activity from the father she must turn to the son and say 'be you my go-between' (473), since there must be a 'go-between from Woman to Production'. This, for Lawrence makes the son, structurally if not actually, the lover of his mother and creates division and pain. The relations between work, the public and the private are thus locked into a necessary pattern, within which individuals must play out the drama of their lives. Work is always outside, apart from the woman, and also carries with it the taint of fixity, inertia and egoism.

We can find this same tension between labour as expression of the shape or pattern of life and labour as deadening toil in some of Lawrence's early poems. 'Dreams Old and Nascent', for example, figures the labouring body centrally in its exploration of time, fantasy and illusion.[5] The poem begins with the image of the world as a 'painted memory', or in an earlier draft as a 'painted fresco'. The world is thus to some extent the product of human invention, either consciously through the artistry of the fresco, or more unconsciously through the shaping power of memory. The painting offers patterns, illumination and the comfort of a dream, but it also acts as a form of constriction and enclosure, 'compelling my life to conform'. The comforting quality of these dreams in the poem fades before the recognition of their power to confine and also before their increasing abstraction, 'They have no hands, they have no bodies, all/These shapes that now are dreams and once were men.' So the substantial human body, whose labour is metonymically represented by its hands, has dissolved into a comforting glow which is also the destructive death of change.

In the second section of the poem 'The surface of dreams is broken, the arras is torn/There's a breach in the walls of the past, lets the daylight through.' This breach lets in 'fluent figures' of working men who are strikingly 'alive, and with something to do'. Their purpose and their activity remove them from the enclosing abstractions of the earlier dream. These active figures each have a secret which 'stirs in his limbs': the secret is never revealed to us but seems to be associated with their vitality and their capacity to 'prove/With a touch the dead and the living'. These working men are certainly on the side of life and of change, but the image rapidly becomes one of violence and conflict:

> They come for strife,
> For the ripping of arras, and smashing of walls, and the fight for life;
> With axe in hand, and the hammer, and the pick-axe over-arching.

The poem pleads for the confining prison of memories to be torn away, for the comforting illusions of habit to be undone, but simultaneously reveals that the breaking down of the prison will reveal horrors as well as release the vital energies of the labouring body: 'the inner rooms are such, they dismay/The heart, all crowded with slaves, most working, some few at play'. The ontological and epistemological status of dreams disturbs the next section of the poem: dreams are 'beloved' and 'sure', but also 'worn out'. The whole world now becomes a house of dreams, where those who dream suffer in, or despite, their oblivion. The dream is now ghastly, no longer the comforting illusions of the beginning of the poem but rather impure, choking and corrupting. The active, fluent lively men have been replaced by 'The ghastly dream of labour' which has become mechanical and industrial. Vitality and energy are choked by images of greed, money, poison and corruption.

Yet the labouring bodies sustain their power to renew and to transform:

> Oh come, oh men along the railway! Oh come as men
> And break the walls of possession of all the wide world!
> Give us air, we cry. Oh, let us but breathe again!

So these labouring bodies which had drifted into the 'ghastly dream of labour' can now be the means of undoing this horror, can refresh and re-vive and can escape the nightmare of acquisitive possession. 'Men with the axe and the pick-axe' will be the means of destroying 'the walls of the filthy dream'. What is left by the end of the poem is neither the comfort-ing illusions of familiarity nor the nightmares of mechanical labour but rather the mere fact of human activity, itself only perceptible as a sort of dreaming:

> And what is life, but the swelling and shaping the dream in the flesh!
> And our bodies molten drops of dream-blood that swirl and swell
> In a tissue, as all the molten cells in the living mesh
> Of a rose-tree move to roses and thorns and a delicate smell.

This attempt to figure the relations between universality and particularity depends again on a parallelism between microcosm and macrocosm, in this instance the individual cell and the rose tree. The vital force of which the poem is dreaming is itself an embodied, fleshly dream and the individual bodies that sustain and contain this vital force are simply small particles, or drops, of a larger and more general substance that is 'dream-blood'. In earlier drafts of the poem this recognition of the parallel substance and form of the particular and the universal is explicitly figured through the activity of labour and more prominently read through the activity of the conscious 'I'. 'The terrible ecstasy of the consciousness that I am life' is expressed through and in tension with 'the miracle of the whole, the widespread, labouring concentration' in a way that locks labour, self-consciousness and the unconscious, by which Lawrence means the non-intellectual, indissolubly together:

Oh the terror of lifting the innermost I out of the sweep of the
    impulse of life,
And watching the great Thing labouring through the whole round
    flesh of the world;
And striving to catch a glimpse of the shape of the coming dream,
As it quickens within the labouring, white-hot metal,
Catch the scent and the colour of the coming dream,
Then to fall back exhausted into the unconscious, molten life!

'IF HE MUST WORK, LET HIM WORK A FEW HOURS A DAY,
A VERY FEW.'[6]

In his 'Study of Thomas Hardy', Lawrence is once more concerned to
capture the dynamic processes characteristic of organic life. His text begins
with the systole and diastole of the beating heart, their opposition and
their repetition expressing the competing forces of self-preservation and
of waste within the individual organism and the species. Self-preservation
is, for Lawrence, an instinct based on fear and conformity, while waste is
the force of risk, creativity and change. The creative energies associated
with waste are figured in images such as the poppy and the phoenix: both
characterized by flaming beauty, transience and renewal. Lawrence places
work forcefully on the side of the deadly and the fearful and repudiates the
tradition which he associates with Carlyle that would make of labour the
means of self-realization.[7]

The importance of Nietzsche's thought for Lawrence's argument here is
unquestionable, indeed we know that Lawrence considered calling his study
'le gai savoir' in homage to Nietzsche's *Gay Science*.[8] Lawrence had been
reading Nietzsche since at least 1910, and had also subscribed to the *New
Age*, a journal edited by A. R. Orage who was an enthusiastic proponent
of Nietzsche's philosophical ideas.[9] Lawrence clearly shared Nietzsche's
conviction about the duality of forces operating upon the human individual
and the human species: Lawrence's systole and diastole giving a biological
resonance to the cultural distinction Nietzsche designated as Dionysian
versus Apollonian.[10] Nietzsche's ethical and historical project articulated a
forceful rejection of idealism, which Lawrence's almost visceral repudiation
of the cynicism of moral and social idealism was to echo. Nietzsche attacked
the idea that reason and altruism could provide comprehensible models of
social or individual behaviour, and argued that only a confrontation of
the darker, chaotic and violent forces that circulate within the social and
the political might allow for a creative understanding of humanity and the

forces that drive it. Nietzsche's concept of the will-to-power was a vehement repudiation of the adequacy of utilitarian models of ethical or social thought which specifically challenged the idea that self-preservation could or should be the aim of the species. In both *Beyond Good and Evil* and *Thus Spake Zarathustra*, Nietzsche struggled to articulate the creative potential of risk and suffering and to overcome the idealist principle that all life is reducible to the 'drive to self-preservation'.[11] Human life, Nietzsche argued, was not a rational and calculated project but a powerful and chaotic vital flux driven by the energy of the will-to-power:

This world . . . my *Dionysian* world of eternal self-creation and eternal self-destruction, this mystery world of twofold voluptuous delight, my 'beyond good and evil', without goal unless the joy of the circle is a goal . . . *This world is the will to power and nothing else besides*. And you too are that will to power, and nothing else besides.[12]

It was the creative potential of that flux that Lawrence was to defend so vigorously in his 'Study of Thomas Hardy' which displays a consistent and intense withdrawal from the teleology and repetition of 'self preservation'. The dichotomy is later articulated in a series of poems exploring selfhood which were published in *Pansies* (1929) where he writes:

To make self-preservation and self-protection the first law of existence
is about as scientific as making suicide the first law of existence,
and amounts to very much the same thing.

A nightingale singing at the top of his voice
is neither hiding himself nor preserving himself nor propagating his species;
he is giving himself away in every sense of the word;
and obviously, it is the culminating point of his existence.[13]

Protection of the self thus paradoxically amounts to the death of the self, as does the reduction of self to a medium for the preservation of the species. Only the waste and excess of the nightingale's song can embody the culminating point of individual existence.

As an activity which makes sense only in terms of rational ends and social identities, productive labour is necessarily a matter of routines and patterns and as such Lawrence argues that it is always a form of imprisonment. Work is 'simply, the activity necessary for the production of a sufficient supply of food and shelter; nothing more holy than that' (*Study of Thomas Hardy*, 423) and we mistake the creative energies that sustain us if we believe they can be found and developed in the activity of human labour. Lawrence even suggests that we may need to be set free from work by technological advances in the mechanization of labour. He does qualify this representation of labour as the negation of creative being in the case of artists, whose labour may indeed be on the side of risk and of waste, but he asserts that 'for the mass, for the 99.9 per cent of mankind, work is a form of non-living, of non-existence' (423).

The individual is most truly himself, Lawrence argues, in moments of excess and of creativity when he is brimming over, bubbling, and 'like a quivering bud'. Again, Lawrence finds in the process of organic growth a metaphor for the energies that are expressed in the fact of individuality. The unstable and anticipatory form of being cannot, he insists, be the subject of intellectual cognition but is susceptible only to uncertainty, and to 'sentient non-knowledge' (425). This form of sentient consciousness is here explicitly represented as the antithesis of the individual and cultural meanings of work. Rational consciousness and work express a movement within human culture which for Lawrence is destructive and embodies a narrative of decline:

> It seems as if the great aim and purpose in human life were to bring all life into the human consciousness. And this is the final meaning of work: the extension of human consciousness. The lesser meaning of work is the achieving of self-preservation. (431)

So Lawrence's assessment of the individual and social significance of work here has become even more damning. Work is associated with self-preservation, with habit and with fear, but now also with the larger project of bringing all forms of being within the categories of conscious knowledge. This, then, is the context in which Lawrence declares that if man must work he should work only a few hours a day: 'then let him have twenty hours for being himself, for producing himself' (429). This production of the self is an asocial activity which can only take place apart from the community or the crowd: 'come away and be separate in your own soul, and live' (429). And this living can only be glimpsed fleetingly, never consciously known and experienced as such.

In the process of organic growth and development there is, Lawrence assumes, a process of differentiation out of which the particular and the individual are formed. An original undifferentiated mass of living flesh is separated out into species and orders of existence, and in man's case some form of consciousness appears to be an important part of the recognition of individuality. Lawrence does seem to concede that the articulation of ideas of self and other does depend on some form of self-consciousness, but this necessary perception of individuality remains transient and precarious within Lawrence's essay. Instead his focus is the destructive tendency within the human species to desire a kind of certainty and fixity within the self, which is always the negation of creative being:

Therefore the unsatisfied soul remains unsatisfied, and chooses work, maybe Good Works, for its incomplete action. It thinks that in work it has being, in knowledge it has gained its distinct self. (434)

But this kind of knowledge can never be anything other than repetitive for Lawrence. He extols the creative potential of 'the fall into the future' (441), the moment, which is out of time, when risk and the unknown interact. This moment, which cannot be the time of labour, may sometimes be expressed in the sexual act. The sexual act is thus the antithesis of work and also one of those moments of risk and waste in which true individuality might be glimpsed. Unable to risk such waste we are condemned to the repetitions of labour; 'so we struggle mechanically, unformed, unbegotten, unborn, repeating some old process of life, unable to become ourselves, unable to produce anything new' (434).

'THE ESSENCE OF WORK . . . LIES IN SINGLE, ABSORBED, MINDLESS PRODUCTIVITY'[14]

The antithesis between work and selfhood developed in the 'Study of Thomas Hardy' emerges from Lawrence's commitment to a particular notion of individuality as transient, unknowable and creative. In his later essay on the 'Education of the People', written in 1918, Lawrence begins to recognize that some of his repudiation of the physical activity of labour may have taken him, rather ironically, towards unhelpful forms of idealism. He remains committed to non-mental forms of consciousness as the fundamental source of individual and cultural knowledges, but he also confronts the implications of his earlier airy dismissal of the 99.9 per cent of the population for whom physical work is the central activity of their lives.

Lawrence's target in this essay is the idealism that he sees as responsible for the distortions of theory and of practice in elementary school teaching. It is symptomatic of a civilization that fears the body and the physical, Lawrence suggests, that education policy proceeds as if all children might be able to aspire to purely mental forms of labour. State education seeks to produce a sense of dissatisfaction with the necessity of physical labour by inviting all pupils to identify with the possibility of 'escape' through education while simultaneously operating a rigorous and competitive selection system that ensures that most children will never in fact be able to experience such escape. This, Lawrence suggests, produces a form of cynicism in both pupils and staff which creates a contempt for any forms of intellectual or abstract inquiry.

Lawrence suggests that such cynicism is destructive for all those involved in formal education, and seeks instead to imagine forms of education that might recognize the inevitability of manual labour while still allowing for the development of significant forms of individuality and of culture. The challenge implicit in Lawrence's argument is immense, and continues to inform the vagaries and innovations of state educational policy today. Lawrence's own prescriptions are singular, but also clearly connected to his developing theories of human psychic and historical processes. First of all he insists that people must be able to make a fair calculation of their economic and material needs. The very cultural and educational forces that encourage people to aspire beyond manual labour simultaneously coerce people into accepting a narrow and constricted version of their own lives because of a fear of failure: the failure that is an inherent part of state education produces a population who are fearful. This fear is Lawrence's first target since 'if you can't cure people of being frightened for their own existence, you'll educate them in vain' (591), and he insists that penury is a real threat only for very few people.

Rejecting the idealism and hypocrisy of current educational curricula, Lawrence insists physical and practical knowledges should be part of the education of all children. For many, indeed, this is to be the major part of their formal education. He argues that a common educational path might be followed from the ages of seven to twelve, but that thereafter pupils' paths would diverge. The choice about which route children will follow will rest with those in authority, and the aim of such a decision should not be the achievement of equality but the realization of the particular talents of distinct individuals. His social model here is hierarchical and organic, expressed in the image of a tree of human life where different functions and natures are expressed in roots, branches and blossom. It is no longer the case that the individual can only come to self-realization through separateness and repudiation of the social, but Lawrence's social model remains far removed from conceptions of the general will. For Lawrence social structure has an immutable and finally unknowable pattern which individuals both inhabit and express: 'Here then is the new ideal for society: not that all men are equal, but that each man is himself' (603).

The forms and relations that express the social are also susceptible to larger movements of history, and these follow distinct patterns of growth and degeneration. Lawrence argues that 'the human soul is drawing near the conclusion of one of its great phases' (615), and insists that this cyclical movement produces both the pathologies of contemporary culture and its radical potentialities. These pathologies assume a number of forms, which

Lawrence addresses with some stridency and considerable violence. Firstly, he condemns the pernicious effects of excessively intellectualizing forms of education, arguing that they produce the form of psychic dysfunction which he describes as neurasthenia:

Away with the imbecile pretence of culture in the elementary schools. Remember the back streets, remember that the souls of the working people are only rendered *neurasthenic* by your false culture. (612)

I will return to the question of neurasthenia below, but at this point simply want to suggest the shift that Lawrence has made here in his analysis. He began by condemning the gap between the aspirations children are offered in schools and the concrete choices available to them, but has now shifted to a more general characterization of cultural education as a matter of 'pretence'. It is not clear, at this point in Lawrence's argument, what a genuine culture could possibly be in the context of state education, or even if such a thing is imaginable. He then moves seamlessly from this repudiation of false culture to a critique of the role of self-consciousness and the cerebral as if they amounted to the same thing.

In terms of the educational curriculum, Lawrence stresses the physical more than the strictly vocational. He suggests that children should be taught to move efficiently through sports, expressive dance, physical fighting and games of skill. If a boy is caught slouching we are entitled to 'throw a book at him' (644) since the posture suggests a failure of physical intelligence. Children should also be taught the skills of basic household management so that they do not need to depend on servants for their physical care, a dependency Lawrence describes as degrading. In so far as they are prepared for work children should be taught to strive for mindless forms of labour. By this Lawrence does not mean mechanical labour but rather forms of work that can absorb the physical self without exciting the nervous or cerebral aspects of selfhood: 'the point about any handwork is that it should not be mindwork' (653). The same ideas are explored in two versions of Lawrence's poem, 'Work'. In the earlier version Lawrence writes

> There is no point in work
> unless it pre-occupies you as well as occupies you.
> When you are only occupied, you are an empty shell.
> A man needs to be independent at his work, so that he can put his
>   own self into it.
>
> When a man puts his own self into his work
> he is living, not merely working.

While in the later he says that:

> There is no point in work
> unless it absorbs you
> . . .
> When a man goes out into his work
> he is alive like a tree in spring,
> he is living, not merely working.

The relations between self, work and consciousness are here rather complex. Work should have a point, that is to say the question of work is an ethical rather than an economic one. But that 'point' is a factor of a particular relation between self and labour. In the earlier version of the poem the individual needs to be independent in order to invest his selfhood in work, but this independence is only possible through an intense pre-occupation. The self must be taken over by work in order to give itself away to work. The image is more intense in the second version where the self is not only preoccupied but actually absorbed. The self disappears into work in order to be really alive. Yet the image of the tree in spring seems false here and actually disrupts the terms of the argument, since a tree does not have mental forms of consciousness which need to be overcome or suspended. Human consciousness may become pre-occupied, it may be absorbed, but it is surely never really sylvan.

The attempt to understand the energies of human labour and the forms of human consciousness through organicism is a recurrent aspect of Lawrence's writing. It emerges in striking terms in 'Education of the People' when he moves from education to the family as the primary site of social and cultural degeneration and seeks to connect the biological process of reproduction to the development of different forms of consciousness. Education's idealism, bullying and hypocrisy then emerge as symptoms of a more fundamental imbalance between different forms of consciousness, an imbalance created primarily by the distortions of maternal love. I will return to Lawrence's theorization of the relations between the biological and the psychic below, but it is worth noting at this point the shock of the irruption of his violent imaging of primary psychic bonds into this essay about education, labour and selfhood. 'How can we help being neurotic when our mothers provoked self-consciousness in us at the breast?' (622), Lawrence asks, shifting his argument once more from the sociological terrain of its beginning. Neurosis and neurasthenia are no longer produced by materialism, by cynical idealism, or by patterns of history, but rather by the provocations of the breast-feeding mother. Lawrence argues that the human individual has a number of primary conscious centres which are located in different parts of the anatomy. Over-stimulation of one centre can have disastrous results for psychic, and ultimately, cultural health. Mothers have a tendency to stimulate the cerebral and self-conscious centres of the infant, and must be forcibly stopped: 'seize babies away from their mothers, with hard, fierce terrible hands' (639). The children also require violent handling in order to overcome the pressure towards deadening forms of self-consciousness produced by their mothers:

Whipping, beating, yes these alone will thunder into the moribund centres and bring them to life. Sharp, stinging, whipping, keen, fierce smacks, and all the roused fury of reaction in the child, these alone will restore us to psychic health. (641)

Connecting this violence to the authority Lawrence has advocated for the establishment of a properly constituted system of education creates an intense unease. He had described this necessary authority, which was to design the educational needs of each child, as 'religious' and there is, of course, no contradiction in the idea of a violent God. Yet, surely the insistent repetitions of violent imagery above suggest something more than a righteous God. There is a building up of violence, from whipping and beating to the keen fierce smacks which makes the conclusion of 'psychic health' both prescriptive and implausible.

This violence gives way briefly to more sober reflections on the meanings of human labour. Returning to his earlier repudiation of idealism, Lawrence argues that work is 'quite a pleasant occupation for a human creature, a natural activity' (648). But the meanings of 'natural' have become much more concrete. It is no longer simply a social fact that most people do land up in manual forms of labour but is somehow connected to the relationships between the different affective centres within the human individual. Work then actively challenges the idealism of our perception of ourselves as nothing but consciousness, and the increasing tendency to experience labour as degrading is a symptom of the extent to which we have become victims of idealism. Tying human labour to a model of human psychobiology, however, produces a much more disturbed and angry figuring of the relationships between gender and labour. Lawrence attributes to a male character of uncertain identity the remark that 'I hate to see a woman trying to be abstract, and being abstract, just as I hate and loathe to see a woman doing mechanical work' (664): the hatred and loathing presumably arising from the fact that both forms of activity are equally foreign to her nature. The essay concludes with the need for men to be ahead of women, to move into the realm of risk and away from the domestic. The domestic, the deadly, and the female are conflated in the concluding remark that 'men who can only hark back to woman become automatic, static' (665).

'HE WORKED SO HARD, AND DID SO LITTLE'[15]

The effort to imagine both the meanings and the pathologies of work has led Lawrence to a knot of questions concerned with biology, history and the will. In engaging with the dynamic process of the human species in the context of a larger map of cultural histories, Lawrence is drawing on a series of unresolved questions within early twentieth-century philosophy, anthropology and psychology. A number of these questions were articulated through the category of 'neurasthenia', a category that Lawrence himself invokes at a number of points. Neurasthenia has attracted the interest of a range of recent cultural critics, perhaps because so many prominent figures in literary modernism, such as Henry James, Olive Schreiner and Marcel Proust, have been associated with the condition.[16] It has also attracted significant interest as a psychological condition somehow expressive of the experience of modernity. As a condition of exhaustion linked to overwork, intellectual labour, the speed of technological change and the intensification of cultural and economic life it has been read as the pathology of modernity, just as stress has been identified as the pathology of the postmodern.[17]

Neurasthenia designates a condition of fatigue, or nervous exhaustion, which many felt was becoming more common by the late nineteenth century. The term had particular prominence in the context of American cultural and medical debates, where it was most explicitly connected to modernization and overwork, but was also common currency in Europe.[18] 'Neurasthenia' designates a condition, but tells us very little about its aetiology. The causes and meanings of neurasthenia were the subject of extensive debate in medical, philosophical and popular literature where they were intimately connected to theorizations of degeneracy and of the will.

The link between neurasthenia and degeneracy depended on the idea that the condition either was, or could become, hereditary. As civilization became more complex, so necessarily did the intellectual and nervous systems of mankind. Greater complexity led to greater vulnerability, and many argued that nervous dysfunction was the necessary result of such increased complexity. The neurasthenic could then pass on this condition, so that the whole race was susceptible to exhaustion and failures of nervous force. Connecting this to anxieties about the growth of the urban underclass led to a conviction that racial and social decline were both persistent and increasing threats since the powers of disorder and dysfunction could readily overwhelm an increasingly exhausted social and psychic order. This conviction of cultural and social degeneracy was certainly shared in important ways by Lawrence, particularly in its emphasis on the pathological consequences of excessive intellectual activity.

Neurasthenia also interacted with energeticist models of human physiology and psychology. Nervous force was the energy necessary for the efficient functioning of human systems and was believed to be a limited resource. To some extent this limitation was seen as historical: the physical concept of entropy sustaining a model in which the generally available resources of human energy showed a tendency to decline. More often, however, the energeticist model led doctors and cultural critics to look for imbalance in the human nervous or muscular system which might provoke a dissipation of energy. In their study of nineteenth-century psychological thought Jenny Bourne Taylor and Sally Shuttleworth discuss the large number of books addressing anxieties about the draining of nervous force in the late nineteenth century and its relation to overwork.[19] Different experts suggest trauma, heredity or sexual excess as contributory factors in the disease, but all share a sense of nervous energy as some kind of material substance subject to scientific laws. When Clifford Allbutt summarizes the current state of medical research on neurasthenia in 1910 he acknowledges the semantic complexity of the term though simultaneously defending its clinical usefulness. He understands the condition primarily in physiological terms, describing the ways in which vital energy 'is clogged by the accumulation of waste products in the blood, or muscles, or both'.[20] This excremental imagining of the destructive power of human waste is markedly different from Lawrence's use of 'waste' to designate the non-functional and the creative expressions of human energy. For Allbutt this waste amounts to a loss of energy, and an inefficient functioning of the energetic system of individual organic life, attributable to the using up of creative energy in 'molecular frictions and other invisible work' ('Neurasthenia', 734). All movements and processes of the human body are 'work' for Allbutt, in the sense that they are an expenditure of energy, but in the neurasthenic this work has become wasteful and its channels have been clogged up.

A similarly energeticist model of human psychology can be read in Freud's accounts of neurasthenia in the 1890s. Freud notes some of the symptoms characteristic of neurasthenia, including an incapacity for work, and is initially prepared to entertain the idea that there might be a hereditary predisposition towards the condition. By 1893, however, he writes that 'I am now asserting that *every* neurasthenia is sexual' by which he means that forms of sexual activity have inappropriately exhausted the patient's nervous energy.[21] Neurasthenia can be readily distinguished from psychoneuroses precisely because the neurasthenic patient can give an account of the ae-tiological factors in sexual life which have led to their condition while the neurotic remains blind to the workings of their unconscious. Again, the source of neurasthenia can be found in a wasting of energy, a mis-direction of energy from its prescribed route, but for Freud the energy is libidinal: 'Neurasthenia can always be traced back to a condition of the ner-vous system such as is acquired by excessive masturbation or arises spon-taneously from frequent emissions.'[22] The image is curiously suspended between the material and the abstract here as 'energy' is displaced by the emission of sexual fluids, a kind of 'wasting' with a much longer cultural history.[23]

Neurasthenia, then, is an exhaustion, a failure to engage with the world and an inability to work. Its prevalence may indicate some deeper and more powerful movement towards degeneration; it may be a symptom of the distortions of everyday life in the modern world; a pathological outcome of brainwork; or an organic imbalance in the distribution of vital energies. It may also be accompanied by feelings of dread and responsibility and, perhaps surprisingly, by a particularly marked sense of the need to work.[24] The cure for neurasthenia, where it can be imagined, amounts to restoring depleted reserves of energy and exciting the activity of the patient's will.

The term 'neurasthenia' is of course rarely used now as either a medical or a cultural category, but as a historical category it may prove illuminating, representing as it does a sedimentation of theorizations of, and anxieties about, exhaustion, history and the dynamic processes of the human body. The images and the narratives invested in the concept of the neurasthenic indeed offer us a particular route into some of Lawrence's fiction and give us another map with which to read its symptomatic concerns and its historical resonances. D. H. Lawrence's short story, 'England, My England' published first in 1915 and then in a substantially revised form in 1922, for example, engages imaginatively with many of the narratives, the arguments and the fears surrounding the cultural phenomenon of the neurasthenic, and particularly with the relations between neurasthenia and work.

This story begins with the phrase, 'He was working' (5), and the early sections of the story explore the meanings and nature of work for its cen-tral character, Egbert. Egbert's work is gardening, which he does not for money but in order to gain a sense of purposeful activity. We learn almost immediately that he is not skilled at this work: the path that he is making will not be straight and the banks he builds up will collapse. Egbert is an isolated figure from the beginning of the narrative, near to his family but separated from them by a heart that is 'hard with disillusion'. He is angry and alienated, but yet 'he worked on. What was there to do but submit!' (5). Imaginatively, Egbert is excited by the creative process of labour and receives a sense of self-confirmation and security from the recognition of the material fruits of his own labour: a garden full of flowers or a hearth piled with wood. Yet the story is concerned overwhelmingly with the failures of his labour and with his inability to work. The imaginative investment in labour as creative process cannot fill the gap between his sense of self and his alienated relation to the world. Clifford Allbutt in his account of neurasthenic patients speaks poignantly of 'their ardent desire to buckle to work' which haunts their actual incapacities and exhaustion[25] and Egbert is similarly haunted by the pleasures and securities of creative work which he can never in fact realize or at least never sustain.

This sense of haunting, of a layering of the self by memories, desires, and fantasies, is exacerbated by the use of free indirect discourse. The narrative voice weaves together interior monologue, memories and self-perceptions with an impersonal and ironic distancing that creates the kind of poignancy between desire and its blockage that Allbutt found in his neurasthenics:

He was not idle, nor was she. There were plenty of things to be done, the house to be put into final repair after the workmen had gone, cushions and curtains to sew, the paths to make, the water to fetch and attend to, and then the slope of the deep-soiled, neglected garden to level, to terrace with little terraces and paths, and to fill with flowers. He worked away, in his shirt-sleeves, worked all day intermittently, doing this thing and the other. And she, quiet and rich in herself, seeing him stooping and labouring away by himself, would come to help him, to be near him. He of course was an amateur – a born amateur. He worked so hard, and did so little, and nothing he ever did would hold together for long. (9)

There is a confusion of subjectivities in this passage, so that it is impossible finally to understand how many of these ideas or images are available to Egbert. There is also a temporal disjunction which adds to the sense of haunting and blurring of subjective boundaries. This story began with Egbert gardening, but the gardening passage above is a moment in the past, which resembles the present of the narrative but lacks its disillusion. The purposiveness of the labour represented is also undermined by its very repetition.

Egbert, it transpires, has never worked for money. Perhaps, the narrative suggests, at a certain point this didn't matter because the romance between Egbert and Winifred, his wife, was what defined their lives. The narrator tell us, however, that 'neither Egbert nor she yet realized the difference between work and romance' (9), and that 'yet' already begins to suggest a revelation to come. We will not believe for long that romance can sustain the same sorts of identities as work. Egbert's incapacity to work is to some extent a matter of conscious choice, 'for Egbert had no intention of coming to grips with life . . . he had no desire to give himself to the world' (10). Here Egbert seems consciously to be rejecting the voices and representations that would require a form of self-sacrifice as a means to construct a significant life narrative. If coming to grips with life here means forming a relationship to the social, Egbert simply refuses the imperative.

But this sense of conscious resistance is always fragile. Firstly, we simply cannot discern to what extent Egbert constructs any counter-narrative of his life. He seems prone to self-delusion and to compensatory fantasies and is never quite present in the time of the narration. We have echoes here of the neurasthenic's repudiation of modernity, and the same ambiguity about whether to read such a repudiation as heroism. Egbert has an enthusiasm for ancient England and imagines his garden 'secret, primitive, savage as when the Saxons first came' (8–9), but this attachment to earlier cultures is soon more harshly represented through the perspective of Winifred: 'He, the higher, the finer, in his way the stronger, played with his garden and his old folk-songs and Morris-dances, just played, and let her support the pillars of the future on her own heart' (13).

The repudiation of modernity and a fascination with other times and cultures is, of course, characteristic of Lawrence's own intellectual and cultural concerns. We know that Lawrence was well-informed about and intrigued by contemporary anthropology, and that he aspired to establish an alternative community, called Rananim, where like-minded individuals could live apart from the amenities and the values of the modern world.[26] But we should not conclude from this that Lawrence, or his narrator, simply endorse Egbert's withdrawal from the contemporary. Lawrence would have known from reading his anthropological sources that any imagining of past or remote cultures was imperfect, enmeshed in fantasy, and never quite what had been looked for. We know, for example, that Lawrence read Leo Frobenius's *Voice of Africa* (1913), and in this text we can find the drama of longing, disappointment and scholarship forcefully acted out. Frobenius's research is driven by a conviction that Africa had important early cultures of which we have become unaware. He set out to uncover artefacts, rituals and beliefs among the African population of the lower Niger, or Yoruba Land, which would give us knowledge of earlier civilizations. His discoveries are, however, always fragmentary, the result of imaginative re-construction, and marked by 'features of the petty latter-day deterioration'.[27]

Egbert's search for a lost savage England is thus thoroughly comprehensible, but, as the story unfolds, increasingly blind. The birth of Egbert and Winifred's children is a crucial moment within the narrative. Before this moment, at least in the revised version of the story, Egbert's desires and memories have been mediated to us largely through his own voice. After he becomes a father, however, he is much more harshly filtered through the consciousness of his wife and his father-in-law. The story is now offering him a place in a patriarchal narrative and his refusal, or inability, to fill this place is pathological and morbid. Egbert 'couldn't link up with the world's work because the basic desire was absent from him' ('England, My England', 14), but this incapacity is increasingly less a matter of resistance and more a question of paralysis. The shadow of the war is already perceptible at this stage of the story.

Winifred's fate is not markedly more creative. She has been seduced by the romanticism of Egbert's detachment, but now finds herself repelled by it. Lawrence represents her as infected by modernity, and thus unable to sustain intuitive and intense relations with her children. She can construct her identity as mother only through the logic of duty, which is simply an increasingly vigorous exercise of the will. To this extent, Winifred might be read as the antithesis of the neurasthenic: Allbutt, after all, recommended the neurasthenic patient to 'exert himself again, to re-educate his will' (787). But the exercise of will is also a potentially destructive imposition of egotism. Winifred's father, Godfrey Marshall is robust with the 'sap-like faith' that keeps man going and as such an admirable organic force, but his robust blood and 'his own will to succeed' (15) can also amount to the eradication of other selves. Godfrey Marshall has the glow and decisiveness of paternal authority, but is also a dark and destructive force who will ultimately precipitate Egbert's departure to the war.

The tension here between will as the enactment of vitality and will as destructive egoism returns us once more to Nietzsche and the circulations of his texts within Lawrence's writing. The sense of will as an impersonal, destructive but necessary force was aligned in Lawrence's reading of Nietzsche with the idea of creative and excessive spending of the self, with the nightingale's song and the poppy's vivid blaze. But in the fictional exploration of what it means to 'come to grips with life' in 'England, My England' Lawrence is driven to a more complex engagement with the contingencies of individuality and the nature of the will, this time mediated both by his own earlier reading of Schopenhauer and by the re-workings of Nietzsche within the project of philosophical and political egoism. As we have seen in chapter 1, Schopenhauer's *The World as Will and Representation* argued that the blind impulses of the will drove all vital processes, both organic and inorganic. His model was dynamic and conflictual, so that constant motion and constant strife became the lot of humanity as much as of any other species. The individual, for Schopenhauer, is the contingent and temporally limited embodiment of the basic vital force that is the will. But this dark and impersonal force of the will, which expresses itself through and is manifest in particular life forms, intersects with the imperative towards conflict and dynamism, to produce a more contingent sense of the willing individual within Schopenhauer's text. The willing and desiring individual will necessarily come into conflict with other willing individuals and out of this conflict will come change, but also an increase in the distinction between the two beings: a mechanism of individuation is set in play which seems to lead the individual beyond the merely impersonal manifestation of the will. David Simpson suggests that this amounts to a 'cluttering' of the individual through the operation of interest, appetite, history and the unconscious.[28] There is an emergent sense of will as designating something double within Schopenhauer's text, a doubleness captured by Schopenhauer's second term, 'representation'. Representation involves processes of distinction and the assumption not simply of individuality but of subjectivity:

man is simultaneously impetuous and dark impulse of willing (indicated by the pole of the genitals as its focal point), and eternal, free, serene subject of pure knowing (indicated by the pole of the brain).[29]

'Will' here begins to assume meanings which are more closely aligned to consciousness and to subjectivity rather than to the biological or materialist sense of the individual. Schopenhauer's will is not simply the vast impersonal force that animates all dynamic processes and modes of being, but also becomes the process of individuation through conflict, and the more everyday understanding of the enacting of desire.

   The understanding of will as the engine of individuation resonates powerfully within the context of egoist philosophical and political discourses, which constructed their imagery and argument from a collage of Schopenhauer, Nietzsche, American transcendentalism and the work of Max Stirner.[30] A journal such as *The Eagle and the Serpent: a Journal of Egoistic Philosophy and Sociology* provides an interesting instance of the movement of such ideas, as well as suggesting the reasons for Lawrence's ultimate repudiation of egoism as a dangerous narrowing of the self. The journal was published between 1898 and 1903 and was edited by Erwin Mac-Call. Like many such small journals it manifests a curious combination of the transient and the rigid: its sub-title changes frequently but its basic cultural and philosophical commitments remain strikingly consistent. The first issue stresses that egoism is finally the only philosophy of liberation conceivable, arguing that all forms of altruism are simply rationalizations of a 'slave morality'.[31] Much of the journal consists of letters from readers who expound variations on the basic principle that the 'I' must be the master rather than the slave of its environment. The writing intersects with various forms of radicalism and historical manifestations of intolerance. Thus, for example, it contains features such as 'Hard Sayings about the Soft Sex' (1 December 1898) which consists of a series of quotations about the fickleness and superficiality of women, and publishes letters including one which asks 'should the exploiting jew be exterminated?' (June 1900). The tone of the journal is strident and the centrality of the ego becomes less a matter of rebellion and more simply a comfortable prejudice as the journal develops. By 1900 its emphasis on the self indeed looks increasingly narcissistic as the project of egoism intersects with the study and practice of dietetics and the launch of a new journal dealing with *Health and Beauty*.

The rebellious and iconoclastic tone of such egoism certainly feeds Lawrence's denunciations of the dominance of conscious will but they lead him to rather different conclusions.

> But what we may sacrifice, if we call it sacrifice, from the self,
> are all the obstructions to life, self-importance, self-conceit,
>   egoistic self-will.[32]

He shares the desire to challenge the idealism of altruism and the tyranny of conformity, but recoils from the unfettered exercise of individual will. Jack Lindsay was to write in another Nietzschean journal of 'Lawrence's blundering primitive contacts, efforts to smudge self out in the blind jungle of matted bodies'.[33] For Lindsay, Lawrence's repudiation of the conscious will was a negation of the transgressive and affirmative quality of human individuality. But Lawrence increasingly articulates his rejection of this conscious egoistic will, favouring instead a more impersonal and biological sense of individuation:

> The self that we are, at its best, is all that we are
> is the very individual flame of life itself
> which is the man's pure self.[34]

This best and pure self is but fleetingly manifested in 'England, My England', where Godfrey Marshall's admired 'will-to-power' (15) rapidly becomes a destructive egoism. He is the embodiment of paternal authority and the power of patriarchy, but his will, particularly since it is unchallenged by any equivalent force in Egbert, becomes pathological. The 'slow, heavy power of will' (26) that sustains the Marshalls ensures a certain vitality, a certain narrative progression, but it is ultimately deadly since it condemns Egbert to death and Winifred to the sterile compulsions of duty.

After the birth of her children, Winifred becomes a coercive figure, driving Egbert to the social while refusing him access to the sexual. His refusal to work becomes then a form of aggression aimed specifically at his wife, 'he simply *would* not give himself to what Winifred called life, *work*' (12). As a couple they become mutually destructive and each represents a form of imbalance between individuality and will. Egbert's increasingly desperate project of refusing authority and responsibility finally culminates in a catastrophic episode of guilt and displaced responsibility. Egbert had left a sickle lying in the grass on which his daughter injures herself badly. She calls desperately for her father, inviting him to take the position of authority and control which the girl repudiates in her mother. Egbert's long, agonized, introspective engagement with the question of his own responsibility intersects only fleetingly with what we learn of the severity of the accident and the inadequacy of the family's response to it. There are moments of intense pain and sympathetic identification with the girl's suffering, but Egbert's more typical responses are irritation and denial:

He had left the sickle there lying on the edge of the grass, and so his first-born child whom he loved so dearly had come to hurt. But then it was an accident – it was an accident. Why should he feel guilty – It would probably be nothing, better in two or three days. Why take it to heart, why worry? He put it aside. (18)

There is an accumulation of guilt, but an inability to assume the position of this guilt, a tendency to put it aside. The tension increases as the child becomes more ill, and Egbert returns over and again to questions of his own guilt. Again, we might be reminded of the neurasthenic in whom 'a fear of doing some wrong returns until it possesses the mind, the besetting thought looms larger and larger until it assumes the garb of a temptation'.[35] Egbert drives himself to moments of activity, 'his heart pinched with anxiety' (19), but the activity produces poor medical care and the wrong diagnosis. The child undergoes painful treatment and suffers extremes of pain, watched by her two parents. Winifred turns away from her own desires completely and constructs her identity through self-sacrifice and a savage form of duty. Egbert simply fails to connect his own intermittent feelings of pain and anxiety to any external form of action in the world: 'He could not bear it. He just could not bear it. He turned aside. There was nothing to do but turn aside. He turned aside and went hither and thither, desultory' (24).

Egbert returns to labour in the garden of his cottage, working erratically but meeting his pressing bodily needs for food and warmth. The sight of his now lame daughter hardens his heart: her damaged body is the limit point of his fantasmatic temporal mobility, an insistent reminder that time can only move in one direction. When the war breaks out it becomes the inevitable narrative conclusion to Egbert's detachment. The narrator lays out exactly the reasons why Egbert should not want to enlist; he was not aggressive, not nationalist, not driven by mass feeling. But it is immediately clear that that is what he will do, because he has lost any sense of imagining or sustaining a life project. Metaphorically he has already assumed the morbidity and meaninglessness that will be lived out in the First World War. If neurasthenia is the disease of modernity then war becomes its most characteristic symptom.

By enlisting, Egbert achieves a form of public identity which ensures his own eradication. He resents the collective and intimate relations of army life and 'an ugly look came on to his face, of a man who has accepted his own degradation' (29). Winfred accepts him in this now 'degraded' but comprehensible identity, and even 'waited for him in a little passion of duty and sacrifice' (29). But their relations are formulaic and he experiences a sense of distance and strangeness when surrounded by his family. By the time that Egbert leaves for Flanders, 'he seemed already to have gone out of life, beyond the pale of life' (30) as his actions become automatic and his consciousness increasingly emptied. In the confrontation with death the loss of self becomes no longer metaphor or strategy. In the earlier version of the story the protagonist is transformed into a violent and impersonal killer, taking a sadistic pleasure in the annihilation of his enemies before the moment of his own death. In the 1922 version the anger and sadism have given way to a moral and epistemological insecurity which struggles to imagine a self in the moment of its disappearance. The story registers Egbert's actions, his punctual responses, the marks of his continuing existence but it simultaneously describes the trajectory towards death. Egbert's separateness, his inability to 'come to grips' with life here achieves a fullness which is also his negation. He is hit by a shell, and knows himself to have been killed:

When faintly something began to struggle in the darkness, a consciousness of himself, he was aware of a great load and a clanging sound. To have known the moment of death! And to be forced, before dying, to review it. (32)

The complex interaction between organism and consciousness is dramatized in the ambiguity of that 'struggling': is this the writhing of an injured body or of a still active consciousness? As death finally approaches, Egbert repudiates the urge towards memory: 'Better the agony of dissolution ahead than the nausea of the effort backwards' (33). Backwards is the movement towards the moment when 'there had been life', but Egbert's being becomes spatial rather than temporal as he lapses 'out on the great darkness' (33). The will has been the force connecting Egbert to temporal and purposeful forms of being, but now the movement forward is a 'terrible work' because it has become impersonal, dark, outside time: 'Let the black sea of death itself solve the problem of futurity. Let the will of man break and give up' (33).

'MUST WE HOLD ON?/OR CAN WE NOW LET GO?'[36]

Lawrence's unease about the social and psychic consequences of egoism becomes an important factor in his theorization of labour and individuality. He is increasingly fascinated by modes of representing the relations between the human individual and the species in terms of microcosm and macrocosm, but also increasingly strident in his repudiation of the dominant conscious will. His poem 'To Let Go or To Hold On –?', published in *Pansies*, dramatizes losing the grip of the conscious individuating will:

> Shall we let go,
> and allow the soul to find its level
> downwards, ebbing downwards, ebbing downwards to the flood?
> till the head floats tilted like a bottle forward tilted
> on the sea, with no message in it; and the body is submerged
> heavy and swaying like a whale recovering
> from wounds, below the deep black wave?
> like a whale recovering its velocity and strength
> under the cold black wave.

What we are letting go of here is the individual will, the sense of agency and the experience of individuality. This does not, however, amount simply to a representation of the fate of the neurasthenic. Rather, we are slipping into the large and amorphous substance that is the ocean, where we can recover from our wounds, the wounds presumably of abrasion and conflict of wills. But this descent is literally chilling, as we float under the cold black wave. The body is submerged, which may represent a recognition of our physical link to other forms of matter and larger cosmic and tidal forces, but the head floats aimlessly, vacuous and abandoned on the sea. The poem goes on to imagine the effort of resisting the pull of such merging:

> or else, or else
> shall a man brace himself up
> and lift his face and set his breast
> and go forth to change the world?
> gather his will and his energy together
> and fling himself in effort after effort
> upon the world, to bring a change to pass?

The active verbs accumulate to suggest the magnitude of the challenge: resisting the pull of the ocean will involve bracing, lifting, setting, going forth, gathering the will and flinging the self. The increasing risk is hardly answered by the rather anti-climactic 'bring a change to pass'. The effort of the will has become an abstraction and we have no sense of the meaning or scale of such a change. The need for purposeful action dominates the stanza, but the meaning and the nature of the action have been obscured.

The poem continues to articulate the conflict between sinking into the larger substance of which we are part or struggling towards individuation. Sinking we shall be like eggs, sperm or germs, powerful images for Lawrence of the inter-relations between the individual and the species. But the imperative to hold on also has its ontological and ethical force: 'go ahead with what is human nature/and make a new job of the human world'. Letting go might allow us to surrender the direction of history and the state of the culture to larger impersonal forces, and thus engender a creative revolution, but the poem ends with the dialectic unresolved:

> Must we hold on?
> Or can we now let go?
>
> Or is it even possible we must do both?

The final question is ethical as well as practical, and is centrally connected to how Lawrence in his later writings imagined the meanings and nature of work. In the next section of this argument I will examine the theoretical and historical writings that fed Lawrence's imaginative rendering of the relations between the individual and the species, and will then consider his own articulation of the psychic and social meanings of individuality in *Psychoanalysis and the Unconscious* and *Fantasia of the Unconscious*.

Lawrence's interest in pre-Socratic Greek philosophy may have derived from his reading of Nietzsche, for whom early Greek philosophy and culture represented the Dionysian impulses of change, conflict and violence that would be repressed by Apollonian reason and ethics. Socrates was cast as the villain in Nietzsche's cultural and historical philosophizing:

I myself was first struck by this impertinent thought, that the great wise men are *declining types*, in the very case where it meets with its strongest opposition from scholarly and unscholarly prejudice: I recognized Socrates and Plato as symptoms of decay, as tools of the Greek dissolution, as pseudo-Greek, as anti-Greek . . . they themselves, these wisest of men, were somehow in *physiological* agreement in order to have – to *have* to have – the same negative attitude towards life.[37]

The impertinence of the thought would certainly be part of its appeal for Lawrence, as would the imagining of cultural phases in terms of the developmental laws of physiology. Lawrence found this commitment to early Greek philosophy much more fully argued in a study by John Burnet published in 1908. Burnet presented the available scholarship on pre-Socratic culture and philosophy, and offered an account of its most prominent thinkers. Burnet is far from nostalgic about pre-modern cultures, insisting that the infancy of civilization is marked less by innocence and truth than by fetishism and fear.[38] His aim is to render the complexity of early Greek philosophy as the product of a culture confronting change, dislocation and violence and to restore its diversity and innovation. Burnet begins by exploring the strangeness of early Greek philosophy, its remoteness from ordinary twentieth-century assumptions about matter, spirit and causality. He finds these early thinkers concerned to elucidate the nature of that 'un-created indestructible reality' which it is the business of their philosophy to grasp: 'these early thinkers tell us [it] was a body, or even matter, if we choose to call it so; but it was not matter in the sense in which matter is opposed to spirit' (16).

What Burnet reveals is a diverse and developing philosophical tradition which assumes that reality can be grasped as substance and as process: 'Anaximander taught . . . that there was one eternal, indestructible substance out of which everything arises, and into which everything once more returns' (55). That the ultimate reality should be material chimes with Lawrence's prioritization of flesh over the Word, and the image of life as a continual making and remaking of a fundamental material form feeds both Lawrence's organicist mode and Nietzsche's fascination with the process of eternal recurrence:

being oneself the eternal joy of becoming – that joy which also encompasses the *joy of destruction* . . . And so again I am touching on the point from which I started out . . . I am taking myself back to the ground from which my willing, my *ability* grows – I, the last disciple of the philosopher Dionysus – I, the teacher of the eternal recurrence.[39]

The shift from an impersonal rendering of the processes of change and development to Nietzsche's more agonized interrogation of 'being one-self' will haunt Lawrence's own engagements with the connection between cosmic forces and the individual life. For Anaximander any process of individuation was unstable and part of a larger dynamic system. Within the originary substance of ultimate reality opposing forces circulate, and their opposition is the engine both of creative change and of destruction. Herakleitos develops this dynamic and conflictual model, but the focus of his inquiry becomes epistemological: 'wisdom is not a knowledge of many things, but the perception of the underlying unity of the warring opposites' (158). It could be argued that the whole project of Lawrence's psychobiological conception of the human individual is in some sense a response to this challenge to articulate the unity within and beyond op-positions, but I will return to this point below. Burnet's exposition of the thought of Anaxagoras shifts this intellectual paradigm subtly once more. Anaxagoras accepted a materialist account of the infinite substance that constitutes life, and also the dynamic and conflictual model of historical and biological change, but also developed an argument about the formal, and even ontological, equivalence of different modes of being. 'What men commonly call coming into being and passing away is really mixture and separation' (303), and thus, Burnet argues, there is a portion of everything in everything. The ambitious pretensions of the conscious will look illusory and even absurd in the face of these articulations of the scale and power of the basic creative processes that govern all forms of life. Our uniqueness is severely compromised by a philosophy that sees in each organism the playing out of an inexorable logic and the repetitive mixing and separating of fundamental organic forms.

Theosophical texts offered Lawrence a mode of thinking that drew on these models of human life as connected to larger forces and patterns of growth, but also explored ways of articulating the creative role of the individual self. Theosophy drew on a number of traditions of religious and philosophical thought, including, importantly, those from the East. That the publisher John Murray issued a series dedicated to the exposition of 'The Wisdom of the East' in the early years of the century is an indicator of the importance of Oriental thought and religion for British intellectual life in the period. Vedic poets assumed 'the existence of a single cosmic matter or world spirit',[40] an image that offers the same interweaving of the material and the spiritual found in Burnet's early Greek philosophers. The concept of 'Brahma', the absolute reality, is realized both in the individual breath of life and the currents of the wind. The breath and the wind push the absolute towards less material forms, but they also offer an image of the relations between the individual and the cosmos. The individual expresses all of the properties of Brahma, but conversely we can glimpse the 'presence of the whole macrocosm, the universal self, in the heart of man' (25).

The same perception of the relations between the microcosm and the macrocosm could be found in theosophical thinking which drew on other religious traditions. Thus, James M. Pryse's study of the Book of Revelations argued that 'all that the universe contains is contained also in man'.[41] Pryse's study claimed to find in the Book of Revelations a manual of spiritual development. He argued that the early Christian church had an esoteric science which revealed to initiates the stages towards revelation, but that this esoteric science has been suppressed by a corrupt priesthood. Pryse aims to uncover this knowledge through a scholarly and imaginative reading of the symbols and patterns of the text. Within his analysis Pryse offers an account of the structure and physiology of the human body as revealing something of the dynamic and hierarchical structures of both knowledge and spiritual truth. Pryse divides the human body into three manifestations, the spiritual, the psychic and the physical, and designates different organs of the body as representative of different faculties of the soul (13). These distinctions relate to Pryse's Platonic model of the orders of human knowledge, from perception, through faith and philosophical reason, to direct cognition. The structure of the human body not only replicates basic epistemological and ontological distinctions, but also offers us a map of these basic forces and relationships. Pryse describes two nervous structures, the cerebro-spinal and the 'sympathetic or ganglionic system' (15) and maps their significance and material manifestation on the individual body. Pryse associates the ganglia, a series of distinct nerve-centres, with the 'chakras' explicated within Hindu religious thinking[42] and argues that the locations and the relations between these chakras can reveal the fundamental structures of the human self. Throughout his analysis, Pryse aims to connect different levels of perception and different forms of being. Thus, for example, in the signs of the zodiac he identifies historical traces of ancient gods, arrangements of the planets and aspects of the human body (21).

Despite being routed through the body, however, Pryse's significant knowledge is ultimately spiritual. He had already described a hierarchy in which the head was associated with the lamb, Christ, and the higher mind, while the genitals were the location and figure of sensuality and the False Seer, and he goes on to argue explicitly that the process of revelation is necessarily connected to 'the complete subjugation of the physical body and its forces, and to liberation from the bondage of physical life' (59). What is uncovered through sacrifice, contemplation and intuition amounts to the 'task of giving birth to oneself' (62), but the self thus perceived has been freed from its accidental materialism:

The attainment of spiritual knowledge is in effect the process of reviving the memory of the incarnating Ego in relation to the supernatural worlds, before it became immured in matter. (96)

Pryse's text, despite its aspiration towards non-material manifestations of the self, was important and influential for Lawrence: he would borrow significantly from its terminology while developing his own map of the nerve centres within the human body and would be spurred on to produce his own interpretation of the psychic and social meanings of revelation. Lawrence does not share Pryse's reverence for the Book of Revelations, and he talks angrily of it as 'the work of a second-rate mind. It appeals intensely to second-rate minds in every country and every century.'[43] He is particularly dismissive of the way it feeds apocalyptic fantasies of revolution in those whose selfhood amounts to no more than conformity. Yet, the Book of Revelations does offer Lawrence a glimpse of the pagan philosophies and religions within its fabric, and reveals our connection 'with the cosmos, with the world, with mankind, with the nation, with the family' (148).

These connections intrigued many thinkers of the early years of the twentieth century who searched for consonance between individual life patterns and the movements of history or the rhythms of cosmic change. Charlotte Despard, for example, a prominent suffrage activist, looked for correlations between the development of vital forces and the growth of the women's movement:

There can be no doubt that woman, with her intuition, her love-instinct and her life-force, will play a large part in the reconstruction of society, which will inevitably follow the era of destruction that seems to lie in front of us.[44]

Despard here yokes the women's movement to larger forces of decline and regeneration, and ultimately to the knowledge that 'we must build up character . . . the character which regards the self of form as but a unit of the Great Self' (*Theosophy*, 34). The women's movement provides the practical experience of duty, sacrifice and collectivity necessary to real philosophical understanding, but also carries within it the forces and narratives of historical change. Edward Carpenter was to reach similar conclusions about both the women's movement and the labour movement, once more on the basis of his encounter with the texts and ideas of theosophy and Eastern religions[45] and he argued that the working man had that more immediate access to 'Life', the Vital and undifferentiated unity which Carpenter sought.[46]

The reading of historical process, cosmic structures and individual lives as expressive of each other was a common strategy in early twentieth-century intellectual and cultural life. Oswald Spengler's *Decline of the West*, for example, a text that appears by name in the fictional world of Lawrence's Lady Chatterley, sought to identify a 'series of stages which must be traversed, and traversed moreover in an ordered and obligatory sequence' which would constitute the morphology of history.[47] T. E. Hulme, in *Speculations*, used his account of the logic of history to overcome the self-evident obviousness of the thought of any particular period. The movement of impersonal historical forces became for him a way of challenging the obviousness of ideology. Drawing on his reading of Bergson, Hulme identified the critical and philosophical stances necessary to permit original and creative thought and concluded, in a manner reminiscent of Lawrence's 'Study of Thomas Hardy' that mankind's involvement in labour and in practical activity was the greatest barrier to true perception: 'If we could break through the veil which action interposes, if we could come into direct contact with sense and consciousness'.[48]

'IT IS THE DESIRE OF THE HUMAN MALE TO BUILD A WORLD'[49]

Lawrence's two volumes, *Psychoanalysis and the Unconscious* (1921) and *Fantasia of the Unconscious* (1922) are an attempt to imagine the relations between will and individuality and between species and history in relation to his understanding of creative selfhood. The use of the term 'psychoanalysis' is perhaps misleading for us, given the dominance of a Freudian model of the unconscious in our contemporary intellectual world. Lawrence does begin by situating his work in relation to Freud, but repudiates Freud's account of the unconscious rapidly and in sweeping terms. Freud's unconscious, Lawrence argues, is 'nothing but a huge slimy serpent of sex, and heaps of excrement, and a myriad repulsive little horrors spawned between sex and excrement'.[50] Lawrence's argument is that the Freudian unconscious is the pathological underbelly of a distorted idealist version of the self, mistakenly read as revealing the essential drives within the human subject. His excremental imagery here evokes other anxieties and preoccupations. We might think of those clogging wastes that affected the neurasthenic, but also of the ways in which Lawrence represented the relations between subjectivity and labour in a poem such as 'All that We have is Life':

> All that we have, while we live, is life;
> and if you don't live during your life, you are a piece of dung
> And work is life, and life is lived in work
> unless you're a wage-slave.
> While a wage-slave works, he leaves life aside
> and stands there a piece of dung.[51]

The individual worker under capitalist social relations becomes, for Lawrence, void and waste. The existential choice dramatized in the first few lines of the stanza, where one can chose whether or not to live one's life, has been negated and the equivalence between the wage-slave and the excremental is absolute. The underbelly of idealism and the individual within capitalist relations of production are both dung, and Lawrence's challenge is to imagine a model of social relations and of the psyche that might escape the necessity of the excremental.

The effort to do this takes Lawrence towards ever more strident and rigid models of the social and the psychic, driven by the impossibility historically and the desperation ethically for social and psychic 'health'. The unconscious, for Lawrence, is the vital force that drives the individual and the species. It has something of the impersonal aspect of the inhuman will, but is also the determining aspect of each individual selfhood: 'Thus it would seem the term *unconscious* is only another word for life. But life is a general force, whereas the unconscious is essentially single and unique in each individual organism' (*Psychoanalysis*, 102).

Lawrence seeks to ground the particularity of the individual within general and knowable biological and psychic structures. He constructs a psychobiological model based on polarity, the equivalence of microcosm and macrocosm, the creative necessity of conflict and the absolute difference of sex. His charting of the nerve centres of the human body is singular, though it draws on some of the terms and images found in a range of theosophical texts. He divides the human organism both horizontally and vertically, and ascribes different affective qualities to different sites within the body. Thus he argues that we have two primary sympathetic nerve centres, the solar plexus and the cardiac plexus. The solar plexus is associated with the lower body, it is the nucleus of the fertilized egg which is the originating moment for the individual organism, and it is the drive towards the triumphantly conscious self. The cardiac plexus is the site of the revelation that 'you are you', the perception of interconnectedness and the realization of species being. Lawrence speaks of the 'primal unconscious pulsing its circuits between two beings: love and wrath, cleaving and repulsion, inglutination and excrementation' (62), and the solar and cardiac plexuses are the location of cleaving, of love and of inglutination. Opposed to these sites are the ganglia, the voluntary centres of separation and repudiation. Again, these are organized in terms of an upper spiritual plane and a lower sensual plane. The voluntary centres are the sites of will, of the desire for integrity and of epistemophilia.

For Lawrence, this model describes the structure of the embryo, the relations between parent and child and the relations between the individual and the social. This belief in a congruence between microcosm and macrocosm was indeed a long-standing one for Lawrence, as we saw in the discussion above of his 'Foreword' to *Sons and Lovers*. In 1915 Lawrence wrote to a friend that:

la race c'*est* moi – la race humaine, c'est *moi*. Let every man say it and be free . . . one is not only a little individual living a little individual life, but that one is in oneself the whole of mankind, and ones fate is the fate of the whole of mankind, and ones charge is the charge of the whole of mankind. Not *me* – the little, vain, personal D. H. Lawrence, but that unnameable me which is not vain and personal, but strong, and glad, and ultimately sure.[52]

Lawrence's organic and psychological system is dynamic, so that each of the centres is constantly in conflict, but the system is also tending towards imbalance and pathology. The overstimulation of voluntary centres is particularly pernicious, and associated above all with the distortions of cerebral and wilful maternal love. Mothers have lost the 'deep bowels of love' that should determine their relations with their children and instead 'what they have is the benevolent spiritual will, the will of the upper self' (*Fantasia*, 55). This pathology haunts Lawrence's texts, and is, for example, forcefully repudiated by a character such as Mellors in *Lady Chatterley's Lover* when he violently rejects what is represented as his daughter's attempt to manipulate his sympathetic will, '"Ah, shut it up, tha false little bitch!" came the man's angry voice, and the child sobbed louder' (58).[53] The overstimulation of the voluntary centres within the individual may result in pathologies of the individual organism, 'any excess in the sympathetic mode from the upper centers tends to burn the lungs with oxygen, weaken them with stress, and cause consumption' (*Fantasia*, 71) but it will also lead to forms of disease within the social: 'In our day, most dangerous is the love and benevolence ideal. It results in neurasthenia, which is largely a dislocation or collapse of the great voluntary centres, a derangement of the will' (59).

Across the two volumes, Lawrence accumulates examples of distortions within the dynamic system of the human organism, which amount to an increasing dominance of the voluntary over the sympathetic centres, a fearful repudiation of the drives and knowledges of the lower centres, and the reduction of human existence to a sterile interplay of will. His biological argument intersects with a historical narrative of decline, and leads to an increasingly dogmatic and rigid account of the proper functioning of the human organism. This proper functioning involves, crucially, the activity of labour:

It is the desire of the human male to build a world: not 'to build a world for you, dear', but to build up out of his own self and his own belief and his own effort something wonderful. (3)

Lawrence attempts to figure this creative activity in terms of the working out of an impersonal organic will, 'Trees that have no hands and faces, no eyes. Yet the powerful sap-scented blood roaring up the great columns. A vast individual life, and an overshadowing will' (44). There is a powerful desire to represent human labour as the necessary expression of the creative impulse, as a working through of the dynamic interrelations between the different nerve centres within the organism. Yet history and agency continually intervene to disrupt this organic model. History appears through the notions of disease and decline, with the tendency towards the cerebral and the ideal being part of the conditions of modern life.[54] But this carries the necessary implication that the individual does not simply act out the logic of its species but may modify, negate or undo the relations between different vital forces.

The anxiety provoked by this recognition produces escalating fantasies of violence within Lawrence's texts which are intimately connected to the question of sexual difference. Lawrence asserts that 'a child is born with one sex only, and remains always single in his sex' (140) and throughout his argument he ascribes distinct drives and characteristics to maleness and femaleness. Specifically, women, or particularly modern women, come to embody the pathological over-emphasis of the will while maleness may more readily express the sympathetic dynamic centres of the human organism. The individual 'building his world' we may note is male not contingently but necessarily, since his struggle towards creative self-expression through labour must first involve the repudiation of the woman's wilful request that he build a world for her. This contrasts interestingly with Lawrence's account of the bee-hive in his 'Foreword' to *Sons and Lovers*, where he had represented the woman in the family home as a source of energy, of transformation and of creative production. But it is perhaps significant that the earlier text dealt with the relations between sons and mothers while *Fantasia of the Unconscious* is examining the dynamic between husbands and wives.

Rigid and absolute sexual difference is crucial to the argument of *Fantasia of the Unconscious*, but it is also something that must continually be won: 'The great thing is to keep the sexes pure . . . we mean pure maleness in a man, pure femaleness in a woman' (279) Lawrence has to assert despite his earlier claim that such distinction was simple and absolute biological fact. By the end of *Fantasia of the Unconscious* the alignment of women with the pathological distortion of the modern will and men with the redeeming power of the sympathetic centres achieves forceful articulation through which men emerge as the historical and ethical bearers of the life force of the human organism:

But fight for your life, men. Fight your wife out of her self-conscious preoccupation with herself. Batter her out of it till she's stunned. Drive her back into her own true mode. Rip all her nice superimposed modern-woman and wonderful-creature garb off her, reduce her once more to a naked Eve, and send the apple flying . . . Make her yield to her own unconscious self, and absolutely stamp on the self that she's got in her head. (284)

'HE SEEMED SO UNLIKE . . . A WORKING MAN'

Some, at least, of the historical and ethical dilemmas articulated in *Fantasia of the Unconscious* emerge in the narrative and the symbolism of *Lady Chatterley's Lover* which is centrally concerned with the dynamic processes of the individual human organism and their expression through the social and sexual relations of early twentieth-century Europe. *Lady Chatterley's Lover* returns constantly to the relations between subjectivity and labour, to the crippling alienation of industrial labour, the desperate compensatory quality of intellectual work, the meanings and significance of physical toil, and the imaginative and ideological work of narrative fiction. The novel begins with the observation: 'The cataclysm has happened, we are among the ruins, we start to build up new little habitats, to have new little hopes. It is rather hard work.' It thus opens with the catastrophe and ruin which Lawrence aims to exemplify and to embody in the physical and psychic failings of his characters, but it also begins with the necessity for hard work.

By the end of the 1920s, Lawrence was increasingly coming to see work as a point of resistance to excessively cerebral conceptions of selfhood, and as the form in which the energies and forces intrinsic to our species could find expression. Work began to figure as the residuum of the physical within social life, an activity whose materiality and temporality cannot be abstracted, despite the progressive tendency towards abstraction and alien-ation inherent in capitalist social and economic relations. When Lawrence recommended, in a letter written in 1927, that his wife's daughter should absorb herself in work he did so not because he particularly wanted women to engage in waged labour but rather out of despair over her capacity to engage in any other ways with the vital and dynamic processes he saw as integral to human subjectivity: 'it is better that she works. The young can neither love nor live. The best is that they work.'[55]

Lady Chatterley's Lover engages with the ways in which work might ex-press, repudiate or unsettle the destructive tendency towards idealism which Lawrence sees as most fully expressed through rapidly advancing industri-alization and mechanization. Commercialism and industrialism are seen as dominating not simply economic relations between classes and between individuals, but also familial, sexual and cultural relations between all the characters in the novel. The novel is set in the industrial Midlands where Clifford Chatterley's country house is surrounded by the collieries that gen-erate his wealth. This industrial landscape is consistently presented by the narrator as embodying broad social and ethical meanings:

With the stoicism of the young she took in the utter, soulless ugliness of the coal-and-iron Midlands at a glance . . . she heard the rattle-rattle of the screens at the pit, the puff of the winding engine, the clink-clink of shunting trucks, and the hoarse little whistle of the colliery locomotives . . . when the wind was that way, which was often, the house was full of the stench of this sulphurous combustion of the earth's excrement. But even on windless days the air always smelt of something under-earth: sulphur, iron, coal, or acid. And even on the Christmas roses the smuts settled persistently, incredible, like black manna from the skies of doom. (13)

The movement of this passage is instructive. It begins with the tentative, even unconscious, recognition by Lady Chatterley of the ugliness of the landscape that surrounds her and it then creates through the insistent rep-etitions of its language an almost physical unease in the reader as it moves towards its conclusion with the skies of doom. That it should be Constance Chatterley who glimpses the ugliness that surrounds her is important for the narrative development of the novel, but so too is her incapacity at this early stage really to grasp the enormity and significance of such ugliness. The narrator drives us towards conclusions Constance Chatterley is far from reaching while also letting us know that she will be capable of such perceptions in the future.

This industrial landscape dominates the lives of those who work in it, turning them from human flesh to soulless mechanism. Working people simply strive to do better within the industrial system: to earn more money. This mechanized greed, a form of 'prostitution to the Money-God' is condemned repeatedly in the novel but political alternatives to capitalism are represented as equally implicated in the logic of mechanism and system: 'You must submerge yourselves in the greater thing, the soviet-social thing. Even an organism is bourgeois: so the ideal must be mechanical . . . Each man a machine-part, and the driving power of the machine, hate: hate of the bourgeois! That, to me, is bolshevism' (38). This remark brings together anxieties over mechanization, objectification and submergence of self in what might seem like a relatively familiar sort of organicist nostalgia, but in fact the relations between mechanism and selfhood are far from stable in the novel as a whole. Representations of selfhood in *Lady Chatterley's Lover* draw on a series of minute but semantically and ideologically significant distinctions between self-consciousness, with its pathological manifestations in the will, and the non-mental consciousness of self Lawrence explored in *Fantasia of the Unconscious*.

Thus, while one character can express anxiety about the ways in which communism necessitates a sacrifice of the self, other voices throughout the novel question the viability and the desirability of self-consciousness and its articulation through the will. This is the conflict between the will as impersonal energy and the will as expression of the egoistic self that has long exercised Lawrence, but in this novel the conflict is personified. Excessive self-consciousness, particularly a mental consciousness with no grounding in bodily experience, is ascribed to many of the characters in this novel. Michaelis, who is Lady Chatterley's lover in the early parts of the novel, is self-contained to the point of pathology, '"*Me* give myself away! ha-ha!" he laughed hollowly, cynical at such an idea' (27) though he also suffers from a 'sad-dog sort of extinguished self' (28). Clifford has a precarious sense of self, 'he needed Connie to be there, to assure him he existed at all' (16), but also has a coercive, bullying self that seeks to eradicate disturbing or unpredictable elements of its own or in others. He has, in other words, will without any substantial individuality. Constance Chatterley's sister Hilda seeks to intervene in her sister's life and is condemned as wilful by Mellors in generalizing terms that move from character analysis to social dogma: 'A stubborn woman an' 'er own self-will: ay, they make a fast continuity, they do' (245).

But it is in the sphere of sexual relationships where the dangers of self-assertion and self-consciousness are most powerfully asserted in this novel. Given Lawrence's theorization of coition as an almost impersonal collision of vital forces which follows a necessary and pre-ordained pattern,[56] any attempt to interpose the self is likely to feature as perversion. Connie's early sexual experiences with a young German student, with whom her primary connections are 'philosophical, sociological and artistic' involve merely 'a queer vibrating thrill inside the body, a final spasm of self-assertion' (8). 'Thrill' and 'spasm' are terms which signal superficiality of experience throughout the novel and are associated with attempts to ward off the creative and the unpredictable. Thus Connie's self-assertion is read through her fearful conformity and the result is a neurotic spasm.

Lady Chatterley's Lover becomes increasingly forceful in its articulation of the forms of authentic selfhood which are desirable and possible. Beginning with a sense that Connie's early sexual experiences might have been transient and superficial but that she is still capable of change and development, the novel begins to see all manifestations of willed selfhood as pernicious and as irremediable. Mellors declares that 'when a woman gets absolutely possessed by her own will, her own will set against everything, then it's fearful, and she should be shot at last' (280). Mellors has been given the power by the novel to distinguish between degenerate and empty forms of subjectivity, such as those associated with his ex-wife and with Clifford Chatterley, and creative forms of self-realization where the individual is justified in pursuing their own ends regardless of the costs.

One of the first things we learn about Mellors is that he is 'sure of himself' and he is represented as intact and as separate to the point of hostility. For Connie, on the other hand, selfhood is a burden, a weight of mental consciousness that she carries from the opening pages of the novel until she 'could bear the burden of herself no more' (117). Connie's affair with Mellors leads to a loss of self which she both celebrates and fears 'she did not want to be effaced' and her will struggles against the forms of knowing associated in the novel primarily with the womb and the bowels: 'She had a devil of self-will in her breast that could have fought the full, soft, heavy adoration of her womb and bowels' (135–36).

Physical consciousness emerges, however fleetingly, as a key point of resistance to mechanization and to the power of commerce in *Lady Chatterley's Lover*. Such consciousness is allied to the proper direction of creative energies and is expressed through and in manual labour. In his poem 'We are the Transmitters', Lawrence writes:

> As we live, we are the transmitters of life.
> And when we fail to transmit life, life fails to flow through us.
>
> That is part of the mystery of sex, it is a flow onwards.
> Sexless people transmit nothing.

And if, as we work, we can transmit life into our work,
life, still more life, rushes into us to compensate, to be ready
and we ripple with life through the days.[57]

The human individual is here conceived as an energetic organism, which can transmit energy and renew itself through the act of sex and the activity of labour. The fragile balance this implies is under threat throughout *Lady Chatterley's Lover*. For example, Clifford Chatterley's nerves function erratically, creating imbalances of energy for him and for the fictional world of the novel. At times he suffers from a collapse of nervous energy, or he wastes nervous energy through self-deception or obsession, and at other moments he is in a 'nervous frenzy'. When not braced up to work Clifford is reduced to 'a net-work of nerves' (139), a circulation of energy which serves simply to mask a dangerous void.

Clifford's condition is named variously. Early in the novel he is suffering from 'vacant depression', while in the later stages of the novel his behaviour is diagnosed as hysterical. Throughout, however, he is associated with wasteful and compulsive spending of nervous energy to no particular end. This lack of 'end' is given forceful, perhaps even crude, expression in his failure to procreate. But it also has more abstract meanings which are associated with his life even before the war. As the inheritor of the legacy of industrial exploitation he is bound to a system that can only accelerate both production and acquisition in an ever more frantic spectacle of industrial growth. As a young intellectual he is similarly caught in a discursive economy that knows no bounds: the intellectual discussions in *Lady Chatterley's Lover* are notably futile and rather prolonged. This forceful indictment of wasteful nervous expenditure sits rather uncomfortably with the fascination with excess and waste we found in his 'Study of Thomas Hardy', but in *Lady Chatterley's Lover* Lawrence displays a horror of non-productive, or non-procreative, expenditures of energy.

In the treatment of neurasthenia doctors recommended rest, but Clifford tries instead to overcome nervous and affective exhaustion by ever-increasing levels of work. His 'work' at the beginning of the novel is writing fiction, an activity that is treated with great scepticism. This scepticism indeed echoes something of the unease Lawrence himself expresses about whether writing amounts in any sense to 'work': 'We've finished the hard work on the ranch here, and I'm hoping for a bit of leisure. I might even try a bit of my own work again.'[58] Joint participation in Clifford's work appears to offer Clifford and Connie some shared and meaningful activity and we are told that 'their interests had never ceased to flow together, over his work' (18). But this shared project is not long sustained: from the out-set we are told that what they had shared was a 'vague life of absorption in Clifford and his work'. The vagueness already tells us about a lack of focus, a certain drifting, the absorption is a loss of self based more on fear and negation than on creative transformation, and finally the absorption is primarily in Clifford and only secondarily in his work, which suggests that such collaborative work cannot mask a more fundamental division. The sentence contrasts strikingly with the narrator's conclusion about Connie and Mellors after they have struggled together to push Clifford's wheelchair uphill: 'It was curious, but this bit of work together had brought them much closer than they had been before' (192), closer presumably than all the sexual intimacies they have shared at this stage of the novel.

Clifford's work is a frenzy of neurotic activity whose aim is worldly suc-cess. Connie's father tells us that as literary texts, his stories are 'void', a judgement that Connie herself will come to share. Connie also comes to resent Clifford's work as a symptom of his self-obsession: 'She wanted to be clear of him, and especially of his consciousness, his words, his obsession with himself – his endless treadmill obsession with himself and his own words' (93). The narrative voice here enacts the futile repetitions of the process it is describing, assaulting us with Clifford's selfhood and his lan-guage. Clifford's writing is simply an enactment of the futility of his speech, with its proliferation of words and its increasing incapacity to name or to know the world, 'when he was alone he tap-tap-tapped on a typewriter, to infinity. But when he was not "working", and she was there, he talked, al-ways talked' (83). The inauthenticity of Clifford's labour is clearly signalled by the inverted commas, as aesthetic creativity is reduced to repetitive and mechanical tapping. Connie's role in this creative work is similarly reduced: 'the thrill had gone out of it. She was bored by his manuscripts. She still dutifully typed them out for him' (99). The creative potential of literary language is here savagely removed by Lawrence from any concerns with the mode of its material production, and the mechanical production of text becomes simply another mode of industrial labour.[59] That Lawrence himself relied so heavily on the labours of women to type up his different manuscript versions of this novel simply adds to the uncomfortable ironies of this moment in the text.

Clifford's work of literary production then is a self-deceiving and self-obsessed exercise in futility, and is indeed an activity he is pleased to re-nounce. As Connie's physical and mental health decline in the first section of the novel, Clifford acquires a nurse, Ivy Bolton, who will oversee the trans-ference of his energies from literary to industrial production. Ivy Bolton is a strange and liminal character: she is the widow of a miner yet her education and professional training gain her an entry to the world of the Chatterleys. She has a fierce sense of class loyalty but also a fascination with the lives and mores of the upper class. As an independent working woman she is particularly susceptible to the corrosive effects of this novel's social and psychic categories which can only read her determination as pathological will. Ivy Bolton is introduced as a woman of some determination driven by a clear desire for economic independence:

Ivy Bolton, went to Sheffield, and attended classes in ambulance, special ambulance, and then the fourth year she even took a nursing course and got qualified. She was determined to be independent and keep her children. So she was assistant at Uthwaite hospital, just a little place, for a while. (81)

This training for independence actually leads her to economic, and later emotional, dependency on the Chatterleys. Her education separates her from the working classes, indeed leads to a sort of contempt for them whilst at the same time identifying her with the progressive movements of industrial capital, if not exactly with progressive capitalists. Mrs Bolton encourages Clifford to shift his energies towards the development of his mines, pointing out in particular the importance of local labour for young girls: 'keep the men going a bit better, and employ the girls' (106). Clifford is pleased to transfer his energies from the 'populace of pleasure to the populace of work' which he finds grim and terrible, but also more substantial: 'the meat and bones for the bitch-goddess were provided by the men who made money in industry' (107). Under Mrs Bolton's influence, Clifford becomes increasingly absorbed in business and in his mines, in the 'brute business of industrial production'.

For Clifford, identification with the processes of industrial labour creates a harmony between labour and selfhood, even if this is a harmony of degradation. Industry and commerce sustain fantasies of potency and agency for Clifford which he had found in no other cultural sphere: 'he really felt, when he had his periods of energy and worked so hard at the question of the mines, as if his sexual potency were returning' (147). For Ivy Bolton, on the other hand, an increasing identification with the process of industrial production serves to disconnect her from her class and from any sustainable notion of 'independence'. By the end of the novel, however, both are destroyed and reduced to mutual dependence and perversity: 'And then he would put his hand into her bosom and feel her breasts, and kiss them in exaltation, the exaltation of perversity, of being a child when he was a man' (291).

The workers in his mines are also reduced and degraded by the results of Clifford's feverish work, which are expressed in the rapidity and momentum of industrial change. Lawrence is particularly forceful in his representation of the impossibility of creative forms of selfhood within the spaces of industrial labour. In two brief poems published in *Pansies* he stages the dichotomy between objects that embody a store of human labour and objects manufactured industrially. Things men have made are 'awake through years with transferred touch' while things made by steel are 'shrouds, they soak the life out of us'.[60] The man-made objects remain warm and alive, while industrially produced objects take the life from those who make them.

In *Lady Chatterley's Lover*, Lawrence works to construct the tension of a dialogue between different characters and the narrative voice, and Constance Chatterley's increasing identification with the terms and convictions embodied in the narrative voice develops slowly and hesitantly throughout the novel and is mediated by her exchanges with Mellors. The working classes, however, are not permitted to enter into such imaginative or intellectual dialogue, but are consistently objectified and offered as emblematic by the narrative voice: their meanings are always already given. This objectification draws to some extent on existing forms of language: the naming of the mine and its associated industries as 'the works' serving to evacuate conceptions of individuality from the process of labour by identifying activity and place. This is a form of abstraction which might be seen as fundamental to the social relations of industrial production under a capitalist economic system, but in a novel that seeks to undo such abstraction and objectification its easy reproduction is striking. Industrial labourers are 'weird distorted, smallish beings like men' (153) whose degradation renders any notion of collectivity impossible. Their physical and moral state makes the idea of common humanity ridiculous, and at the sight of them Connie's 'bowels fainted' (159).

The working classes have been reduced, by industrialization and by education, to false consciousness and coercive will. Connie overhears working-class children singing in their new school, a building which resembles both a chapel and a prison, and responds with horror:

Anything more unlike song, spontaneous song, would be impossible to imagine: a strange, bawling yell that followed the outlines of a tune. It was not like savages: savages have subtle rhythms. It was not like animals: animals *mean* something when they yell. It was like nothing on earth, and it was called singing. Connie sat and listened with her heart in her boots, as Field was filling petrol. What could possibly become of such a people, a people in whom the living intuitive faculty was dead as nails, and only queer mechanical yells and uncanny will-power remained. (152)

We can have no access to what this sort of singing exercise might mean to these children, or to whether they might elsewhere do other sorts of singing. Rather, they are condemned to represent the corrosive effects of industrialization on human intuition and creativity. Working men are also read as expressive only of a system that contains them absolutely, 'men not men, but animas of coal and iron and clay' (169). They are identified completely with the materials and with the mechanism of industrial production while working women are barely perceptible at all. Working people are determined by the system that produces the forms of their labour and the details of their work are thus profoundly insignificant.

There is, apparently, no redemption for the destructive effects of industrial labour. Certainly, the elderly Squire Winter suggests that industrial work may in fact be the saving of the race when he says to Clifford: 'you may again employ every man at Tevershall. – Ah, my boy! – to keep up the level of the race, and to have work waiting for any man who cares to work! –' (150) but since this comment is made in the course of a speech in which the Squire congratulates Clifford on his future paternity its perspicacity is in some doubt. Mellors tells us, on the other hand, that working for money has turned men 'into labour-insects, and all their manhood taken away, and all their real life' (220).

The hopelessness of this analysis continually disturbs the narrative and imagery of *Lady Chatterley's Lover*, but the possible recovery of 'manhood' through labour is imagined, through the activities of the gamekeeper, Oliver Mellors. We learn very early in the novel that Mellors maintains his own domestic space through his own labour.[61] He has handed the daily care of his daughter over to his mother, but tends to his own garden and does his own housework. His domestic work is the condition of his separateness and allows him to control his environment and the rhythms of his day. Mellors's 'little railed-in garden in the front of the house' is also a measure of his control of his own environment. Interestingly it evokes a markedly less sensual engagement with gardening than Connie is to experience later in the novel: 'Connie especially felt a delight in putting the soft roots of young plants into a soft black puddle, and cradling them down. On this spring morning she felt a quiver in her womb, too' (162).

Connie discovers Mellors in the woods: drawn by the sound of his hammering she finds him in his shirt-sleeves, kneeling and at work. He resents the intrusion, but she is apparently fascinated by the spectacle. She enters his hut and sees a carpenter's bench, tools and nails, an axe, a hatchet and 'things in sacks': the paraphernalia of artisanal labour. She then settles down to watching 'the man at work'. This fascination carries with it its own forms of objectification, with Mellors imagined simply as 'the man', but this is surely abstraction to an essence rather than reduction to an emblem. For Connie, her earlier glimpse of Mellors washing merges with her attentive observation of his labour:

So Connie watched him fixedly. And the same solitary aloneness she had seen in him naked, she now saw in him clothed: solitary and intent, like an animal that works alone, but also brooding, like a soul that recoils away, away from all human contact . . . It was the stillness, and the timeless sort of patience, in a man impatient and passionate, that touched Connie's womb. (89)

Such stillness contrasts markedly with the fevered toiling of Clifford or the mechanized repetitions of industrial labour. Mellors's labour is individual and artisanal, and his intentness is distinct from the 'vague absorption' of intellectual labour. Mellors is the son of a collier who after receiving an education at Sheffield Grammar School becomes a clerk. He later 'chucked up my job at Butterley because I thought I was a weed clerking there' (201) and found work instead as a blacksmith on the pit-brow. As a blacksmith he is curiously placed in relation to mechanized labour since the blacksmith points both backwards to a vanishing form of agricultural production and forwards to the dependence of labourers on a functioning machine. He spends some time in the army, displaying a particular knack for working with horses and winning the support and affection of one of his officers. He gains a commission, but following the death of his friend gives up army life to return to manual labour. This narrative of Mellors's career stresses his agency, his capacity to chose particular places and forms of labour, and Connie's observation that 'he seemed *so* unlike a gamekeeper, so un-like a working-man anyhow' (68) captures something of this anachronistic quality.

But how are such forms of work possible within an economic and moral system that had seemed so destructive of productive labour? The answer may lie in some theory of uneven development, with Mellors emerging as an anachronistic figure whose very oddness might provide a resource for utopian imaginings, the kind of figure of medieval labour that Lawrence indeed had specifically disavowed in his 'Study of Thomas Hardy'. Certainly there are suggestions at a number of points that physical and manual labour were not always the alienated thing that they appear to be in *Lady Chatterley's Lover* as a whole. At one point we are told that in the late Victorian period miners were 'good working men', though Mellors himself sees the decline as rather earlier: 'it's a shame, what's been done to people these last hundred years: men turned into nothing but labour-insects' (220). This uncertain periodization is not simply a matter of carelessness, but a symptom of the particular interactions of myth and history within the novel: it is necessary for *Lady Chatterley's Lover* to imagine more integrated forms of labour, but not really to examine how or when they might have been realized.

Mellors's version of work is pre-industrial and he insists that 'I know nothing at all about all these mechanical things' (187), although as a trained blacksmith that is likely to be a question of willed ignorance. He extricates himself imaginatively from the economic relations and industrial forms of production that dominate the world around him: 'bit by bit, let's drop the whole industrial life an' go back' (219). Since working for money can only lead to physical and moral deformity, and there is no solution to the 'wage squabble' except not to care, Mellors 'refused to *care* about money' (148).

Yet in the sphere of labour, it is far from clear how these transformations can possibly be brought about. We have already been told that the 'individual asserts himself in his disconnected insanity in these two modes: money and love' (97), and without dwelling on the disconnected insanity we can indeed see that money and love are privileged modes of experience and relationship within *Lady Chatterley's Lover*. The transformative possibilities of sexual relationship can be figured within the novel as a matter of unique and private forms of human relationship and as the outcome of the work of writing. It is certainly true that sexual behaviour is constantly metaphorized and pathologized in the novel and given public meanings, but, nonetheless, it is possible for two individuals, Connie and Mellors, to create forms of intimacy and passion that the novel represents as transformative and transgressive. In some sense the novel draws on the 'privacy' of sexual relations which it elsewhere denies in order to render alternative moral and sexual economies imaginable. It also builds up the symbolic and affective meanings of a series of terms, such as 'blindly', 'intuitively' and 'queer' in order to allow for the imaginative apprehension of new modes of selfhood. I do not intend to suggest that *Lady Chatterley's Lover* constructs some sort of sexual utopia: Mellors's hatred of 'mouth kisses' his murderous dislike of lesbians, and his distaste for black women who are 'a bit like mud' (204) all suggest that fear and phobia continue to circulate within his sexual fantasies and knowledges. Equally Connie's increasing horror of other women, 'to be free of the strange dominion and obsession of *other women*. How awful they were, women!' (253) suggests that her new ways of knowing and experiencing the world are not without their rather brutal exclusions. Nonetheless, it remains the case that the novel can, through its own literary work, construct another version of sexual relationship with a freedom that is simply unavailable in the case of economic relations.

At the end of the day, and at the end of the novel, Mellors has to have a job: 'I've got to work, or I should die' (167). This need is not a matter of economic stringency, since he has an army pension, but is a question of having something to keep him occupied and 'working with the immediate quiet absorption that was characteristic of him' (198). He has to work in order to function creatively as an individual and he has to work for someone else in order to have the discipline of labour, but he refuses to participate in the 'wage-struggle'. The dilemma is simply exacerbated by his relationship with Connie who could, after all, keep both of them financially secure. But Mellors makes it clear that his involvement in productive and waged labour is a condition of the viability of their relationship.

There is never any question that Connie might need work as a culmination of her selfhood since the narrative of her life is created out of affective and domestic relationships. It is pregnancy that delivers her from inertia and motherhood is set to become her primary occupation. For Mellors, however, his life must have some sense of movement and purpose which is connected to his role as productive labourer: 'Living is moving and moving on . . . A man must offer a woman *some* meaning in his life, if it's going to be an isolated life, and if she's a genuine woman. – I can't be just your male concubine' (276).

By the end of the novel Connie and Mellors are living apart, presumably temporarily. She is waiting to have their baby and he is learning to become a farmer:

And for six months he should work at farming, so that eventually he and Connie could have some small farm of their own, into which he could put his energy. For he would have to have some work, even hard work, to do, and he would have to make his own living, even if her own capital started him. (298)

Connie's capital sits uncomfortably beside Mellors's desire to make his own living because the acknowledgement of the need for capital allows social relations and economic structures to intrude into the unmediated exchange of work and individual selfhood that Mellors projects. Mellors ends by invoking the 'great groping white hands' (300) that will seek to crush all those who would live outside the norms of money and will, but in the face of the novel's incapacity really to imagine any such space except in the most abstract terms, these white hands become ghostly and even fantastical. The work of the novel has taken us so far from the contingencies and materiality of productive labour that even its vivid fears and passionate denunciations begin to feel less solid. The symbolic invocation of degeneration and decline cannot sustain its rootedness as we are taken from the physicality and economic contingency of manual labour to the ghostly abstractions of those groping white hands.

Thus a text in which Lawrence has tried to expose the alienation of the physical as the condition of modernity lands up re-enacting the process of abstraction through the rigidity of its imaginative and intellectual categories. Something similar seems to happen to Lawrence at this period when he returns to painting. Lawrence produced a series of paintings in the 1920s, in which there was a predominance of flesh, and specifically of male flesh within the canvas. In his own introduction to these images, Lawrence constructs a narrative of modernity as a progressive fear and withdrawal from physicality, which achieve its most extreme expression in contemporary aesthetic theory. Against this tendency, Lawrence praises Cézanne, for his struggle to represent physicality, materiality and 'thereness', and he clearly intends we read his own images through this drive to evoke the substantial and the material existence of flesh. Yet the lure of allegory and abstract symbolism is powerful for Lawrence, as is clear not only within the images themselves but also in their titles, such as 'Resurrection', 'Flight back into Paradise' or 'Leda'.

The figures in these paintings are massive, in the sense that they have large bodies and small heads, but in the repetitive rendering of the same basic physique, the paleness of the flesh, and the abstract quality of the locations, the paintings tend to evoke ideas more powerfully than materialities. Lawrence's own comments on the paintings seem to push us towards allegorical engagement rather than the intensity of intuitive response he has described in his Introduction. He describes the 'Flight back into Paradise' as an image of Eve retreating from the modern world while Adam struggles with the angel at the gates.[62] We may even here be returning to the naked Eve Lawrence represented as the antithesis of modern woman in *Fantasia of the Unconscious*. The painting offers a very tightly structured rendering of both the struggle and the retreat: it is divided diagonally, with the top left-hand side of the image containing factories, chimneys, smoke and fire, while the bottom contains the three naked figures. The woman is tied to the nightmarish industrial scene by an abstractly represented rope while the Adam figure seems to evoke an intensity of psychic distress, though it may also be an extremity of physical pain. The image as a whole has little power beyond the ways in which it articulates a basically intellectual struggle.

The paintings were attacked in the late 1920s as gross, as coarse and as hideous, and were also deemed to be obscene.[63] My own reading of the paintings, however, would be that they are insufficiently coarse or gross to capture the intuitive and physical response Lawrence seems to yearn for. He has written himself into such a rigid set of oppositions and created such a tight symbolic and political alignment of aspects of the contemporary that his paintings become merely illustrative, rather than being challenging or disruptive images in their own right. They also strikingly avoid any substantial representation of labour, despite the fact that physical labour has become so important to Lawrence's sense of possible redemption by this time. Even a painting such as 'Accident in Mine' creates symbols of suffering rather than approaching the physicality of manual labour underground. His miners stand up tall and seem not to be constricted by their environment while their facial expressions are almost blank. They have become form more than substance.

The abstraction and allegory found in these paintings tends to undercut Lawrence's avowed commitments to physicality and in particular to manual labour, as expressed in his 1929 article, 'Men must Work and Women as Well'. Here he explicitly repudiates his earlier argument that material and mechanical progress could free us from the burden of toil, associating such inverted utopianism with 'great magnates of industry like Mr Ford'.[64] Indeed, the aspiration to free ourselves from physical labour becomes simply another manifestation of the repudiation of material forms of subjectivity: 'one of the greatest changes that has ever taken place in man and woman is this revulsion from physical effort, physical labour and physical contact, which has taken place within the last thirty years' (584). Having craved freedom from physical work, we are now doomed to resent all physical demands on our time and energies and the result is 'some form of collective social madness' (591). Lawrence condemns the pernicious effects of such fastidiousness, arguing that all that it has produced is angry and resentful individuals who are nonetheless still required to undertake a series of manual tasks. Yet his language suggests that his earlier aspiration to escape from the brute demands of physical labour has not entirely disappeared: 'the labouring masses are and will be, even if all else is swept away: because they must be. They represent the gross necessity of man, which science has failed to save us from' (587). Even allowing for the ironic tone in which he represents this 'gross necessity', it is hard not to hear some lingering regret over science's failure. And even within this powerful defence of physical labour as the biological and ethical end of man, we can still find the imaginative aspiration for a world in which we have been set free from the repetitive and exhausting business of physical toil.

Imaginative aspiration is also the subject of the next and final chapter, which examines the theorization of 'the general strike' in the late nineteenth and early twentieth centuries. Here we will find both the aspiration towards historical agency we discussed in relation to Sylvia Pankhurst, as well as the imaginative intervention in the possibilities of modern selfhood we have seen in Lawrence's writing. These will come together particularly in relation to the forms and modes of temporality which can be imagined through the category of 'modern labour', as expressed in the myth and the experiences of a general strike.

CHAPTER FIVE

The general strike: labour and the future tense

In this final chapter I will examine the 'general strike' as an event and a process which, perhaps paradoxically, had an integral relationship to the imagination and the experience of human labour in the early years of the twentieth century. I will be looking particularly at the complex temporalities set in play by images and narrative of the general strike, with the aim of understanding the versions of selfhood these different temporalities might imply. I will also try to illuminate the ways in which narratives and images of the general strike enable, but also constrain, a temporality directed towards the future.

The general strike is a cessation of labour, but is nonetheless only imaginable in relation to the activity and the institutions that define labour at any particular historical moment. The general strike reaches beyond the confines of one particular place of work or one particular trade. It is an inherently modern phenomenon, in the sense that it depends on the division of labour and its resultant organization of workers into large groups, often located in factories, and also relies on the interdependence of different aspects of the labour process. The general strike needs industrial organization and modern communications, both to initiate and to sustain it. Both as a remembered or imagined historical experience and as a theoretical category it raises a series of questions about the relation between human labour and historical agency that it will be the aim of this chapter to explore. Historical, political, artistic and mythical temporalities are all invoked in the explosion of imaginative and political activity that surrounds the general strike.

SYNDICALISM AND THE GENERAL STRIKE

The idea and the practice of the general strike were of fundamental importance for political theorists and activists in the early years of the twentieth century. Indeed, Donald Sassoon has argued that, for socialism in Western Europe, 'of far greater importance than the issue of revolutionary violence was the debate over the uses of the general or "mass" strike as a political weapon'.[1] Syndicalism, a form of political organization that drew on the disruptive potential of action taken at or near the point of production, included the general strike, along with direct action, boycott or sabotage, in its range of tactics for achieving profound industrial and social change.[2] Syndicalism was an increasingly significant presence in the industrial and political landscape of Britain and of Europe from the late nineteenth century, and reached its most powerful and developed forms in the years between 1905 and the First World War. In considering the cultural and political significance of the general strike between 1890 and 1929, it will thus also be necessary to examine the development of syndicalism as a political rhetoric and as a political practice during these years.

The first theoretical articulation of the nature and the significance of the general strike can be found in William Benbow's *Grand National Holiday and Congress of the Productive Classes* of 1832.[3] Benbow was a political activist and polemicist, writing and working at a period of intense industrial and political agitation. He was a member both of the National Union of the Working Classes, which was founded in 1831, and of the more moderate National Political Union. He became active in the Chartist movement and was arrested on a number of occasions for his political activities.[4] His 1832 pamphlet sets out the case for a general cessation of labour for a period of one month. He begins this polemic by citing biblical texts denouncing the greed and sinfulness of the rich and the oppressive nature of landowners. Like earlier radical theorists, Benbow divides the world between the productive and unproductive classes, or between the useful worker and the parasite: 'they exist on disease and blood: crime and infamy are the breath of their nostrils' (4). His case is that the present distribution of wealth gives power and liberty to the parasitic few, and denies ease and happiness to the useful worker. Benbow argues that 'Life, when good for anything, consists of ease, gaiety and pleasure, and consequently of happiness' (3), and thus seems to associate work with oppression and a lack of happiness. Being condemned to ceaseless labour leaves the working classes unable to achieve a meaningful sense of identity: 'How is it that the people have never existed – that is, have never enjoyed ease, gaiety, pleasure and happiness?' (5). It is not entirely clear whether Benbow's objection is to the fact of labour, or to the alienating conditions under which it must be performed by the mass of the labouring poor, though he certainly insists that 'our labour is of no use to us, since what it produces goes into the hands of others' (9). The idea that inequality constitutes a negation of selfhood is a powerful one in Benbow's text, and it is developed in a series of images of working people as sleeping, or as supine.

The overcoming of this negation will require sustained political activism, realizable partly in the general strike. Thus Benbow says that when working people fight for themselves, 'then will they live' (4). He asks working people to join in his proposed holiday, for the sake of liberty and of happiness: 'If you, O people, do not rouse yourselves you will leave to posterity a nation of the most miserable slaves' (6). Benbow's plan is for a cessation of labour for a period of a month, which is to be paid for from loan funds, from funds originally meant for relief of the poor, and from political donations: 'The reformers of the united kingdom will hold out an open hand to support us during our festival' (13). His vision of a festival, or a holiday, is not, however, a vision of idleness. Working people are to cease from toil in order to begin to study. Research and political organization are to be the activities undertaken during the general strike, so that working people can overcome the ignorance that condemns them to collude passively in a social system that is oppressive and unequal, and deprives the labouring classes even of their labour.

Although there were many examples of concerted and generalized industrial unrest in the early years of the nineteenth century, Benbow's vision of a sustained period of political activism and political education was never achieved by the majority of labouring men and women. Nonetheless, the rhetoric and the argument of Benbow's text made a significant contribution to the development of what we would now call a syndicalist consciousness later in the century. Syndicalism depended absolutely on Benbow's vision of class antagonism, as well as on his personal and ethical sense of the need for the political and historical awakening of the working classes. The growth of syndicalism, as a political practice and as a theory, was tightly connected, even if often oppositionally, to the growth in the membership and power of trade unions. Trade union membership grew, in Britain and also throughout Europe, from the early 1870s. In Britain membership exceeded 1 million in 1874, and then, following a few years of decline, doubled between 1889 and 1891.[5] Unions became increasingly aware of socialist and collectivist ideas, and this period saw the development of more general unions, rather than the narrowly defined craft unions that had been so important to the industrial landscape of nineteenth-century Europe. Following the Taff Vale decision of 1901, the industrial and political priorities of the trade union movement in Britain were substantially inflected towards the struggle for parliamentary representation of the interests of labour. The Taff Vale decision held that unions were liable for financial losses incurred as a result of strike action, and the consequences for trade unions and their official policies were substantial. The first few years of the twentieth century saw a decrease in industrial conflict in Britain, and the growth of collective bargaining procedures and national pay schemes.

By 1905, however, industrial militancy was once more increasing. The early years of the century saw a rise in the cost of living and a fall in wage levels driven by poor rates of growth and overseas competition.[6] The rail and the coal industries were particularly badly affected. In 1906 and 1907 there were a series of disputes in the South Wales coalfield; in 1907 there was a dispute in the railway industry that nearly culminated in a general strike; in 1908 there was a prolonged strike in the cotton industry; in 1911 there were a series of transport strikes, and in 1912 there was a general strike by miners for a minimum wage.[7] Across Europe, the general strike was widely employed as a tactic within a sustained conflict between capital and labour. Rudolf Rocker, in his 1938 study of anarcho-syndicalism, mentions general strikes in Barcelona (1902); in Bilbao and in Belgium (1903); in Russia (1905); in Catalonia and in Sweden (1909).[8] Unsurprisingly, then this period, between 1905 and 1914 was one of intense theoretical discussion of the nature and the political legitimacy of the general strike.

Syndicalism was an international movement and body of ideas, and there was a significant knowledge within Britain of syndicalist texts and movements from France, Russia, Germany and the United States. When Wilf McCartney wrote in 1942 about his own involvement in syndicalism in the early years of the century, he made this kind of internationalism explicit.[9] McCartney worked in the catering trade, which was particularly badly affected by low rates of pay and poor working conditions and was not well served by established trade unions. Around 1900, McCartney records that he attended lectures on syndicalism in a hall in Little Newport Street. These lectures were attended mainly by catering workers, and concentrated on techniques of industrial militancy: 'we realized there is no other basis but direct action at the point of production for the catering trade workers' (*Dare to be a Daniel*, 8). In 1905 the French Cooks' Syndicate was formed to fight for better pay and conditions in the industry. The constitution of this Syndicate insisted on direct action as the primary tactic of industrial militancy. McCartney stresses the scepticism members of the Syndicate felt about the leaders of established trade unions, who were seen as sacrificing the interests of their members for the sake of their own comfort. As McCartney rather coyly puts it, the International Workers of the World appealed rather more.

The International Workers of the World was a movement founded in the United States in 1905. Borrowing the rhetoric of internationalism from the Socialist International, which had been reformed in 1889, this movement nonetheless sought to distinguish itself sharply from the theoretical and political positions it associated with the labour movement and its political institutions. One of its most prominent activists and theorists was Daniel de Leon. De Leon had risen to prominence in the American Socialist Labour Party at the end of the nineteenth century. Already, by 1898, de Leon is articulating a fierce opposition to the timidity and self-interestedness of trade unions, and insisting on the necessity of class war. In an address to striking workers, he sets out to 'enlighten them on the great issue before them, and the great historical drama in which most of them are still unconscious actors'.[10] He castigates union leaders, particularly those in Britain, for their weak and corrupt leadership but insists that working men can 'preserve manhood' through the constant activity of 'the rebellion that is implied in a strike' (*What Means*, 4). The key elements of syndicalist thought are present in this brief address: commitment to class war, suspicion of the institutions and leaders of the labour movement, and a belief that participation in industrial militancy is a form of rebellion that can sustain selfhood, here explicitly gendered as 'manhood', in the face of overwhelming oppression. By 1905, de Leon is explicitly committed to syndicalism and to the International Workers of the World. In an Address on the subject of industrial unionism, he again insists that class conflict is unavoidable, and that there is no possibility of a consensus between the interests of capital and labour, but he now argues very forcefully for a new political and cultural project based explicitly on the militant activity of 'toilers', and with no affiliation to any political party.[11] He describes trade union leaders as the 'watch-dog of capitalism' and argues instead for industrial unionism as a form of collective struggle whose power comes through the general strike. As he tellingly puts it: 'Industrialism means Might. Craft Unionism means Impotence' (*Principles*, p. 29). This sexualized imagery picks up de Leon's earlier concern with manhood, suggesting that what is at stake for him in the general strike is masculinity at least as much as humanity.

Rosa Luxemburg's metaphorical investment in the general strike is, as might be expected, rather more inclusive. Her study of the general strike, *The Mass Strike, the Political Party and the Trade Unions*, was written in 1906 and is primarily concerned with the history of industrial and political conflict in Russia between 1896 and 1905. She aims to understand the energies that create and sustain such industrial conflict, but also to think about how it might be possible to re-imagine the notion of political leadership through and beyond the general strike. In the history of the mass strike in Russia, Luxemburg argues, 'we see a bit of pulsating life of flesh and blood, which . . . is connected with all parts of the revolution by a thousand veins'.[12] The vitalism of this image suggests that Luxemburg sees the general strike as an organic process, and also as an articulation of the energies of an impersonal Will. She insists that it cannot be understood within rigid categories, and that it cannot ever be captured as a completed process: 'the mass strike in Russia displays such a multiplicity of the most varied forms of action that it is altogether impossible to speak of "the" mass strike' (*Mass Strike*, 23). Given the multiplicity and the amorphous nature of the general strike, Luxemburg argues that the task of a progressive political leadership does not lie in preparation for or direction of the strike, but rather in a more abstract political leadership of the working classes as a whole.

All theorists of the general strike stress its capacity to energize and to radicalize, but in doing so also invoke the passive and negative condition that is the consequence of modern forms of labour. Arnold Roller argues that the general strike is a form of activism that can produce consciousness, agency, and purposeful activity where before there was slumber or indifference:

Large masses of the working people, who never paid any attention . . . ; who never have been aroused by the ballot; and who would never have followed the call of the revolution, because their life never was anything else but a uniform vegetating between obtuse slumber and enervating labor, are now at once put on the street.[13]

Labour thus has a tendency to enervate and to pacify, but it is also the space in which innovation can be imagined and achieved. This creative and imaginative dimension of labour is explicitly invoked by Graham Wallas in his analytic presentation of syndicalism in the *Sociological Review* of 1912. Wallas presents an account of the philosophical and political issues he sees as implicit in the development of syndicalist thought in the early years of the twentieth century, in which he stresses the ways in which the creative ambitions of the movement move into the realm of the aesthetic: 'again and again in the French literature of Syndicalism came the analogy of the arts. It was urged that in any industry organized syndically the mechanic would become an artist.'[14] Even given the rhetorical defensiveness of ascribing such an aesthetic project to the French, it is striking that Wallas feels the need to move his account of the general strike into the space of artistic creativity. Of course, the idea that labour and creativity have shared social and psychological roots is not new, but what is striking is the modernism of Wallas's account. The aesthetic impulse is defined by its vitalism, its disruption and its break with inherited structures. It is also associated not with the rhythms and traditions of craft, but with the new social and economic relations of unskilled labour.

Within syndicalist thought, manual labour, and specifically unskilled manual labour, have a central place. This is both because such labour creates the alienation that requires the vitality of the general strike, and also because the social relations that result from these forms of labour make new forms of organization imaginable. Bob Holton, in his analysis of British Syndicalism between 1900 and 1914, argues that 'skill-displacing technological change was an important aspect of the economic context to syndicalism'.[15] This point is also developed by Tom Brown, who was himself a syndicalist activist in the mid-twentieth century. Brown sees syndicalism as a movement that grew on the discontent of the unskilled who felt their interests were ill served by existing union structures.[16] In the same spirit, W. W. Craik sees the displacement of the skilled craftsman as the central fact that has to be grasped in any historical understanding of labour and its organizations in the early years of the twentieth century: 'machinery has made new conquests. The sub-division of the labour-process has increased. The "dilution of labour" is not only an actual fact on a scale hitherto unknown and unimagined, but is destined to become a *permanent* fact' (*A Short History*, 110). This permanence is rhetorically powerful, but also significantly disabling for a theoretical text that aspires to imagine a different future, or to grasp the possibility of revolutionary change.

GEORGES SOREL AND THE MYTH OF THE GENERAL STRIKE

Experiences of industrial militancy, and the related theorizations of the general strike in the early years of the twentieth century, set in play a series of images and arguments about the relation between labour and selfhood. These embodied an historical argument about the particularity of modern forms of labour as well as a political argument about the possibilities of action orientated towards the future. Within this urgent and polemical series of writings, one theorist is of particular interest for any attempt to understand the relations between the imagination of labour and of selfhood in this period. Georges Sorel's prolific historical and theoretical writings engage explicitly with economic history, political philosophy and the history of ideas, in the context of an activism that seeks to connect the experience of labour to a narrative of historical liberation. He embodies in his writings the intensity and imagist concentration of literary high modernism, while also showing a broader commitment to modernity in his fascination with technique, technology and the motors of historical change. His interest in form is historical, political and aesthetic, and his writings provide a fascinating place in which to understand the possible connections between these different modes of thought and inquiry in the early years of the twentieth century.

Georges Sorel's writings on labour, political struggle and the general strike weave through the conceptual and imaginative landscape of late nineteenth- and early twentieth-century thought. His writings are eclectic, polemical and formally innovative: Ramsay MacDonald indeed described him as 'more a poet than anything else'.[17] They also engage with many of the central philosophers of the modern condition, including Marx, Vico, Proudhon, William James and Henri Bergson, and constitute an intellectually complex and challenging body of political argument. Sorel's political and theoretical ambition have made his legacy far from comfortable. He has been claimed by a range of political positions as one of their own and has been read as both a radical and a reactionary. My aim in this chapter is not to re-appropriate Sorel, but rather to argue that in the structure, the imagery and the rhetoric of his arguments it is possible to grasp the ways in which the experience of labour could be understood as enabling new and distinctively modern forms of subjectivity. It is also possible, within these images and rhetorical devices, to grasp something of the modernism of Sorel's cultural and political project, and to move beyond Michael Roe's observation that 'in political doctrine . . . probably the major modernist was Georges Sorel' towards a more general appreciation of the interconnection of political and cultural modernisms.[18]

Georges Sorel was born in Cherbourg, in Northern France, in 1847. He trained as an engineer and worked as a civil servant. His first published articles, which appeared when Sorel was in his forties, were concerned with psychophysics: that scientific and specifically physiological articulation of the mechanisms of sensation and feeling whose power and prevalence in the late nineteenth century has so intrigued cultural historians such as Anson Rabinbach.[19] Sorel's first major book, *The Trial of Socrates* (1889), developed an argument about the regressive impact of Socratic reason on Greek civilization and consequently on all civilizations that followed the Greeks.[20] In this detailed philosophical study Sorel acknowledged the importance of Socrates' philosophical method, but regretted both his political and his ethical conclusions, which Sorel insisted confounded the moral, the legal and the scientific in a way that could only generate relativism and arbitrariness. Sorel concedes that Socrates is not the only villain of his piece, and that the 'trial' he is staging is in that sense largely symbolic, but he nonetheless sustains this symbolism to the point of identifying the philosophical and political impasses of the opening years of the twentieth century with the legacy of Socrates' philosophical writings.

Sorel's method and his conclusions in this epochal history are not idiosyncratic, but resonate with a range of philosophical or fictional writings of this period, including texts by Nietzsche, Spengler, D. H. Lawrence, or to some extent Freud.[21] In *The Trial of Socrates*, Sorel demonstrates a strong predilection for the military and moral values of pre-Socratic Greece. This preference is represented by Sorel as broadly democratic, but it is articulated within a powerful rhetoric of the interconnections between family, heroism and labour: 'Sorel unquestionably adheres to the morality of old Athens. He recommends the moral value of work, of the family, of heroism.'[22]

This commitment to the socially redemptive qualities of labour also informs Sorel's encounter with Marxist thought in the 1890s. Sorel's were among the first serious and sustained engagements with Marx's thought in France, and Sorel's Marx was above all a scientific thinker, committed to the social and cultural liberation of *homo faber*. In the intensity of philosophical and political debate about the revision of Marx's ideas that followed the death of Engels in 1895, Sorel's particular contribution lay in his commitment to the centrality of *syndicats*, or trade unions, for any analytic or imaginative account of the contemporary historical process. Thus, for example, in *L'Avenir socialiste des syndicats* (1898) he undertook to explicate Marx's ideas, as distinct from the policies and the pragmatic positions of the political parties who claimed to act in his name: 'This study provides a good illustration of the doctrines of Marx.'[23] He argued that revolutionary social structures could only emerge from institutions that were both collective and orientated to the experience of labour. Movement and action were, Sorel argued, the sources of new knowledges and intellectuals should no longer assume any leadership role, but should rather work directly for the *syndicats*. *Syndicats*, for Sorel, were the formal articulation of the intimate relations between labour and selfhood and they represented the ways in which the experience of labour could facilitate historical progress. As J. R. Jennings puts it 'it appeared that the *syndicats* were capable of engendering amongst the working class the qualities of hard work, personal responsibility and initiative, and devotion to their comrades'.[24]

These *syndicats* are not understood as the last resort of the alienated labourer. Sorel saw in the division of labour, an increasingly distinctive feature of industrial processes from the late eighteenth century, not simply an oppressive and dehumanizing process, but rather a necessary extension and development of the relations of production that had facilitated social and economic progress in the early modern period. In *The Illusions of*

Progress (1908) Sorel follows Marx in mapping 'the organization of work in modern times' and his discussion of 'the advance towards socialism' is couched in terms of a history of the division of labour derived primarily from *Capital*.[25] He thus describes the transition from family workshops to factory production as an 'immense social revolution' (194) in which relations of production and technological possibilities combine to produce the 'new seedbeds of industry' (195). The revolution imagined in this text is relatively gradual. Sorel notes the violent contestation of new rhythms and relations of labour and acknowledges that the factory system necessitated 'iron discipline', but he reads the developments as broadly progressive: a move from the primitive to the modern – and Sorel is an ardent modernist.

Sorel certainly describes the deleterious social and individual consequences of the 'forced cooperation' produced by the imposition of the factory system: 'the advance of the worker towards a completely mindless life seems to be the ideal of the leaders of this forced cooperation' (195), but like Marx he sees in the experience of forced cooperation the potential for new modes of collectivity in which 'we will see the work of freely associated men acting consciously' (196). Importantly, for Sorel, de-skilling and repetitive labour are not the culmination of modernity but rather constitute a phase in which the possibility of 'free cooperation' can be grasped.

Sorel's method here is dialectical, as the title, *The Illusions of Progress*, might already suggest. His interest in this volume is both in the philosophical history through which we have come to think the idea of 'progress' but also in the objective unfolding of distinctively new forms of social identity. Sorel's ideology critique leads him to argue that bourgeois ideology has exhausted itself, and that the belief in evolution, enlightenment and consensual democracy have fallen into their negation as decadence. But he nonetheless refuses the conclusion that such decadence is the only story to be told, and argues instead that new times are coming for which labouring people must prepare themselves through discipline and study. Sorel thus employs a rigorous historicism to dispel the obviousness of bourgeois conceptualizations of 'progress'.

Sorel's argument is that the logic of industrial production will require ever-greater degrees of technical skill and critical knowledge in the workforce and that this will create the conditions for new forms of intellectual work. Philosophy will thus move beyond the fragmented individual and towards the constitution of skilled workers capable of diverse forms of intelligent labour. You could say that he foresaw Bill Gates but not Ronald MacDonald. Sorel is positively Brechtian in his relish for collectively produced forms of critical reason and the pursuit of practical understanding:

'the socialist workshop could bring together producers whose minds would always be alert to criticize the techniques being learned . . . and who would be supervised by engineers who would speak to their men as a teacher speaks to his pupils' (197). This leads him to a series of concrete suggestions about future developments in technical education that might facilitate the production of such conscious and critical modes of collectivity.

Sorel's narrative of the gradual revelation of the possibilities of social co-operation and its relation to practical forms of knowledge oscillates between the epochal and the everyday. The 'everyday' forms a spatial antithesis to the temporal unfolding of a particular logic: a glutinous space both of resistance and of blindness. But this does not make it impossible to glimpse such a temporal logic in its unfolding. There are, Sorel argues, distinct historical phases within the relations of production of the industrialized world that necessitate the division of labour, the de-skilling of the worker, and then the gradual restoration of the critical and self-conscious collectivity expressed in the early years of the twentieth century by the *syndicats*. The heroic agency of the skilled worker is the relatively smooth culmination of an unfolding historical drama.

The smooth temporality of this version of historical progress is radically undercut by Sorel's more famous publication of 1908, *Reflections on Violence*, a political and philosophical examination of the meaning and the potential of the general strike. That a discussion of the general strike should take place under the sign of 'violence' is not simply a question of rhetoric: between 1906 and 1908, 'nineteen workers were killed and over seven hundred were injured in industrial disputes' in France.[26] *Reflections on Violence* is concerned with the question of freedom; a question, which Sorel elsewhere suggested, was connected to 'the intimate joy' of manual labour.[27] The question of freedom in *Reflections* draws strongly on Henri Bergson's conceptualization of the psychic and social importance of 'duration'. Duration, for Bergson, is a temporality that is characterized by the mingling of past and present, and by the simultaneous presence of consciousness and memory. For Bergson, 'the free act takes place in time which is flowing', and 'to act freely is to recover possession of oneself, and to get back into pure duration'.[28]

Sorel draws on Bergson's work to suggest the philosophical and social importance of a temporality that cannot be assimilated to the repetitive, but which articulates itself as simultaneously intensive and extensive. He maps Bergson's commitment to duration on to his own specific concern with the potential for creative, and even revolutionary, thought: a mode of thought which overcomes the lures of the habitual. If we are unfree when we are caught in the superficial and the habitual, then, Sorel argues, it is in the intensity of duration that we can glimpse the possibility of a creative moment. This moment will have both individual and collective resonance. As Bergson argued in *Time and Free Will*, 'is there not much to be said for the hypothesis of a conscious force or free will which, subject to the action of time and storing up duration, may thereby escape the law of the conservation of energy' (154).

Sorel argues that 'it is very evident that we enjoy this liberty pre-eminently when we are making an effort to create a new individuality in ourselves' (*Reflections*, 30). The correlation between liberty and hard work Sorel implies here is also forcefully articulated by Bergson: 'to recover the fundamental self, a vigorous effort of analysis is necessary' (*Time*, 129). Stripping away the habitual and recognizing the 'succession of qualitative changes which melt into and permeate one another, without precise outlines, without any tendency to externalise themselves in relation to one another, without any affiliation with number' (104), involves an intellectual and a physical effort, it is, in other words, hard work. This commitment to hard work may well have been part of Sorel's appeal for T. E. Hulme, who translated *Reflections* in 1916.[29] Hulme's version of modernism as a rigorous, structured and concrete repudiation of the dangerously ambitious optimism of the Romantics[30] resonates with aspects of Sorel's commitment to discipline and to hard work.[31]

The effort towards liberty, for Sorel, leads to an orientation towards the future. It suggests the possibility of agency; 'to say that we are acting implies that we are creating an imaginary world placed ahead of the present world and composed of movements which depend entirely on us' (*Reflections*, 30). We cannot consider ourselves to be acting as conscious beings unless we are able to imagine and to think in the future tense. The recognition of selfhood implicit in the experience of duration leads, Sorel argues, to the possibility of glimpsing historical agency as an orientation towards the future derived from a personal sense of responsibility. This relation to the future is not one of continuous progression, but rather one of shocking discontinuity. It depends for its viability and power on the imaginative resources of the myth of the general strike.

Drawing so significantly on Bergson's account of the liberating potential of the experience of duration leads Sorel to an epistemological preference for intuition over reason. Bergson believed that duration was not susceptible to analysis, which would serve only to resolve it into a series of separate states. Rather, it could only be glimpsed fleetingly in privileged moments of insight through the process of intuition. Sorel seeks to find in the social institution or practice of the general strike the possibility of such moments of insight, and much of the formal innovation of *Reflections on Violence* is bound up with his attempt to represent the possibility of intuitive knowledge. The general strike is both a social event and a myth for Sorel: 'myths are not descriptions of things, but expressions of a determination to act' (32). They are thus not susceptible to quantitative or comparative analysis but must be grasped intuitively as an expression of will: 'when the masses are deeply moved it then becomes possible to trace the outlines of the kind of representation which constitutes a social myth' (31). A myth is thus an expression of will, an overflowing of passion, and a moment of privileged epistemological insight. A myth is also a necessary imaginative link to future action:

Men who are participating in a great social movement always picture their coming action as a battle in which their cause is certain to triumph. These constructions, knowledge of which is so important for historians, I propose to call myths. (22)

Projection into the future is a necessary element of effective political action in the present. But Sorel is clear that this does not amount to a utopianism. Myth does not represent an ideal state, and it is not particularly important whether is represents an achievable state. Its importance lies in its capacity to unpick the obviousness of the contemporary. We have already seen that for Sorel acting in the present can only take place in relation to an imaginary future world. But not simply any world will do. It must be a myth that has the capacity to animate the masses: to trace the outlines of the kind of representation which constitutes a social myth the masses must be deeply moved. The need to break through the bonds of habitual thought can only be answered by a myth that is both revolutionary and catastrophic.

Sorel seeks to distance his theorization of agency through the elaboration of myth from any notion of calculated historical change. He was by 1908 contemptuous of the policies and procedures of mainstream socialist parties and their attempts to plan for the future. He believed that socialist activism throughout the nineteenth century had had the deleterious consequence of reinforcing the power of the State without re-imagining its capacity to represent the mass of the population.[32] Sorel's myth had to articulate discontinuity, catastrophe and a completely new temporal horizon. His chosen mechanism for the articulation and promulgation of this myth was the general strike: 'the general strike has a character of *infinity* because it puts on one side all discussion of definite reforms and confronts men with a catastrophe' (27).

The general strike thus partakes of a distinct temporality that is infinity. It has no located place in the unfolding of a continuous historical narrative, but rather breaks down boundaries between past, present and future. This is true, however, only of the general strike conceived as an embodied myth, not when it is conceived as a contingent political strategy. Sorel distinguishes the 'political General Strike' from the 'Proletarian General Strike' which he sees as diametrically opposed. The political strike is calculating, centralized and modest in its ambitions whereas the proletarian strike 'must be considered as an undivided whole' (139) and can only be revolutionary in its aspirations. The wholeness of the proletarian general strike is a symptom and a guarantor of its integrity: its relation to the innovative temporalities of duration or of infinity.

Why does the general strike have such imaginative and political power in Sorel's analysis? One answer lies in its connection to violence. As a violent manifestation of class interest and feeling it tends to exacerbate social divisions, and to drive the middle classes into opposition, thus clarifying the landscape of class war. Violence, Sorel argues 'can, in an indirect manner, so operate on the middle class as to awaken them to a sense of their own class sentiment' (88), thus subjecting the bourgeoisie to the same injection of vital energies and conscious selfhood that earlier syndicalists had imagined only in terms of the proletariat. This leads Sorel to a series of associations between the proletarian general strike and a state of war which test his temporal location of the general strike in infinity; wars after all are powerfully historically located, often read as the hinges of historical time but rarely conceived outside it.

Sorel also discusses the general strike in relation to the untimeliness of capitalism and its capacity to anticipate in imaginative forms the structures on which it itself depends – otherwise known as the law of uneven development. Thus Sorel writes that 'capitalism . . . prepares the coming of social reforms which it did not intend to produce' (85). But the temporal complexity of capitalist development here seems to mirror rather than strictly to oppose the catastrophic temporality of the general strike, since the practice of the general strike is closely related to cycles of capitalist development and to periods of technological innovation. Actual participation in violent strikes will tend to produce the collective conditions for further class antagonism. In this sense the general strike as a myth emerges from particular located historical experiences: 'the practice of strikes engenders the notion of a catastrophic revolution' (71). But these experiences must be articulated collectively in order for the general strike to assume its role as animating myth, and this is the role of syndicalism at a particular historical movement;

'revolutionary syndicalism keeps alive in the minds of the masses the desire to strike, and only prospers when important strikes, accompanied by
violence, take place' (43).

The general strike is thus both infinite and temporally located, and the
tension between these two understandings drives much of the polemic of
Sorel's argument. He strives to establish the integrity and the uniqueness
of the general strike as a myth. He returns again and again to images of
wholeness and completeness when trying to capture its nature. Thus, for
example, the general strike draws on the noblest and deepest sentiments
of the proletariat and 'groups them in a co-ordinated picture, and, by
bringing them together, gives to each one of them its maximum of intensity'
(137). But this enabling and ennobling myth threatens always to slip into
inauthenticity, repetition and finally into the contingency of the everyday.
Even when talking about the strategy of revolutionary syndicalism, Sorel
cannot sustain his sense of the general strike's integrity nor of its infinity.
He admires the intensity with which syndicalism, like a kind of imagist
condensation, concentrates the whole project of socialism within the drama
of the general strike:

They restrict the whole of socialism to the general strike; they look upon every
combination as one that should culminate in this catastrophe; they see in each
strike a reduced facsimile, an essay, a preparation for the great upheaval. (127)

Within this narrative of catastrophic change, however, lurks the ghost of
the reduced facsimile, and the legacy of repetition. The strike itself cannot
be unique, but only the idea of the strike: 'the idea of the general strike has
such power behind it that it drags into the revolutionary track everything
it touches' (145). The idea of the strike thus has the power to pull social
and psychic structures behind it as it opens an imaginative route towards
the future. Sorel is not here talking about specific experiences of industrial
militancy, but rather of 'a body of images' (130), which can be discerned
'by intuition alone'. It is this Bergsonian intuition that can rescue the
general strike from its contingency and enable its perception as a whole,
enable it moreover to evoke 'as an undivided whole the mass of sentiments
which corresponds to the different manifestations of the war undertaken
by Socialism against modern society' (131). But Sorel's commitment to the
general strike as a myth that can be grasped only intuitively cuts across
his argument about the particularity and even the everydayness of the
experience of labour. He argues:

The general strike corresponds to a kind of feeling which is so closely related to
those which are necessary to promote production in any very progressive state of

industry, that a revolutionary apprenticeship may at the same time be considered as an apprenticeship which will enable the workman to occupy a high rank among the best workmen of his own trade. (35)

The temporality of apprenticeship, which suggests a gradual and structured acquisition of knowledges and skills, sits uneasily with Sorel's catastrophic imagining of history. Indeed, *Reflections on Violence* ends on this progressive temporal coming to agency of skilled labour, suggesting that the idea of continual progress can finally be realized in the social experience of a workshop of free labourers, where 'consistent improvement in quality and quantity will be thus assured to production' (286).

In *Reflections on Violence*, Sorel has tried to fashion a conceptual scheme that would allow us to imagine the possibility of revolutionary change and to act with a viable orientation to the future. The contingency and the temporal locatedness of labour are, he admits, a problem: 'Socialism is necessarily very obscure, since it deals with production, *i.e.*, with the most mysterious part of human activity' (164) yet he also argues that this 'mysteriousness' is largely an illusion produced by our habitual use of language. Having embraced mysteriousness, infinity and intuition as enabling revolutionary thought he here seems to repudiate these very aspects of thought in the name of integrity and clarity. Moving through the fluid uncertainties that characterize the experience of duration, the troubling temporality of infinity, the anticipatory quality of syndicalist action, and the risk of repetition implicit in the 'reduced facsimile', Sorel seems to settle on balance for a surely illusory realist coherence, rather than for the heroism of modernist imagination. Productive labour may be, to some extent, mysterious, but Sorel argues that this:

does not in the least prevent us picturing the proletarian movement in a way that is exact, complete, and striking, and this may be achieved by the aid of that powerful construction, which the proletarian mind has conceived in the course of social conflicts, and which is called the general strike. (164)

But this is the instantaneousness of the photograph, rather than the disruptive temporality of Bergson's duration, or even the complex temporal layering of the modernist image. Labour as the founding experience of a myth that is infinite and infinitely heroic, gives way to a rigidity of picturing that is 'exact, complete, and striking', but also, I would argue, relatively static.

This reading of the temporalities of Sorel's thought is intended to suggest the ways in which his imagining of time might illuminate the logic of his representations of labour and of selfhood. My suggestion is that Sorel's modernism is expressed in his search for the epiphanic moment within the historical process that can lead to significant social change. He is preoccupied by the need for images and experiences of collectivity and conflict to animate the historical process and to break the bonds of the habitual. These images are to be produced in and through the myth of the general strike that opens the way to that new and disruptive temporality which Sorel names as infinity. But another set of commitments, to the productive and located experience of skilled labour, pushes Sorel in a very different direction, and towards a very different temporality. Here he finds the gradual acquisition of skills and knowledges, the uneven development, that is characteristic more of the everyday than of the infinite. Sorel's polemical theorization, riven by the different temporalities of the general strike and generalized labour, opens up the historical adventure of modernist imagining to the recalcitrance of the everyday and thus makes it possible to imagine modernism itself as a moment in and of history:

By accepting the idea of the general strike, although we know that it is a myth, we are proceeding exactly as a modern physicist does who has complete confidence in his science although he knows the future will look upon it as antiquated. (167)

Sorel's image here is characteristically committed to the dynamism of science, accepting both its necessity and its impossibility within the logic of a historically progressive contradiction. His dialectical method offers him a way to articulate this contradiction, and even a way to experience it as something other than trauma. What however, does this contradictory temporality offer to writers who do not have the philosophical and psychological comforts of Sorel's dialectic? Can they see the temporality of the general strike, or the temporalities of labour, as anything other than trauma and loss?

JOHN WAUGH SCOTT: SYNDICALISM, REALISM AND WORK

One answer to these questions can be found in the philosophical and political writings of the Scottish philosopher John Waugh Scott. Scott was a lecturer in Moral Philosophy at Glasgow University from 1905 to 1920, and then Professor of Logic and Philosophy in Cardiff from 1920 to 1944. He is not a particularly well-known figure in the history of philosophy, though his work reached a broad readership in the 1920s and '30s. As well as publishing an impressive range of book-length studies, he also wrote articles on philosophical topics for the *Encyclopaedia Britannica*, and published in the *New Age* under the pseudonym of W. D. Law. His importance for this study, however, lies not in his prominence or his innovation, but rather in the way in which his work as a whole reveals something about the philosophical languages available for thinking about labour in the 1920s. His published philosophical work engages directly with questions related to syndicalism, labour and ethical and economic value, and draws on a range of philosophical traditions, from empiricism, to Kantianism, to Marxism, which are nonetheless yoked together in a way that illuminates the methods and concerns of British, and particularly Scottish, philosophy as a discipline in the period.

Scott's 1919 study, *Syndicalism and Philosophical Realism: a Study in the Correlation of Contemporary Social Tendencies*, engages directly and in detail with the arguments of Sorel and Bergson outlined above, but also develops an account of the ways in which syndicalism might be read as sharing crucial and damaging assumptions and positions with the contemporary tradition of philosophical realism which he associates above all with Bertrand Russell.[33] Scott's linking of Russell and syndicalism is not in itself unusual. Russell had, after all, published a study of syndicalism, socialism and anarchism in the previous year, in which he chastized syndicalism for its lack of a mechanism for mediating conflicts between different groups of producers and advocated instead the 'guild socialism' of G. D. H. Cole which had much more articulated mechanisms for balancing the interests of producers with the interests of the community as a whole.[34] What is distinctive and important about Scott's study, however, is that he does not limit his discussion of syndicalism and philosophical realism to such overt areas of common concern, but rather develops a more complex argument about historically rooted tendencies within these very different philosophical traditions:

Our most recent philosophical thought, all unconsciously, is swimming in the same current with that general social movement which has been making itself felt during the last decade or two within the socialistic camp. (*Syndicalism*, 1)

The 'general social movement' to which Scott is referring here is syndicalism, which he characterizes initially in terms of 'waves of unrest, spasmodic manifestations of a popular thirst for combined action' (6). He sees syndicalism as a spontaneous and popular movement, which creates the possibility and the necessity of mass action. It is, he argues, 'an instance, almost, of pure mass action' (14), and as such expresses a distinctive and defining aspect of the modern industrial world. The hesitation here, in that 'almost' pure instance, reveals something of Scott's ambivalence about syndicalism and its ethical and political implications. Having evoked this historically produced expression of spontaneous popular feeling, Scott moves swiftly to the limitations of such spontaneity and such feeling: 'with its economic character is connected a disintegrating influence which spells a certain kind of failure' (15). Scott argues that the narrowly economic focus of syndicalism makes it finally a destructive and partial political movement: 'the placing of the chief end of man in economics and in the salvation of a class is of the nature of a relapse. It is the outcome of a certain weariness' (30). These images of fall and decline are repeated throughout Scott's text as he turns to examine in detail the disintegrative tendencies of syndicalism.

To some extent, Scott's target here is the quite explicit reliance of syndicalism on the image of class war, and of antagonistic classes with mutually exclusive interests. This economic and antagonistic model, Scott argues, cannot encompass the range of ethical and legal issues that are normally designated by the notion of 'the political'. In this sense, syndicalism is seen as a symptom of a certain weary inability to sustain a model of justice and community in the face of the traumas of contemporary economic struggle. Despite Sorel's insistence on the necessity of discipline and of hard political work, Scott accuses him of a form of ethical and intellectual laziness. Sorel's insistence on the need for continued and continuing industrial militancy is, for Scott, negative and constraining because it abandons any responsibility for thinking about the legitimacy of the eventual ends of such action. Indeed, notions of legitimacy and duty disappear, and thought stops at the point that striking begins.

Syndicalism is destructive, then, because it displaces the political in favour of the economic and it suspends questions of duty, justice and legitimacy. But Scott argues that it is also guilty of fragmentation precisely in relation to the ways in which it imagines temporality: the innovative temporality that had for Sorel been the basis of its claim to integrity and wholeness. Scott points out that syndicalist unions had few of the financial and institutional mechanisms for mutual support, which were so important for craft unions. Syndicalism does not imagine or construct collective identities across time: 'the newer organizations do not rally their members to a strong, close, brotherhood prepared to stand a long siege in a just cause' (51). Rather, syndicalism brings together disparate groups of workers for a moment of collective action, 'a widespread violent effort for an immediate gain when the moment has come' (51), and for Scott this cannot be the basis of a sustainable political or collective identity. Sorel's epiphanic moments are for Scott simply a failure of political will and a kind of theoretical and practical laziness.

Laziness is also a charge Scott has in store for Bergson, following a detailed exposition and critique of his philosophical method. Bergson is, in many ways, the hinge of Scott's overall argument about 'contemporary social tendencies', since he has close affiliations with syndicalism, with Russell and with 'philosophical realism' as Scott defines it.[35] For Scott, philosophical realism refers broadly to a non-Kantian empirical tradition. He invokes Berkeley, Locke and Hume as the sources of this tradition, and includes both Russell and Bergson in its contemporary manifestations. Scott sees this tradition of philosophical realism as a passive acceptance of the atomism of the given, with a necessary tendency towards both scepticism and fragmentation, and 'the only way out of the impasse is the way Kant took' (64).

Bergson's route into this impasse is laid out in its complexity. Scott admits that Bergson's epistemological assumptions do not amount to an atomism of the self, but rather stress the interpenetration of object and perceiving subject. Similarly, Bergson's version of selfhood creates a vision of ideas and memories as interpenetrated rather than as separated, and Scott argues that for Bergson, 'Ideas are not separate. They are bone of each other's bone, and flesh of each other's flesh' (96). Despite this, Bergson does risk a kind of solipsism, and this is the result of his scepticism about reason and his preference for intuitive modes of inquiry: 'thought when it comes is the failure of selfhood, its dispersal' (99). The displacement of reason, Scott argues, amounts not only to a dispersal of the self, but also to the fragmentation of community, which depends on shared modes of rational inquiry. Both the antagonism to analytic thought and the commitment to intuition, Scott suggests, are centrally connected to the problem of time in Bergson's work. Bergson imagines a process of development and change in which a radically different future is imaginable, but he cannot sustain this vision beyond the momentary insight of intuition which for Scott carries within it no future tense. Bergson also, like Sorel, can make no calculations based on a relation to the future, but relies rather on the energy of an impersonal will in the process of its movement. Bergson's will tends away from system and from calculation, while for Scott it is the business of politics to discipline, and even to sublimate the energies of this will.

Bergson then favours the incalculable and the intuitive over the planned and the reasoned, which Scott suggests amounts finally to a form of anti-intellectualism and also to a dispersal of the social. If, for Bergson, the self cannot reveal itself either in language or in social institutions, then Scott suggests his philosophical method can never address the domain of the political. In fact, Scott puts the point more forcefully by insisting that

Bergson's philosophical system amounts to a kind of quietism: '[Bergson] says that the real is intuited; and we have replied that to intuit is to accept' (144).

Not only is intuition a form of political abstention, it is also a symptom of intellectual laziness. Bergson suggests that intuition, a mode of perception that relies on the overcoming of habitual categories and assumptions, might be more readily accessed in a state of somnolence, and Scott jumps at such a concession: 'Bergson's own expressions . . . seem to justify us in taking intuition as an idle occupation compared with thought' (148). Scott is aware of Bergson's presentation of his philosophical method as intense, strenuous and a matter of great effort, but he finds this in the end deeply implausible:

If this characterization is sound, the realistic spirit as we have defined it can be strenuous. It, nevertheless, still is what we have taken it to be, the desire to take the given as given, and not to do anything to it. In the literal sense of the words, it is against work . . . Many lazy people are strenuous – when they are avoiding work. There is no end to what they will undertake with that in view. (139)

Scott describes intuition as a strenuous effort to be idle, and finds in Bergson's philosophical method ultimately an acceptance of the given as given. He does not deny the effort involved in intuiting the self as complex and temporally intermingled, but finds that this effort does not amount to substantial work. Indeed he suggests that rather than reading the intuitive apprehension of the self as the possibility of freedom, 'there is always the possibility that it may be quite the reverse, mere passion, the return of the self towards the animal, the negation and undoing of all the characteristic work which man does' (155).

So Scott takes issue precisely with the ways in which Bergson's philosophical method might connect work and freedom. Rather than seeing in it, as Sorel does, a method for connecting productive labour and future liberation, Scott finds in Bergson an easy acceptance of the status quo and a withdrawal from the project of collective political struggle. The danger in philosophical realism, and indeed in syndicalism, for Scott is not, however, simply a matter of its refusal to imagine a form of critical reason. Scott is also concerned by what he perceives to be a narrowness, both of vision and of method, and it is this narrowness of which he finds Russell particularly culpable. Scott describes his reading of Russell as an attempt to historicize philosophical categories and methods: 'we must try to apprehend his mind's point of incidence upon current culture, the place where the thought impinges upon the general thought of the time' (174). He begins with Russell's obvious differences from Bergson, arguing that while Bergson begins with what is immediately given in consciousness Russell begins with what is given to it, and that while Russell seeks the stable object, Bergson seeks the flowing. Nonetheless, Scott argues that the two philosophers are both implicated in realism's disintegrative tendency: 'realism is by its nature a breaker-up of the constructive rational order' (176).

It is Russell's ethical and social writings that Scott finds most compromised by a realism that makes collective political practice unimaginable. Thus, Russell's views on marriage seem to Scott to concede too much to the instinctive passions of the individual and too little to the centrality of social institutions: 'the accentuated idiosyncrasies of the modern individual are accepted as one of the inevitabilities, and before that fact other things are simply to make way' (203). Scott suggests that Russell simply overlooks the integrity of social bonds, or the extent to which selfhood may in fact be social rather than individual. Thus he suggests:

In all his plea for liberation, Mr Russell assumes that the thing is there to be liberated. There is only the breaking of bonds to be done. What he does not reckon with is the possibility that the bonds may be the man's own very sinews; and that by the time he has broken them all there may be no man. (204)

But Scott finally concludes that Russell is aware of this disintegrative tendency and works to overcome it through the notion of 'self-possession': 'he is conscious that man must somewhere or somehow meet the ultimate and be braced into self-possession by its presence' (207). This bracing into self-possession through an encounter with transcendence is Scott's way of pointing ahead, and avoiding the disintegrative tendency he has perceived in both syndicalism and philosophical realism. Curiously, however, Scott's final position, with its emphasis on duty, family and labour is strikingly reminiscent of Georges Sorel's early writings, and in particular of *The Trial of Socrates*, with its commitment to the duty and heroism of pre-Socratic Greece. Sorel's subsequent philosophical and political journey took him to the dialectical tension between the revolutionary energies of the unskilled syndicalist worker and the historically progressive potential of the skilled and self-conscious industrial proletariat. Scott's subsequent philosophical and political journey will lead him to some of the by-ways of economic and political theory of the 1920s, including Distributism and Social Credit, that are of considerable significance for any cultural history of this period.

After completing his study of syndicalism and philosophical realism, Scott turned his attention initially to Marx, publishing *Karl Marx on Value* in 1920. Scott describes this book as intended for 'earnest students of all social classes who are seeking a better understanding of the present phase of social development'.[36] It is a detailed and informed analysis of the Labour Theory of Value as developed by Marx, examining its ethical, economic and philosophical coherence and considering the extent to which it might help us to grasp the nature and significance of labour in modern industry. Scott acknowledges the political and ethical significance of the theory, but finds it finally incomplete and thus inadequate because it cannot make a solid historical connection between abstract labour and particular instances or practices of labour as experienced by concrete subjects: 'how do you get from "abstract labour" to real human labour in any specific instance?' (51). Scott becomes increasingly concerned with this aporia, moving towards theoretical positions and political organizations that focus particularly on the material and historical experience of labour. This can be clearly seen in his 1925 study, *Unemployment: a Suggested Policy*.[37]

Scott's study of unemployment begins by describing unemployment as the '*bête noir* of contemporary life' (5), and goes on to develop an alternative system for the organization of useful labour and also a philosophy of the significance of labour for human character. It is interesting that here, as in theorizations of the general strike, it is the confrontation with an absence or cessation of labour that produces particular insights into the meaning of human labour. Scott's response to the disruptive and destructive character of unemployment is to advocate a move towards a radically different organization of labour as imagined in what he calls 'the Home Croft Plan for combating industrial unemployment' (5). This amounts to moving the emphasis of human labour away from the production of industrial commodities and towards the production of food, mostly for consumption directly by the family who produce it. Under Scott's scheme, industrial workers are to be given up to an acre of land and they will be expected to work two shifts a day, 'one shift at his industrial work, earning wages, and another shorter shift, with his wife and children in his garden, producing food' (10). The clear expectation here is that the man will be the only wage earner in this family, a position that is of course at some odds with actual patterns of employment in the 1920s. It is also assumed that the industrial worker will share Scott's own commitment to work as 'the basis of character' (48), and will thus be unconcerned by its significant extension.

Part of the rationale for Scott's Home Croft Plan lies in the security it offers to industrial workers who are otherwise subject to the fluctuations of the employment market, or the catastrophic consequences of industrial conflict. Land and the supplies of food it can produce are reliable, and the worker can depend on his land 'to help him to hold out, during a strike or lock-out, a spell of unemployment or almost any other kind of disaster which interrupts his pay' (14). So the worker's acre is to be a kind of insurance against the inherent instability of capitalist production. Scott has already conceded a lot here that he was not willing to concede in the earlier study of syndicalism. As we have seen, one of his objections to syndicalism was that it did not build up the structures of mutual support and financial aid that were an integral aspect of the older types of trade union. By 1925, Scott has lost his confidence in this union structure to maintain the industrial worker in times of difficulty, and his commitment to mutuality and communal support has been displaced on to a vision of the industrial family as a viable economic unit: 'every worker a self-feeder, then: that is the only ultimately stable basis for any industrial civilization' (63).

Scott's commitment to the Home Croft Plan is not simply pragmatic, however, but reflects a judgement about the fundamental relation between labour and the soil: 'not everybody sees that industry will go neurotic and die if it does not stand on the soil' (29). The idea that industrial capitalism is decayed and dying is a common one in the early twentieth century but Scott's attribution of neurosis adds an interesting dimension. Neurosis, after all, might be susceptible to a cure, and for Scott, this cure involves industrialism planting its feet firmly back on the soil (8). The incoherence of such an image is striking, and the tension between mechanism and organism within the image is palpable. In an attempt to locate his argument within a broader social movement, Scott points us towards the work of William Smythe. Smythe published a volume on the philosophy and practice of the 'home-in-a-garden' in 1921, where he laid out the social and individual benefits of agriculture and animal husbandry within the context of an industrial home and garden.[38] Smythe begins his volume by invoking an Emersonian vision of the integral relations between land, labour and freedom, but the system of agricultural production he goes on to advocate could be called nothing other than industrial. He recommends battery farming of poultry, 'the intensive hen to go with the intensive garden' (*City Homes*, 123), and suggests that rabbits should be fattened quickly in small pens 'to prevent their getting too much exercise' (259). So, in Smythe's text, the tension between mechanism and organism is resolved by industrializing agricultural production, in itself an historically acute judgement about the possibilities of human labour within developing industrial capitalism. Scott seems to resolve the tension however by simply not noticing it. He divides his industrial worker in two, and leaves the organization of industrial processes themselves untouched. Scott argues that his Home Croft Plan represents a way ahead rather than a return to the past, and suggests that it allows for the development of a new kind of industrialism. This innovation is not, however, to touch on the relations of production or the techniques of labour within industrial capitalism. Scott argues that industrialism has miscarried, and has had obviously negative effects on our civilization. Yet, he argues, this is not the result of the division of labour, which on the contrary transforms manual labour into automatic movement and thus leaves the worker's mind free. Rather, the problem with industrialism is a problem of distribution, and this is what the Home Croft Plan would address. Poor and overcrowded housing, instability of employment, poverty and hunger are the evils Scott sets out to address through his advocacy of the Home Croft Plan as a mechanism for self subsistence for the labouring family.

This emphasis on ownership of a small piece of land, and on equal distribution of resources resonates with the economic and cultural project of the Distributist League in the early decades of the twentieth century. Distributism was a particular articulation of anti-capitalism, which opposed the monopolistic tendencies of capitalism, in relation both to industrial production and to cultural production in areas such as the press. The movement's most prominent spokesmen were G. K. Chesterton and Hilaire Belloc, whose polemical and engaged writing gave the movement the capacity to enthuse supporters from the political, cultural and religious (broadly Catholic) contexts with which it intersected.[39] The basic position of Distributism was that property should be divided up among the largest possible number of people, since the ownership of property is a basic right and its concentration the greatest possible threat to liberty. Distributism campaigned against the concentration of economic and political power and supported small-scale economic and manufacturing enterprises such as small shops or small-scale crafts. They particularly opposed the concentration of power and the distortion of social priorities brought about by the increasing role of international finance. Distributism supported to an extent certain existing forms of working class organization, including trade unions, as 'a defensive reaction to attempted exploitation' but was antipathetic to organized socialist movements as simply another form of manipulation and exploitation of working people.[40] One Distributist text of the late 1920s even describes the whole history of trade unionism in Britain as one of compromise and treachery culminating in the historic 1926 'betrayal of the General Strike'.[41]

Distributism was centrally committed to work as the main enjoyment of life, and was suspicious of socialist movements that seemed to organize so consistently simply to reduce the amount of work done. Whereas socialist groups sought to reduce work and increase leisure, the Distributists argued that they sought to reintegrate work by reconnecting it to the liberty provided by the ownership of property:

If the development of personality, that is liberty – the exercise of each human will in doing what it thinks best – is the object of leisure in a socialist state, it is the object of the 24 hours of the day. Men's work must be personal as well as their leisure. To the owner, conscious of independence and the satisfaction of human dignity and freedom, work is one of the enjoyments of life. (Humphries, *Liberty and Property*, 25)

This vision explicitly connects work to the defence of individual liberty. Chesterton argued that 'the commercial and industrial progress which began by professing individualism has ended with the complete swamping of the individual' and the explicit aim of the Distributist League was to reverse this process by restoring to working people the liberty inherent in property ownership.[42]

The coincidence between Distributism and Scott's vision of the Home Croft Plan in 1925 becomes more striking over the next decade and Scott's *Self-Subsistence for the Unemployed* (1935) and *Barter: a Study in the Economics of the Smaller Group* (1938) both align themselves explicitly with Chesterton and with Distributism.[43] Indeed *Barter* appeared first as a series of articles in *G. K.'s Weekly*, and was then published as a complete volume by the Distributist League. In these later volumes, Scott reports on the progress of the Home Croft Plan, including the building and equipping of a number of Home Crofts following a public appeal for funds. Scott argues that the movement has sustained its vision that 'all real renewal of life must come from the soil' (*Self-Subsistence*, 74), and also that the family holds the key to a new economic vision. The search for renewal, sustainability, and an alternative future leads, Scott argues, 'beyond problems of production to the more vital problems of distribution' (*Barter*, 7) and he demonstrates the ways in which the Home Croft Plan has tackled such historical and economic problems.

Running through these two later volumes, however, is a rather distinct current of thought, which is concerned more fully with the socially and psychologically destructive effects of key aspects of international finance. Scott argues against the iniquitous effects of the gold standard as an economic distortion that ensures global inequality. He also turns to an examination of what he describes as 'parasitic occupations', a category in which he includes landlords, middlemen and clerks.[44] These categories of occupation generate no wealth and serve rather to throw the economic order into 'progressive disarray' (*Self-Subsistence*, 152). The rhetoric of parasitism has emerged in other chapters in this book: we saw it in the work of Olive Schreiner, where it designated a gendered state of social uselessness based on the decline of women's traditional social roles; and we also saw it above in William Benbow's condemnation of the non-labouring classes. In Scott's text, however, the rhetoric, combined with the condemnation of international finance, picks up a racialized, anti-semitic, dimension that is also expressed in Scott's desire to articulate 'an economics of the island community'.[45] Scott is concerned to maintain boundaries that are racial as well as territorial. He is also concerned to sustain the possibility of a rooted and coherent version of the self, as the title 'self-subsistence' indeed suggests. He argues that we have lost any grasp of what is authentic or important, as our needs and desires are produced by images and by a series of strategies of the parasitic classes: 'the new demands, needs, tastes which are forced into being by urban populations churning on themselves' (*Self-Subsistence*, 155). Scott craves transparency, rootedness and self-reliance in economic as well as in social institutions, and is concerned that the present economic order has become both oppressive and arbitrary.

The arbitrariness of economic relations and the distortions of international finance were also of great concern to those involved in arguments about Social Credit in the 1920s, particularly C. H. Douglas and A. R. Orage whose collaborations in the period following the First World War were to have a profound influence on their contemporary culture. Douglas's and Orage's intellectual and political roots were in Guild Socialism, a British inflection of syndicalism that was powerfully influential from around 1913. G. D. H. Cole described Guild Socialism as 'a proposal for the co-management of industry by the state and the trade unions', while Bertrand Russell described it as 'the best practicable system . . . which concedes what is valid both in the claims of the state socialist and in the syndicalist fear of the state'.[46] Guild Socialism stressed the role of the producers in shaping industry, and also offered to the worker a more creative relationship to labour:

We must never forget when we speak of National Guilds in being, first, that the Guildsmen would be the men and the sons of the men who had fought and won their battle from wage-slavery to industrial democracy; secondly, that they would be enabled to look upon their work, its purposes and its conditions with a nobler outlook than any we know of in industry today.[47]

To change the economic relations of production is to change the experience of labour, and is thus to move from servility to freedom. The emphasis on men and the sons of men in Reckitt and Bechhhofer's analysis is far from unusual for writing within this anti-capitalist tradition, which is frequently explicit in its gendered narratives of decline. Writing in 1912, for example, A. R. Orage made an explicit link between the intensification of labour, the interests of international finance, and the forced entry of women into industrial labour, concluding that each plays out the destructive tendencies of capitalist development.[48]

A key site for the elaboration of arguments about Guild Socialism, and later about Social Credit, was the journal *New Age* which from 1907 was co-owned by Orage. This journal developed a series of cultural and economic arguments that had their root in traditions of socialist thought, and was also an important journal of modernist cultural and literary innovation. It had financial support from George Bernard Shaw, and published early work by T. E. Hulme, Katherine Mansfield and Storm Jameson.[49] The economic, and ultimately the cultural, arguments developed within the Social Credit Movement contain much of the anxiety about rootlessness and mystification we found in Scott's texts of the 1930s. Social Credit was, above all opposed to debt, and specifically to the ways in which an economy based on debt created the necessity of continuous, but unsustainable, growth. Douglas argued that 'cash credits', roughly equivalent to income (A), plus payments for raw materials (B) must be equivalent to the cash price for all consumer goods. This A + B Theorem led Douglas to produce an account of the distortions implicit in capitalist economic relations, and to advocate the payment of 'social credit dividends' to correct what he saw as a current imbalance. Investment should always relate to increased production and should never be financed through borrowing. A national dividend should be paid to all citizens, and should again be an expression, rather than a distortion, of national wealth. The aim of all these policies was the establishment of a more equitable, and a more transparent, mechanism for the distribution of goods and of money: 'to make finance, or the money system, reflect facts, and cease to let it control them'.[50] Work was essential to this vision, but it should not be the monotonous labour associated with the wage slave: 'the performance of one mechanical operation devoid of interest, requiring little skill'.[51] This desire to re-found economics on the basis of transparency and authenticity, however, once more had its rhetorical and political casualties. Douglas's condemnation of escalating credit led to a condemnation of the international financiers who sustained and benefited from it, and an anti-semitic discourse of usury circulated throughout the economic, cultural and literary texts influenced by the Social Credit Movement, most strikingly, of course, in the poetry of Ezra Pound.[52]

John Waugh Scott's work in the 1920s and early 1930s has taken us to the heart of thinking about the relations between labour and selfhood in the period. Each of the traditions he addresses, or with which his work intersects more tangentially, put the moral and the economic significance of labour at the heart of their attempt to think the future and to imagine radical change. In the final section of this chapter I want to develop this analysis of the relations between labour, selfhood and the general strike by looking not at philosophical or political arguments but at fictional representations of the general strike as an event and as a myth. I will focus this analysis on fictional texts that engage with what is undoubtedly the central 'general strike' within British cultural and political history; the General Strike of 1926.

REPRESENTING AND REMEMBERING A GENERAL STRIKE: 1926

On 4 May 1926, 'The largest strike in British history and the only one organized by the TUC had begun' when nearly two million workers went on strike.[53] The strike followed a period of conflict within the coal industry. The state of the coal industry, the largest industry in Britain in the post-War period, had been a matter of grave concern since the early years of the century. Coal was a crucial part of the infrastructure of industrial production throughout Britain, and the industry employed over one million workers. In 1919, the Sankey Commission was appointed to report on the state of the industry and concluded that there needed to be increased levels of wages, reduced working hours and a system of public ownership of coal. The government accepted the first two of these recommendations, but did not agree to nationalization of the industry, a decision that for some commentators planted the seeds of the General Strike to come:

The chief villain of the piece is Lloyd George. He promised to do whatever the Sankey Commission recommended. He was told by Big Business that he must not nationalize. He did not keep his promise. All the trouble since 1919 has been trouble arising out of that broken pledge.[54]

In 1921, the government decided that they would no longer seek to control wages and hours in the coal industry, and the coal-owners announced significant wage reductions and issued notice of a lock-out for all those who would not work at the new rates. Sympathetic strike action was planned by railway and transport workers, but on 15 April, subsequently dubbed 'Black Friday', the strike was called off. The economic difficulties of the industry continued, as they were bound to in the absence of any radical intervention.

For an economist such as Keynes, indeed, the difficulties in the industry were the logically necessary outcome of a flawed economic policy, driven by Churchill, which sought to restore the gold standard through modifications in the exchange rate. The result was to drive down wages, and 'like other victims of economic transition in past times, the miners are to be offered the choice between starvation and submission'.[55] By 1925, when Sterling had once again been tied to the gold standard, the government found itself intervening in the coal industry again. Following threats of industrial militancy, and specifically the decision of the General Council of the Trades Union Congress on 31 July 1925 ('Red Friday') to support sympathetic strike action, the Baldwin government agreed to grant a subsidy to the industry for nine months and to set up a further commission of inquiry. The Samuel Commission reported in March 1926, and its recommendations included the necessity for an agreed wage cut, but did not accept the need for longer working hours. In response, the coal-owners announced wage cuts and increases in working hours, and also issued notices of a lock-out. In response, the General Council of the Trades Union Congress called for a General Strike involving workers in transport, printing, building, electricity and gas industries in support of the case of the locked-out miners. This was far from being the triumphant expression of a syndicalist project, however:

None but a few crazy idealists had ever wanted a General Strike. Now the very people who have always been most strongly opposed to it are forced to admit that there is no other way for the Trade Unions to carry out their pledge of support to the miners.[56]

In Sorel's terms, this is a vision of a political rather than a proletarian general strike, where the aim is the achievement of particular political and economic concessions, rather than any revolutionary challenge to the State. Certainly, the Trade Union leadership and the leadership of the Labour Party were keen to disavow any association with revolutionary political struggle, Ramsay MacDonald declaring in the House of Commons that 'with the discussion of general strikes and Bolshevism and all that kind of thing, I have nothing to do at all'.[57] Nonetheless, the scale of the strike, and the solidarity of those who participated, meant that it was experienced by many commentators as at least acting out the possibilities of large-scale industrial militancy. The advance planning for the Strike by the TUC had been minimal, but most towns had strike committees who organized pick-eting and related activities with little violence. The government established an Organization for Maintenance of Supplies (O.M.S.), and volunteers came forward in their thousands to drive buses or trains, or to work in

other essential industrial areas. Much of this volunteering was largely symbolic, since those who came forward often lacked the basic skills necessary
for the job, but this symbolism drew on the clear sense of the Strike as
point of crisis where sides needed not simply to be taken but also to be
aggressively represented.

After nine days, the General Strike ended at noon on 12 May. The TUC
leadership argued that the Strike was in danger of crumbling, a judgement
for which there is scant evidence, and advocated the acceptance of the
recommendations of the Samuel Report on the coal industry. The miners,
however, remained locked-out through the following months, and finally
suffered a total defeat by the end of November 1926. For all the workers who
had participated in the Strike, the consequences were serious. The miners
had to accept lower wages and longer hours. Other groups of workers
were subject to victimization, and often returned to face poorer working
conditions and rates of pay. As Margaret Morris argues, 'the General Strike
was a traumatic experience for the Trade Union movement',[58] and this
trauma led to a generalized reluctance to think creatively towards the future,
to a kind of atrophy of utopian thinking. This sense of the 1926 Strike as
trauma, the vision of it as an historical turning point, and the notion of it
as both a repetition and a culmination of earlier conflicts are all powerfully
present in imaginative writing that draws in some way on the General Strike.
In what follows, I will examine the ways in which such fiction draws on
the complex temporalities of the General Strike: as repetition, as traumatic
break, as painful suspension of historical time, or as an uncanny doubling
of time. I will consider the ways in which imaginative representations of
the General Strike struggle to constitute the liberating or at least enabling
temporality of the future tense, and will also examine the relations between
this difficulty and the dynamic between labour and selfhood as imagined
in different texts. The novels I will discuss are: H. G. Wells, *Meanwhile:
the Picture of a Lady* (1927); Virginia Woolf, *To the Lighthouse* (1927); John
Galsworthy, *Swan Song* (1928); Harold Heslop, *The Gate of a Strange Field*
(1929); Ellen Wilkinson, *Clash* (1929); and Wyndham Lewis, *The Apes of
God* (1930).

One recurring rhetorical strategy in representations of the General Strike
is the constructions of historical and political continuities between May
1926 and earlier moments of national crisis. Trauma can of course be rendered banal by repetition, and the insistent comparison between the 1926
Strike and earlier moments of national conflict is at least partly a way
of warding off its most disturbing effects. The favoured historical moment for such comparisons is the First World War. This comparison is

perhaps overdetermined, given the centrality of conflict and of national self-articulation to both events, but the modes of comparison found across different texts are complex and their contradictions uncover something of the contested meanings of this social and political moment. The insistence of military imagery in representations of the Strike was clear at the time: *The Guardian* leader of the 4 May 1926 remarking that 'some people, unfortunately, like war, and the evening papers were full of the forms and phrases of a state of war' and citing the use of phrases such as 'the call for volunteers', or the 'demand for surrender'.[59] For the Home Secretary, William Joynson-Hicks, the Strike was a conflict between class interest and national interest, and its violent climax was both inevitable and desirable. When Baldwin agreed a temporary subsidy to the mining industry in 1925, Joynson-Hicks asserted 'The danger is not over. Sooner or later this thing has got to be fought out by the people of this land.'[60] And when the strike was announced, he sought to legitimize and strengthen the government's position by calling for sacrifice as the necessary psychological and social investment in peace: 'surely that unselfishness which caused men to sacrifice all that they held dear for the sake of their country in the Great War will lead them once more to obey the call of their country to sacrifice on both sides of what they deem to be their rights in order to preserve peace in our land.'[61]

In John Galsworthy's *Swan Song* there is an insistent series of attempts to understand the Strike through the frame of the First World War. In the opening pages, Michael, who is a Member of Parliament whose sympathies lie with the miners, reflects on the psychological and political effects of moments of national crisis: 'When "The Great War" broke out, though just old enough to fight, he had been too young to appreciate the fatalism which creeps over human nature with the approach of crisis.'[62] Michael argues that 'face-saving' is the case and meaning of both events, 'it caused the war; it's causing the strike now' (5). The parallel between these two moments is largely psychological for Michael: 'As before the war, there was a profound longing for the humiliation and dejection of the enemy' (5), while for the younger Jon Forsyte, the parallel is more closely connected to ideas of agency and collective national identity. Jon Forsyte 'left his wife and mother in Paris – said he'd missed the war and couldn't afford to miss this' (11).

The landscape and iconography of the war also feature in numerous contemporary cartoons. An image from the *British Gazette*, the pro-government paper edited by Winston Churchill, portrays John Bull standing defiant in a ruined landscape, which speaks at least as much of the trenches as the industrial landscape of Britain, while the Union Jack confronts the flag of the General Strike.[63] In a *Punch* cartoon produced after the end of the Strike, John Bull appears once more, standing by Baldwin as he steers his ship through the rocks of the coal crisis. Here conflict is read through the image of natural disaster, but also visualized in terms of the defence of an island nation.[64] The parallel is certainly not lost on Galsworthy's Michael, when the end of the Strike is announced: 'For a minute he sat motionless with a choky feeling, such as he had felt when the news of the Armistice had come through' (*Swan Song*, 54).

The parallel between the Strike and the war does not always engender such comfortable collective identification, however. We have already noted Joynson-Hicks call for sacrifice 'on both sides' and this recognition of mutual sacrifice tends to undermine the stable sense of collective struggle Joynson-Hicks would like to imagine, and actually articulates the division within the nation even as it seeks to overcome it through memories of a shared national goal. It is striking, indeed, that such rhetoric of sacrifice, or negation of selfhood, is also used by supporters of the Strike: 'Nothing like this unanimous sacrifice for a largely unselfish end has been seen since August 1914.'[65] In Wilkinson's *Clash*, narrative attention is overwhelmingly directed on active participants in the Strike, or on those who are drawn into activism by this historical event. One such character is Gerry Blain, a badly wounded war hero, who throws himself into political organization at great risk to his own emotional and physical health. Gerry constantly evokes parallels between the Strike and the recent war, starting from the very moment when the certainty of this new 'war' is announced:

'Wouldn't have missed it for worlds. We are in for it now. It's worth having come through that war for. I've often wondered lately why I did. We'll show the beggars . . . fighting their war and, and then our men getting treated like dogs!' The young ex-Air officer was nearly delirious with excitement.[66]

Joan Craig, full-time union organizer, encourages Blain to use his experience of the war to build new forms of solidarity, '"You had better talk class solidarity, Gerry. It ought to be your line. 'You stuck together in the trenches lads, the same spirit here,'"' (78). Despite his earlier excited anticipation of the new conflict, Blain does in fact express some unease about the ways in which historical crises can generate a marked enthusiasm for sacrifice, believing that '[i]f the men who sacrificed themselves in the war had put in a spot of work previously as ordinary citizens to get peace, that beastly horror need not have happened' (97). As the novel develops, parallels between the strike and the war are increasingly treated with suspicion. A Chief Constable's wife gives strikers cups of tea, simply because she 'had spent the entire War handing out cups of tea to British Tommies' (133), but since she equally cheerfully hands out tea to volunteers working for the O.M.S. the effect of this revival of wartime spirit is to suggest the woman's political and historical naïveté rather than her identification with national struggle. Later, when Mary Maud Meadowes, an upper-middle-class sympathizer with the strike, expresses bitterness and vindictiveness towards a woman who has helped to support the O.M.S. she is condemned by the narrator in a way that invokes wartime experience as some sort of ethical grounding: 'hers was the bitterness of the non-combatant, familiar enough in all wars' (151), but which clearly emphasizes the pathology rather than the constitutive heroism of such wartime experiences.

A poem by Eleanor Farjeon published in the labour movement paper, the *British Worker*, finds in the 'twelve year echo' of the war resonances of betrayal:

> 'STAND BY!'
>
> 'Stand by me!' said the Government
> Twelve years since, in 'Fourteen,
> 'The Country's in a fix, lads,
> And needs you on the scene.
> Stand by the Country's Standard
> And see the trouble through –
> And when the War is over
> Count on Us to stand by you!'
>
> 'Stand by us!' says the Government
> In nineteen-twenty-six,
> 'There's trouble in the air, lads,
> And the State is in a fix.'
> 'Stand by us!' says the government,
> 'And see the trouble through –
> And when the Strike is over
> Count on us to stand by you!'
>
> Oh hark! the twelve years' Echo:
> 'Count on Us to stand by You! . . .'[67]

Here Farjeon disrupts the identification between industrial activists and the national enemy, uncovering ideological and linguistic struggles over the categories of 'us' and 'you' as they are indistinctly echoed across a gap of twelve years. The same strategy can be found in a letter to the *British Worker* during the Strike from 'An Englishwoman who feels undying gratitude to the men who protected her in the Great War, and whose only crime now is standing by the British hero of the mines.'[68] She writes, 'Memory hurts. I walk on to the station. The eyes of the picket there are the eyes of a man who lay for hours on the battlefield, broken and torn, and spent months in hospital being patched up, but who will suffer from his wounds until his death' (66). The miners have here become the hero, and the strikers embody the violent traumas of trench warfare and the sacrifices such experiences entailed. The rhetoric of sacrifice here sustains a painful memory of past suffering rather than a triumphant assertion of the legitimacy of national self-definition, as it had for Joynson-Hicks.

The idea that the General Strike is a repetition, hovering somewhere between tragedy and farce, of the First World War, gives way in some texts to a more developed sense of the Strike as the culmination of a longer historical process of which the War was simply one manifestation. The novelist Harold Heslop places the General Strike at the heart of his *Bildungsroman*, *The Gate of a Strange Field*. This novel is structured in relation to the career of its protagonist, Joe, a miner and Trade Union official, with its four sections: Adolescence, The Awakening, Strife, and Deliverance, characterizing both the stages of his life and the development of industrial conflicts in the period: 'It was strife from now until the end. They could not escape it. Upon the inevitableness of the coming struggle was built a strong psychology that needed careful analysis.'[69] This 'psychology' must capture both the sense of an unfolding historical narrative and the sometimes painful loss of individual agency within the movement of this impersonal historical process. Heslop's narrator says, 'and so the world and its people plunged into the days that were to bring them nearer the gate of a strange field' (203) and the 'plunging' suggests both an immersion in the tide of history and a dangerous loss of control. Joe's disorientation is palpable, 'It crashed through his brain. A General Strike! A General Strike! Heavens! Events were hurrying the stream of life. Was it to be the end? Or the beginning? Or . . .' (205)

This catastrophic and conflictual movement of the stream of life speaks at least as much of the philosophical influence of Schopenhauer or of Sorel as it does of the legacy of Marx. The temporality of events and the energies of a stream of life crash painfully through Joe's brain, leaving him unable to know whether a process is beginning or ending, or whether some completely distinct temporality is in the process of being articulated.

H. G. Wells's *Meanwhile: the Picture of a Lady* signals its interest in temporality in its title. The novel opens at a dinner party in Monte Carlo, where guests include Colonel Bullace, an admirer of Joynson-Hicks and a fascist sympathizer, as well as Mr Sempack, a writer on utopia. Sempack's after-dinner conversation turns to the question of work: 'He was saying: "Work. We have to work for the sake of the work and take happiness for the wild-flower it is."'[70] His discourse continues with an observation that happiness may be expected in the future, but 'meanwhile –' we have to accept that our pleasures may be simply partial or somehow incomplete, an observation to which another guest replies 'I perceive that I have been meanwhiling all my life. Meanwhiling . . . Have I been living? You make me question it. Have I just been meanwhiling away my life?' (22). Working, waiting and really living become mutually implicated in this curious exchange with its pragmatic and its utopian energies so curiously intertwined.

Sempack is an explicit advocate of the importance and the possibility of historical progress, 'I am for progress. I believe in progress' (29), and he is also a strong believer in the value of work. His early advocacy of discipline and patience as the tools of the social radical, 'the minds of people have to be adjusted to new ideas before there is an end to this sweating of men in the darkness' (32) invokes a Leninist conceptualization of the relations between philosophy and history that confronts both the confused liberalism and the proto-fascism of other characters in the novel.

Sempack's austere and rigorous social analysis is, however, crucially modified by a brief but intense experience of sexual desire, and the focus of his analysis shifts tellingly from the movement of history to the conflicts and movements of erotic life. The novel has set up a conflict between the temporal incompleteness of 'meanwhile', the moment we inhabit by default as we wait for the unfolding of historical progress, and the experience of the vitality of life. Sempack declares that 'life that ceases to struggle away from whatever it is towards something that it isn't is ceasing to be life' (59), an assertion that undercuts the 'almost inhuman' patience of his earlier acceptance of the necessary incompleteness of the 'meanwhile'. He goes on to suggest, 'we human things; what are we? Channels through which physical energy flows into decision and act and creative achievement' (75) but the direction of this physical energy perturbs him. Unlike the fascist supporter, Colonel Bullace, who has no doubt about the direction of historical movement ('The General Strike, the Social Revolution in England is timed for the first of May, this first of May. The attack is as certain as the invasion of Belgium was in August 1914' (96)), Sempack is forced to confront the difficulty of shaping or channelling the circulation of powerful historical energies. He concedes that 'Idea must clothe itself in Will' (135), admitting that his ideas may need to be handed over to more practical men in the hope that vision and pragmatism can somehow be brought into the same time-frame.

Galsworthy's *Swan Song* explores a similarly vitalist notion of Will as the energy that can act on the world, an energy that is as evasive as it is impersonal:

What a world! The Eternal Mood at work! And if you died, like that old boy, and lay for ever beneath a crab-apple tree – well, it was the Mood resting a moment in your still shape – no! not even resting, moving on in the mysterious rhythm that one called life. (347)

The temporality of history is here displaced by the imagining of eternal vital processes, which are both constitutive of yet antithetic to the human.

Such vitalism was deeply antipathetic to Wyndham Lewis, whose philosophical and fictional writings in this period are fundamentally concerned with time and labour, as well as with the General Strike. Anne Wyndham Lewis suggests, in her Preface to the 1982 edition of *Blasting and Bombardiering*, that Lewis saw the General Strike as the inevitable result of the disillusion, despair and decay of the twenties: 'All this is captured here and shown to lead to the horror of the General Strike.'[71] Certainly, Lewis begins his conclusion to this text with an explicit reference to the Strike, and goes on to identify 1926 as 'the moment when politics began for me in earnest' (339). Lewis had, in fact, been involved in arguments about time, selfhood and labour for some time before 1926. He attended Bergson's lectures at the Collège de France before the War, and had an extensive knowledge of Sorel's political and philosophical writings.[72] In *The Art of Being Ruled* (1926) Lewis describes Sorel as 'the key to all contemporary political thought' and the whole volume is an extended meditation on Sorel's legacy, on syndicalism and on the role of the intellectual.[73]

Lewis is, however, no enthusiast either for Bergson or for Sorel, and his reservations are centrally connected to the ways in which both writers handle concepts of time. Lewis is critical of Sorel's aspiration towards a truly revolutionary temporality, achieved though the catastrophic imagining of a general strike: 'all his exhortation to the workers is to conceive their class-struggle *epically*. Workmen, of course, have other ideas about their destiny' (*Art*, 329). He is also uneasy with what he sees as a fundamental formlessness in the thought of both Sorel and Bergson. Lewis argues that art should be concerned primarily with structure and with 'the outsides of things', whereas Sorel and Bergson are endlessly drawn to 'the *vitals* of things' and to *vitalist* enthusiasms' (403). This unease finds fuller expression in *Time and Western Man* (1927) where Lewis mounts a major critique of what he sees as the dominant philosophical and cultural movements of the 1920s – his targets include Pound, Joyce and Stein as well as Bergson and Whitehead. Lewis argues that time has come to dominate cultural representation and philosophical speculation at the expense of space. Time, for Lewis is associated with flux, with divided subjectivities, with blind striving and with passivity; space is connected to stability, form, the visual, and with action.

This preference for spatial forms of imagination is realized in Lewis's novel *The Apes of God* (1930). This novel constructs an anthropology of the manners and mores of intellectual and artistic London in the twenties. Its characters include the physically repulsive but intellectually gifted Horace Zagreus, a disciple of the super-intellectual Pierpoint, and Daniel Boleyn a young Irishman whom Zagreus hopes to initiate into the secrets of the 'ape world' that is his contemporary society. The organization of the novel is architectural rather than narrative, and incidents, both farcical and tragic, follow one another at a dizzying pace: Dan lurches from disaster to disaster as he moves through the houses and along the streets of a rather alien city.

The final disaster of this novel is the General Strike. Lewis writes with no sympathy for either the strikers or the government, but rather uses Dan's profound alienation to construct a sense of distance from the events as they occur. The General Strike is presented as symptom, rather than as historical event, although it does also have the power to animate and to drive the novel towards some sort of resolution. Lewis had considerable sympathy with views about the distorting effects of debt and credit discussed above. Indeed these led him to write a sympathetic study of Hitler in 1931, on the basis that Hitler was opposed to usury and would act to curb the destructive effects of international finance.[74] He thus represents the General Strike not as a resolution of any basic conflict, or as a historical turning point, but rather as a kind of pathology.

In the final section of the novel, Dan emerges into the London streets unaware of the Strike, and is struck first of all by an inexplicable disruption of social, and even sexual, mores. The first thing he notices is that men in a car are following him. They are in fact volunteers, eager to offer him a lift to his place of work, but Dan is never able to accept or to understand this new freedom for strangers to approach him in the street. He blushes, feels ashamed, and despises such 'low familiarity coming from strangers'.[75] Turning away in horror from such unwelcome solicitations, Dan finds himself staring at women's underwear in a shop window, 'He blushed all the way up the backs of his legs. He had a centripetal shame in him' (*Apes of God*, 639). Scarcely recovered from such shaming encounters,

Dan then finds himself in the company of pickets; an equally unsettling experience:

Some men were standing . . . and laughing in a cruel and repulsive fashion as if they did not wish to laugh at all, at the driver – who had a policeman up with him upon the box. The men who were in check caps were ridiculing the driver for something, and he heard them pass some very horrid remarks but the driver did not answer them, and the policeman did not seem to mind. Someone said it was a picket. (641)

Dan then seeks refuge in the house of a friend, but there he finds only fear and boredom, produced by the disruptions and uncertainties of everyday life during the Strike.

The novel ends with a deeply pessimistic, incoherent and rather distasteful sexual coupling, directly produced by the Strike. Zagreus goes to visit Lady Fredigonde, an elderly woman from whom he had been trying to extract a substantial sum of money. Her husband is apparently asleep. Lady Fredigonde insists that Sir James is simply pretending to sleep as a way of expressing his anger about the General Strike, 'Today he is very aggravating! The Strike has upset him, I think' (645). But Sir James is, in fact, dead. With barely a pause in the rhythm of their conversation, Lady Fredigonde draws attention to her improved financial position following her husband's death and then asks Zagreus to marry her. Zagreus promptly agrees and, '[t]he two crippled stumps of her arms went out – the short way that they could, and aspired to rise the necessary inches to circumscribe her splendid groom. A dark spasm visited the corpse-like carcass beneath' (649). As they kiss, noises are heard from the street: a 'mechanistic rattle' and a drum beat that might be the sound of strikers or might be the death rattle that brings all these narrative adventures to an end. Decay, corruption, death and 'dark spasm' are the legacy of the General Strike whose rattle invades the very core of the couple's embraces.

Powerful forces associated with reproduction and with desire constantly disrupt the narrative temporalities of fictional representations of the 1926 Strike. In Wells's *Meanwhile*, Cynthia Ryland is the hostess who is first encountered at the dinner party in her home discussed above. She encourages her husband to return to England where he can play an active role in the coming General Strike, but decides her pregnancy makes any such activism impossible for her. Cynthia 'was sustained by this deep life stream that had entered into her and taken control of her once uneasy self' (108). Despite the grotesqueness of her self-description as 'three parts vegetable for a bit now – and then a sort of cow' (88), she actually sustains a significant political and practical role in the novel. Finally, when a young man stumbles into her garden, pursued by fascists, she 'thought very quickly. This man had to be saved. She was on his side' (187). She hides the man and later helps him to escape to France.

In Lewis Grassic Gibbon's rather later novel, *Cloud Howe* (1933), part of his trilogy *A Scots Quair*, Chris Guthrie also experiences the General Strike through the temporality and the physicality of pregnancy.[76] She miscarries after trying to warn the strikers of the disastrous consequences of their planned bombing of a railway line. She passes the final days of the Strike unconscious, and wakes to the realization of trauma and loss: 'The baby had been born, then, it wasn't born dead, though it died soon after . . . that was days ago, two or three days before the Strike ended' (309). Chris's distress over the loss of her baby becomes indistinguishable from the trauma of defeat in the Strike, and historical and biological processes are represented as sharing a temporality and an impersonal vitality.

This same temporal elision frames the overall structure of Wells's *Meanwhile*, where the contested meanings of the strike are finally displaced by the birth of a son to Cynthia and Philip. This son is the physical incarnation of his father's intellectual alignment with the discourse of progress as well as the realization of the vital energies circulating in and through Cynthia's pregnancy. He is the only sort of answer the novel provides to the larger historical questions set in play by earlier discourses on work, agency and the future.

The creative and vital energies associated with reproduction thus create one of the temporal frames for imagining the process and the significance of the General Strike. Similarly, the energies and disruptions associated with sexual passion provide a metaphorical language for representing the Strike in a number of texts, and the temporal framework of the Strike is often mapped onto the unfolding of a sexual narrative. In Heslop's *The Gate of a Strange Field*, Joe meets his estranged wife, Molly, at the very moment when the Strike is declared. He begins an affair with her which absorbs his energies in the early days of the Strike, 'they spent a blissful weekend while the world outside reverberated with the tumult of a coming strife' (218) and as the narrative continues Joe feels himself increasingly powerless and disabled by the intensity of his desire. The affair ends and Joe returns to the North, where his personal and professional lives fall apart. Towards the end of the novel Joe asserts that 'mankind cannot endure such volcanic eruptions and continue on exactly the same plane' (249), an assertion that might be read either as a repudiation of the volcanic eruptions or as a commitment to the inevitability of change. But in the final section Joe is trapped underground after an 'eruption' in the pit. He is entombed for seventeen days and although he survives he is reduced to a state of passivity and physical collapse, a conclusion that seems to leave little hope for the creative energies of the volcanic.

In Galsworthy's *Swan Song* the General Strike produces the practical and the moral circumstances necessary to the renewal of the affair between Jon Forsyte and Fleur. Both characters have married since they were last romantically involved, but Fleur's working at the canteen for volunteers and Jon's return to London mean that they meet once more. The renewal of their affair is catastrophic, generating distress, disappointment and for Fleur a depression that is so encompassing that it amounts to giving up on life. This failed erotic encounter weaves through the narrative of the Strike, with its small fears and its modest achievements, to produce a sense of failure, and paralysing incapacity to act that in the end casts its shadow over the whole world of the Forsytes.

In Wilkinson's *Clash*, sexual desire constantly unsettles the narrative centre of the novel, as Joan Craig's journeys and speeches during the Strike are re-read as erotic display. The dilemma is articulated in the opening pages of the novel. When Joan first becomes aware of the approach of the Strike, she reacts with enthusiasm and excitement, provoking in her employer a series of erotic musings:

Royd was outwardly placid, but his jaw was locked on his pipe stem. The grace of her thin body, her tousled black hair above her white neck, went to his head. He was too physically strong for the life he was leading. The transition from heavy manual work to a sedentary life had been too abrupt. Though his own marriage was a perfectly happy and peaceful one, the wild strain in Joan appealed to deep fires in Royd's nature. He ached to stand behind her now, grip her wrists, and force that alive body against his. (13)

Throughout the novel the 'clash' of industrial militancy is articulated and imagined through the energies and frustrations of other sorts of conflict. Joan is caught in a clash between individual vocation and collective identification, between the cultural values of North and South, between the intense passion of one lover and the more measured affection of another, and finally between work and sexuality as ways of living her identity as modern woman. Desired for her energy, her agency and her vision, Joan is nonetheless offered only different forms of frustration. She is at the edge of the historical struggle that is the Strike, gaining access to its inner spaces of power and decision only through subterfuge of a distinctly implausible kind. In concentrating her political energies on women in the mining communities she knows she is confirming that marginality, though she also sees no other way of sustaining any sort of collective identification. Joan repeatedly talks of the importance of work; both for her own sake and because it is the space in which she can imagine liberation of some sort. Throughout the Strike, she is working extremely hard. 'I'll work my head off' (27), she announces at the outset, and then drives herself on to attend meetings, deliver speeches and to fulfil a range of practical political duties. By the end of the novel, she is faced with a stark choice by one of her lovers: she must give up work and dedicate herself to passion and to family life, or she must renounce this passion and pursue her future career as an MP. She settles in the end for a companionate marriage with the war hero Gerry Blain, entered into on the explicit understanding that 'the work comes first' (310). The conclusion is far from triumphant, and the novel ends with rather laboured humour, uncharacteristic ellipses, and coy allusions to the possibility of sexual fulfilment in the future. Joan's frustrated passion is the result of a clear and deliberate choice about the areas of life in which she is most likely to find fulfilment, but the novel's continual allusions to sacrifice seep from the narrative of the General Strike to the narrative of this protagonist who has been so prophetically cast as 'Joan of Arc' (62). She does not emerge from the fire in a very good state.

In many imaginative treatments of the General Strike, the events of 1926 offer characters the chance to feel part of history, to connect their own life narratives to a national drama. This sense of historical project is intimately connected to the experience of work. In *Meanwhile*, Cynthia suggested to her husband: 'Go to England, dear one. Things are happening there. Trouble and muddle. Men – men ought to work' (88). In *Swan Song*, the nine days bring the Forsytes together in the shared experience of labour. Jon Forsyte declares 'I must go and get a good, dirty job. I should like to stoke an engine' (19) and finds an 'extraordinary pleasure in being up against it – being in England again, doing something for England' (37).

The psychic and social meanings of labour are central to novelistic representations of the General Strike. For some, the meaning of the Strike is a liberation from the necessity of repetitive labour. Thus Heslop's narrator notes that 'by noon, quiet humour assailed the crowd of city workers. They laughed, not because they were enjoying the strike, but because they would be late for work. Time, the thing that counts in industry, was slipping past and they were still walking' (*The Gate*, 228). Such release from the repetitions and compulsions of labour was part of the meaning of the strike. Thus, for example, the Cardiff Strike Committee advised its members on how to pass their time agreeably while on strike, 'WHAT CAN YOU DO:

Keep smiling. Refuse to be provoked. Get into your garden. Look after the wife and kiddies.'[77] There is an echo here of William Benbow, for whom the General Strike was imagined as a space in which collective and individual forms of being could be both constructed and celebrated precisely in the hiatus created by industrial militancy.

In marked contrast to this craving for the cessation of work among workers, volunteers experienced their unaccustomed manual labour as a form of liberation. The anthropologist Rachelle Saltzman comments dryly that during the Strike 'representatives of the upper and upper-middle classes defended their right not to do manual labour by doing it – temporarily'.[78] Fleur and Michael, in *Swan Song*, launch upon the project of providing a canteen for volunteers almost immediately the Strike is announced: 'It'll mean frightfully hard work; and getting anybody we can to help' (6). The ending of the Strike is experienced by Fleur as a moment of loss and disappointment since:

She had a first-rate crew of helpers of all ages, most of them in society. They worked in the manner properly attributed to negroes . . . they got up at, or stayed up to, all hours. They were never cross and always cheery. In a word, they seemed inspired. (59)

Similarly, in *Clash*, the rather cold and passionless Helen Dacre becomes animated by the prospect of volunteering: 'The excitement and unaccustomed energy had quickened her blood. Her face was flushed and her eyes bright and eager . . . Mrs Dacre was as eager to overwork herself as ever Joan could be' (121). Since this very work will drive her husband, temporarily, into Joan Craig's arms, its capacity to excite and animate Helen is even more striking.

Many volunteers approached their labour with a similar spirit of adventure and purposefulness, seeking to combine the carnivalesque with the rhetoric of righteous toil. But this fantasy was not without its pathology. Wells represents this emphatically through the character of Lady Catherine. Lady Catherine begins *Meanwhile* as a vacuous society woman, but she is transformed by the announcement of the Strike: 'This has stirred me like great music' (112). She instantly decides to return to England as a volunteer, finding in this identity a profound self-confirmation, '"Now it has come," said Lady Catherine, "I am glad it has come," and sat still for some moments with a quiet smile on her handsome animated face' (115). On her return to England, however, Lady Catherine becomes both cruel and manipulative, finally killing a man during the Strike; having run the man over in her car she simply drives off. This violent conclusion to Catherine's inspired sense of historical mission is explicitly contrasted with Cynthia's heroic saving of a young man from fascist persecution, but also with her comfortable acceptance of domesticity.

We have seen how the General Strike has been imagined as a repetition, as a traumatic moment of crisis, and as a space for the knotted and clotted temporalities of sexuality and reproduction to achieve some sort of stability. But for some writers, the General Strike was 'untimely' in a rather different sense: it was simply happening at the wrong time. In his history of the General Strike, Julian Symons begins by pointing out that 'The General Strike which lasted from May 3–12 1926, was, Leopold Amery said afterwards, thirty years out of date.'[79] This sense of the Strike as being already too late permeates a number of accounts and it is particularly marked in retrospective accounts. For example in his memoirs, Leonard Woolf talks about his memories of the Strike and then advances the hypothesis that 'the perpetual tragedy of history is that things are perpetually being done ten or twenty years too late'.[80] Similarly, a character in Storm Jameson's *None Turn Back* (1936) declares the Strike doomed: 'the miners are beaten – they were beaten before they came out of their holes. They lost their chance in nineteen-nineteen. That was the last moment for a general strike.'[81]

The uncanniness of the Strike as a moment in history reverberates in Virginia Woolf's formally innovative and philosophically challenging exploration of time in *To the Lighthouse*. This novel has a most unusual structure: it has three parts which though linked in both narrative and thematic terms are also relatively distinct. The first part introduces us to the Ramsay family and their houseguests. The action in this part takes place in one day, during which a trip is planned to visit the lighthouse and to bring gifts to the lighthouse keeper. The final part of the novel also takes place in one day, when remaining members of the family return to their house and finally manage to complete their trip to the lighthouse. Between these two developed narrative explorations of the intersubjective relations of the Ramsay family and their friends, there is a third short, stylistically distinct part called 'Time Passes'. Here, in a series of brief, densely written, poetically resonant sections, Woolf seeks to represent the collision of human and non-human temporalities. The Ramsay's house is empty and suffers decay as its borders and boundaries become increasingly permeable. Years pass, and central characters die, of illness, in the war, or in childbirth. These deaths are represented in a way that is shocking as well as painful: they appear in parentheses, as they are part of a quite different time scale from the seasonal, monumental temporality of this central part of the novel. Compared to the movements of seasons, and the unfolding temporal energies of natural forces, the individual lives with which we became so involved in the first part of the novel can be understood only as a minute episode. Woolf was very aware of the formal challenges of capturing in a narrative text forms of temporality that are neither linear nor humanized. She wrote in her diary, 'here is the most difficult abstract piece of writing – I have to give an empty house, no people's characters, the passage of time, all eyeless and featureless with nothing to cling to'.[82]

'Time Passes' was, as Kate Flint has pointed out, written during the General Strike, and that 'passage of time . . . with nothing to cling to' will turn out to have quite particular historical resonances.[83] Woolf's diary records her responses to the Strike in some detail. On 5 May, she suggests that 'an exact diary of the Strike would be interesting' (77) and she briefly attempts to record her impressions of crowded motor cars, the absence of buses, placards and newspapers. But this exact record quickly gives way to the more fragmentary, layered and speculative mode that is characteristic of Woolf's diary writing. Indeed, by 13 May, she is no longer able to grasp that sense of historical urgency that made an exact record seem both timely and interesting, writing instead, 'I suppose all pages devoted to the Strike will be skipped, when I read over this book. Oh that dull old chapter, I shall say. Excitements about what are called real things are always unutterably transitory' (85). Yet if Woolf's impulse towards the exact record was to prove transitory, her imaginative reworking of the dislocations and temporal disruptions of the Strike in 'Time Passes' would be a far more enduring cultural record.

Woolf talks about the Strike as producing a sense of mingled anticipation and boredom, with a resultant paralysis of the will: 'It is all tedious and depressing, rather like waiting in a train outside a station . . . one does not know what to do'.[84] She also registers an intellectual and emotional disorientation, 'I notice how frequently we break of [f] with "Well, I don't know." Leonard says this is due to the lack of papers' (78). This absence of newspapers, as an unsettling marker of the disruption of temporality is recorded in numerous texts about the experience of the Strike, including Lewis's *The Apes of God*: 'The absence of newspapers fostered every report of disorder' (643).

'Time Passes' opens with the phrase 'Well, we must wait for the future to show.'[85] This is a curious phrase, suggesting both passivity and creative anticipation, but it is one that alerts us at the outset to the importance of the future in this part of a novel that is elsewhere so saturated with memories.[86] 'Time passes' explores different temporal frames. It craves the epiphanic moment of completeness: 'the hare erect; the wave falling; the boat rocking' (174), because such moments seem to contain an energy and focus that create their own kind of unity. Yet the text also acknowledges the processes of fragmentation and change that undo such moments: 'For our penitence deserves a glimpse only; our toil respite only' (174) and the moment cannot be held on to for long. The formal completeness that is 'loveliness and stillness' is exemplified in 'Time Passes' in the figure of a distant pool: 'solitary like a pool at evening, far distant, seen from a train window, vanishing so quickly that the pool, pale in the evening, is scarcely robbed of its solitude, though once seen' (176). The pool's solitude is a metaphor for the evacuation of human relations from the imagining of time: the pool is distant, seen but not seen, or at least not transformed by the fact of being looked at. Yet these human relations are simultaneously restored by the glance and by the train window. Writing about the Strike, Woolf had said, 'It is all tedious and depressing, rather like waiting in a train outside a station', and this metaphorical representation of frustrated anticipation illuminates the fictional resonances of the train window which here stage a fantasy of disconnection and separateness.

The shimmering pool returns later in 'Time Passes', where 'stirring the pool' uncovers 'imaginations of the strangest kind' which struggle to articulate the possible relations between inner vision and external sensation: 'In those mirrors, the minds of men, in those pools of uneasy water, in which clouds for ever turn and shadows form, dreams persisted' (179). These dreams are dreams of a stable and ethical social order where 'good triumphs, happiness prevails, order rules' (180), but they are as evanescent, immediately undercut by the cruel arbitrariness of Prue Ramsay's death, since 'They said nobody deserved happiness more.'

The unfolding of monumental time, the temporality of nature, of impersonal vital forces, is both precarious and violent in Woolf's novel. It threatens to destroy all that we have known of the family and of their material existence in space. Yet as 'Time Passes' continues this temporality is answered, and even redeemed, in rather an unexpected way. Quite another temporality is introduced by the labour of the domestic servant, Mrs McNab, 'tearing the veil of silence with hands that had stood in the wash-tub, grinding it with boots that had crunched the shingle' (177). Hers is not the time of epiphany, anticipation or creative dreaming, but the time of repetitive labour, 'bringing things out and putting them away again' (178). In a curious inversion of modernist sensibilities about habit and repetition, this repetitive and manual labour is ultimately redemptive. After all, in 'Time Passes', at the end of nine sections, just like the end of the nine days of the Strike, 'peace had come. Messages of peace breathed from the sea to the shore' (193), and we are back again to the sustainability of the island nation restored to peace and to useful labour. Yet this peace is far from comfortable, marked as it is by the trauma of waking nightmares: 'her eyes opened wide. Here she was again, she thought, sitting bolt upright in bed. Awake' (194).

Woolf's textual imagining of a future peace is unsettled by the image of a waking nightmare. The capacity of violence to emerge in the contexts of political, philosophical or fictional explorations of a different future for labour has emerged strikingly throughout this chapter, as indeed through-out this book as a whole. The apparently redemptive character of 'hands that had stood in the washtub' has finally to confront the physical and the psychical traumas that drive such blank and desperate staring into the future, if labour is to have a future tense.

Notes

INTRODUCTION

1. See M. Godelier, 'Work and its Representations: a Research Proposal', *History Workshop Journal*, 10 (1980), 164–74.
2. See 'labour', in Raymond Williams, *Keywords: a Vocabulary of Culture and Society* (Glasgow: Collins, 1976), pp. 145–48.
3. Eric Hobsbawm, *The Age of Empire 1875–1914* (London: Sphere Books, 1989), p. 5.
4. Jonathan Rose, *The Edwardian Temperament, 1895–1919* (Athens, Ohio: Ohio University Press, 1986), p. xii.
5. See for example Paul Fussell, *The Great War and Modern Memory* (London: Oxford University Press, 1975) and Trudi Tate, *Modernism, History and the First World War* (Manchester: Manchester University Press, 1998).
6. Adriano Tilgher, *Work: what it has Meant to Men through the Ages*, trans. D. C. Fisher (London: George G. Harrap, 1931), p. 63.
7. Krishan Kumar, 'From Work to Employment and Unemployment: the English Experience', in R. E. Pahl (ed.), *On Work: Historical, Comparative and Theoretical Approaches* (Oxford: Basil Blackwell, 1988), pp. 138–64 (p. 138).
8. Eric Hobsbawm, 'The Making of the Working Class, 1870–1914', in *Uncommon People: Resistance, Rebellion and Jazz* (London; Weidenfeld and Nicolson, 1998), p. 60.
9. See Kumar, 'From Work to Unemployment', p. 164. Hobsbawm, *The Age of Empire* p. 195, suggests that only 12 percent of married women were working in the 1890s, so the reduction after the 1850s seems to have been quite rapid.
10. David Feldman, 'The Importance of Being English: Jewish Immigration and the Decay of Liberal England', in David Feldman and Gareth Stedman Jones (eds.), *Metropolis London: Histories and Representations since 1800* (London: Routledge, 1989), pp. 56–84.
11. Robert H. Sherard, *The Child-Slaves of Britain* (London: Hurst and Blackett, 1905), pp. 65–66.
12. Paul Thompson, *The Edwardians: the Remaking of British Society*, 2nd edition (London: Routledge, 1992), p. 270; John Burnett (ed.), *Useful Toil: Autobiographies of Working People from the 1820s to the 1920s* (London: Allen Lane, 1974), p. 280.

13. Frederick Winslow Taylor, *Principles of Scientific Management* (New York and London: Harper and Brothers Publishers, 1911).

14. James F. Knapp, *Literary Modernism and the Transformation of Work* (Evanston, Ill.: Northwestern University press, 1988), p. 129.

15. Harry Braverman, *Labor and Monopoly Capital: the Degradation of Work in the Twentieth Century* (London: Monthly Review Press, 1974).

16. As Braverman notes, Lenin was an enthusiastic proponent of Taylor's work.

17. Rita Felski, 'The Gender of Modernity', in Sally Ledger, Josephine McDonagh and Jane Spencer (eds.), *Political Gender: Texts and Contexts* (London: Harvester, 1994), pp. 144–55 (p. 151).

18. Ann L. Ardis, *New Women, New Novels: Feminism and Early Modernism* (London: Rutgers University Press, 1990), p. 20.

19. For discussion of this point, see John Burnett, Introduction to *Useful Toil*; Harriet Bradley, 'Changing Social Divisions: Class, Gender and Race', in Robert Bocock and Kenneth Thompson (eds.), *Social and Cultural Forms of Modernity* (Cambridge: Polity Press, 1992), pp. 12–67; Sonya Rose, *Limited Livelihoods: Gender and Class in Nineteenth-Century England* (London: Routledge, 1992), p. 46; and Louise Tilly and Joan W. Scott, *Women, Work and Family* (New York: Holt, Rinehart and Winston, 1978), p. 77.

20. See Jane Lewis, 'The Working-Class Wife and Mother and State Intervention, 1870–1918', in Jane Lewis (ed.), *Labour and Love: Women's Experience of Home and Family, 1850–1940* (Oxford: Basil Blackwell, 1986), pp. 99–120.

21. See Tilly and Scott, *Women, Work and Family*, p. 151.

22. Veronica Beechey, *Unequal Work* (London: Verso, 1987), p. 65.

23. Deborah Thom, 'Free from Chains? The Image of Women's Labour in London, 1900–1920', in David Feldman and Gareth Stedman Jones (eds.), *Metropolis London* (London: Routledge, 1989), pp. 85–99.

24. See Kristin Huneault, '"Living Tableaux of Misery and Oppression": Sweated Labour on Tour', in Valerie Mainz and Griselda Pollock (eds.), *Work and the Image II. Work in Modern Times: Visual Mediations and Social Processes* (Aldershot: Ashgate, 2000), pp. 11–31.

25. Sally Alexander, Introduction to *Women's Fabian Tracts* (London: Routledge, 1988), pp. 1–13.

26. See, for example, B. L. Hutchins, 'Home Work and Sweating: the Causes and Remedies', in Alexander, *Women's Fabian Tracts*, pp. 33–52.

27. See Denise Riley, '"The Free Mothers": Pronatalism and Working Women in Industry at the End of the Last War in Britain', *History Workshop Journal*, 11 (1981), 59–118.

28. Clementina Black, Introduction to Clementina Black (ed.), *Married Women's Work* (London: G. Bell, 1915), pp. 1–15 (p. 4).

29. See Jane Marcus (ed.), *The Young Rebecca: Writings of Rebecca West, 1911–1917* (London: Macmillan, 1982), p. 41.

30. David Meakin, *Man and Work: Literature and Culture in Industrial Society* (London: Methuen, 1976), p. 2.

31. Ruth Danon, *Work in the English Novel: the Myth of Vocation* (London: Croom Helm, 1985), p. 171.
32. Knapp, *Literary Modernism*, p. 3.
33. Richard Godden, *Fictions of Labor; William Faulkner and the South's Long Revolution* (Cambridge: Cambridge University Press, 1997).
34. Keith Thomas (ed.), *The Oxford Book of Work* (Oxford: Oxford University Press, 1999).

1 PHILOSOPHIES OF LABOUR AND SELFHOOD

1. Hannah Arendt, *The Human Condition* (London: University of Chicago Press, 1958), p. 127.
2. *Ibid.*, p. 101.
3. Peter Laslett, Introduction to John Locke, *Two Treatises of Government* (New York; Cambridge University Press, 1960), p. 114.
4. Locke 'Second Treatise of Government', chapter 5, 'Property', *ibid.*, p. 329.
5. Johannes Rohbeck, 'Property and Labour in the Social Philosophy of John Locke', *History of European Ideas*, vol. 5, no. 1 (1984), 65–77 (73).
6. See Adam Smith, *The Wealth of Nations* (London: Everyman's Library, 1991), vol. 1, book 1, chapter 2.
7. Kathryn Sutherland, Introduction to Adam Smith, *An Inquiry into the Nature and Causes of the Wealth of Nations* (Oxford: Oxford University Press, 1993), p. xxviii.
8. For discussion of this idea see Raymond Williams, *Culture and Society, 1780–1950* (Harmondsworth: Penguin, 1958).
9. G. W. F. Hegel, *Elements of the Philosophy of Right*, ed. Allen W. Wood, trans. H. B. Nisbet (Cambridge; Cambridge University Press, 1991). For a discussion of Hegel's reading of Smith, see Tom Rockmore, *Before and After Hegel: a Historical Introduction to Hegel's Thought* (London: University of California Press, 1993), p. 129.
10. Richard J. Norman, *Hegel's 'Phenomenology': a Philosophical Introduction* (Aldershot: Gregg Revivals, 1991), p. 108.
11. Rockmore, *Before and After Hegel*, p. 53.
12. G. W. F. Hegel, *Phenomenology of Spirit*, translated by A. V. Miller (Oxford: Oxford University Press, 1977), pp. 104–19.
13. Raymond Plant, *Hegel: an Introduction* (Oxford: Basil Blackwell, 1983), p. 114.
14. Arthur Schopenhauer, *The World as Will and Idea*, trans. R. B. Haldane and J. Kemp, 3 vols. (London: Trübner and Co., 1883–86). See also the discussion of the journal *The Eagle and the Serpent* in chapter 3.
15. Christopher Janaway, *Self and World in Schopenhauer's Philosophy* (Oxford: Clarendon Press, 1989).
16. Arthur Schopenhauer, *The World as Will and Representation*, trans. E. F. J. Payne, 2 vols. (Indian Hills, Colo.: Falcon's Wing Press, 1958), vol. 1, p. 37.

17. See 'The World as Will', in Arthur Schopenhauer, *Philosophical Writings* (New York; Continuum, 1994), pp. 125–98.

18. See discussions of Sylvia Pankhurst and of D. H. Lawrence in chapters 3 and 4.

19. G. B. Tennyson, introductory remarks on *Sartor Resartus*, in G. B. Tennyson (ed.), *A Carlyle Reader: Selections from the Writings of Thomas Carlyle*, (Cambridge: Cambridge University Press, 1984), p. 122.

20. A particularly intriguing rhetorical identification by a man who was, of course, Scottish.

21. All three quotations are from Thomas Carlyle, *Chartism* (London: The Holerth Press, 1924), p. 20.

22. Thomas Carlyle, 'Past and Present' in *Lectures* (London: Chapman and Hall, 1890), pp. 69–302 (p. 185).

23. C. J. Arthur, *Dialectics of Labour: Marx and his Relation to Hegel* (Oxford: Basil Blackwell, 1986).

24. Jonathan Beecher and Richard Bienvenu (eds.), *The Utopian Vision of Charles Fourier: Selected Texts on Work, Love, and Passionate Attraction* (London: Jonathan Cape, 1972), p. 142.

25. For discussion of this point see Warren Breckman, *Marx, the Young Hegelians, and the Origins of Radical Social Theory: Dethroning the Self* (Cambridge: Cambridge University Press, 1999) and Dirk J. Struik, 'Introduction' in Karl Marx, *Economic and Philosophic Manuscripts of 1844*, ed. Dirk J. Struik (London: Lawrence and Wishart, 1970).

26. Marx, *Economic and Philosophic Manuscripts*, p. 112.

27. For further discussion of debates about the employment of women, see chapter 3.

28. For a very different representation of the relations between labour and freedom, see the discussion of Olive Schreiner below.

29. 'These labourers, who must sell themselves piecemeal, are a commodity', Karl Marx and Friedrich Engels, *The Communist Manifesto*, ed. David McLellan (Oxford: Oxford University Press, 1992), p. 9.

30. Karl Marx and Friedrich Engels, *The German Ideology: Part One*, ed. C. J. Arthur (London: Lawrence and Wishart, 1977), p. 92.

31. G. A. Cohen, 'The Dialectic of Labour in Marx', in *History, Labour, and Freedom: Themes from Marx* (Oxford: Clarendon Press, 1988), pp. 183–208 (p. 189).

32. *Ibid.*, p. 190.

33. Karl Marx, *Capital: Volume One*, trans. Eden and Cedar Paul (London: J. M. Dent and Sons, 1972), p. 169.

34. See, for example, Eric Hobsbawm, *Labouring Men: Studies in the History of Labour* (London: Weidenfeld and Nicolson, 1968).

35. William Smart, 'John Ruskin His life and Work' (1883), reprinted in William Smart and J. A. Hobson, *'John Ruskin His life and Work' and 'John Ruskin, Social Reformer'* (London: Routledge/Thoemmes Press, 1994), p. 36.

36. John Ruskin, 'Work', in *The Crown of Wild Olive* (London: Routledge/Thoemmes Press, 1994), p. 32.

37. See John Ruskin, *Time and Tide, by Weare and Tyne: Twenty-Five Letters to a Working Man of Sunderland on the Laws of Work* (London: Routledge/Thoemmes Press, 1994).
38. See John Ruskin, *Unto this Last* (London: Routledge/Thoemmes Press, 1994).
39. *Ibid.*, pp. 80–85.
40. John D. Rosenberg discusses this in his Introduction to John Rosenberg (ed.), *The Genius of John Ruskin: Selections from his Writings* (London: RKP, 1979).
41. See chapter 5 for further discussion of this point.
42. J. A. Hobson, in Smart and Hobson, *John Ruskin*, p. 307.
43. William Morris, 'Useful Work versus Useless Toil', in Asa Briggs (ed.), *William Morris: 'News for Nowhere' and Selected Writings and Designs* (Harmondswoth; Penguin, 1984), pp. 117–36.
44. In Briggs, *William Morris* pp. 183–300.
45. See Ruth Levitas, 'Utopian Fictions and Political Theories: Domestic Labour in the Work of Edward Bellamy, Charlotte Perkins Gilman and William Morris', in Val Gough and Jill Rudd (eds.), *A Very Different Story: Studies of the Fiction of Charlotte Perkins Gilman* (Liverpool: Liverpool University Press, 1998), pp. 81–99.
46. See Duncan Large, 'Introduction', in Friedrich Nietzsche, *Twilight of the Idols* (Oxford: Oxford University Press, 1998), p. xv.
47. See David S. Thatcher, *Nietzsche in England: 1890–1914* (Toronto: University of Toronto Press, 1970). For an indication of the persistence of Nietzsche's presence in British intellectual life, see two journals: *The Eagle and the Serpent* (1890s) and *London Aphrodite* (1920s).
48. Friedrich Nietzsche, *Daybreak: Thoughts on the Prejudices of Morality*, eds. Maudemarie Clark and Brian Leiter, trans. R. J. Hollingdale (Cambridge: Cambridge University Press, 1997), p. 206.
49. See *Gay Science*, trans. W. Kaufman, (New York: Random House, 1974), p. 158.
50. Friedrich Nietzsche, *Untimely Meditations*, translated by R. J. Hollingdale (Cambridge: Cambridge University Press, 1983), p. 127.
51. Friedrich Nietzsche, *Human, All too Human*, trans. Marion Faber and Stephen Lehmann (Harmondsworth: Penguin, 1984), p. 254, para. 611.
52. For a discussion of Brittain's interest in Schreiner, see Alan Bishop, '"With suffering and through time": Olive Schreiner, Vera Brittain and the Great War', in Malvern Van Wyk Smith and Don Maclennan (eds.), *Olive Schreiner and After* (Claremont, R.S.A.: David Philip, 1983), pp. 80–92.
53. B. L. Hutchins, *Conflicting Ideals of Woman's Work* (London: T. Murby and Co., 1916), p. 16.
54. D. H. Lawrence, *The Rainbow*, ed. Mark Kinkead-Weekes (London: Penguin, 1995), p. 379.
55. See Ralph Iron (Olive Schreiner), *Dream Life and Real Life* (London: T. Fisher Unwin, 1893), pp. 65–93.
56. See Carolyn Burdett, *Olive Schreiner and the Progress of Feminism: Evolution, Gender, Empire* (Basingstoke: Palgrave, 2001), p. 57.

57. *Olive Schreiner's Thoughts about Women*, compiled by Anna Purcell (Cape Town: Women's Enfranchisement League, 1909).

58. Olive Schreiner, *Woman and Labour* (London: T. Fisher Unwin, 1911), p. 334.

59. See Herbert Spencer, *The Principles of Ethics*, 2 vols. (London: Williams and Norgate, 1893) vol. 1, 329.

60. See, for example, Burdett, *Olive Schreiner*, and Nancy L. Paxton, *George Eliot and Herbert Spencer: Feminism, Evolution and the Reconstruction of Gender* (Princeton, N.J.: Princeton University Press, 1991).

61. Both essays are in Sigmund Freud, *Civilization, Society and Religion*, ed. Albert Dickson, The Penguin Freud Library, 15 vols. (Harmondsworth: Penguin Books, 1985), vol. 12, pp. 179–340.

2 TECHNOLOGIES OF LABOUR: WASHING AND TYPING

1. See, for example, Marshall McLuhan, *Understanding Media: the Extensions of Man* (Cambridge, Mass.: MIT Press, 1998); Roger Chartier, *Cultural History: between Practices and Representations*, trans. Lydia G. Cochrane (Cambridge: Polity Press, 1988).

2. See Friedrich A. Kittler, *Discourse Networks 1800/1900*, trans. Michael Metteer with Chris Cullens (Stanford, Calif.: Stanford University Press, 1990).

3. See Ruth Schwartz Cowan, *More Work for Mother: the Ironies of Household Technology from the Open Hearth to the microwave* (London: Free Association Books, 1989), p. 4.

4. Tim Armstrong, *Modernism, Technology and the Body: a Cultural Study* (Cambridge: Cambridge University Press, 1998); Mark Seltzer, *Bodies and Machines* (London: Routledge, 1992).

5. Anson Rabinbach, *The Human Motor: Energy, Fatigue and the Origins of Modernity* (Berkeley, Calif.: University of California Press, 1992).

6. Kittler, *Discourse Networks* and *Gramophone, Film, Typewriter*, trans. Geoffrey Winthrop-Young and Michael Wutz (Stanford, Calif.: Stanford University Press, 1999).

7. David E. Wellbery, Foreword to Kittler, *Discourse Networks*, pp. vii–xxxiii (p. xxii).

8. Mark Seltzer, 'The Postal Unconscious', *Henry James Review*, 21/3 (2000), 197–206 (200).

9. Seltzer, *Bodies and Machines*, p. 10.

10. Jennifer Wicke, 'Vampiric Typewriting: *Dracula* and its Media', *ELH*, 59 (1992), 467–93 (467).

11. The chapter entitled 'Queen's Sacrifice' is the most opaque section of *Discourse Networks*: Kittler begins with the Lacanian observation that 'La[barred]femme n'existe pas', but then goes on to tease out the meanings of women's professional prominence and of the 'desexualization' offered by technologically mediated writing (pp. 347–57).

12. Cited in Wilfred A. Beeching, *Century of the Typewriter* (Bournemouth: British Typewriter Museum Publishing, 1990), p. 35.

13. Frank J. Romano, *Machine Writing and Typesetting* (Salem, N. H.: Gama, 1986), p. 15.

14. Margery W. Davies, *Woman's Place is at the Typewriter: Office Work and Office Workers 1870–1930* (Philadelphia, Penn.: Temple University Press, 1982). See also Ellen Jordan, 'The Lady Clerks at the Prudential: the Beginning of Vertical Segregation by Sex in Clerical Work in Nineteenth-Century Britain', *Gender and History*, 8(1) (1996), 65–81 and Sharon Hartman Strom, *Beyond the Typewriter: Gender, Class and the Origins of Modern American Office Work, 1900–1930* (Urbana, Ill.: University of Illinois Press, 1992).

15. Jacques Boyer, 'Are Men Better Typists than Women?: Interesting tests made by J. M. Lahy', *Scientific American*, 109 (1913), 316 and 326–27 (327).

16. David Lockwood, *The Blackcoated Worker: a Study in Class Consciousness* (London: George Allen and Unwin, 1958), p. 14.

17. See Ellen Jordan, 'The Lady Clerks'.

18. Krishan Kumar, 'From Work to Employment and Unemployment: the English Experience', in R. E. Pahl (ed.), *On Work: Historical, Comparative and Theoretical Approaches* (Oxford: Basil Blackwell, 1988), pp. 138–64 (p. 164).

19. Davies, *Woman's Place*, p. 78.

20. Strom, *Beyond the Typewriter*, p. 10.

21. Teresa Davy, '"A Cissy Job for Men; a Nice Job for Girls": Women Shorthand Typists in London 1900–1939', in Leonore Davidoff and Belinda Westover (eds.), *Our Work, Our Lives, Our Words: Women's History and Women's Work* (Totoway, N.J.: Barnes and Noble, 1986), pp. 124–44 (p. 142) and Kay Sanderson, '"A Pension to Look Forward To . . .?": Women Civil Service Clerks in London 1925–1939' in Davidoff and Westover, *Our Work*, pp. 145–60 (p. 156).

22. René Wellek and Austin Warren discuss this question briefly in *Theory of Literature* (Harmondsworth: Penguin, 1973), suggesting that while the issue is important 'no empirical investigation has been made' as yet (p. 87).

23. Christopher Middleton (ed.), *Selected Letters of Friedrich Nietzsche* (London: University of Chicago Press, 1969), p. 178.

24. Friedrich Nietzsche, *Briefe* eds. by Elisabeth Forster-Nietzsche and Peter Gast, 5 vols. (Leipzig, 1902–09), vol. 4, p. 97.

25. Ronald Hayman, *Nietzsche: A Critical Life* (London: Weidenfeld and Nicolson, 1980), p. 23.

26. Letters from Georg Brandes of 7 March 1888 and 6 October 1888 both mention Nietzsche's handwriting and its surprising strength, see O. Levy (ed.), *Friedrich Nietzsche: Selected Letters* (London: Soho Book Company, 1985), p. 333 and 352.

27. Kittler, *Discourse Networks*, p. 196.

28. For further discussion of James and the typewriter, see Pamela Thurschwell, 'Henry James and Theodora Bosanquet: on the Typewriter, in the Cage, at the Ouija Board', *Textual Practice*, 13(1) (1999), 5–23.

29. Theodora Bosanquet, *Henry James at Work* (London: Hogarth Press, 1924), p. 7.

30. Sharon Cameron, *Thinking in Henry James* (London: University of Chicago Press, 1989), p. 32.

31. Willard Bohn, *The Aesthetics of Visual Poetry 1914–1928* (Cambridge; Cambridge University Press, 1986), p. 3.

32. Madame Asa L'Orme, 'Letter', *The Author: the Organ of the Society of Authors*, 3(11) (1893), 411.

33. *The Author*, 3(9) (1893), 320–21.

34. See letter from Auden Amyand, *The Author*, 9(5) (1898), 118.

35. *The Author*, 16(9) (1906), 276.

36. Kittler, *Gramophone, Film, Typewriter*, p. 229.

37. Letter to Bryher, Summer 1924, in Gloria G. Fromm (ed.), *Windows on Modernism: Selected Letters of Dorothy Richardson* (London:University of Georgia Press, 1995), p. 106. I am grateful to Howard Finn for drawing this to my attention.

38. Mark Kinkead-Weekes, *D. H. Lawrence; Triumph to Exile, 1912–1922* (Cambridge: Cambridge University Press, 1996), p. 332.

39. Letter of 22 April 1922, in Henry Maas (ed.), *The Letters of A. E. Housman* (London: Rupert Hart-Davis, 1971), p. 193.

40. Letter of 15 June 1922, *Letters*, p. 197.

41. For discussion of a number of fictional texts relevant to this discussion but not included in this chapter see Michael North, *Reading 1922; a Return to the Scene of the Modern* (Oxford; Oxford University Press, 1999), pp. 183–85.

42. Sir Arthur Conan Doyle, 'A Case of Identity', in *The Complete Illustrated Sherlock Holmes* (Ware, Herts.: Omega Books, 1986), pp. 127–38 (p. 129).

43. *Ibid.*, p. 135.

44. Sir Arthur Conan Doyle, 'The Adventure of the Solitary Cyclist', in *Complete Illustrated Sherlock Holmes*, pp. 586–97 (pp. 586–87).

45. George Gissing, *The Odd Women* (London: Penguin, 1993), p. 23.

46. Olive Pratt Rayner (Grant Allan), *The Type-Writer Girl* (London: C. Arthur Pearson, 1897).

47. Bram Stoker, *Dracula* (London: Penguin, 1993), p. 450.

48. Wicke, 'Vampiric Typewriting: *Dracula* and its Media'.

49. Ménie Muriel Dowie, *Love and his Mask* (London: Heinemann, 1901), p. 1.

50. D. H. Lawrence, 'Cocksure Women and Hensure Men', in *D. H. Lawrence: Selected Essays* (Harmondsworth: Penguin, 1981), pp. 31–34 (p. 34).

51. See further discussion of the significance of laundry in this section of the poem, see below.

52. T. S. Eliot, 'The Waste Land', in *Selected Poems* (London: Faber and Faber, 1973). pp. 49–74, line 242.

53. Ivy Low (Litvinov), *The Questing Beast* (London: Martin Secker, 1914), p. 30. See also Sophie Treadwell, 'Machinal', in Judith E. Barlow (ed.), *Plays by American Women: 1900–1930* (New York: Applause Theatre Book Publishers, 1985), pp. 171–255 for a dramatic representation of the deadening and alienating rhythms of work as a typist.

54. Rebecca West, *The Judge* (London: Virago, 1980), p. 10.

55. Seltzer, *Bodies and Machines*, p. 4.

56. Strom, *Beyond the Typewriter*, p. 2.

57. Tom Gallon, *The Girl Behind the Keys* (London: Hutchinson, 1903), p. 11.

58. James Joyce, *Ulysses* (Harmondsworth: Penguin, 1975), p. 369.

59. *Ibid.*, p. 80.

60. Emile Zola, *L'Assommoir (The Dram Shop)*, translated by Robin Buss (London, Penguin, 2000).

61. J. M. Synge, 'The Aran Islands', in *Collected Works*, ed. Alan Price 4 vols. (London, Oxford University Press, 1966), vol. 1 pp. 47–184 (p. 76).

62. Caroline Davidson, *A Woman's Work is never Done: a history of housework in the British Isles 1650–1950* (London: Chatto and Windus, 1982), chapter 7.

63. For discussion of the working conditions of the laundress, see for example, Gareth Stedman Jones, *Outcast London: a Study in the Relationship Between Classes in Victorian Society* (Oxford: Oxford University Press, 1971).

64. See, for example, M. E. Headdon, *Housework and Domestic Economy* (London: George Philip and Son, 1893), and Christina Hardyment, *From Mangle to Microwave: the Mechanization of Household Work* (Cambridge: Polity Press, 1988), p. 60

65. Cowan, *More Work for Mother*, p. 93.

66. See Hardyment, *From Mangle*, p. 63, Claire Duchen, 'Occupation Housewife: the Domestic Ideal in 1950s France', *French Cultural Studies*, 2 (1991), 1–11, and Jennifer A. Loehlin, *From Rags to Riches: Housework, Consumption and Modernity in Germany* (Oxford: Berg, 1999).

67. Kristin Ross, *Fast Cars, Clean Bodies: Decolonization and the Reordering of French Culture* (Cambridge, Mass.: MIT Press, 1996) and Claire Duchen, 'Occupation Housewife'.

68. See Susan Strasser, *Never Done: a History of American Housework* (New York: Pantheon Books, 1982), p. 73.

69. See, for example, N. Clifton Reynolds, *Easier Housework by Better Equipment* (London: Country Life Ltd., 1929), and The Council of Scientific Management in the Home, *Housework with Satisfaction*, ed. Mildred Wheatcroft (London: National Council of Social Service, 1960).

70. John Mepham, *Virginia Woolf: a Literary Life* (London: Macmillan, 1991), p. xvii.

71. Virginia Woolf, *The Years* (Oxford: Oxford University Press, 1992), p. 3.

72. Entry for Monday 19 March 1934, *The Diary of Virginia Woolf, vol. IV: 1931–1935*, ed. Anne Olivier Bell, assisted by Andrew McNellie (London: Penguin, 1983), p. 205.

73. In April 1925, Woolf wrote in her diary, 'I'm out to make £300 this summer by writing, & build a bath & hot water range at Rodmell', while in June 1926 she remarked that 'Rodmell is a perfect triumph . . . The bath boils quickly; the water closets gush and surge (not quite sufficiently though)', *The Diary of Virginia Woolf, vol. III: 1925–1930*, ed. Anne Olivier Bell, assisted by Andrew McNellie (London: Penguin, 1982), p. 9 and p. 89.

74. Virginia Woolf, 'Introductory Letter' to Margaret Llewellyn Davies (ed.), *Life As We have Known It, by Cooperative Working Women* (London: Virago, 1977), p. xxii.

75. Katherine Mansfield, 'Pictures', in *The Collected Stories of Katherine Mansfield* (Harmondsworth: Penguin, 1981), p. 120.
76. Joyce, *Ulysses*, p. 593.
77. A relation between Bloom's interest in hygiene and his Jewishness emerges at several points in the text. For example in 'Lestrygonians': 'Kosher. No meat and milk together. Hygiene that was what they call it now. Yom Kippur fast spring cleaning of the inside' (p. 171).
78. Dorothy Richardson, 'Pointed Roofs', in *Pilgrimage*, 4 vols. (London, Virago, 1979), vol. 1, pp. 60–61.
79. The bicycle is the technology most powerfully associated with freedom in the whole of *Pilgrimage*. As Miriam says, 'To be able to bicycle would make life utterly different; on a bicycle you feel a different person; nothing can come near you, you forget who you are' (p. 149).
80. *Life is hard; for women.*

3 SYLVIA PANKHURST: LABOUR AND REPRESENTATION

1. For the connections between suffrage activists and philosophical explorations of modernity, see, for example, Bruce Clarke, *Dora Marsden and Early Modernism, Gender, Individuation, Science* (Ann Arbor, Mich.: University of Michigan Press, 1996); Suzanne Raitt, *May Sinclair: a Modern Victorian* (Oxford: Clarendon Press, 2000); and Barbara Winslow, *Sylvia Pankhurst: Sexual Politics and Political Activism* (London: University College London Press, 1996).
2. E. Sylvia Pankhurst, in Emma Alice Margaret, Countess of Oxford and Asquith (ed.), *Myself When Young: by Famous Women of Today* (London: Frederick Muller, 1938), pp. 259–312 (p. 262).
3. There has been a significant degree of reticence among Pankhurst's critics and biographers on this point. A recent study by Mary Davis, *Sylvia Pankhurst: a Life in Radical Politics* (London: Pluto Press, 1999) speaks only of a 'close friendship', but both Winslow, *Sylvia Pankhurst* and Patricia E. Romero, *E. Sylvia Pankhurst: Portrait of a Radical* (New Haven, Conn.: Yale University Press, 1987) suggest that Pankhurst and Keir Hardie had an affair that lasted ten years.
4. Lenin's critique of Pankhurst can be found in '"Left-Wing" Communism in Great Britain', in *'Left-Wing' Communism: an Infantile Disorder* (Moscow: Novosti Press Agency, 1970), pp. 79–94.
5. See *Germinal*, 1 (July) 1923.
6. A clipping of this story can be found in the 'David Mitchell Suffragette Collection' at the Museum of London, accession number 73.83/20.
7. Davis, *Sylvia Pankhurst*, p. 109.
8. Pankhurst, in *Myself When Young*, p. 288.
9. See Carolyn Burdett, *Olive Schreiner and the Progress of Feminism: Evolution, Gender, Empire* (Basingstoke: Palgrave, 2001), p. 57.

10. Olive Schreiner, *Woman and Labour* (London: T. Fisher Unwin, 1911), p. 100.

11. Constance Lytton, *Prisons and Prisoners* (London; William Heinemann, 1914), p. ix. Schreiner's *Woman and Labour* was dedicated to Constance Lytton.

12. Elizabeth Robins, *The Convert* (London: Methuen, 1907).

13. Bruce Clarke, *Dora Marsden and Early Modernism: Gender, Individualism, Science* (Ann Arbor, Mich.: University of Michigan Press, 1996); see also Charles Ferrall, 'Suffragists, Egoists, and the Politics of Early Modernism', *English Studies in Canada*, 18:4 (1992), 433–46.

14. Suzanne Raitt, *May Sinclair: a Modern Victorian* (Oxford: Clarendon Press, 2000).

15. Pankhurst's plans for a book are mentioned in *Votes for Women*, 26 August 1910, 776.

16. Lisa Tickner, *The Spectacle of Women: Imagery of the Suffrage Campaign 1907–1914* (London: Chatto and Windus, 1987), p. 102.

17. Robert Sherard, 'The White Slaves of England: – the Chainmakers of Cradley Heath', *Pearson's Magazine*, 2 (July–December) (1896), 408–14.

18. For discussion of opposition to Factory Acts within the suffrage movement, see Lisa Tickner, *Spectacle*.

19. Sylvia Pankhurst, 'The Chain Makers of Cradley Heath' unpublished typescript, *The Papers of Sylvia Pankhurst, 1882–1960*, Internationaal Instituut voor Social Geschiedenis, Amsterdam. On Microfilm, published by Adam Matthew Publications, 1991, reel 16, pp. 1–22 (p. 1)

20. E. Sylvia Pankhurst, *The Suffragette Movement: an Intimate Account of Persons and Ideals* (London: Longmans, Green and Co., 1931), p. 215. For a discussion of Jefferies's complex political legacy, see Raymond Williams, *The Country and the City* (London: Hogarth Press, 1985), pp. 191–96.

21. Pankhurst, in *Myself When Young*, p. 262.

22. Griselda Pollock, 'The Dangers of Proximity: the Spaces of Sexuality and Surveillance in Word and Image', *Discourse*, 16:2 (1993–94), 3–50.

23. For examples of some of the images in Munby's collection, see *ibid.*

24. Sylvia Pankhurst, 'Pit brow women', *Votes for Women*, 11 August 1911, 730, reprinted in Kathryn Dodd (ed.), *A Sylvia Pankhurst Reader* (Manchester: Manchester University Press, 1993), pp. 36–41.

25. Sylvia Pankhurst 'The Pit Brow Lassies' unpublished typescript, *Papers of Sylvia Pankhurst*. On Microfilm, reel 16, pp. 1–8 (p. 1).

26. For discussion of the match girl as a figure of urban degeneracy see Judith R. Walkowitz, *City of Dreadful Delight: Narratives of Sexual Danger in Late-Victorian England* (London: Virago, 1992), p. 78.

27. Pankhurst, in *Myself When Young*, p. 288.

28. Sylvia Pankhurst, 'The Potteries', unpublished typescript, *Papers of Sylvia Pankhurst*. On Microfilm; reel 16, p. 13.

29. See Raitt, *May Sinclair*, particularly chapter 7.

30. Pankhurst, *Suffragette Movement*, p. 285.

31. Sylvia Pankhurst, 'A minimum wage for women', *The Woman's Dread-nought*, 12 September 1914, reprinted in Kathryn Dodd (ed.), *A Sylvia Pankhurst Reader* (Manchester: Manchester University Press, 1993), pp. 60–63 (p. 60).

32. Sylvia Pankhurst, 'The Woman Boot Makers of Leicester', unpublished type-script, *Papers of Sylvia Pankhurst*. On Microfilm, reel 16, p. 6.

33. Sylvia Pankhurst's writing on women agricultural workers exists in two forms: in an unpublished typescript, 'The Agricultural Labourers of the Border Counties' which is part of a larger study, 'Women's Work in the Fields and Farmsteads', *Papers of Sylvia Pankhurst*. On Microfilm, reel 16, pp. 1–25, and as 'Women Farm Labourers in the Border Counties', *Votes for Women* (26 August) (1910) 776–77. Both versions begin in the same way.

34. Sylvia Pankhurst, 'The Scotch Fisher Lassies', unpublished typescript, *Papers of Sylvia Pankhurst*. On Microfilm, reel 16, p. 2.

35. Pankhurst, *Myself When Young*, p. 265.

36. Sylvia Pankhurst, 'The Workgirl', *Germinal*, 1:1 (1923); this journal can be found in *Papers of Sylvia Pankhurst*. On Microfilm, reel 2.

37. Tickner, *Spectacle*, p. 28.

38. The murals are described in great detail in the *Programme* for the WSPU Exhibition, 13–26 May 1909. A copy of this programme can be consulted in the Museum of London, accession number 60.15/28.

39. Sylvia Pankhurst, 'The Potato Pickers', part of a larger study, 'Women's Work in the Fields and Farmsteads', *Papers of Sylvia Pankhurst*. On Microfilm, reel 16, pp. 26–35; and 'The potato-pickers', *Votes for Women*, 28 January 1909, 294, reprinted in Dodd, *Sylvia Pankhurst Reader*, pp. 34–36.

40. Gill Davies, 'Foreign Bodies: Images of the London Working Class at the end of the Nineteenth Century', *Literature and History*, 14:1 (1988), 64–80 (69). The importance of Davies's analysis is mentioned in the introduction to Dodd, *Sylvia Pankhurst Reader*, 11.

41. Pankhurst, *Suffragette Movement*, p. 155.

42. Pankhurst, *Myself When Young*, p. 259.

43. Pankhurst, *Suffragette Movement*, p. 215.

44. Paula Gillett, *Worlds of Art: Painters in Victorian Society* (New Brunswick, N.J.: Rutgers University Press, 1990); and Jan Marsh, 'Women and Art 1850–1900', in Jan Marsh and Pamela Gerrish Nunn, *Pre-Raphaelite Women Artists* (Manchester: Manchester City Art Galleries, 1997), pp. 10–53.

45. For an early twentieth-century view on the importance of watercolour for English art, see Charles Holme (ed.), *English Water-Colour; with Reproductions of Drawings by Eminent Painters* (London: The Studio, 1902).

46. Walter Crane, *Line and Form* (London: George Bell and Sons, 1900), p. 219.

47. Letter from Elsa Frankael, dated 21 November 1965, *David Mitchell Suffragette Collection*, Museum of London, accession number 73.83/21.

48. Letter of August 1959 in Register Packet for portraits of Keir Hardie (3978 and 3979) in National Portrait Gallery, London.

49. Letter of 27 February 1957, in Register Packet, Keir Hardie.

50. *Votes for Women*, 22 July 1919, 713.
51. Pankhurst, *Suffragette Movement*, p. 263.
52. Pankhurst did also produce a portrait of a farm girl, also unfinished, with upturned head and flowing cap, reminiscent of the 'self portrait' which is now in the National Portrait Gallery.
53. Letter of 2 February 1964, Register Packet, Pankhurst's Self-Portrait (4999), National Portrait Gallery, London.
54. These sketches and drawings can be found in *Papers of Sylvia Pankhurst*. On Microfilm, reel 2.
55. Barbara Winslow, *Sylvia Pankhurst: Sexual Politics and Political Activism* (London: University College London Press, 1996), p. 12.
56. Jackie Duckworth, 'Sylvia Pankhurst as an Artist', in Ian Bullock and Richard Pankhurst (eds.), *Sylvia Pankhurst: from Artist to Anti-Fascist* (London: Macmillan, 1992), pp. 36–57 (p. 57).
57. Tickner, *Spectacle*, p. 28.
58. Richard Pankhurst, *Sylvia Pankhurst: Artist and Crusader* (London: Paddington Press, 1979), p. 21.
59. This poster is reproduced in Jackie Duckworth, 'Pankhurst as an Artist', pp. 36–57 (p. 53).
60. Barbara Green, 'From Visible *Flâneuse* to Spectacular Suffragette? the prison, the Street, and the Sites of Suffrage', *Discourse*, 17:2 (1994/5), 67–97.
61. Charles Harrison, *English Art and Modernism 1900–1939* (London: Yale University Press), p. 18.
62. *Ibid.*, p. 19.
63. Lucking Tavener, *Labour, as seen in Recent Painting, being the substance of three lectures delivered at Walthamstow Brotherhood Church* (London: Brotherhood Press, 1905).
64. T. J. Clark, *Farewell to an Idea: Episodes from a History of Modernism* (New Haven, Conn., and London: Yale University Press, 1999), pp. 55–137.
65. C. H. Collins Baker, *Dutch Painting of the Seventeenth Century* (London: The Studio, 1926).
66. William H. Sewell, Jr., 'Visions of Labour: Illustrations of the Mechanical Arts before, in, and after Diderot's *Encyclopédie*', in Steven Laurence Kaplan and Cynthia J. Koepp (eds.), *Work in France: Representations, Meaning, Organization, and Practice* (Ithaca, N.Y. and London: Cornell University Press, 1986), pp. 258–86 (p. 277).
67. For the economic and ideological importance of dress within the suffrage movement see Joel H. Kaplan and Sheila Stowell, *Theatre and Fashion: Oscar Wilde to the Suffragettes* (Cambridge: Cambridge University Press, 1994), especially chapter 5: 'The Suffrage Response'.
68. Pankhurst, *Suffragette Movement*, p. 354.
69. Harrison, *English Art and Modernism*, p. 49.
70. Sylvia Pankhurst, 'Co-Operative Housekeeping', the *Workers' Dreadnought*, 28 August 1920; reprinted in Kathryn Dodd, *Sylvia Pankhurst Reader*, pp. 104–08.
71. Pankhurst, *Suffragette Movement*, p. 218.

4 D. H. LAWRENCE: LABOUR, ORGANICISM AND THE INDIVIDUAL

1. James Knapp, *Literary Modernism and the Transformation of Work* (Evanston, Ill.: Northwestern University Press, 1988), particularly chapters 3 and 4.
2. Bruce Clarke, *Dora Marsden and Early Modernism: Gender, Individualism, Science* (Ann Arbor, Mich.: The University of Michigan Press, 1996).
3. D. H. Lawrence, 'Foreword' to *Sons and Lovers*, eds. Helen Baron and Carl Baron (Cambridge: Cambridge University Press, 1992), pp. 467–73 (p. 471).
4. See also the discussion of Schopenhauer in chapter 1.
5. D. H. Lawrence, 'Dreams Old and Nascent', in *Complete Poems*, eds. Vivian de Sola Pinto and Warren Roberts (Harmondsworth: Penguin, 1993), pp. 173–76; earlier drafts can be found pp. 908–12.
6. D. H. Lawrence, 'Study of Thomas Hardy', in *Phoenix: the Posthumous Papers of D. H. Lawrence*, ed. Edward D. McDonald (London; William Heinemann Ltd., 1936), pp. 389–516 (p. 429).
7. Lawrence's relation to Carlyle is in fact more complex than this repudiation suggests. Lawrence may reject Carlyle's elevation of work to a spiritual and moral good but he shares his distaste for Utilitarianism. Carlyle's argument in *Sartor Resartus*, for example, which stresses the need to reject received forms of knowledge and to assert the singularity of imaginative insight was important for Lawrence.
8. See George Zytaruk and James T. Boulton (eds.), *The Letters of D. H. Lawrence*, vol. 2: *June 1913–October 1919* (Cambridge: Cambridge University Press, 1981) for allusions to possible Nietzschean titles for the 'Study of Thomas Hardy'.
9. John Worthen, *D. H. Lawrence: the Early Years 1885–1912* (Cambridge: Cambridge University Press, 1991), p. 210.
10. See Friedrich Nietzsche, *The Birth of Tragedy*, trans. Walter Kaufmann (New York: Vintage Books, 1967).
11. Friedrich Nietzsche, *Beyond Good and Evil*, trans. R. J. Hollingdale (Harmondsworth: Penguin, 1973), p. 26.
12. Friedrich Nietzsche, *The Will to Power*, trans. Walter Kaufmann and R. J. Hollingdale (New York: Vintage Books, 1968), Section 1067, p. 550.
13. D. H. Lawrence, 'Self-Protection', in *Complete Poems*, eds. Vivian de Sola Pinto and Warren Roberts (Harmondsworth: Penguin, 1993), p. 523.
14. D. H. Lawrence, 'Education of the People', in *Phoenix*, pp. 587–665 (p. 655).
15. D. H. Lawrence, 'England, My England', in *England, My England and Other Stories*, ed. Bruce Steele (Cambridge: Cambridge University Press, 1990), p. 9.
16. See for example, Michael R. Finn, 'Neurasthenia, Hysteria, Androgyny: the Goncourts and Marcel Proust', *French Studies*, 51 (1997), 293–304; Barbara Will, 'Nervous Systems 1880–1915', in Tim Armstrong (ed.), *American Bodies: Cultural Histories of the Physique* (Sheffield; Sheffield Academic Press, 1996), pp. 86–100; and Janet Oppenheim, *'Shattered Nerves': Doctors, Patients and Depression in Victorian England* (Oxford: Oxford University Press, 1991), chapter 3, 'Nerve Force and Neurasthenia'.

17. Barbara Will ('Nervous Systems') discusses the claims of neurasthenia to be the condition of modernity.

18. For the specifically European debate on neurasthenia see Janet Oppenheim, *'Shattered Nerves'*; and Brigid Doherty, '"See: *We are all Neurasthenics!*", or The Trauma of Dada Montage', *Critical Inquiry*, 24 (1997), 82–132.

19. Jenny Bourne Taylor and Sally Shuttleworth (eds.), *Embodied Selves: an Anthology of Psychological Texts 1830–1890* (Oxford: Clarendon Press, 1998).

20. Clifford Allbutt, 'Neurasthenia', in Clifford Allbutt and Humphry Davy Rolleston (eds.), *A System of Medecine*, 9 vols. (London: Macmillan, 1910), vol. 8 pp. 727–91 (p. 733).

21. Sigmund Freud, 'Extracts from the Fleiss Papers: Draft B, the Aetiology of the Neuroses', in *The Standard Edition of the Complete Psychological Works of Sigmund Freud*, 8 vols. ed. James Strachey (London: Hogarth Press, 1966), vol. 1, pp. 179–84 (p. 179).

22. *Ibid.*, pp. 263–85 (p. 268).

23. For fuller discussion of the ways in which Freud's work relates to the models and terminology of nineteenth-century biology, see Frank J. Sulloway, *Freud, Biologist of the Mind: beyond the Psychoanalytic Legend* (Cambridge, Mass.: Harvard University Press, 1992).

24. See Allbutt, 'Neurasthenia', pp. 735 and 748.

25. *Ibid.*, p. 736.

26. Lawrence was excited by the possibility of establishing Rananim in early 1915, the year when he was also working on the first version of 'England, My England': 'My pet scheme. I want to gather together about twenty souls and sail away from this world of war and squalor and found a little colony where there shall be no money but a sort of communism as far as the necessaries of life go, and some real decency', Letter to William Hopkin, 18 January 1915, in Zytaruk and Boulton, *The Letters of D. H. Lawrence*, vol. 2, p. 259.

27. Leo Frobenius, *The Voice of Africa, Being an Account of the Travels of the German Inner African Exploration in the Years 1910–1912*, 2 vols. (London: Hutchinson, 1913), vol. 1, p. 65.

28. David Simpson (ed.), *German Aesthetic and Literary Criticism: Kant, Fichte, Schelling, Schopenhauer and Hegel* (Cambridge: Cambridge University Press, 1984), Introduction.

29. Arthur Schopenhauer, extract from *The World as Will and Representation*, in Simpson, *German Aesthetic and Literary Criticism*, p. 179.

30. See also Bruce Clarke's *Dora Marsden*.

31. *The Eagle and the Serpent: a Journal of Egoistic Philosophy and Sociology*, 1 (15 February 1898), 5.

32. Lawrence, 'Self-Sacrifice', in *Complete Poems*, p. 678.

33. Jack Lindsay, 'The Modern Consciousness', *The London Aphrodite*, 1 (1928), 3–24 (20).

34. Lawrence, 'Self-Sacrifice', in *Complete Poems*, p. 679.

35. Allbutt, 'Neurasthenia', p. 748.

36. Lawrence, 'To Let Go or To Hold On –?', *Collected Poems*, pp. 428–29.

37. Friedrich Nietzsche, *Twilight of the Idols*, trans. Duncan Large (Oxford: Oxford University Press, 1998), p. 11.

38. John Burnet, *Early Greek Philosophy* (London: Adam and Charles Black, 1908).

39. Nietzsche, *Twilight of the Idols*, p. 81.

40. L. D. Barnett, *Brahma-Knowledge: an Outline of the Philosophy of the Vedanta as set forth by the Upanishads and by Sankara* (London: John Murray, 1907).

41. James M. Pryse, *The Apocalypse Unsealed, being an Esoteric Interpretation of the Initiation of Iôannês, Commonly called the Revelation of [St] John* (London: John M. Watkins, 1910).

42. It is hard to be clear about how close Pryse assumes the relation between the physiological term 'ganglion' and the Hindu term 'chakra' (meaning disc) to be; he may simply find the association helpful to his argument. In her Introduction to Lawrence's *Apocalypse and the Writings on Revelation* (Cambridge: Cambridge University Press, 1980), Mara Kalnins says that 'chakra' is generally translated as 'plexus', p. 5. This renders Lawrence's insistent distinction between 'plexus' and 'ganglion' in *Fantasia of the Unconscious* rather more opaque.

43. Lawrence, *Apocalypse*, p. 66.

44. Charlotte Despard, *Theosophy and the Women's Movement* (London: Theosophical Publishing Society, 1913).

45. For an interesting discussion of Carpenter and the cultural movements of modernism, see Linda Dalrymple Henderson, 'Mysticism as the "Tie that Binds": the Case of Edward Carpenter and Modernism', *Art Journal*, 46:1 (1987), 29–37.

46. See Edward Carpenter, *Love's Coming-of-Age: a Series of Papers on the Relations of the Sexes* (Manchester: Labour Press, 1896).

47. Oswald Spengler, *The Decline of the West*, vol. 1: *Form and Actuality*, trans. Charles Francis Atkinson, first published 1918 (London: George Allen and Unwin, 1926).

48. T. E. Hulme, *Speculations: Essays on Humanism and the Philosophy of Art*, ed. Herbert Read, first published 1924 (London: Routledge and Kegan Paul, 1987), p. 147.

49. D. H. Lawrence, *Fantasia of the Unconscious* (New York: Thomas Seltzer, 1922), p. 3.

50. D. H. Lawrence, *Psychoanalysis and the Unconscious* (New York: Thomas Seltzer, 1921), p. 15.

51. D. H. Lawrence, 'All That We Have is Life', *Collected Poems*, pp. 449–50.

52. Lawrence, Letter to Gordon Campbell, March 1915, in *Letters*, vol. , pp. 301–02.

53. The historical dimension of this argument is more fully articulated in 'Introduction to these Paintings', in *The Paintings of D. H. Lawrence* (London: The Mandrake Press, 1929).

54. D. H. Lawrence, *Lady Chatterley's Lover*, ed. Michael Squires (Cambridge: Cambridge University Press, 1993), p. 68.

55. Lawrence, Letter to Baroness Anna von Richthofen, 14 April 1927, in James T. Boulton and Margaret H. Boulton with Gerald M. Lacy (eds.), *The Letters of*

D. H. Lawrence, vol. VI: *March 1927–November 1928* (Cambridge: Cambridge University Press, 1991), p. 34.

56. Lawrence, *Fantasia*.
57. Lawrence, 'We are the Transmitters', *Collected Poems*, p. 449.
58. D. H. Lawrence, Letter to Curtis Brown, 7 June 1924, in James T. Boulton and Lindeth Vasey (eds.), *The Letters of D. H. Lawrence*, vol. V, *March 1924–March 1927* (Cambridge: Cambridge University Press, 1989), p. 55.
59. See the discussion of Lawrence's own experience of typing in chapter 2.
60. Lawrence, 'Things Men have Made' and 'Things made by Iron', *Collected Poems*, p. 448.
61. There is an echo here of the evident pride Lawrence displays in his own manual labours, something registered throughout his letters. See, for example, letters to Amy Lowell, S. S. Koteliansky and Edward Marsh, 22–25 August 1915, *Letters*, vol. II, on whitewashing his house.
62. See David Ellis, *D. H. Lawrence, Dying Game, 1922–1930* (Cambridge: Cambridge University Press, 1998), p. 183.
63. For discussion of responses to the paintings and the closing of Lawrence's exhibition, see Colin Wilson and John Cohen, 'The Paintings of D. H. Lawrence', *The Studio*, 164:834 (October 1962), 130–35.
64. D. H. Lawrence, 'Men Must Work and Women as Well', in Warren Roberts and Harry T. Moore (eds.), *Phoenix II: Uncollected, Unpublished and Other Prose Works* (London: Heinemann, 1968), pp. 582–91 (p. 583).

5 THE GENERAL STRIKE: LABOUR AND THE FUTURE TENSE

1. Donald Sassoon, *One Hundred Years of Socialism: the West European Left in the Twentieth Century* (London: I. B. Tauris, 1996), p. 20.
2. See, for example, Rudolf Rocker, 'The Methods of Anarcho-Syndicalism', in *Anarcho-Syndicalism*, 1st edn. 1938 (London: Pluto Press, 1989), pp. 109–30.
3. William Benbow, *The Grand National Holiday and Congress of the Productive Classes* (1832), pamphlet and associated material edited by A. J. C. Rüter, *International Review for Social History*, 1 (1936), 217–56.
4. See Rüter's introduction to *Grand National Holiday* for discussion of Benbow's career and his broader political affiliations.
5. John Lovell, 'British Trade Unions 1875–1933', in L. A. Clarkson (ed.), *British Trade Union and Labour History: a Compendium* (London: Macmillan, 1990), pp. 71–136.
6. See Bob Holton, *British Syndicalism 1900–1914: Myths and Realities* (London: Pluto Press, 1976), pp. 27–36.
7. W. W. Craik, *A Short History of the Modern British Working-Class Movement* (London: The Plebs League, 1919); John Lovell, 'British Trade Unions'.
8. Rudolf Rocker, *Anarcho-Syndicalism* (London: Pluto Press, 1989), p. 120.
9. Wilf McCartney, *Dare to be a Daniel. A History of one of Britain's Earliest Syndicalist Unions* (London: KSL, 1992).

10. Daniel de Leon, *What Means this Strike?* (Edinburgh: Socialist Labour Press, n.d.), p. 4.
11. Daniel de Leon, *Principles of Industrial Unionism* (Glasgow: Socialist Labour Press, n.d.).
12. Rosa Luxemburg, *The Mass Strike, the Political Party and the Trade Unions* (London: Bookmarks, 1986), p. 46.
13. Arnold Roller, *The Social General Strike* (Chicago, Ill.: The Debating Club, 1905), p. 9.
14. Graham Wallas, 'Discussion on Syndicalism', *Sociological Review*, 5 (1912), 247–57 (249).
15. Holton, *British Syndicalism*, p. 30.
16. Tom Brown, *British Syndicalism: Pages of Labour History* (London: Kate Sharpley Library, 1994).
17. Ramsay MacDonald, 'Discussion on Syndicalism', *Sociological Review*, 5 (1912), 247–57 (254).
18. Michael Roe, *Nine Australian Progressives: Vitalism in Bourgeois Social Thought 1890–1960* (St Lucia, Queensland: University of Queensland Press, 1984), p. 5.
19. See Anson Rabinbach, *The Human Motor. Energy, Fatigue, and the Origins of Modernity* (Berkeley, Calif.: University of California Press, 1992), p. 166–72.
20. Georges Sorel, *Le Procès de Socrate; examen critique des thèses Socratiques* (Paris: Librairie Félix Alcan, 1889).
21. Friedrich Nietzsche, *Birth of Tragedy*, trans. Walter Kaufmann (New York: Vintage Books, 1967) and *on the Genealogy of Morals* (Oxford: Oxford University Press, 1998), Oswald Spengler, *The Decline of the West*, trans. Charles Francis Atkinson, 2 vols. (London: George Allen and Unwin, 1926–28) and rather later, *Civilization and its Discontents* SE, vol. 21 (London: Hogarth Press, 1930).
22. J. R. Jennings, *Georges Sorel: the Character and Development of his Thought* (London: Macmillan, 1985), p. 29.
23. Georges Sorel, *L'Avenir socialiste des syndicats* (Paris: Librairie de l'art social, 1898), p. 30.
24. Jennings, *Georges Sorel*, p. 75.
25. Georges Sorel, *The Illusions of Progress*, trans. John and Charlotte Stanley, (Berkeley, Calif.: University of California Press, 1969), p. 194.
26. Jennings, *Georges Sorel*, p. 117.
27. Georges Sorel, 'A Critique of *Creative Evolution*', in John L. Stanley (ed.), *From Georges Sorel; Essays in Socialism and Philosophy*, (New York: Oxford University press, 1976), pp. 284–90 (p. 288). An earlier version of this critique of Bergson first appeared in *Le Mouvement socialiste*, 12 (1907).
28. Henri Bergson, *Time and Free Will*, trans. F. L. Pogson (London: George Allen and Unwin, 1910), p. 221 and pp. 231–32. The second remark is cited in Sorel, *Reflections on Violence*, trans. T. E. Hulme (London: George Allen and Unwin, 1916), p. 29.
29. In *Modernist Writing and Reactionary Politics* (Cambridge: Cambridge University Press, 2001).
30. T. E. Hulme, *Speculations*.

31. Hulme praises Sorel's grasp of the limited nature of man and the consequent need for discipline in his preface to *Reflections on Violence*, pp. vi–vii. Charles Ferrall points out that this preface first appeared in the *New Age*, a publication that, as we shall see, was an important site for the exploration of alternative economic and cultural theories in the period.

32. See Sorel's introductory 'Letter to Daniel Halévy' in *Reflections on Violence*, pp. 1–42.

33. J. W. Scott, *Syndicalism and Philosophical Realism: a Study in the Correlation of Contemporary Social Tendencies* (London: A. and C. Black, 1919).

34. Bertrand Russell, *Roads to Freedom: Socialism, Anarchism, and Syndicalism* (London: George Allen and Unwin, 1918); G. D. H. Cole, *The World of Labour: A Discussion of the Present and Future of Trade Unionism* (London: G. Bell and Sons, 1913), particularly chapter 9.

35. Scott draws particularly on Russell's *The Philosophy of Bergson* (Cambridge: The Heretics, 1914) to provide the focus of his comparative discussion.

36. J. W. Scott, *Karl Marx on Value* (London: A. and C. Black, 1920), epigraph.

37. J. W. Scott, *Unemployment: a Suggested Policy* (London: A. and C. Black, 1925).

38. William E. Smythe, *City Homes on Country Lanes: Philosophy and Practice of Home-in-a-Garden* (New York: Macmillan, 1921).

39. Hilaire Belloc, *The Servile State* (London: Constable and Co., 1927) makes the links between these contexts explicit. He associates Christianity initially with the overthrowing of slavery, but then sees Protestantism as complicit with capitalism, and thus with the development of new forms of servility. Distributism is advanced as the only viable oppositions to this process.

40. See A. M. Currie and G. C. Heseltine, *Trade Unions* (London: The Distributist League, 1927).

41. H. E. Humphries, *Liberty and Property. An Introduction to Distributism* (London: The Distributist League, 1928).

42. G. K. Chesterton, 'The Purpose of the League', published in a pamphlet with K. L. Kenrick, 'What is Distributism?' (London: The Distributist League, 1926), p. 6. Anthony Cooney discusses the relation between this position and the Catholic doctrine of the late nineteenth and early twentieth centuries in *Distributism* (London: Gild of St George, 1986).

43. J. W. Scott, *Self-Subsistence for the Unemployed: Studies in a New Technique* (London: Faber and Faber, 1935); *Barter: a Study in the Economics of the Smaller Group* (London: The Distributist League, 1938).

44. See chapter 14 of *Self-Subsistence*.

45. See the Preface to *Barter*.

46. Cole, *The World of Labour*, p. 363; Russell, *Roads to Freedom*, p. 13.

47. M. B. Reckitt and C. E. Bechhofer, *The Meaning of National Guilds* (London: Cecil Palmer and Hayward, 1918), p. 308.

48. See A. R. Orage, *Political and Economic Writings*, arranged by Montgomery Butchart (London: Stanley Nott, 1936), particularly pp. 17–57.

49. For further discussion of this journal see Frances Hutchinson and Brian Burkitt, *The Political Economy of Social Credit and Guild Socialism* (London: Routledge, 1997).

50. Major C. H. Douglas, *Reconstruction: the 'Glasgow Evening Times' Articles of May, 1932, on Social Credit* (Liverpool: K. R. P. Publications Limited, 1943), p. 7.
51. Major C. H. Douglas, *Economic Democracy* (London: Cecil Palmer, 1919), p. 34.
52. See Douglas's discussion of the relations between Judaism and monopoly capitalism in *Social Credit* (London: Eyre and Spottiswoode, 1937), and Ezra Pound, whose poetic writing is saturated with references to economic theory, to usury, and to the pernicious nature of credit and the international control of capital.
53. Margaret Morris, *The General Strike* (London: The Journeyman Press, 1980), p. 21.
54. Hamilton Fyfe, *Behind the Scenes of the Great Strike* (London: The Labour Publishing Co., 1926), p. 9.
55. J. M. Keynes, *The Economic Consequences of Mr Churchill* (London: Hogarth Press, 1925), p. 23.
56. Fyfe, *Behind the Scenes*, p. 7.
57. See A. J. Cook, *The Nine Days: the Story of the General Strike Told by the Miners' Secretary* (London: Co-operative Printing Society, 1926).
58. Morris, *General Strike*, p. 274.
59. *The Guardian*, 4 May 1926. The contents of the much-reduced *Guardian* which came out during the Strike can be found in R. H. Haigh, D. S. Morris and A. R. Peters, *The Guardian Book of the General Strike* (Aldershot: Wildwood House, 1988).
60. See Morris, *General Strike*, p. 146.
61. *Guardian*, 3 May 1926, Haigh, Morris and Peters, *Guardian Book*, p. 15.
62. John Galsworthy, *Swan Song* (London: William Heinemann Ltd, 1928), p. 3.
63. See *British Gazette*, 12 May 1926.
64. See *Punch*, 26 May 1926.
65. R. W. Postgate, Ellen Wilkinson, M. P., and J. F. Horrabin, *A Workers' History of the Great Strike* (London: The Plebs League, 1927), p. 96.
66. Ellen Wilkinson, *Clash* (London: Virago, 1989), p. 48.
67. The poem is included in Hamilton Fyfe, *Behind the Scenes*, p. 61.
68. Cited in Fyfe, *Behind the Scenes*, p. 66.
69. Harold Heslop, *The Gate of a Strange Field* (London: Brentano, 1929), p. 202. This novel takes its title from a phrase in Wells's *Meanwhile: the Picture of a Lady* which describes the General Council of the TUC as being 'like sheep at the gate of a strange field'. See John Lucas's discussion of the novel in, *The Radical Twenties: Aspects of Writing, Politics and Culture* (Nottingham: Five Leaves Publications, 1997), p. 238.
70. H. G. Wells, *Meanwhile: the Picture of a Lady* (London: Ernest Benn Ltd., 1927), p. 21.
71. Preface to Wyndham Lewis, *Blasting and Bombardiering* (London: John Calder, 1982).
72. See Paul Edwards, Introduction and Afterword to Wyndham Lewis, *Time and Western Man*, ed. Paul Edwards (Santa Rosa, Calif.: Black Sparrow Press, 1993).

73. Wyndham Lewis, *The Art of Being Ruled* (London: Chatto and Windus, 1926), p. 128.
74. See Wyndham Lewis, *Hitler* (London: Chatto and Windus, 1931). In this text Lewis also advances the view that Hitler is no militarist threat, so we can see that Lewis's understanding of fascism was far from complete.
75. Wyndham Lewis, *The Apes of God* (Harmondsworth: Penguin, 1965), p. 638.
76. Lewis Grassic Gibbon, *A Sots Quair* (Harmondsworth: Penguin Books, 1986).
77. See Postgate, Wilkinson, Horrabin, *A Workers' History*, p. 40.
78. Rachelle H. Saltzman, 'Folklore as Politics in Great Britain: Working-Class Critiques of Upper-Class Strike Breakers in the 1926 General Strike', *Anthropological Quarterly*, 67:3 (1994), 105–21 (116).
79. Julian Symons, *The General Strike: a Historical Portrait* (London: Cresset Press, 1957), p. 3.
80. Leonard Woolf, *Downhill All the Way: an Autobiography of the Years 1919–1939* (London: Hogarth Press, 1967), p. 225.
81. Storm Jameson, *None Turn Back* (Virago: 1984), p. 22.
82. Anne Olivier Bell (ed.), *The Diary of Virginia Woolf, vol. III: 1925–1930* (London: Hogarth Press, 1980), p. 76.
83. See Kate Flint, 'Virginia Woolf and the General Strike', *Essays in Criticism*, 36:4 (1986), 219–334.
84. Anne Olivier Bell (ed.), *Diary of Virginia Woolf*, p. 77.
85. Virginia Woolf, *To the Lighthouse* (Oxford: Oxford University Press, 1992), p. 171.
86. For an interesting discussion of the representation of the future in *To the Lighthouse*, see Ann Banfield, 'Tragic Time: the Problem of the Future in Cambridge Philosophy and *To the Lighthouse*', *Modernism/Modernity*, 7:1 (1999), 43–75.

Bibliography

Alexander, Sally, 'Becoming a Woman in London in the 1920s and 1930s', in *Becoming a Woman and other Essays in Nineteenth- and Twentieth-Century Feminist History* (London: Virago, 1994), pp. 203–24.

Alexander, Sally (ed.), *Women's Fabian Tracts* (London: Routledge, 1988).

Allbutt, Clifford, 'Neurasthenia', in Clifford Allbutt and Humphry Davy Rolleston (eds.), *A System of Medicine* (London: Macmillan, 1910), vol. 8, pp. 727–91.

Allen, Eleanor, *Home Sweet Home. A History of Housework* (London: A. and C. Black, 1979).

Amyand, Auden, 'Letter', *The Author*, 9:5 (1898), 118.

Ansell-Pearson, Keith, *An Introduction to Nietzsche as Political Thinker* (Cambridge: Cambridge University Press, 1994).

Anthony, P. D., *The Ideology of Work* (London: Tavistock, 1977).

Ardis, Ann L., *New Women, New Novels: Feminism and Early Modernism* (London: Rutgers University Press, 1990).

Arendt, Hannah, *The Human Condition* (London: University of Chicago Press, 1958).

Armstrong, Terence Ian Fytton (writing under pseudonym of John Gawsworth), *Apes, Japes and Hitlerism: a Study and Bibliography of Wyndham Lewis* (London: Unicorn Press, 1932).

Armstrong, Tim, *Modernism, Technology and the Body: a Cultural Study* (Cambridge: Cambridge University Press, 1998).

Armytage, W. H. G., *Heavens Below* (London: Routledge, 1961).

Arnall, Philip, 'The Typewriter', *The Fortnightly*, 142, new series (1937), 700–13.

Arnot, R. Page. *The Miners: Years of Struggle from the Year 1910 Onwards* (London, 1953).

Aron, Cindy S., '"To Barter Their Souls for Gold": Female Clerks in Federal Government Offices, 1862–1890', *The Journal of American History*, 67:4 (1981), 835–53.

Art Journal Issue on Mysticism and Occultism in Modern Art, 46:1 (1987).

Arthur, C. J., *Dialectics of Labour: Marx and his Relation to Hegel* (Oxford: Basil Blackwell, 1986).

Banfield, Ann, 'Tragic Time: the Problem of the Future in Cambridge Philosophy and *To the Lighthouse*', *Modernism/Modernity*, 7:1 (1999), 43–75.

Banks, Olive, *Faces of Feminism: a Study of Feminism as a Social Movement* (Oxford: Martin Robertson, 1981).

Barash, Carol L., 'Virile Womanhood: Olive Schreiner's Narrative of a Master Race', in Elaine Showalter (ed.), *Speaking of Gender* (London: Routledge, 1989), pp. 269–81.

Barnett, L. D., *Brahma-Knowledge: an Outline of the Philosophy of the Vedanta as set forth by the Upanishads and by Sankara* (London: John Murray, 1907).

Barrie, J. M., 'The Twelve-Pound Look', *The Plays of J. M. Barrie* (London: Hodder and Stoughton, 1928).

Beard, George M., *American Nervousness: its Causes and Consequences* (New York, 1991).

Beecher, Jonathan and Richard Bienvenu (eds.), *The Utopian Vision of Charles Fourier: Selected Texts on Work, Love, and Passionate Attraction* (London: Jonathan Cape, 1972).

Beechey, Veronica, *Unequal Work* (London: Verso, 1987).

Beeching, Wilfred A., *Century of the Typewriter* (Bournemouth: British Typewriter Museum Publishing, 1990).

Bell, Clive, *Civilization: an Essay* (London: Chatto and Windus, 1928).

Bell, Ian F. A., '"Work Unbartered": Labour and Time in Pound's Cantos of the late 1930s', *Symbiosis: A Journal of Anglo-American Literary Relations*, 1:2 (1997), 159–71.

Belloc, Hilaire, *The Servile State* (London: Constable and Co., 1927).

Benbow, William, *The Grand National Holiday and Congress of the Productive Classes* (1832), pamphlet and associated material edited by A. J. C. Rüter, *International Review for Social History*, 1 (1936), 217–56.

Bennett, Arnold, *The Journals*, ed. Frank Swinnerton (Harmondsworth; Penguin, 1971).

Bergson, Henri, *Time and Free Will. An Essay on the Immediate Data of Consciousness*, trans. F. L. Pogson (London: George Allen and Unwin, 1910).

Creative Evolution, trans. Arthur Mitchell (London: Macmillan, 1911).

Bishop, Alan, '"With suffering and through time": Olive Schreiner, Vera Brittain and the Great War', in Malvern Van Wyk Smith and Don Maclennan (eds.), *Olive Schreiner and After* (Claremont, S.A.: David Philip, 1983), pp. 80–92.

Black, Clementina, *Married Women's Work* (London: G. Bell, 1915).

Black, Michael (ed.), *D. H. Lawrence: the Early Philosophical Works. A Commentary* (London: Macmillan, 1991).

Blatchford, Robert, *Merrie England* (London: Clarion, 1894).

Bohn, Willard, *The Aesthetics of Visual Poetry 1914–1928* (Cambridge: Cambridge University Press, 1986).

Bosanquet, Theodora, *Henry James at Work* (London: Hogarth Press, 1924).

Boulton, James T. and Lindeth Vasey (eds.), *The Letters of D. H. Lawrence*, vol. 5, *March 1924–March 1927* (Cambridge: Cambridge University Press, 1989).

Boulton, James T. and Margaret H. Boulton with Gerald M. Lacy (eds.), *The Letters of D. H. Lawrence*, vol. 6, *March 1927–November 1928* (Cambridge: Cambridge University Press, 1991).

Boyer, Jacques, 'Are Men Better Typists than Women?: Interesting tests made by J. M. Lahy', *Scientific American*, 109 (1913) 316 and 326–27.

Bradley, Harriet, *Men's Work, Women's Work: a Sociological History of the Sexual Division of Labour in Employment* (Cambridge: Polity Press, 1989).

'Changing Social Divisions: Class, Gender and Race', in Robert Bocock and Kenneth Thompson (eds.), *Social and Cultural Forms of Modernity* (Cambridge: Polity Press, 1992), pp. 12–67.

Braverman, Harry, *Labor and Monopoly Capitalism: the Degradation of Work in the Twentieth Century* (London: Monthly Review Press, 1974).

Breckman, Warren, *Marx, the Young Hegelians, and the Origins of Radical Social Theory: Dethroning the Self* (Cambridge: Cambridge University Press, 1999).

Briggs, Asa (ed.), *William Morris: 'News for Nowhere' and Selected Writings and Designs* (Harmondsworth: Penguin, 1984).

Britain, Ian, *Fabianism and Culture: a Study in British Socialism and the Arts 1884–1918* (Cambridge: Cambridge University Press, 1982).

Britton, Derek, *Lady Chatterley: the Making of the Novel* (London: Unwin Hyman, 1988).

Brown, Tom, *British Syndicalism: Pages of Labour History* (London: Kate Sharpley Library, 1994).

Bullock Ian, and Richard Pankhurst (eds.), *Sylvia Pankhurst: from Artist to Anti-Fascist* (London: Macmillan, 1992).

Burdett, Carolyn, *Olive Schreiner and the Progress of Feminism: Evolution, Gender, Empire* (Basingstoke: Palgrave, 2001).

Burnet, John, *Early Greek Philosophy*, 2nd edn (London: Adam and Charles Black, 1908).

Burnett, John (ed.), *Useful Toil: Autobiographies of Working People from the 1820s to the 1920s* (London: Allen Lane, 1974).

Butler, Samuel, *The Way of All Flesh* (Oxford: Oxford University Press, 1993).

Bynum, W. F., E. J. Browne and Roy Porter (eds.), *Dictionary of the History of Science* (London: Macmillan, 1981).

Caine, Hall, *Our Girls: Their Work for the War* (London: Hutchinson, 1916).

Caldwell, William, *Schopenhauer's System in its Philosophical Significance* (Edinburgh: William Blackwood and Sons, 1896).

Cameron, Sharon, *Thinking in Henry James* (London: University of Chicago Press, 1989).

Carlyle, Thomas, 'Past and Present', in *Lectures* (London: Chapman and Hall, 1890), pp. 69–302.

Chartism (London: Holerth Press, 1924).

A Carlyle Reader: Selections from the Writings of Thomas Carlyle, ed. G. B. Tennyson (Cambridge: Cambridge University Press, 1984).

Carpenter, Edward, *Love's Coming-of-Age: a Series of Papers on the Relations of the Sexes* (Manchester: Labour Press, 1896).

Cave, Terence, *Pré-Histoires. Textes troublés au seuil de la modernité* (Geneva: Librairies Droz, 1999).

Center, Stella S. (ed.), *The Worker and his Work: Readings in Present-Day Literature Presenting Some of the Activities by Which Men and Women the World over Make a Living* (London: Limmincott, 1920).

Chartier, Roger, *Cultural History: between Practices and Representations*, trans. Lydia G. Cochrane (Cambridge: Polity Press, 1988).

Chesterton, G. K., 'The Purpose of the League', published in a pamphlet with K. L. Kenrick, 'What is Distributism?' (London: The Distributist League, 1926).

Claeys, Gregory, *Citizens and Saints: Politics and Anti-Politics in early British Socialism* (Cambridge: Cambridge University Press, 1989).

Clark, T. J., *Farewell to an Idea: Episodes from a History of Modernism* (New Haven, Conn., and London: Yale University Press, 1999).

Clarke, Bruce, *Dora Marsden and Early Modernism: Gender, Individualism, Science* (Ann Arbor, Mich.: University of Michigan Press, 1996).

Clifton Reynolds, N., *Easier Housework by Better Equipment* (London: Country Life Ltd., 1929).

Cohen, G. A., *History, Labour, and Freedom: Themes from Marx* (Oxford: Clarendon Press, 1988).

Cole, G. D. H., *The World of Labour: a Discussion of the Present and Future of Trade Unionism* (London: G. Bell and Sons, 1913).

Collins Baker, C. H., *Dutch Painting of the Seventeenth Century* (London: The Studio, 1926).

Colls, Robert, and Philip Dodd (eds.), *Englishness: Politics and Culture 1880–1920* (London: Croom Helm, 1986).

Conan Doyle, Sir Arthur, *The Complete Illustrated Sherlock Holmes* (Ware, Herts: Omega Books, 1986).

Connolly, James, *Socialism Made Easy* (Glasgow: Socialist Labour Press, 1917).

Cook, A. J., *The Nine Days: the Story of the General Strike Told by the Miners' Secretary* (London: Co-operative Printing Society, 1926).

Cooney, Anthony, *Distributism* (London: Gild of St George, 1986).

Corbin, Alain, *Le Miasme et la jonquille* (Paris: Aubier Montaigne, 1982).

Council of Scientific Management in the Home, *Housework with Satisfaction*, ed. Mildred Wheatcroft (London: National Council of Social Service, 1960).

Cowan, Ruth Schwartz, *More Work for Mother: the Ironies of Household Technology from the Open Hearth to the Microwave* (London: Free Association Books, 1989).

Craik, W. W., *A Short History of the Modern British Working-Class Movement* (London: The Plebs League, 1919).

Crane, Walter, *Line and Form* (London: George Bell and Sons, 1900).

Current, Richard N., *The Typewriter and the Men who Made it* (Urbana, Ill.: University of Illinois Press, 1954).

Currie, A. M., and G. C. Heseltine, *Trade Unions* (London: The Distributist League, 1927).

Dalrymple Henderson, Linda, 'Mysticism as the "Tie that Binds": the Case of Edward Carpenter and Modernism', *Art Journal*, 46:1 (1987), 29–37.

Daly, Macdonald, 'D. H. Lawrence and Labour in the Great War', *The Modern Language Review*, 89:1 (1994), 19–38.

'D. H. Lawrence and the 1912 Miners' Strike', *English Studies: a Journal of English Language and Literature*, 75:2 (1994), 133–45.

Danon, Ruth, *Work in the English Novel: the Myth of Vocation* (London: Croom Helm, 1985).

'David Mitchell Suffragette Collection', Museum of London.

Davidson, Caroline, *A Woman's Work is Never Done: a History of Housework in the British Isles 1650–1950* (London: Chatto and Windus, 1982).

Davies, Gill, 'Foreign Bodies: Images of the London Working Class at the end of the Nineteenth Century', *Literature and History*, 14:1 (1988), 64–80.

Davies, Margery W., *Woman's Place is at the Typewriter: Office Work and Office Workers 1870–1930* (Philadelphia, Penn. Temple University Press, 1982).

Davis, Mary, *Sylvia Pankhurst: a Life in Radical Politics* (London: Pluto Press, 1999).

Davy, Teresa, "'A Cissy Job for Men; a Nice Job for Girls": Women Shorthand Typists in London 1900–1939', in Leonore Davidoff and Belinda Westover (eds.), *Our Work, Our Lives, Our Words: Women's History and Women's Work* (Totoway, N.J.: Barnes and Noble, 1986), pp. 124–44.

Derrida, Jacques, *Ulysse gramophone: deux mots pour Joyce* (Paris: Editions Galilée, 1987).

Despard, Charlotte, *Theosophy and the Women's Movement* (London: Theosophical Publishing Society, 1913).

Dodd, Kathryn (ed.), *A Sylvia Pankhurst Reader* (Manchester: Manchester University Press, 1993).

Doherty, Brigid, "'See: *We are all Neurasthenics!*", or The Trauma of Dada Montage', *Critical Inquiry*, 24 (1997), 82–132.

Donaldson-Evans, Mary, 'The Morbidity of *Milieu*: *L'Assommoir* and the Discourse of Hygiene', in Alain Toumayan (ed.), *Literary Generations* (Lexington, Ken.: French Forum Publishers, 1992), pp. 150–62.

Douglas, Major C. H., *Economic Democracy* (London: Cecil Palmer, 1919).

Social Credit (London: Eyre and Spottiswoode, 1937).

Reconstruction: the 'Glasgow Evening Times' Articles of May 1932, on Social Credit (Liverpool: K. R. P. Publications Limited, 1943).

Dowie, Ménie Muriel, *Love and his Mask* (London: Heinemann, 1901).

Draznin, Yaffa Claire (ed.), *'My Other Self': the Letters of Olive Schreiner and Havelock Ellis, 1884–1920* (New York: Peter Lang, 1992).

Duchen, Claire, 'Occupation Housewife: the Domestic Ideal in 1950s France', *French Cultural Studies*, 2 (1991), 1–11.

Duckworth, Jackie, 'Sylvia Pankhurst as an Artist', in Ian Bullock and Richard Pankhurst (eds.), *Sylvia Pankhurst: from Artist to Anti-Fascist* (London: Macmillan, 1992), pp. 36–57.

Dyhouse, Carol, *Feminism and the Family in England 1880–1939* (Oxford: Basil Blackwell, 1989).

Edinburgh College of Domestic Science, *The Edinburgh Handbook of Housework* (London: Thomas Nelson and Sons, 1934).

Eliot, T. S., *Selected Poems* (London: Faber and Faber, 1973).

Ellis, David, 'Lawrence and the Biological Psyche', in Mara Kalnins (ed.), *D. H. Lawrence: Centenary Essays* (Bristol: Bristol Classical Press, 1986), pp. 89–109.

D. H. Lawrence, Dying Game, 1922–1930 (Cambridge: Cambridge University Press, 1998).

Feldman, David, and Gareth Stedman Jones, *Metropolis London: Histories and Representations since 1800* (London: Routledge, 1989).

Felski, Rita, 'The Gender of Modernity', in Sally Ledger, Josephine McDonagh and Jane Spencer (eds.), *Political Gender: Texts and Contexts* (London: Harvester, 1994), pp. 144–55.

Fernihough, Anne, *D. H. Lawrence: Aesthetics and Ideology* (Oxford: Clarendon Press, 1993).

Ferrall, Charles, *Modernist Writing and Reactionary Politics* (Cambridge: Cambridge University Press, 2001).

Ferrall, Charles, 'Suffragists, Egoists, and the Politics of Early Modernism', *English Studies in Canada*, 18:4 (1992), 433–46.

Fine, Ben, *Women's Employments and the Capitalist Family* (London: Routledge, 1992).

Finn, Michael R., 'Neurasthenia, Hysteria, Androgyny: the Goncourts and Marcel Proust', *French Studies*, 51 (1997), 293–304.

First, Ruth, and Ann Scott, *Olive Schreiner* (London: Andrew Deutsch, 1980).

Flint, Kate, 'Virginia Woolf and the General Strike', *Essays in Criticism,* 36:4 (1986), 219–334.

Fourier, Charles, *The Theory of the Four Movements*, eds. Gareth Stedman Jones and Ian Patterson (Cambridge: Cambridge University Press, 1996).

Frazer, J. G., *Totemism and Exogamy: a Treatise on Certain Early Forms of Superstition and Society*, 4 vols. (London: Macmillan and Co., 1910).

Freud, Sigmund, 'Extracts from the Fleiss Papers: Draft B, the Aetiology of the Neuroses', in *The Standard Edition of the Complete Psychological Works of Sigmund Freud*, vol. 1, ed. James Strachey (London: Hogarth Press, 1966), pp. 179–84.

'Sexuality in the Aetiology of the Neurosis', *The Standard Edition of the Complete Psychological Works of Sigmund Freud*, vol. 1, ed. James Strachey (London: Hogarth Press, 1966), pp. 263–85.

Civilization, Society and Religion, ed. Albert Dickson, The Penguin Freud Library, vol. 12 (Harmondsworth: Penguin Books, 1985), pp. 179–340.

Frobenius, Leo, *The Voice of Africa, Being an Account of the Travels of the German Inner African Exploration in the Years 1910–1912*, 2 vols. (London: Hutchinson, 1913).

Fromm, Gloria G. (ed.), *Windows on Modernism: Selected Letters of Dorothy Richardson* (London: University of Georgia Press, 1995).

Fussell, Paul, *The Great War and Modern Memory* (London: Oxford University Press, 1975).

Fyfe, Hamilton, *Behind the Scenes of the Great Strike* (London: The Labour Publishing Co., 1926).

Gallon, Tom, *The Girl Behind the Keys* (London: Hutchinson, 1903).

Galsworthy, John, *Swan Song* (London: William Heinemann Ltd, 1928).

General Council of the Trades Union Congress, *Mining Dispute, National Strike. Supplementary Report of the General Council to the Conference of Executives of Affiliated Unions, 20 January 1927* (London: TUC, 1927).

Giedion, Siegfried, *Mechanization Takes Command a Contribution to Anonymous History* (New York: Oxford University Press, 1948).

Gillett, Paula, *Worlds of Art: Painters in Victorian Society* (New Brunswick, N.J.: Rutgers University Press, 1990).

Gissing, George, *The Odd Women* (London: Penguin, 1993).

Glucksmann, Miriam, *Women Assemble: Women Workers and the New Industries in Inter-War Britain* (London: Routledge, 1990).

Godden, Richard, *Fictions of Labor: William Faulkner and the South's Long Revolution* (Cambridge: Cambridge University Press, 1997).

Godelier, M., 'Work and its Representations: a Research Proposal', *History Workshop Journal*, 10 (1980), 164–74.

Gordon, Eleanor, *Women and the Labour Movement in Scotland 1850–1914* (Oxford: Oxford University Press, 1991).

Grassic Gibbon, Lewis, *A Sots Quair* (Harmondsworth: Penguin Books, 1986).

Green, Barbara, 'From Visible *Flâneuse* to Spectacular Suffragette? The Prison, The Street, and the Sites of Suffrage', *Discourse*, 17:2 (1994/5), 67–97.

Gura, Philip F. and Joel Myerson (eds.), *Critical Essays on American Transcendentalism* (Boston, Mass.: G. K. Hall, 1982).

Haigh, R. H., D. S. Morris and A. R. Peters, *The Guardian Book of the General Strike* (Aldershot: Wildwood House, 1988).

Hardyment, Christina, *From Mangle to Microwave: the Mechanization of Household Work* (Cambridge: Polity Press, 1988).

Harris, Wendell V., *The Omnipresent Debate: Empiricism and Transcendentalism in Nineteenth-Century English Prose* (DeKalb, Ill.: Northern Illinois University Press, 1981).

Harrison, Charles, *English Art and Modernism 1900–1939* (London: Yale University Press, 1994).

Hartman Strom, Sharon, *Beyond the Typewriter: Gender, Class and the Origins of Modern American Office Work, 1900–1930* (Urbana, Ill.: University of Illinois Press, 1992).

Hayman, Ronald, *Nietzsche: a Critical Life* (London: Weidenfeld and Nicolson, 1980).

Headdon, M. E., *Housework and Domestic Economy* (London: George Philip and Son, 1893).

Hegel, G. W. F., *Phenomenology of Spirit*, trans. A. V. Miller (Oxford: Oxford University Press, 1977).

    Elements of the Philosophy of Right, ed. Allen W. Wood, trans. H. B. Nisbet (Cambridge: Cambridge University Press, 1991).

Heslop, Harold, *The Gate of a Strange Field* (London: Brentano, 1929).

Hobsbawm, Eric, *Labouring Men: Studies in the History of Labour* (London: Weidenfeld and Nicolson, 1968).

Worlds of Labor (New York: Pantheon, 1984).

The Age of Empire 1875–1914 (London: Sphere Books, 1989).

'The Making of the Working Class, 1870–1914', in *Uncommon People: Resistance, Rebellion and Jazz* (London: Weidenfeld and Nicolson, 1998), pp. 57–74.

Hoffman, Nancy, and Florence Howe, *Women Working: an Anthology of Stories and Poems* (New York: The Feminist Press, 1979).

Holme, Charles (ed.), *English Water-Colour; with Reproductions of Drawings by Eminent Painters* (London: The Studio, 1902).

Holton, Bob, *British Syndicalism 1900–1914: Myths and Realities* (London: Pluto Press, 1976).

Hudson, Pat, and W. R. Lee (eds.), *Women's Work and the Family Economy in Historical Perspective* (Manchester: Manchester University Press, 1990).

Hulme, T. E., *Speculations: Essays on Humanism and the Philosophy of Art*, ed. Herbert Read (London: Routledge and Kegan Paul, 1987).

Humphries, H. E., *Liberty and Property. An Introduction to Distributism* (London: The Distributist League, 1928).

Huneault, Kristin, '"Living Tableaux of Misery and Oppression": Sweated Labour on Tour', in Valerie Mainz and Griselda Pollock (eds.), *Work and the Image. Work in Modern Times: Visual Mediations and Social Processes* (Aldershot: Ashgate, 2000), pp. 11–31.

Hunt, Lynn (ed.), *The New Cultural History* (Berkeley, Calif.: University of California Press, 1989).

Hunt, Violet, *The Workaday Woman* (London: T. Werner Laurie, 1906).

Hutchins, B. L., *Homework and Sweating The Causes and the Remedies*, Fabian Tract no. 130 (London: Fabian Society, 1907).

The Working Life of Women, Fabian Tract no. 157 (London: Fabian Women's Group, 1911).

Women in Modern Industry (London: G. Bell and Sons, 1915).

Conflicting Ideals of Woman's Work (London: T. Murby and Co., 1916).

Hutchinson, Frances and Brian Burkitt, *The Political Economy of Social Credit and Guild Socialism* (London: Routledge, 1997).

Hynes, Samuel, *The Edwardian Turn of Mind* (London: Pimlico, 1968).

Jameson, Storm, *None Turn Back* (London: Virago, 1984).

Janaway, Christopher, *Self and World in Schopenhauer's Philosophy* (Oxford: Clarendon Press, 1989).

Jeffrey, Keith, and Peter Hennessy, *States of Emergency: British Governments and Strikebreaking since 1919* (London: Routledge and Kegan Paul, 1983).

Jennings, J. R., *Georges Sorel: the Character and Development of his Thought* (London: Macmillan, 1985).

Joannou, Maroula, *'Ladies, Please Don't Smash these Windows': Women's Writing, Feminist Consciousness and Social Change, 1918–1938* (Oxford: Berg, 1995).

Joannou, Maroula and June Purvis (eds.), *The Women's Suffrage Movement: New Feminist Perspectives* (Manchester: Manchester University Press, 1998).

John, A. V. (ed.), *Unequal Opportunities; Women's Employment in England 1800–1918* (Oxford: Basil Blackwell, 1986).

Jordan, Ellen, 'The Lady Clerks at the Prudential: the Beginning of Vertical Segregation by Sex in Clerical Work in Nineteenth-Century Britain', *Gender and History*, 8:1 (1996), 65–81.

Joyce, James, *Ulysses* (Harmondsworth: Penguin, 1975).

Joyce, Patrick (ed.), *The Historical Meanings of Work* (Cambridge: Cambridge University Press, 1987).

Kalnins, Mara (ed.), *D. H. Lawrence: Centenary Essays* (Bristol: Bristol Classical Press 1986).

Kaplan, Joel H., and Sheila Stowell, *Theatre and Fashion: Oscar Wilde to the Suffragettes* (Cambridge: Cambridge University Press, 1994).

Kaplan, Steven Laurence, and Cynthia J. Koepp (eds.), *Work in France: Representations, Meaning, Organization, and Practice* (Ithaca, N.Y., and London: Cornell University Press, 1986).

Keating, Peter (ed.), *Into Unknown England 1866–1913: Selections from the Social Explorers* (Glasgow: Collins, 1976).

Kessler-Harris, Alice, *Women have always Worked: a Historical Overview* (New York: The Feminist Press, 1981).

Keynes, J. M., *The Economic Consequences of Mr Churchill* (London: Hogarth Press, 1925).

Kiely, Robert, 'Out on Strike: the Language and Power of the Working Class in Lawrence's Fiction', in Michael Squires and Keith Cushman (eds.), *The Challenge of D. H. Lawrence* (Madison, Wis.: University of Wisconsin Press, 1990), pp. 89–102.

Kinkead-Weekes, Mark, *D. H. Lawrence: Triumph to Exile, 1912–1922* (Cambridge: Cambridge University Press, 1996).

Kirk, Neville, *Change, Continuity and Class: Labour in British Society, 1850–1920* (Manchester: Manchester University Press, 1998).

Kittler, Friedrich A., *Discourse Networks 1800/1900*, trans. Michael Metteer with Chris Cullens (Stanford: Stanford University Press, 1990).
    Gramophone, Film, Typewriter, trans. Geoffrey Winthrop-Young and Michael Wutz (Stanford, Calif.: Stanford University Press, 1999).

Knapp, James F., *Literary Modernism and the Transformation of Work* (Evanston, Ill.: Northwestern University Press, 1988).

Kumar, Krishan, 'From Work to Employment and Unemployment: the English Experience', in R. E. Pahl (ed.), *On Work: Historical, Comparative and Theoretical Approaches* (Oxford: Basil Blackwell, 1988), pp. 138–64.

Lawrence, D. H., 'The Crown', *The Signature*, 1–3 (1915).
    'England, My England', *The English Review*, 21 (1915), 238–52.
    Psychoanalysis and the Unconscious (New York: Thomas Seltzer, 1921).
    Fantasia of the Unconscious (New York: Thomas Seltzer, 1922).
    'John Galsworthy', in Edgell Rickword (ed.), *Scrutinies* (London: Lawrence and Wishart, 1928), pp. 52–72.

The Paintings of D. H. Lawrence, privately printed for subscribers only (London: Mandrake Press 1929).

'Men Must Work and Women as Well', in *Assorted Articles* (London: Martin Secker, 1930), pp. 126–45.

'Education of the People', in *Phoenix: the Posthumous Papers of D. H. Lawrence*, ed. by Edward D. McDonald (London: William Heinemann Ltd., 1936), pp. 587–665.

Phoenix: the Posthumous Papers of D. H. Lawrence, ed. Edward D. McDonald (London: William Heinemann Ltd., 1936).

'Study of Thomas Hardy', in *Phoenix: The Posthumous Papers of D. H. Lawrence*, ed. Edward D. McDonald (London: William Heinemann Ltd., 1936), pp. 398–516.

Phoenix: Uncollected, Unpublished and Other Prose Works, eds. by Warren Roberts and Harry T. Moore (London: Heinemann, 1968).

Studies in Classic American Literature (Harmondsworth: Penguin, 1977).

Apocalypse and the Writings on Revelation, ed. Mara Kalnins (Cambridge: Cambridge University Press, 1980).

'Cocksure Women and Hensure Men', in *D. H. Lawrence: Selected Essays* (Harmondsworth: Penguin, 1981), pp. 31–34.

Ten Paintings (Manchester: Carcanet, 1982).

England, My England and Other Stories, ed. Bruce Steele (Cambridge: Cambridge University Press, 1990).

Selected Poetry and Non-Fictional Prose, ed. John Lucas (London and New York: Routledge, 1990).

Sons and Lovers, eds. Helen Baron and Carl Baron (Cambridge: Cambridge University Press, 1992), pp. 467–73.

Complete Poems, eds. Vivian de Sola Pinto and Warren Roberts (Harmondsworth: Penguin, 1993).

Lady Chatterley's Lover, ed. Michael Squires (Cambridge: Cambridge University Press, 1993).

The Rainbow, ed. Mark Kinkead-Weekes (London: Penguin, 1995).

Laybourn, Keith, *Britain on the Breadline: a Social and Political History of Britain Between the Wars* (Gloucester: Alan Sutton, 1990).

The General Strike of 1926 (Manchester: Manchester University Press, 1993).

Leffingwell, W. H., *Scientific Office Management* (London: A. W. Shaw, 1917).

Lenin, V. I. '"Left-Wing" Communism in Great Britain', in *'Left-Wing' Communism: an Infantile Disorder* (Moscow: Novosti Press Agency, 1970), pp. 79–94.

Leon, Daniel de, *Principles of Industrial Unionism* (Glasgow: Socialist Labour Press, n.d.).

What Means this Strike? (Edinburgh: Socialist Labour Press, n.d.).

Lerner, Laurence, 'Olive Schreiner and the Feminists', in Malvern Van Wyk Smith and Don Maclennan (eds.), *Olive Schreiner and After* (Claremont, S.A.: David Philip, 1983), pp. 67–79.

Levitas, Ruth, 'Utopian Fictions and Political Theories: Domestic Labour in the Work of Edward Bellamy, Charlotte Perkins Gilman and William Morris', in

Val Gough and Jill Rudd (eds.), *A Very Different Story: Studies of the Fiction of Charlotte Perkins Gilmam* (Liverpool: Liverpool University Press, 1998), pp. 81–99.

Levy, O. (ed.), *Friedrich Nietzsche: Selected Letters* (London: Soho Book Company, 1985).

Lewis, Jane (ed.), *Labour and Love: Women's Experience of Home and Family. 1850– 1940* (Oxford: Basil Blackwell, 1986).

Lewis, Wyndham, *The Art of Being Ruled* (London: Chatto and Windus, 1926).
   Hitler (London: Chatto and Windus, 1931).
   The Apes of God (Harmondsworth: Penguin, 1965).
   Blasting and Bombardiering (London: John Calder, 1982).
   Time and Western Man, edited by Paul Edwards (Santa Rosa, Calif.: Black Sparrow Press, 1993).

Lindsay, Jack, 'The Modern Consciousness', *The London Aphrodite*, 1 (1928), 3–24.

Llewelyn Davies, Margaret (ed.), *Life As We have Known It, By Cooperative Working Women* (London: Virago, 1977).

Locke, John, *Two Treatises of Government* (New York: Cambridge University Press, 1960).

Lockwood, David, *The Blackcoated Worker: a Study in Class Consciousness* (London: George Allen and Unwin, 1958).

Loehlin, Jennifer A., *From Rags to Riches: Housework, Consumption and Modernity in Germany* (Oxford: Berg, 1999).

L'Orme, Madame Asa, 'Letter', *The Author: the Organ of the Society of Authors*, 3:11 (1893), 411.

Lovell, John, 'British Trade Unions 1875–1933', in L. A. Clarkson (ed.), *British Trade Union and Labour History: a Compendium* (London: Macmillan, 1990), pp. 71–136.

Low (Litvinov), Ivy, *The Questing Beast* (London: Martin Secker, 1914).

Lucas, John, *The Radical Twenties: Aspects of Writing, Politics and Culture* (Nottingham: Five Leaves Publications, 1997).

Luey, Beth, 'Publishers, Authors, and Technology: a Look Backward and Forward', *Book Research Quarterly*, 4 (Winter 1988–89), 57–64.

Luxemburg, Rosa, *The Mass Strike* (London: Bookmarks, 1986).

Lyon, Janet, 'Militant Discourse, Strange Bedfellows: Suffragettes and Vorticists before the War', *Differences: a Journal of Feminist Cultural Studies*, 4:2 (1992), 100–33.

Lytton, Constance, *Prisons and Prisoners* (London; William Heinemann, 1914).

Maas, Henry (ed.), *The Letters of A. E. Housman* (London: Rupert Hart-Davis, 1971).

MacDonald, Ramsay, 'Discussion on Syndicalism', *Sociological Review*, 5 (1912), 247–57.

Macdougall, Ian, *Working Lives: Photographs of Workers and their Work in Scotland 1897–1997* (Hamilton: Scottish Library Association, 1997).

Mainz, Valerie and Griselda Pollock (eds.), *Work and the Image. Work, Craft and Labour: Visual Representations in Changing Histories* (Aldershot: Ashgate, 2000).

Work and the Image II. Work in Modern Times: Visual Mediations and Social Processes (Aldershot: Ashgate, 2000).

Mann, Tom, *Memoirs* (London: The Labour Publishing Company, 1923).

Mansfield, Katherine, *The Collected Stories of Katherine Mansfield* (Harmondsworth: Penguin, 1981).

Marcus, Jane, *Suffrage and the Pankhursts* (London: Routledge and Kegan Paul, 1988).

Marcus, Jane (ed.), *The Young Rebecca: Writings of Rebecca West, 1911–1917* (London: Macmillan, 1982).

Marriott, John, 'Sensation of the Abyss: the Urban Poor and Modernity', in Mica Nava and Alan O'Shea (eds.), *Modern Times: Reflections on a Century of English Modernity* (London: Routledge, 1996), pp. 77–100.

Marrot, H. V., *The Life and Letter of John Galsworthy* (London: William Heinemann, 1935).

Marsh, Jan, and Pamela Gerrish Nunn, *Pre-Raphaelite Women Artists* (Manchester: Manchester City Art Galleries, 1997).

Marson, Dave, *Children's Strikes in 1911*, History Workshop Pamphlet no. 9 (Oxford: History Workshop, 1973).

Marton, Peter, *The Vital Science: Biology and the Literary Imagination, 1860–1900* (London: George Allen and Unwin, 1984).

Marx, Karl, *Economic and Philosophic Manuscripts of 1844*, ed. Dirk J. Struik (London: Lawrence and Wishart, 1970).

  Capital: Volume One, trans. Eden and Cedar Paul (London: J. M. Dent and Sons, 1972).

  Capital: Volume Three, trans. David Fernbach (Harmondsworth: Penguin, 1981).

  Early Political Writings, ed. Joseph O'Malley (Cambridge: Cambridge University Press, 1994).

Marx, Karl, and Friedrich Engels, *The German Ideology: Part One,* ed. C. J. Arthur (London: Lawrence and Wishart, 1977).

  The Communist Manifesto, ed. David McLellan (Oxford: Oxford University Press, 1992).

McCartney, Wilf, *Dare to be a Daniel. A History of one of Britain's Earliest Syndicalist Unions* (London: KSL, 1992).

McLuhan, Marshall, *Understanding Media: the Extensions of Man* (Cambridge, Mass.: MIT Press, 1998).

Meakin, David, *Man and Work: Literature and Culture in Industrial Society* (London: Methuen, 1976).

Mepham, John, *Virginia Woolf: a Literary Life* (London: Macmillan, 1991).

Middleton, Christopher (ed.), *Selected Letters of Friedrich Nietzsche* (London: University of Chicago Press, 1969).

Milner, Susan, *The Dilemmas of Internationalism: French Syndicalism and the International Labour Movement 1900–1914* (New York: Berg, 1990).

Moore, G. E., *Principia Ethica*, rev. edn, ed. Thomas Baldwin (Cambridge: Cambridge University Press, 1993).

Mores, George Carl, *The History of the Typewriter* (London: Guilbert Pitman, 1909).

Morris, Margaret, *The General Strike* (London: Journeyman Press, 1980).

Morris, William, 'News from Nowhere', in Asa Briggs (ed.), *William Morris: 'News for Nowhere' and Selected Writings and Designs* (Harmondsworth: Penguin, 1984), pp. 183–300.

'Useful Work versus Useless Toil', in Asa Briggs (ed.), *William Morris: 'News for Nowhere' and Selected Writings and Designs* (Harmondsworth; Penguin, 1984), pp. 117–36.

Nava, Mica, and Alan O'Shea (eds.), *Modern Times: Reflections on a Century of English Modernity* (London: Routledge, 1996).

Nietzsche, Friedrich, *Briefe*, eds. Elisabeth Forster-Nietzsche and Peter Gast, 5 vols. (Leipzig, 1902–09).

The Birth of Tragedy, trans. Walter Kaufmann (New York: Vintage Books, 1967).

The Will to Power, trans. Walter Kaufmann and R. J. Hollingdale (New York: Vintage Books, 1968).

Beyond Good and Evil, trans. R. J. Hollingdale (Harmondsworth: Penguin, 1973).

Gay Science, trans. W. Kaufman (New York: Random House, 1974).

Untimely Meditations, trans. R. J. Hollingdale (Cambridge: Cambridge University Press, 1983).

Human, All too Human, trans. Marion Faber and Stephen Lehmann (Harmondsworth: Penguin, 1984).

Twilight of the Idols, trans. Duncan Large (Oxford: Oxford University Press, 1998).

Daybreak: Thoughts on the Prejudices of Morality, eds. Maudemarie Clark and Brian Leiter, trans. R. J. Hollingdale (Cambridge: Cambridge University Press, 1997).

Norman, Richard J., *Hegel's 'Phenomenology': a Philosophical Introduction* (Aldershot: Gregg Revivals, 1991).

Norquay, Glenda, *Voices and Votes: a Literary Anthology of the Women's Suffrage Campaign* (Manchester: Manchester University Press, 1995).

North, Michael, *Reading 1922: a Return to the Scene of the Modern* (Oxford: Oxford University Press, 1999).

O'Brien, Robert Lincoln, 'Machinery and the English Style', *The Atlantic Monthly*, 94 (1904), 464–72.

Olney, Martha L., *Buy Now, Pay Later: Advertising, Credit, and Consumer Durables in the 1920s* (Chapel Hill, N.C.: University of North Carolina Press, 1991).

Oppenheim, Janet, *The Other World: Spiritualism, and Psychical Research in England, 1850–1914* (Cambridge: Cambridge University Press, 1985).

'Shattered Nerves': Doctors, Patients, and Depression in Victorian England (New York and Oxford: Oxford University Press, 1991).

Orage, A. R., *Political and Economic Writings*, arranged by Montgomery Butchart (London: Stanley Nott, 1936).

Oxford and Asquith, Emma Alice Margaret, Countess of (ed.), *Myself When Young: by Famous Women of Today* (London: Frederick Muller, 1938).

Pahl, R. E., *Divisions of Labour* (Oxford: Basil Blackwell, 1984).

Pahl, R. E. (ed.), *On Work: Historical, Comparative and Theoretical Approaches* (Oxford: Basil Blackwell, 1988).

Pankhurst, E. Sylvia, 'Women Farm Labourers in the Border Counties', *Votes for Women,* 26 August 1910, 776–77.

Writ on Cold Slate (London: The Dreadnought Publishers, 1922).

The Suffragette Movement: an Intimate Account of Persons and Ideals (London: Longmans, Green and Co., 1931).

The Papers of Sylvia Pankhurst, 1882–1960, Internationaal Instituut voor Social Geschiedenis, Amsterdam. On Microfilm, published by Adam Matthew Publications, 1991. This can be consulted in the National Women's Library, London.

'A minimum wage for women', *The Woman's Dreadnought,* 12 September 1914, reprinted in Kathryn Dodd (ed.), *A Sylvia Pankhurst Reader* (Manchester: Manchester University Press, 1993), pp. 60–63.

'Co-Operative Housekeeping', the *Workers' Dreadnought,* 28 August 1920; reprinted in Kathryn Dodd (ed.) *A Sylvia Pankhurst Reader* (Manchester: Manchester University Press, 1993), pp. 104–08.

'Pit brow women', *Votes for Women,* 11 August 1911, 730, reprinted in Kathryn Dodd (ed.), *A Sylvia Pankhurst Reader* (Manchester: Manchester University Press, 1993), pp. 36–41.

'The potato-pickers', *Votes for Women,* 28 January 1909, 294, reprinted in Kathryn Dodd (ed.), *A Sylvia Pankhurst Reader* (Manchester: Manchester University Press, 1993), pp. 34–36.

Pankhurst, Richard, *Sylvia Pankhurst: Artist and Crusader* (London: Paddington Press, 1979).

Paxton, Nancy L., *George Eliot and Herbert Spencer: Feminism, Evolution and the Reconstruction of Gender* (Princeton, N.J.: Princeton University Press, 1991).

Pichardie, Jean-Paul, *D. H. Lawrence: La Tentation utopique. De Rananim au Serpent à Plumes* (Rouen: l'Université de Rouen, 1988).

Plant, Raymond, *Hegel: an Introduction* (Oxford: Basil Blackwell, 1983).

Pollock, Griselda, 'The Dangers of Proximity: the Spaces of Sexuality and Surveillance in Word and Image II, *Discourse* 16:2 (1993–94), 3–50.

Porter, Roy, and Mark S. Micale (eds.), *Discovering the History of Psychiatry* (New York and Oxford: Oxford University Press, 1994).

Postgate, R. W., Ellen Wilkinson, M. P., and J. F. Horrabin, *A Workers' History of the Great Strke* (London: The Plebs League, 1927).

Pratt Rayner, Olive (Grant Allan), *The Type-Writer Girl* (London: C. Arthur Pearson, 1897).

Programme for the WSPU Exhibition, 13–26 May 1909, Museum of London, accession number 60. 15/28.

Pryse, James M., *The Apocalypse Unsealed, Being an Esoteric Interpretation of the Initiation of Iôannês, Commonly called the Revelation of [St] John* (London: John M. Watkins, 1910).

Rabinbach, Anson, *The Human Motor. Energy, Fatigue, and the Origins of Modernity* (Berkeley, Calif.: University of California Press, 1992).

Rado, Lisa (ed.), *Rereading Modernism: New Directions in Feminist Criticism* (New York: Garland Publishing, 1994).

Ragussis, Michael, *The Subterfuge of Art: Language and the Romantic Tradition* (Baltimore, Md. and London: Johns Hopkins University Press, 1978).

Rainey, Lawrence, *Institutions of Modernism: Literary Elites and Public Culture* (London: Yale University Press, 1998).

Raitt, Suzanne, *May Sinclair: a Modern Victorian* (Oxford: Clarendon Press, 2000).

Reckitt, M. B. and C. E. Bechhofer, *The Meaning of National Guilds* (London: Cecil Palmer and Hayward, 1918).

Register Packet for portraits of Keir Hardie (3978 and 3979) in National Portrait Gallery, London.

Register Packet for Pankhurst's Self-Portrait (4999), National Portrait Gallery, London.

Richards, G. Tilgham, *Handbook of the Collection Illustrating Typewriters* (London: HMSO, 1948).

Richardson, Dorothy, *Pilgrimage*, 4 vols. (London, Virago, 1979).

Riley, Denise, '"The Free Mothers": Pronatalism and Working Women in Industry at the End of the Last War in Britain', *History Workshop*, 11 (1981), 59–118.

Robbins, Bruce, *The Servant's Hand: English Fiction from Below* (New York: Columbia University Press, 1986).

Roberts, Warren, *A Bibliography of D. H. Lawrence*, 2nd edn (Cambridge: Cambridge University Press, 1982).

Robins, Elizabeth, *The Convert* (London: Methuen, 1907).

Rocker, Rudolf, *Anarcho-Syndicalism* (London: Pluto Press, 1989).

Rockmore, Tom, *Before and After Hegel: a Historical Introduction to Hegel's Thought* (London: University of California Press, 1993).

Roe, Michael, *Nine Australian Progressives: Vitalism in Bourgeois Social Thought 1890–1960* (St. Lucia, Queensland: University of Queensland Press, 1984).

Rohbeck, Johannes, 'Property and Labour in the Social Philosophy of John Locke, *History of European Ideas*, 5:1 (1984), 65–77.

Roller, Arnold, *The Social General Strike* (Chicago, Ill.: The Debating Club, 1905).

Romano, Frank J., *Machine Writing and Typesetting* (Salem, N.H.: Gama, 1986).

Romero, Patricia W., *E. Sylvia Pankhurst: Portrait of a Radical* (New Haven, Conn.: Yale University Press, 1987).

Rose, Jonathan, *The Edwardian Temperament, 1895–1919* (Athens, Ohio: Ohio University Press, 1986).

Rose, M. *Reworking the Work Ethic* (London: Batsford, 1985).

Rose, Sonya O., *Limited Livelihoods: Gender and Class in Nineteenth-Century England* (London: Routledge, 1992).

Rosenberg, John (ed.), *The Genius of John Ruskin: Selections from his Writings* (London: RKP, 1979).

Ross, Kristin, *Fast Cars, Clean Bodies: Decolonization and the Reordering of French Culture* (Cambridge, Mass.: MIT Press, 1996).

Rothstein, Andrew, *The Soldiers' Strikes of 1919* (London: Macmillan, 1980).

Ruskin, John, *Time and Tide, by Weare and Tyne: Tweny-Five Letters to a Working Man of Sunderland on the Laws of Work* (London: Routledge/Thoemmes Press, 1994).

Unto this Last (London: Routledge/Thoemmes Press, 1994).

'Work' in *The Crown of Wild Olive* (London: Routledge/Thoemmes Press, 1994).

Russell, Bertrand, *The Philosophy of Bergson* (Cambridge: The Heretics, 1914).

Roads to Freedom: Socialism, Anarchism, and Syndicalism (London: George Allen and Unwin, 1918).

In Praise of Idleness and Other Essays (London: Unwin Paperbacks, 1976).

Saltzman, Rachelle H., 'Folklore as Politics in Great Britain: Working-Class Critiques of Upper-Class Strike Breakers in the 1926 General Strike', *Anthropological Quarterly*, 67:3 (1994), 105–21.

Sand, Shlomo, *L'Illusion du politique; Georges Sorel et le débat intellectuel 1900* (Paris: la Découverte, 1985).

Sanderson, Kay, '"A Pension to Look Forward To . . .?": Women Civil Service Clerks in London 1925–1939' in Leoncre Davidoff and Belinda Westover (eds.), *Our Work, Our Lives, Our Words: Women's History and Women's Work* (Totoway, N.J.: Barnes and Noble, 1986), pp. 145–60.

Sassoon, Donald, *One Hundred Years of Socialism: the West European Left in the Twentieth Century* (London: I. B. Tauris, 1996).

Scanlon, Joan, 'Bad Language *vs* Bad Prose? *Lady Chatterley* and *The Well*', *Critical Quarterly*, 38:3 (1996), 3–13.

Schopenhauer, Arthur, *The World as Will and Idea*, trans. R. B. Haldane and J. Kemp, 3 vols. (London: Trübner and Co., 1883–86).

The World as Will and Representation, trans. E. F. J. Payne, 2 vols. (Indian Hills, Colo.: Falcon's Wing Press, 1958).

Philosophical Writings (New York: Continuum, 1994).

Schreiner, Olive (writing as Ralph Iron), *Dream Life and Real Life* (London: T. Fisher Unwin, 1893).

Olive Schreiner's Thoughts about Women, compiled by Anna Purcell (Cape Town: Women's Enfranchisement League, 1909).

Woman and Labour (London: T. Fisher Unwin, 1911).

Schreiner, Olive, *From Man to Man* (London: Virago, 1982).

Schreuder, M. Wilhelmina, and Margaret Schrevel, *Inventory of the E. Sylvia Pankhurst Papers 1863–1960* (Amsterdam: International Institute of Social History, 1989).

Scott, J. W., *Barter: a Study in the Economics of the Smaller Group* (London: The Distributist League, 1938).

Scott, Gillian, *Feminism and the Politics of Working Women: the Women's Cooperative Guild, 1880s to the Second World War* (London: University College London Press, 1989).

Scott, J. W., *Syndicalism and Philosophical Realism: a Study in the Correlation of Contemporary Social Tendencies* (London: A. and C. Black, 1919).

Karl Marx on Value (London: A. and C. Black, 1920).

Kant on the Moral Life (London: A. and C. Black, 1924).

Unemployment: a Suggested Policy (London: A. and C. Black, 1925).

Self-Subsistence for the Unemployed: Studies in a New Technique (London: Faber and Faber, 1935).

Seltzer, Mark, *Bodies and Machines* (London: Routledge, 1992).

'The Postal Unconscious', *Henry James Review*, 21:3 (2000), 197–206.

Sewell, Jr., William H., 'Visions of Labour: Illustrations of the Mechanical Arts before, in, and after Diderot's *Encyclopédie*', in Steven Laurence Kaplan and Cynthia J. Koepp (eds.), *Work in France: Representations, Meaning, Organization, and Practice* (Ithaca, N.Y. and London: Cornell University Press, 1986), pp. 258–86.

Shakers of Shaker Village, N.H., *Improved Shaker Washing Machine: Designed Particularly for Hospitals, Hotels, Laundries etc.* (Shaker Village, N.H.: 1860 [date attributed by BL Catalogue]).

Sherard, Robert, 'The White Slaves of England: IV – The Chainmakers of Cradley Heath', *Pearson's Magazine*, 2 (July–December, 1896), 408–14.

The Child-Slaves of Britain (London: Hurst and Blackett, 1905).

Shorter, Edward, 'Women's Work What Difference did Capitalism Make?' *Theory and Society*, 3 (1976), 513–27.

From the Mind into the Body: the Cultural Origins of Psychosomatic Symptoms (New York: Free Press, 1994).

Siep, Ludwig, 'Individuality in Hegel's *Phenomenology of Spirit*', in Karl Amariks and Dieter Sturma (eds.), *The Modern Subject: Conceptions of the Self in Classical German Philosophy* (Albany, N.Y.: State University of New York Press, 1995), pp. 131–48.

Simpson, David (ed.), *German Aesthetic and Literary Criticism: Kant, Fichte Schelling, Schopenhauer, Hegel* (Cambridge: Cambridge University Press, 1984).

Sinclair, May, 'Type-Writing: a Protest', *The Author*, 15:5 (1905), 147–48.

Smart, William, 'John Ruskin his Life and Work' (1883), reprinted in William Smart and J. A. Hobson, *'John Ruskin His Life and Work' and 'John Ruskin, Social Reformer'* (London: Routledge/Thoemmes Press, 1994).

Smith, Adam, *The Wealth of Nations* (London: Everyman's Library, 1991).

An Inquiry into the Nature and Causes of the Wealth of Nations, ed. Kathryn Sutherland (Oxford: Oxford University Press, 1993).

Smythe, William E., *City Homes on Country Lanes: Philosophy and Practice of Home-in-a-Garden* (New York: Macmillan, 1921).

Sorel, Georges, *Le Procès de Socrate; examen critique des thèses Socratiques* (Paris: Librairie Félix Alcan, 1889).

L'Avenir socialiste des syndicats (Paris: Librairie de l'art social, 1898).

Reflections on Violence, trans. T. E. Hulme (London: George Allen and Unwin, 1916).

The Illusions of Progress, trans. John and Charlotte Stanley (Berkeley, Calif.: University of California Press, 1969).

'A Critique of Creative Evolution', in *From Georges Sorel; Essays in Socialism and Philosophy*, ed. John L. Stanley (New York: Oxford University Press, 1976).

Spalding, Frances, *British Art Since 1900* (London: Thames and Hudson, 1986).

Spencer, Herbert, *The Principles of Ethics*, 2 vols. (London: Williams and Norgate, 1893).

Political Writings, ed. John Offer (Cambridge: Cambridge University Press, 1994).

Spengler, Oswald, *The Decline of the West*, trans. Charles Francis Atkinson, 2 vols. (London: George Allen and Unwin, 1926–28).

Civilization and its Discontents, SE, vol. 21 (London: Hogarth Press, 1930).

Stanley, John L., *From Georges Sorel; Essays in Socialism and Philosophy* (New York: Oxford University Press, 1976).

Stedman Jones, Gareth, *Outcast London; a Study in the Relationship between Classes in Victorian Society* (Oxford: Oxford University Press, 1971).

Stoker, Bram, *Dracula* (London: Penguin, 1993).

Strasser, Susan, *Never Done: a History of American Housework* (New York: Pantheon Books, 1982).

Sulloway, Frank J., *Freud, Biologist of the Mind: beyond the Psychoanalytic Legend* (Cambridge, Mass.: Harvard University Press, 1992).

Sutherland, Kathryn, Introduction to Adam Smith, *An Inquiry into the Nature and Causes of the Wealth of Nations* (Oxford: Oxford University Press, 1993).

Swanwick, H. M., *I Have Been Young* (London: Victor Gollancz, 1935).

Swift, Edgar J., 'The Acquisition of Skill in Type-Writing', *The Psychological Bulletin*, 1:9 (1904), 295–305.

Symons, Julian, *The General Strike: a Historical Portrait* (London: Cresset Press, 1957).

Synge, J. M., 'The Aran Islands', in *Collected Works*, vol. 2, ed. Alan Price (London: Oxford University Press, 1966), pp. 47–184.

Tarkington, Booth, *Alice Adams* (New York: Doubleday, 1921).

Tate, Trudi, *Modernism, History and the First World War* (Manchester: Manchester University Press, 1998).

Tavener, Lucking, *Labour, as seen in Recent Painting, being the Substance of three Lectures delivered at Walthamstow Brotherhood Church* (London: Brotherhood Press, 1905).

Taylor, Charles, *Sources of the Self: the Making of the Modern Identity* (Cambridge: Cambridge University Press, 1989).

Taylor, Frederick Winslow, *The Principles of Scientific Management* (New York and London: Harper and Brothers Publishers, 1911).

Taylor, Jenny Bourne, and Sally Shuttleworth (eds.), *Embodied Selves: an Anthology of Psychological Texts 1830–1890* (Oxford: Clarendon Press, 1998).

Taylor, Rosemary, *In Letters of Gold: the Story of Sylvia Pankhurst and the East London Federation of the Suffragettes in Bow* (London: Stepney Books, 1993).

Thatcher, David S., *Nietzsche in England, 1890–1914* (Toronto: University of Toronto Press, 1970).

The Eagle and The Serpent: a Journal of Egoistic Philosophy and Sociology 1898–1903.

Thom, Deborah, 'Free From Chains? The Image of Women's Labour 1900–1920', in David Feldman and Gareth Stedman Jones (eds.), *Metropolis London: Histories and Representations since 1800* (London: Routledge, 1989), pp. 85–99.

Thomas, Keith (ed.), *The Oxford Book of Work* (Oxford: Oxford University Press, 1999).

Thompson, E. P., 'Time, Work-Discipline and Industrial Capitalism', *Past and Present*, 38 (1967).

The Making of the English Working Class (London: Penguin, 1980).

Thompson, P. *The Nature of Work* (London: Macmillan, 1983).

The Edwardians: the Remaking of British Society (London: Routledge, 1992).

Thoreau, Henry David, *Walden and Civil Disobedience* (Harmondsworth: Penguin, 1983).

Thurschwell, Pamela, 'Henry James and Theodora Bosanquet: On the Typewriter, In the Cage, at the Ouija Board', *Textual Practice*, 13:1 (1999), 5–23.

Tickner, Lisa, *The Spectacle of Women: Imagery of the Suffrage Campaign 1907–1914* (London: Chatto and Windus, 1987).

Tilgher, Adriano, *Work: What it has Meant to Men Through the Ages*, trans. D. C. Fisher (London: George G. Harrap, 1931).

Tilly, Louise A., and Joan W. Scott, *Women, Work and Family* (New York: Holt, Rinehart and Winston, 1978).

Torgovnick, Marianna, *The Visual Arts, Pictorialism and the Novel: James, Lawrence and Woolf* (Princeton, N.J.: Princeton University Press, 1985).

Treadwell, Sophie, 'Machinal', in Judith E. Barlow (ed.), *Plays by American Women: 1900–1930* (New York: Applause Theatre Book Publishers, 1985).

Tsuzuki, Chushichi, *Tom Mann 1856–1941* (Oxford: Clarendon Press, 1991).

Vicinus, Martha, *Independent Women: Work and Community for Single Women, 1850–1920* (London: Virago, 1985).

Walkowitz, Judith R., *City of Dreadful Delight: Narratives of Sexual Danger in Late-Victorian England* (London: Virago, 1992).

Wallas, Graham, 'Discussion on Syndicalism', *Sociological Review*, 5 (1912), 247–57.

Webb, Sidney and Beatrice, 'What Syndicalism Means: an Examination of the Origin and Motives of the Movements with an Analysis of its Proposals for the Control of Industry', Supplement to *The Crusade Against Distributism*, 3 (August 1912), 136–54.

Weir Mitchell, Silas, *Wear and Tear, or Hints for the Overworked* (Philadelphia, Penn.: Lippincott, 1871).

Wellbery, David E., 'Foreword' to Friedrich A. Kittler, *Discourse Networks 1800/1900*, trans. Michael Metteer with Chris Cullens (Stanford, Calif.: Stanford University Press, 1990) pp. vii–xxxiii.

Wellek René, and Austin Warren, *Theory of Literature* (Harmondsworth: Penguin, 1973).

Wells, H. G., *Meanwhile: the Picture of a Lady* (London: Ernest Benn Ltd., 1927).

West, Rebecca, *The Judge* (London: Virago, 1980).

White, John J., 'The "Typographical Revolution" and Futurism's Exploration of the Iconic', in *Literary Futurism: Aspects of the First Avant-Garde* (Oxford: Clarendon Press, 1990), pp. 8–72.

Wicke, Jennifer, 'Vampiric Typewriting: *Dracula* and its Media', *ELH*, 59 (1992), 467–93.

Wilkinson, Ellen, *Clash* (London: Virago, 1989).

Will, Barbara, 'Nervous Systems 1880–1915', in Tim Armstrong (ed.), *American Bodies: Cultural Histories of the Physique* (Sheffield: Sheffield Academic Press, 1996), pp. 86–100.

Williams, Raymond, *Culture and Society, 1780–1950* (Harmondsworth: Penguin, 1958).

   Keywords: a Vocabulary of Culture and Society (Glasgow: Fontana, 1976).

   The Country and the City (London: Hogarth Press, 1985).

Wilson, Colin and John Cohen, 'The Paintings of D. H. Lawrence', *The Studio*, 164:834 (October 1962), 130–35.

Winslow, Barbara, *Sylvia Pankhurst: Sexual Politics and Political Activism* (London: University College London Press, 1996).

Woolf, Leonard, *Downhill All the Way: an Autobiography of the Years 1919–1939* (London: Hogarth Press, 1967).

Woolf, Virginia, *The Diary of Virginia Woolf*, Vol. III: *1925–1930*, ed. Anne Olivier Bell, assisted by Andrew McNellie (London: Penguin, 1982).

   The Diary of Virginia Woolf, Vol. IV: *1931–1935*, ed. Anne Olivier Bell, assisted by Andrew McNellie (London: Penguin, 1983).

   The Years (Oxford: Oxford University Press, 1992).

   To the Lighthouse (Oxford: Oxford University Press, 1992).

Worthen, John, *D. H. Lawrence: the Early Years 1885–1912* (Cambridge: Cambridge University Press, 1991).

Wrigley, Chris, 'Local History. Part One: the Government's Volunteers', *The Local Historian* 16:1 (1984), 36–49.

Zola, Émile, *L'Assommoir (The Dram Shop)*, trans. Robin Buss (London: Penguin, 2000).

Zoll, Allan R., 'Vitalism and the Metaphysics of Love: D. H. Lawrence and Schopenhauer', *The D. H. Lawrence Review*, 11:1 (1978), 1–20.

Zytaruk, George J. (ed.), *The Quest for Rananim: D. H. Lawrence's Letters to S. S. Koteliansky, 1914–1930* (London: McGill-Queen's University Press, 1970).

Zytaruk, George and James T. Boulton (eds.), *The Letters of D. H. Lawrence*, vol. 2: *June 1913–October 1919* (Cambridge: Cambridge University Press, 1981).

Index